KYOTO-CSEAS SERIES ON ASIAN STUDIES 22
Center for Southeast Asian Studies, Kyoto University

UNRAVELING MYANMAR'S TRANSITION

KYOTO-CSEAS SERIES ON ASIAN STUDIES 22
Center for Southeast Asian Studies, Kyoto University

UNRAVELING MYANMAR'S TRANSITION

Progress, Retrenchment, and Ambiguity Amidst Liberalization

Edited by
Pavin Chachavalpongpun,
Elliott Prasse-Freeman, and Patrick Strefford

NUS PRESS
Singapore

in association with

KYOTO UNIVERSITY PRESS
Japan

The publication of this book is funded by the Japan Society for the Promotion of Science (JSPS KAKENHI Grant Number: JP19HP5136) as Grant-in-Aid for Publication of Scientific Research Results.

NUS Press
National University of Singapore
AS3-01-02, 3 Arts Link
Singapore 117569
http://nuspress.nus.edu.sg

ISBN 978-981-325-107-6

Kyoto University Press
Yoshida-South Campus, Kyoto University
69 Yoshida Konoe-cho, Sakyo-ku
Kyoto 606-8315
Japan
http://www.kyoto-up.or.jp

ISBN 978-4-8140-0245-0

National Library Board, Singapore Cataloguing in Publication Data

Name(s): Chachavalpongpun, Pavin, editor. | Prasse-Freeman, Elliott, editor. | Strefford, Patrick, editor.
Title: Unraveling Myanmar's transition: progress, retrenchment, and ambiguity amidst liberalization / edited by Pavin Chachavalpongpun, Elliott Prasse-Freeman, and Patrick Strefford.
Description: Singapore: NUS Press; Kyoto, Japan: Kyoto University Press, [2020] | Series: Kyoto-CSEAS series on Asian studies 22. | Includes index.
Identifier(s): OCN 1119661837 | ISBN 978-981-32-5107-6 (paperback)
Subject(s): LCSH: Burma--Politics and government--21st century. | Burma--Economic conditions--21st century. | Burma--Social conditions--21st century. | Rohingya (Burmese people)
Classification: DDC 303.4825910905--dc23

Cover design: Wasin Pathomyok

Cover image: Myanmar traditional fabric pattern (CPOR/Shutterstock.com ID 732116158).

Printed by: Mainland Press Pte Ltd

CONTENTS

LIST OF ILLUSTRATIONS

Tables

Figures

FOREWORD

David I. Steinberg
Distinguished Professor of Asian Studies Emeritus
Georgetown University

Myanmar/Burma studies have taken the proverbial great leap forward in the past two decades. If the political, economic, and social progress that Myanmar has made is still less than optimal and less than observers hoped for or expected, and while significant and widespread challenges remain as a new administration takes over state power following the 2020 election, the study of this important country and its multiple, complex cultures has vastly improved over this score of years. This volume is a reflection and microcosm of those positive changes.

The academic transformation and improvement of research in Myanmar is indeed apparent. Through the improved training in technological and research methodologies, the far broader exposure of its intellectuals to international standards, the greater availability of data, the freedom with which its internal intellectuals and its diaspora can explore salient issues, and the access to better training of foreign specialists on that country and the problems that it faces, the sophistication of Myanmar studies has broadened and deepened. Even under the repressive junta administration following the coup of 1988, until 2010 more access was available for indigenous and foreign scholars to explore many important societal issues than in the previous half-century, when even most internal, even mundane, research was classified. This later access was apparent both through the availability throughout the major cities of that country of influential texts in English and other languages critical of the administration of Myanmar, when they had previously been banned and had to be smuggled into the country, and even now through the legal and extra-legal translations of many such works into Burmese. Since 1988 until 2018, over 2,133 books and hardcover major reports (and excluding myriad chapters and op-eds) in English have been published, testifying to the attractions of that country, the importance of its influence in the region, and the lessons to be learned from the nature and scope of its problems.[1] Although the government had tried to control information, technological advances prohibited the regime from successfully isolating the state from the international community and Burmese citizens from international contacts and material; eventually it had to recognize the need for change, if not complete transparency, and became far more accessible.

Foreign interest and competence on Myanmar is also reflected in the growth of various institutes devoted to Myanmar issues. These include two in Australia (Canberra and Melbourne), one in Kunming (China), one in Chiang Mai (Thailand), one in Manipur (India), and one in the United States in Illinois. They sponsor research, seminars and conferences, and courses on Myanmar issues. Their activities are augmented by research and scholarship in Europe, Japan, Singapore, and internationally in a wide variety of institutions, and at many centers of Southeast Asian studies worldwide. These collaborative editorial efforts of three scholars from Japan, Singapore, and Australia reflect these welcome developments, as does the inclusion of a number of scholars from other areas, including, of course, Myanmar.

This volume contains some important chapters on the perpetual issues in contemporary Myanmar, such as on civil-military relations, foreign policy, Buddhism, aspects of the polity and economy, but it also includes works on current issues, such as the environment and extractive industries, urban real estate, ethnic education, the capacity of foreign assistance, and on motherhood and women's labor among the Rohingya. As a whole, it offers important perspectives (both more traditional and contemporary) on the society and some of the issues that the new administration will have to confront. It is thus a welcome addition to the bourgeoning literature on that important country.

The title of the volume includes the term "transition," and as the opening chapter indicates, the volume has witnessed the maturation of some of the anticipated transition issues, their potential, but at the same time it "critiques the *concept* of transition simultaneously." That seminal chapter transcends the rather jejune, journalistic connotations (and often foreign policy statements) of an inevitable transition from some beginning to an end, especially a positive political result. Rather, the authors regard it as a "discursive context," which is an important step in the analytical thinking on Myanmar's future. It allows for more nuanced considerations of the ramifications of policy choice and outcomes.

This is wise, for the challenges that any new regime in Naypyitaw will have to face will be multiple, daunting, and interconnected—internal socio-economic, ethnic, and political factors influencing each other but also interacting with foreign problems at both regional and international levels. These are likely to be compounded by intrusive and traditional cultural concepts of power and authority that may be in variance with contemporary, sometimes idealized, international standards of governance and the role of the military in modern societies. This work explores some of these issues.

This volume, then, is a concrete result of the increased accessibility of scholarly inquiry on Myanmar, but it also is a harbinger of the sophisticated paths that future scholarship on that country will take. This is an important volume. It is for the serious observer of the Myanmar scene and for those who formulate policies towards that country.

Note

1. Andrew Selth, *Burma (Myanmar) since the 1988 Uprising: A Select Bibliography* (Brisbane: Griffith Asia Institute, Griffith University, 2018), 3rd edition.

INTRODUCTION

Elliott Prasse-Freeman, Pavin Chachavalpongpun, and Patrick Strefford

As this introduction is finalized in mid-2018, Myanmar stands at a strange juncture in its so-called "transition" to democracy. Just a number of years earlier Burmese people of many ethnicities and faiths had rejoiced when long-imprisoned dissidents, such as Nobel Laureate Aung San Suu Kyi (hereafter referred to as Daw Suu), swept national elections in 2015; foreign states, especially from the West, had eagerly embraced the opportunity to assist with the political liberalization that the military, which had ruled the country since 1962, initiated in 2011; investors had salivated at the promise of new markets as the military acceded some control of an economy that began to grow at nearly 8 per cent per year. Peace was promised and optimism urged. Yes, structural problems persisted—including ethnic marginalization and on-going conflict, a natural resource dependent economy, an embedded military elite, inadequate public services, and an under capacitated civilian bureaucracy—but they would be overcome through hard work, dedication, and the "Union Spirit." These feelings of ebullience have, however, subsided. They have been displaced, or at least inundated, by a malaise, a sense of unease about the present and uncertainty, even foreboding, about the future. The suspicion now is that those persistent challenges are actually entrenched, structural, and enduring. More importantly, the fear is that the transition, by liberalizing critical sectors and expanding certain freedoms—such as political and legal opportunities for expression and mobilization—yet while *not* addressing those entrenched problems, has created a toxic environment in which classism, racism, and bigotry are rending apart Myanmar's already delicate social fabric. This volume's title hints at a fundamental question: is Myanmar itself unraveling?

The displacement of the Rohingya population of Northern Rakhine State has played a pivotal role in this creeping transition in the way the "transition" is imagined. The world watched the ethnic cleansing unfold slowly (with incidents of expulsion during this recent era occurring in 2012 and 2016—even earlier extrusions transpired under the cover of the military state) before it peaked in a massive clearance campaign in August 2017 that drove 700,000 people into Bangladesh and left nearly 7,000 Rohingya dead.[1] The extent of the horror and destruction has disrupted broader narratives of amelioration in the country. Hence, even as the most recent cleansing campaign has compelled a reassessment of the earlier conflagrations, prompting many to begin conceiving the events together as genocide, the Rohingya ejection has compelled a reconsideration of the country's general problems, throwing them into critical relief.

To wit, given that the Rohingya extrusion was enabled by an army insulated from civilian strictures, the country's resurgent civil wars and its other communal and religious conflicts seem less amenable to reconciliation. Indeed, while the National League for Democracy (NLD) enjoyed an electoral triumph that appeared to move Myanmar out of the military's direct control, because the 2008 Constitution assigns the military 25 per cent of the seats in the legislature, gives the military control of three major ministries (border affairs, defense, and home affairs), and also requires a majority of more than 75 per cent to approve any constitutional amendment,[2] the military has maintained the ability to freely assert itself in affairs it has deemed relevant to national security. This is alarming enough, but given that the Rohingya conflict was also presided over by a complicit civilian leadership, endorsed by empowered Buddhist-nationalist political entrepreneurs, seemingly ratified by observing publics, and magnified by a virulent social media, it is no longer possible to simply blame the military. The Rohingya conflict has exposed, or generated, fissures that risk further dividing the multi-ethnic and multi-religious polity.

Moreover, while international capital originally returned to Myanmar, its flows have waned,[3] a phenomenon which some attribute to the Rohingya crisis.[4] But as importantly, Foreign Direct Investment (FDI) remains mostly focused on extractive industries (which have few linkages with labor-intensive sectors), meaning that livelihoods are not improving at a pace or in a manner as to meet expectations.[5] It also means that peasants are being dispossessed of land or are finding it impossible to get land returned to them that had been stolen during the military era. In this context it is perhaps not surprising that internecine conflicts (especially against Muslims or people with apparent South Asian physiognomy) are being fueled by a xenophobic discourse that presents people who have long lived in Myanmar as threats to the prosperity of the "nation." In other words, the brutalities against the Rohingya should not be seen as ancient hatreds becoming unleashed after the withdrawal of an appropriately coercive force,[6] but rather as a function of the current political changes, including political economic dislocations. Indeed, the Rohingya crisis and the challenges faced by peasants in the Burmese heartland should be understood together, as outcomes of the same historical moment.

And yet, when Burmese people protest their economic conditions in the midst of the country's natural resources being "sold off" to the highest bidder, state juridical institutions such as the courts and police continue to function much as they have done for over two decades: with impunity at worst, and with disregard for many citizen rights at best. This regressive approach has been enabled by the new "democratic" administration; indeed, Daw Suu's party has even pushed through—with little respect for democratic process and no consultation with civil society—a public assembly law far more repressive than that of the military's proxy party that ruled from 2011 to 2015.[7]

Transition to Where?

This brief discussion of Myanmar's ongoing challenges seeks to illuminate the ambiguity of the current moment, where previous advantages are suddenly reinterpreted as *also* potential risks. For instance, Myanmar's vast oil and gas reserves, as well as timber and valuable metals, that previously were viewed as a windfall that could drive rapid development may now be perceived as fuel for the so-called "resource curse." While Myanmar's strategic position in the region—nestled between the world's two most populous countries—was once heralded as a strategic opportunity, it has now been identified as a source of anxiety that is driving Buddhist-nationalist jingoism. While new free speech and assembly freedoms were identified as advantages in that they allowed a national conversation to develop after years of a military-dominated public sphere, there are now concerns that social media has been harnessed by the state to advance its own agenda—such as when Daw Suu's social media account labeled sexual assault of Rohingya women as "fake rape"[8] and insisted that "fake news" and "hate narratives" come from abroad.[9] And finally, while Daw Suu's maneuver to become the de facto leader of the country was initially identified as a great hope, now—given concerns about her inability to delegate responsibility, her coziness with the military, her chauvinism against non-Bamar peoples, and her authoritarian streak that brooks no dissent—it seems also a significant risk, even a detriment.

Given this sort of messiness, as various apparently unrelated phenomena increasingly appear deeply entangled and intertwined, and as social facts evade easy interpretation, we turn to the concept of "transition" itself. Critically, the contributions collected here were written at a novel moment in Myanmar's contemporary history, and reflect the ambiguity alluded to. While earlier volumes on Myanmar's transition have, as was appropriate, stressed the break with the country's military past,[10] while warning of risks on the *horizon*, the contributors to this volume penned their chapters across a time period that saw many of those risks actually *materialize*. Hence the volume is something of a hybrid—it considers the *potential* of the transition, *assesses* the transition, and critiques the *concept* of transition simultaneously.

The transition concept itself, as articulated in political science literature and conventional journalistic accounts, focuses on the political processes involved in the evolution or conversion of authoritarian states systems into ones more liberal (if not necessarily democratic). In these transitions, Dankwart Rustow, one of the founders of transition theory, argued in a seminal article for rejecting "what are sometimes proposed as preconditions of democracy, e.g., high levels of economic and social development or a prior consensus either on fundamentals or on the rules."[11] Scholars building on this insight came to stress that "the very process of transition from authoritarian rule, independently of the conditions that generated it, helps determine not only the prospects of democratic consolidation but also the success of the transition to democracy in the first place."[12] Indeed, "different types of democracy ... emerge from distinctive modes of regime transition" and have divergent "potential political, economic, and social consequences."[13] One of these distinctive modes, particularly relevant for Myanmar, is what has been called the "pacted transition" model, in which previous authoritarians negotiate with democratic elites, remaining close to or becoming fully incorporated into the new "democratic" regime. "Under such circumstances," writes the originator of the term "pacted transition," "major and irreversible shifts in the distribution of resources that can be converted into power and influence are more or less ruled out."[14] In fact, even after the period of "early uncertainty"—the delimited "transition"—ends, such pacts "tempt elites to extend their agreements" and "reinforce a pattern of collusion between political parties that generates corruption and citizen disillusionment."[15]

This description would seem to fit today's Myanmar well, as civil society activists express frustration at being systematically excluded from participating in the NLD's social policies,[16] as lower-class Burmese convey their disappointment at Daw Suu's unwillingness to address rising costs of daily living,[17] and as ethnic nationalities communicate concerns that Daw Suu has ceded leadership to the military in matters concerning the elusive peace process,[18] and accuse her of generally extending rather than reducing Burmanization of the nation.[19]

While the transitions literature is illuminating in this regard, we also want to mark a cautious distance from some of the presuppositions the term may imply. Indeed, "transition" suggests a starting point and also a destination—a linear progression within a time-bound period. All of these seem suspect assumptions given that Myanmar's past has not been eclipsed and various unrealized futures are being imagined by multiple actors.[20] In this volume, in fact, we have encouraged respective authors to interpret Myanmar's "transition" in their own ways—hence, some mark it as beginning after 2011/12, some in the mid-2000s, one goes back to 1988, while still others avoid the term entirely. Ultimately, we treat "transition" not as a concept that regulates and circumscribes our analysis of this particular political moment in Myanmar, but as a *discursive context* in which Myanmar has been placed, one which has real effects on the ground. For instance, not only are expectations of improved livelihoods described in the paragraph above generated in part by the transition framing, but the putative brittleness of the "transition" is used to police and restrict certain demands—from interventions that might help spur democratization[21] all the way to pleas to stop nascent ethnic cleansing[22]—suppressing them as "too much" or "too soon."

Unraveling the Challenges

These ambiguities and entanglements—of temporalities, objectives, visions, social phenomena—described above highlight another meaning of "unravel" contained in *Unraveling Myanmar*: if the country seems to be unraveling, this volume also focuses on the ways in which the challenges plaguing Myanmar need to be unraveled—identified, analyzed, and deconstructed. If the country no longer appears like it is democratizing, if inter-ethnic peace no longer seems possible, if industrial development appears out of reach, what are the factors coalescing to create intractable barriers to change? Animating the volume is the way its contributors bring unique perspectives and methodologies in their attempts at unraveling the challenges. Whether it is through discerning corruption by analyzing the country's real estate bubble, looking at the Rohingya issue through ethnographic description of Rohingya women's labor exploitation, assessing civil society advocacy capacity through its participation in attempts to regulate the extractive industry, or gauging the strength—and surprising weakness—of Myanmar's military (or Tatmadaw) through the electoral failures of its proxy party (the Union Solidarity and Development Party, USDP), the volume employs unconventional approaches and analytical rigor to draw out unique insights.

The Content of the Book

This book discusses a range of different issues—from economic development, political reforms, civil-military relations, foreign affairs, the changing religio-political landscape, the importance of education among ethnic groups, environmental governance, to the state of foreign assistance to Myanmar—to try to unravel the reasons for the persistence of some of the critical hurdles facing the country. It is based on a project financially supported by the Japan Society for the Promotion of Science (JSPS). The JSPS granted a four-year financial assistance to researchers at the Center for Southeast Asian Studies (CSEAS) at Kyoto University. Leading the project, Pavin Chachavalpongpun outlined the research proposal and the scope of study. Participating in this project are professors from CSEAS—Yoko Hayami, Koichi Fujita, Fumiharu Mieno, and Yoshihiro Nakanishi. The project began in 2013 and ended in 2017. In February 2016, a workshop was organized as a part of fulfilling the objective of the project entitled, "Critical Hurdles to Myanmar's Opening Up Process." The organizers invited experts in Myanmar studies to present their work, the result of which forms the basis of this book.

In terms of the book's structure, there are four main sections: politics, political-economy, social-cultural issues, and the Rohingya conflict. The first section sets the stage with contributions outlining some of the significant political challenges Myanmar faces. Chapter One offers a broad picture of the post-election landscape in Myanmar, delving into options, opportunities, as well as challenges in the political realm. Aung Tun analyzes Myanmar's historical 2015 election, in which mass participation in a largely free and fair poll resulted in the NLD's landslide victory and consequent formation of a government. In analyzing the elections, the chapter appraises some factors contributing to the defeat of major political parties, such as the ousted military-backed USDP and ethnic-based parties. Regarding the USDP, ultimately it was not so much that it *lost*, argues Aung Tun, but that the NLD *won*: the widespread and exuberant support for Daw Suu's party was too great to overcome. As for ethnic parties, however, the resounding defeat was less anticipated. Aung Tun presents evidence from Burmese commentators that argues that voters deployed a sophisticated pooling strategy—choosing to give their votes to the NLD, which could form a government, rather than risk "splitting" the opposition to the incumbent USDP. This was especially true given that the existence of multiple ethnic parties vying for the "ethnic vote" meant that voters already perceived the ethnic vote as at risk of being diluted. Looking forward, this chapter draws attention to the risks now borne by the NLD given the electoral faith placed in it by ethnic voters, especially given the rising authoritarianism from within the party that Aung Tun notes.

Chapter Two by Yoshihiro Nakanishi takes on the civil-military relationship, inverting the typical perspective and analyzing the transition from the Tatmadaw's perspective. Nakanishi argues that while the military junta sought to create political stability by introducing a formal electoral system that would enable the military's institutionalization in politics, things have not in fact gone quite according to plan. On one hand, this attempt appeared successful during President Thein Sein's rule (2011–15), under which the government reached detente with the NLD, improved its relationship with Western countries, and presided over a high economic growth rate. However, the NLD's 2015 electoral victory clearly showed that early achievements were not sufficient to promise the miltary's party a second term. Because the USDP was resoundingly defeated, the Tatmadaw lost its coalition partner, in turn forfeiting "some of the political leverage necessary to impose its will on the government." Further, the new NLD government proceeded to pack the Constitutional Tribunal with sympathetic judges, meaning that the NLD can accomplish many goals through legislation, as the military lacks the influence to initiate the Constitutional review process. And despite the Rohingya expulsion giving the Tatmadaw popularity it had never before enjoyed—with nationalists supporting it, and foreign nations casting opprobrium especially on Daw Suu[23]—it is unclear that the Tatmadaw can translate that popularity into electoral support for its USDP. As a result, the military finds itself in a new role: no longer hegemonic and setting policy, but able to act as a potential spoiler, creating a dangerous and unstable position for the country, to be sure.

Chapter Three, co-authored by Moe Thuzar and Pavin Chachavalpongpun, elaborates on the country's foreign relations and how they have been affected by the on-going opening up process. It critically examines Myanmar's foreign policy positions and trajectories across different time periods in the country's post-independence era up to the present. The authors focus on the current three major powers (the US, China, and Japan) as having the most impact or influence (politically, economically, strategically) on foreign policy, and the aim of this chapter is to offer a prism of interpreting Myanmar's foreign policy moves rather than analyzing its bilateral relations per se. The authors' main argument is that while the fundamentals of the country's independent and neutral stance in foreign policy remain essentially unchanged, the different exigencies of external and domestic circumstances have influenced the practice of foreign policy towards the current active engagements on both bilateral and multilateral fronts, even as the country grapples with serious legacy issues as it emerges from its cocoon. Yet, while recent governments have attempted to move away from an encroaching China, the Rohingya crisis has driven Myanmar back in that direction and away from the West. One question is whether the country can remain neutral now that, as the authors put it, "The NLD government's foreign policy actions and pronouncements will now be viewed mainly through the prism of the Rohingya crisis."

The book's second section drills down into the political-economic challenges the country has been facing during this period. Chapter Four, by Fumiharu Mieno, investigates the way the current corporate and financial systems in Myanmar currently impact its long-term growth trajectory. Mieno describes the necessity of developing financial intermediation and corporate governance institutions that can efficiently allocate "long-term" capital necessary for countries seeking to structurally transform from being primary product producers to becoming advanced manufacturers. In a system without institutionalized reforms in either sector, often corporations become financiers, and Mieno describes the trajectories that so-called "cronies" in Myanmar have taken to become these kinds of conglomerates. This crucial insight provides a new way of viewing these much-discussed cronies—rather than simply parasites on military patrons, cronies have become essential cogs in Myanmar's (admittedly dysfunctional) political economy.[24] Mieno also notes that while the economy has experienced decent growth since the beginning of the SLORC reforms in 1990, the composition of exports and GDP, after a brief moment of potential industrialization, has remained dominated by primary product extraction, a harbinger of bleak economic prospects.

Acting as a useful partner to the previous chapter, Chapter Five, written by Bo Bo Nge, takes the insightful approach of using Myanmar's real estate bubble to draw conclusions about illicit capital flows and money laundering in the country. The chapter begins by observing that in Myanmar people store value in real assets because of the "inflation tax" applied to cash and bank deposits. The author then demonstrates that the real estate market is effectively used to launder illicit money, highlighting a tax amnesty from 2007 to 2012 during which time taxes were slashed on monies for which holders could not prove legal provenance. Then, finding vastly more illicit capital inflows into Myanmar than outflows, Bo Bo Nge speculates that these incentives provided money-laundering opportunities not only for domestic capital, but for *foreign* capital as well. As a result of this "official whitewashing privilege," the author notes that it should be no surprise that a real estate bubble has formed, especially given the vast illicit economy in Myanmar (jade, as documented by Global Witness,[25] has been estimated to produce US$31b off-books revenue). Bo Bo Nge concludes by considering the economic impacts of an inflated real estate sector, demonstrating that by using it as collateral, financial institutions give out loans to those who can afford real estate, not to those with economically viable proposals. Such distortions can lead to the misallocation of capital, while the real estate bubble, it bursts, may lead to a significant economic contraction.

In Chapter Six, on environmental governance and the Extractive Industries Transparency Initiative (EITI) in Myanmar, co-authors Marjanneke J. Vijge and Adam Simpson explain how Myanmar's recent liberalization has brought opportunities as well as challenges in the extractive sector. Though the exploitation of natural resources in Myanmar has historically been prioritized over environmental protection, the country has recently embarked on an environmental governance transition, part of which involves the implementation of the Myanmar Extractive Industries Transparency Initiative (MEITI). Taking MEITI as a case study, the authors assess its ability to contribute to the sustainable governance of the extractive industry sector. In particular, the authors analyze whether and how the MEITI (dis)empowers civil society organizations from addressing the environmental and social impacts of extractive industries in Myanmar, uncovering an interesting set of tensions in which Civil Society Organizations (CSOs) identify how the same MEITI platforms on which they are able to raise issues and put pressure on government also run the risk of co-opting them in a set of processes that ultimately act as fig leaves covering systematic environmental exploitation.

Chapter Seven, commencing the third section on social changes, acts as a bridge with the previous one, given its focus on international development economics. Patrick Strefford's article addresses development aid in Myanmar, specifically focusing on capacity development (CD) in this transitional period, arguing that technical assistance for CD has become a key modality for disbursing development aid. Capacity, in terms of the ability to set and achieve goals, has become regarded by donors and partners alike as both a goal of, and prerequisite for, development. However, this perspective concerns only the capacity shortfall *within* the recipient country, here Myanmar. While there is no doubt that the ability of the Myanmar government to provide the public services that the citizens require is indeed limited, Strefford's chapter focuses instead on the ability of the donor community to provide the services that the government requires. Do donors have the capacity required to disburse effective development assistance? In answering such questions, this chapter investigates the capacity of donors, showing how donor-driven aid is a significant phenomenon that limits the capacity of donors to provide effective aid for development. It gestures towards considering an under-appreciated aspect of capacity: the capacity to *translate* technocratic assistance into political idioms and implementable policies that allow domestic governments (and recipients) to have ownership of the projects, and hence implement them successfully. Hence donor-driven agendas may themselves *inhibit* donors from cultivating the critical capacity that is the unique skill of cultural translation.

Chapter Eight by Patrick McCormick underlines the importance of ethnic education in "Burma," the name he prefers for referring to the country. McCormick's initial review of the education sector serves to dampen enthusiasm at near-term prospects for rapid "development" or "industrialization" in Myanmar, at least if development is meant to be led by human capital dependent sectors. McCormick not only relays sobering details on low enrolment and achievement metrics, but highlights an education system oriented towards an "agrarian, monarchical, hierarchical society," rather than a more highly-differentiated and egalitarian one. Turning to ethnic education systems, the author shows how the systems are meant to address the educational needs of ethnic minority students in areas where government services have been either unavailable (due to a history of warfare) or inadequate. In examining the systems of the Mon, Kachin, and Karen, McCormick shows that each system reflects the contingencies of politics and history: with the British, with the central Burmese state, and with their respective experiences with armed conflict and ceasefires. Attitudes towards using ethnic languages as a medium of instruction and towards participating in Burmese national life by using the Burmese language all vary across the systems. For many, it is important that students who have gone through the ethnic systems have the possibility of taking examinations to enter government high schools. For others, conversely, life is oriented *outside* or *away* from Myanmar, an important takeaway for those presuming a multi-ethnic federal future in Myanmar. Hence, if greater integration of the ethnic systems into the government system is seen as a realistic long-term goal, efforts to solve problems in terms of qualifications and recognition of students and teachers must be redoubled. The state of the ethnic education systems sheds light on processes of decentralization and on the hurdles the country faces in efforts to allow greater autonomy while also serving the educational needs of ethnic minority students. Particularly in this aspect, the matters the ethnic education systems raise overlap with larger questions of mother tongue education and improving educational outcomes by using minority languages, wherever in the country those communities live.

In Chapter Nine, Matthew J. Walton tackles the issue of religion in politics and society, positing that Myanmar's current political transition has provided additional political space for the expression of Buddhist perspectives and concerns in the public sphere, some of which support democratic reform and some of which express a more regressive agenda. For the latter group, political, economic, and social changes have created an environment of uncertainty in which both Buddhism and the dominant sense of Burmese national identity as Buddhist have been perceived as under threat. This chapter explores some of the aspects of Myanmar's political transition that seem to have enabled or supported the rise of Buddhist activist groups, especially those that have taken a leading role in anti-Muslim protests and violence. It considers several different factors that may have promoted the rise of these groups or conditioned the dynamics of Buddhist-Muslim conflict, including changing communication practices and technologies, the influence of global anti-Muslim discourse and sentiment, the reorganization of democratic space (including lifting restrictions on speech and expression), the aforementioned anxieties about Buddhism, and perceived threats to monks' authority and role in society.

The book concludes with a special section devoted to the Rohingya crisis, with two chapters commissioned after the events of August/September 2017. The first, Chapter Ten by Shae Frydenlund provides an alternative to the many current one-dimensional accounts of Rohingya suffering, instead portraying what real on-the-ground existence is like for Rohingya women. While many descriptions of Rohingya focus on horrific abuses, implicitly presenting Rohingya as completely cut off from the rest of Myanmar (and the world), the author shows how certain modes of Rohingya exclusion lead to other forms of *inclusion*: as formal labor markets are denied to them because of their ethnicity, they are reabsorbed in systems of non-remunerated affective labor. Their work as caregivers "subsidize[s] the low wages paid by brick factories and leather tanneries in Sittwe and Cox's Bazaar, as well as the meatpacking factories that employ large numbers of refugees in Colorado." By paying careful ethnographic attention to the networks and relationships that Rohingya women forge after dislocation, Frydenlund provides rare insight into the ways in which Rohingya women are intimately involved in capitalist accumulation and global systems. This has the dual benefit of re-humanizing and re-politicizing people who have been mostly represented as bare life. Further, the author observes how Rohingya women are increasingly choosing to wear the *burqa* in public, but analyzes it not (as some have) as denoting increasing Islamization, but as a defensive tactic against their increasing public exposure. The unfortunate consequence is that as Rohingya women are made increasingly vulnerable, they pursue survival strategies—such as wearing the *burqa*—that are interpreted as rejections of Myanmar culture, intensifying their vulnerability.

The final chapter, by Elliott Prasse-Freeman and Kirt Mausert, is a speculative reconsideration of archaeological, genetic, linguistic, historiographical, and ethnographic sources on Arakan and southeastern Bengal (Chittagong) from the 8th century to the present. The authors argue that while colonial imaginaries, adopted and reproduced by the current Burmese regime, insist that people who "look" Southeast Asian and practice Buddhism "belong" in Myanmar, while people who "look" South Asian and practice Islam "belong" in Bangladesh, the past suggests that there was a complex, fluid, and interpenetrating set of trans-ethnic relations that incorporated Arakan/Chittagong Bengal into a broad social system. While Arakan's first civilizations (Veshaili, Lemro) were Indic Buddhist, and 16th- and 17th-century Arakan incorporated Chittagong and managed vast Muslim populations in both rural and urban domains, it was only later that religious identity became a dominant and exclusive marker of personhood, that the shared past of both Rakhine and Rohingya became appropriated by the former as its exclusive patrimony, and the Naf river (today the border with Bangladesh) became a civilizational dividing line. By deconstructing many of the assumptions about the region, the authors challenge and critique the dominant versions of Myanmar's indigeneity discourse, showing that it crumbles under intense scrutiny.

Acknowledgment

We would like to sincerely thank the JSPS for its financial support for this project. We are grateful to the members of this JSPS-funded project and all the contributors, for their cooperation, patience, and commitment. Without them, this book would have been impossible.

Notes

1. Medicins Sans Frontiers, "Myanmar/Bangladesh: MSF surveys estimate that at least 6,700 Rohingya were killed during the attacks in Myanmar," 12 December 2017 <http://www.msf.org/en/article/myanmarbangladesh-msf-surveys-estimate-least-6700-rohingya-were-killed-during-attacks> [accessed 18 June 2018].
2. Renaud Egreteau, *Caretaking Democratization: The Military and Democracy in Myanmar* (Oxford: Oxford University Press, 2016).
3. Motokazu Matsui, "Myanmar braces for 30% drop in foreign investment," *Nikkei Asian Review*, 21 March 2017 <https://asia.nikkei.com/Politics/Myanmar-braces-for-30-drop-in-foreign-investment> [accessed 18 June 2018].
4. Gwen Robinson, "The Rohingya Crisis Gives Investors in Myanmar Cold Feet," *Nikkei Asian Review*, 9 February 2017 <https://asia.nikkei.com/Economy/The-Rohingya-crisis-gives-investors-in-Myanmar-cold-feet> [accessed 16 September 2018]; Thiha Ko Ko, "Western FDI to fall in 2018 as Rakhine Crisis Continues," *Myanmar Times*, 8 January 2018 <https://www.mmtimes.com/news/western-fdi-fall-2018-rakhine-crisis-continues.html> [accessed 16 September 2018].
5. Elliott Prasse-Freeman and Phyo Win Latt, "Class and Inequality in Contemporary Myanmar," in *Routledge Handbook of Contemporary Myanmar*, ed. Adam Simpson, Nicholas Farrelly, and Ian Holliday (Oxon and New York: Routledge, 2018), pp. 404–18.
6. Contrast with Jacques Leider's ancient hatreds argument in "Competing Identities and the Hybridized History of the Rohingyas," in *Metamorphosis: Studies in Social and Political Change in Myanmar*, ed. Renaud Egreteau and François Robinne (Singapore: NUS Press, 2015), pp. 151–2.
7. Aye Thein, "Democratizing the Public Space in Myanmar," *Tea Circle Oxford*, 26 March 2018.

8. Jonah Fisher, "Hounded and Ridiculed for Complaining of Rape," *BBC*, 11 March 2017 <https://www.bbc.com/news/magazine-39204086> [accessed 16 September 2018].
9. Reuters, "'Hate Narratives' from Abroad Drive Myanmar Communities Apart, Suu Kyi Says," *Reuters*, 21 June 2018 <https://www.reuters.com/article/us-myanmar-rohingya/hate-narratives-from-abroad-drive-myanmar-communities-apart-suu-kyi-says-idUSKBN1JH0I9> [accessed 16 September 2018]. On the general issue of social media and its effects in Myanmar, see Matthew Schissler, "New Technologies, Established Practices: Developing Narratives of Muslim Threat in Myanmar," in *Islam and the State in Myanmar: Muslim-Buddhist Relations and the Politics of Belonging*, ed. Melissa Crouch (Oxford: Oxford University Press, 2016), pp. 211–33.
10. See International Crisis Group, "Reform in Myanmar: One Year On," Briefing 136/Asia, 11 April 2012; Skidmore, Monique and Trevor Wilson, "Interpreting the Transition in Myanmar," in *Myanmar's Transition: Openings, Obstacles, and Opportunities*, ed. Monique Skidmore, Trevor Wilson, and Nick Cheesman (Singapore: Institute of Southeast Asian Studies, 2012); Renaud Egreteau and François Robinne, eds., *Metamorphosis: Studies in Social and Political Change in Myanmar* (Singapore: NUS Press, 2015); David I. Steinberg, ed., *Myanmar: The Dynamics of an Evolving Polity* (Colorado: Lynne Rienner, 2015); Adam Simpson, Nicholas Farrelly, and Ian Holliday, "Introduction: Explaining Myanmar in Flux and Transition," in *Routledge Handbook of Contemporary Myanmar*, ed. Simpson, Farrelly, and Holliday (Oxon and New York: Routledge, 2018).
11. Dankwart Rustow, "Transitions to Democracy: Toward a Dynamic Model," *Comparative Politics* 2, no. 3 (1970): 362.
12. Gerardo L. Munck and Carol Skalnik Leff, "Modes of Transition and Democratization: South America and Eastern Europe in Comparative Perspective," *Comparative Politics* 29, no. 3 (1997): 344.
13. Terry Lynn Karl, "Dilemmas of democratization in Latin America," *Comparative Politics* 23, no. 1 (1990): 1.
14. Philippe C. Schmitter, "Twenty-five years, fifteen findings," *Journal of Democracy* 21, no. 1 (2010): 20.
15. Schmitter 2010: 23.
16. Elliott Prasse-Freeman, "The New Burma is Starting to Look Too Much Like the Old Burma," *Foreign Policy*, 28 June 2016 <http://foreignpolicy.com/2016/06/28/the-new-burma-is-starting-to-look-too-much-like-the-old-burma/> [accessed 16 September 2018].
17. Richard Paddock, "After Aung San Suu Kyi's First Year in Power, Dismay Swirls in Myanmar," *New York Times*, 8 April 2017 <https://www.nytimes.com/2017/04/08/world/asia/myanmar-aung-san-suu-kyi-first-year.html> [accessed 16 September 2018].

18. "Myanmar's Failing Peace," *The Irrawaddy*, May 2018. <https://www.irrawaddy.com/opinion/editorial/myanmars-failing-peace.html> [accessed 16 September 2018]; Lawi Weng, "Peace Process Entirely in Military's Hands, Karen Group Says," *The Irrawaddy*, 6 June 2018.
19. Nyein Nyein, "Analysis: Where Some See Respect, Ethnic Groups See Burmanization and Loss of Rights," *The Irrawaddy*, 16 June 2018, <https://www.irrawaddy.com/news/analysis-see-respect-ethnic-groups-see-burmanization-loss-rights.html> [accessed 16 September 2018]; Paddock 2017.
20. Courtney Wittekind, "Transition and its Temporalities," *Tea Circle*, 10 January 2017.
21. Prasse-Freeman 2016.
22. Elliott Prasse-Freeman, "Scapegoating in Burma," *Anthropology Today* 29, no. 4 (August 2013).
23. Ben Dunant, "It's Good to Be the Tatmadaw," *The Diplomat*, 11 May 2017 <https://thediplomat.com/2017/05/its-good-to-be-the-tatmadaw/> [accessed 16 September 2018].
24. See also Michele Ford, Michael Gillan, and Htwe Htwe Thein, "From Cronyism to Oligarchy?: Privatisation and Business Elites in Myanmar," *Journal of Contemporary Asia* 46, no. 1 (2016).
25. Global Witness, "Jade: Myanmar's 'Big State Secret'," October 2015.

References

Aye Thein. 2018. "Democratizing the Public Space in Myanmar." *Tea Circle Oxford*, 26 March.

Crouch, Melissa and Tim Lindsey. 2014. "Introduction: Myanmar, Law Reform and Asian Legal Studies." In *Law, Society and Transition in Myanmar*, ed. Melissa Crouch and Tim Lindsey. New South Wales: Bloomsbury Publishing.

Dunant, Ben. 2017. "It's Good to Be the Tatmadaw." *The Diplomat*, 11 May <https://thediplomat.com/2017/05/its-good-to-be-the-tatmadaw/> [accessed 16 September 2018].

Egreteau, Renaud. 2016. *Caretaking Democratization: The Military and Democracy in Myanmar*. Oxford: Oxford University Press.

Egreteau, Renaud and François Robinne, eds. 2015. *Metamorphosis: Studies in Social and Political Change in Myanmar*. Singapore: NUS Press.

Fisher, Jonah. 2017. "Hounded and ridiculed for complaining of rape." *BBC*, 11 March <https://www.bbc.com/news/magazine-39204086> [accessed 16 September 2018].

Ford, Michele, Michael Gillan, and Htwe Htwe Thein. 2015. "From Cronyism to Oligarchy? Privatisation and Business Elites in Myanmar." *Journal of Contemporary Asia* 46, no. 1: 18–41.

Global Witness. 2015. "Jade: Myanmar's 'Big State Secret'," October.

International Crisis Group. 2012. "Reform in Myanmar: One Year On." Briefing 136 / Asia, 11 April.

Irrawaddy. 2018. "Myanmar's Failing Peace." *The Irrawaddy*, May <https://www.irrawaddy.com/opinion/editorial/myanmars-failing-peace.html> [accessed 16 September 2018].

Karl, Terry Lynn. 1990. "Dilemmas of Democratization in Latin America." *Comparative Politics* 23, no. 1: 1–21.

Lawi Weng. 2018. "Peace Process Entirely in Military's Hands, Karen Group Says." *The Irrawaddy*, 6 June.

Leider, Jacques. 2015. "Competing Identities and the Hybridized History of the Rohingyas." In *Metamorphosis: Studies in Social and Political Change in Myanmar*, ed. Renaud Egreteau and François Robinne. Singapore: NUS Press.

Matsui, Motokazu. 2017. "Myanmar braces for 30% Drop in Foreign Investment," *Nikkei Asian Review*, 21 March <https://asia.nikkei.com/Politics/Myanmar-braces-for-30-drop-in-foreign-investment> [accessed 16 September 2018].

Medicins Sans Frontiers. 2017. "Myanmar/Bangladesh: MSF surveys estimate that at least 6,700 Rohingya were killed during the attacks in Myanmar," 12 December <http://www.msf.org/en/article/myanmarbangladesh-msf-surveys-estimate-least-6700-rohingya-were-killed-during-attacks> [accessed 18 June 2018].

Munck, Gerardo L. and Carol Skalnik Leff. 1997. "Modes of Transition and Democratization: South America and Eastern Europe in Comparative Perspective." *Comparative Politics* 29, no. 3: 343–62.

Nyein Nyein. 2018. "Analysis: Where Some See Respect, Ethnic Groups See Burmanization and Loss of Rights," *The Irrawaddy*, 16 June <https://www.irrawaddy.com/news/analysis-see-respect-ethnic-groups-see-burmanization-loss-rights.html> [accessed 16 September 2018].

Paddock, Richard. 2017. "After Aung San Suu Kyi's First Year in Power, Dismay Swirls in Myanmar." *New York Times*, 8 April <https://www.nytimes.com/2017/04/08/world/asia/myanmar-aung-san-suu-kyi-first-year.html> [accessed 16 September 2018].

Prasse-Freeman, Elliott. 2016. "The New Burma is Starting to Look Too Much Like the Old Burma." *Foreign Policy*, 28 June <http://foreignpolicy.com/2016/06/28/the-new-burma-is-starting-to-look-too-much-like-the-old-burma/> [accessed 16 September 2018].

Prasse-Freeman, Elliott and Phyo Win Latt. 2018. "Class and Inequality in Contemporary Myanmar." In *Routledge Handbook of Contemporary Myanmar*, ed. Adam Simpson, Nicholas Farrelly, and Ian Holliday. Oxon and New York: Routledge, pp. 404–18.

Reuters. 2018. "'Hate Narratives' from Abroad Drive Myanmar Communities Apart, Suu Kyi Says." *Reuters*, 21 June <https://www.reuters.com/article/us-myanmar-rohingya/hate-narratives-from-abroad-drive-myanmar-communities-apart-suu-kyi-says-idUSKBN1JH0I9> [accessed 16 September 2018].

Robinson, Gwen. 2017. "The Rohingya Crisis Gives Investors in Myanmar Cold Feet." *Nikkei Asian Review*, 9 February <https://asia.nikkei.com/Economy/The-Rohingya-crisis-gives-investors-in-Myanmar-cold-feet> [accessed 16 September 2018].

Rustow, Dankwart A. 1970. "Transitions to democracy: Toward a dynamic model." *Comparative Politics* 2, no. 3: 337–63.

Schissler, Matthew. 2016. "New Technologies, Established Practices: Developing Narratives of Muslim Threat in Myanmar." In *Islam and the State in Myanmar: Muslim-Buddhist Relations and the Politics of Belonging*, ed. Melissa Crouch. Oxford: Oxford University Press, pp. 211–33.

Schmitter, Philippe C. 2010. "Twenty-five Years, Fifteen Findings." *Journal of Democracy* 21, no. 1: 17–28.

Simpson, Adam, Nicholas Farrelly, and Ian Holliday. 2018. "Introduction: Explaining Myanmar in Flux and Transition." In *Routledge Handbook of Contemporary Myanmar*, ed. Simpson, Farrelly, and Holliday. Oxon and New York: Routledge.

Skidmore, Monique and Trevor Wilson. 2012. "Interpreting the Transition in Myanmar." In *Myanmar's Transition: Openings, Obstacles, and Opportunities*, ed. Monique Skidmore, Trevor Wilson, and Nick Cheesman. Singapore: Institute of Southeast Asian Studies.

Steinberg, David I., ed. 2015. *Myanmar: The Dynamics of an Evolving Polity*. Colorado: Lynne Rienner.

Thiha Ko Ko. 2018. "Western FDI to fall in 2018 as Rakhine crisis continues." *Myanmar Times*, 8 January <https://www.mmtimes.com/news/western-fdi-fall-2018-rakhine-crisis-continues.html> [accessed 16 September 2018].

Wittekind, Courtney. 2017. "Transition and its Temporalities." *Tea Circle*, 10 January.

SECTION ONE
The Political Landscape

CHAPTER 1

Post-Elections Myanmar: Options, Opportunities or Challenges?

Aung Tun

The 2015 election was a landmark political moment in Myanmar.[1] The international community recognized it as the most free and fair election in the last 25 years of Myanmar's political history.[2] Ninety-two political parties participated in the 8 November election, presenting a diversity of political views, fielding over 6,000 candidates, using a variety of campaign methods, and finally utilizing massive manpower through extensive mobilization operations in various constituencies.[3] Every party made an enormous effort to put forward its individual political goals and programs for the next five years. Undoubtedly, this was an extremely important political moment that would shape the future for every citizen in Myanmar.

Myanmar's General Election in November 2015 determined the members of the Assembly of the Union (*Pyidaugsu Hluttaw*), which is comprised of the Lower House of parliament (People Assembly, *Pyithu Hluttaw*) and the Upper House (National Assembly, *Amyotha Hluttaw*) as well as the regional assemblies of the 14 states and regions. The Lower House has not more than 330 *Pyithu Hluttaw* representatives elected from the prescribed 330 townships across Myanmar, plus 110 *Pyithu Hluttaw* representatives from the army. The Upper House is composed of 168 *Amyotha Hluttaw* representatives elected in an equal number of 12 representatives from each region or state, plus 56 representatives from the army. The principle underpinning this is to ensure "good representation" among population, ethnicity or races. Their duties are similar to that of the US Upper and Lower Houses; to make laws, to scrutinize the executive and ensure accountability.

In the 2015 election a total of 1,171 seats were contested—330 seats (323 seats in actuality as elections in the seven Shan constituencies were not held due to security concerns) in the Lower House, 168 seats in the Upper House, and 673 seats (659 in reality due to the fact that elections in four Shan constituencies were not held for the same security concerns) in the Regional Assembly. In the bicameral General Assembly, the National League for Democracy (NLD) won 79 per cent of the total elected seats, granting it a supermajority of 59 per cent of the total parliamentary seats including the military ones—60 per cent in the Upper House (*Amyotha Hluttaw*) and 59 per cent in the Lower House (*Pyithu Hluttaw*). A detailed explanation of the election follows below.

Pyithu Hluttaw (Lower House)

Of the 92 registered parties, 82 parties fielded a total of 1,745 candidates for 330 seats (323 seats) in the Lower House (this included 84 independent candidates). The NLD won 255 seats of those 323 contested seats, securing 59 per cent of "total seats" in the Lower House and 78 per cent of "total contested seats."[4] The Union Solidarity and Development Party (USDP) won 30 seats, finishing in second place, while the Arakan National Party (ANP) and the Shan Nationalities League for Democracy (SNLD) took 12 seats each. The remaining 14 seats were shared by other ethnic parties including one independent candidate from the Shan State. Given that the NLD secured a supermajority of the seats in the Lower House, the party was in a good position to shape the political agenda in the next parliamentary session. This is because the Lower House has almost two times more seats in the Assembly than the Upper House, as the former is based on population while the latter on geographic areas of 14 states and regions.[5]

Amyotha Hluttaw (Upper House)

Of the 92 registered parties, 72 parties (10 parties less than the number that contested for the *Pyithu Hluttaw*) fielded a total of 886 candidates for 168 seats in the Upper House, including 2 independent candidates. The NLD won 135 seats, thereby securing 60 per cent of "total seats" in the Upper House and 80 per cent of "total contested seats."[6] The USDP party won only 11 seats in the Upper House, a major humiliating defeat. The ANP took 10 seats, while the SNLD took 3 seats. Other ethnic parties, including two independent candidates from the Chin and Kayah

States, shared the remaining 12 seats.[7] Again, in the Upper House, as in the Lower House, the NLD won a landslide, putting itself in a strong political position to shape the future of the country.

Regional *Hluttaw* (Regional Parliaments)

Of the 92 registered parties, 90 parties fielded a total of 3,443 candidates for Regional *Hluttaw* (a total of 673 seats), including 177 independent candidates. The NLD won a landslide in all the seven regions and in five states, sweeping the seats except in the Shan and Rakhine States. The table below shows how the NLD fared in each state and region.[8]

States/Regions	*NLD (%)*	*Remark*
Chin	50	Majority
Kachin	49	Majority
Kayah	55	Majority
Kayin	57	Majority
Mon	61	Majority
Rakhine	19	ANP 49% by majority
Shan	16	USDP + Military 51% by majority
Ayeyarwaddy	71	Majority
Bago	72	Majority
Mandalay	63	Majority
Sagaing	68	Majority
Tahnintharyi	75	Majority
Yangon	72	Majority

Source: Union Election Commission (UEC), Myanmar and ICG 2015.

As a result of this outstanding performance in the regional elections, the NLD unseated all the existing USDP Chief Ministers, as well as their Cabinet Members and Regional Parliamentary Speakers.

Expectations from the NLD's Success

Since the NLD repeated a landslide—as in the 1990 election—and won a supermajority in both houses of Parliament (*Phyidaungsu Hluttaw*), the NLD-led *Hluttaw* elected U Htin Kyaw in March 2016 and then U Win Myint in March 2018 [upon the former's resignation] as President and U Henry Van Thio (of Chin ethnicity) as the Second Vice President. Meanwhile, the military elected an ex-general, U Myint Swe (the military has the constitutional right to appoint one of the vice presidents), as the First Vice President. Aung San Suu Kyi (hereafter referred to as Daw Suu) became the de facto leader of the country, being appointed as State Counselor, Minister of President's Office, as well as Foreign Minister. She is in charge of the peace process, the stability in the Rakhine State as well as presiding over other high-level committees. Prior to the formation of the new administration, she declared herself to be "above the president," and the new administration ensured her powerful position.[9] In fact, this is also concerned with the Tatmadaw's recognition of her political position as State Counselor particularly in her important roles on peace process and so forth. For example, in the 2008 constitution, there is nothing mandated for State Counselor position, and it remains very unclear that the Tatmadaw will treat her as State Counselor [the de facto leader] or just a Foreign Minister in terms of her working relationship with them. Despite this uncertainty, with the perhaps surprisingly peaceful transfer of power, the new administration headed by the NLD leadership has the political mandate to run the country for the next five years. But many critical questions have emerged regarding expectations on how this change would transform the political landscape.

Legislatively, many positive results were expected from the NLD-led *Hluttaws*. Many civil and political rights-related laws and articles as well as provisions were expected to make the nation more democratic.[10] For instance, *Pyithu Hluttaw* had attempted to revoke the notorious law known as the 1950 Emergency Provisions Act, which was used to arrest politicians and activists by successive Burmese regimes.[11] However, it is very important to point out that Myanmar's legislative system is based on an Affairs Committee System rather than a Debate System.[12] Those committees principally demand better technical understanding of issues and subject matters to formulate bills or to discuss any proposals or issues beforehand, rather than in open debate in parliament. In other words, the committee system emphasizes working together intellectually in the committee rather than open debate. For instance, the work of the Public Account Committee definitely requires members who understand well the technicalities of public budgeting and related oversight. Without the understanding of the technical matters on those issues to be decided in the parliaments, it would be difficult to move the nation forward because many technical laws (such as business and financial laws) enacted during the socialist economy period need to be amended or revoked because they are outdated. How this will work in the NLD government remains to be seen.

In addition, because of its remarkable victory, the NLD had the right to elect several "heavyweight political positions"—all Chief Ministers for Region and State governments, Speakers for the State and Region *Hluttaws,* Ministers for those governments, Attorney General of the Union, Chairman of the Union Election Commission as well as of Anti-Corruption Commission.[13] The NLD-led government streamlined the number of ministries from 36 to 25, mainly to reduce the government expenditure.[14] Obviously, a successful implementation will benefit not only the public at large but also the NLD itself since this could be a critical determinant for the result in the next elections. The NLD implementation process, therefore, tests the ability of the NLD to meet the public's expectations.

In addition to a myriad of new political tasks in its upcoming administration, the NLD also faces many challenges. Perhaps the most important challenge is how the NLD deals with the National Defense and Security Council (NDSC). The NDSC is led by the President and its functions are prescribed in Article 201 of the Constitution. However, it seems that the President has considerable discretion regarding the timing and contents of the NDSC meeting.[15] In this Council, power is largely shared with the military. The Council is composed of 11 powerful members: the President, two Vice Presidents, two Speakers of the Lower and Upper Houses, the Commander-in-Chief of the Defense Services, the Deputy Commander-in-Chief of the Defense Services, the Minister for Defense, the Minister for Foreign Affairs, the Minister for Home Affairs, and the Minister for Border Affairs.[16] Given that the military already has the constitutional right to appoint three key ministers and two Commanders-in-Chief (Chief and Deputy) as well as one Vice President to that Council, the NLD is only granted the right to appoint five Council members.[17] This means that it will be extremely difficult for the NLD to gather a majority of the votes or the voices, particularly if any "state emergency" issue would arise. In this way, it is obvious that the military has the ultimate power to shape "the rules of the game" in town. Dealing with this powerful Council on important matters such as security issues and the peace process will be a crucial challenge for the NLD. Myanmar's peace process definitely rests on the Council's decisions rather than the new government's, unless a commitment from both sides were to be secured. Upon taking in office for two and a half years, the NLD government has never called any NDSC meeting, which deals with declaration of a state of emergency and martial law issues even for the Rakhine crisis.[18] By not calling any NDSC meeting, NLD demonstrates that it does not recognize the role of NDSC in the new administration's important decisions, even though NDSC has the constitutional rights to exist for those decisions. Thus, it is very important to mention that NLD still insist on the constitutional amendments and that the working relationship between the Tatmadaw and NLD-led government is perceived to be based on informal political setting, not a legitimate way as is set in the 2008 constitution.

The Failure of the USDP

The 2015 general election made the USDP, the ruling party, the big loser and the NLD, the major opposition party, the big winner. There are several significant reasons why the USDP performed so poorly and suffered such an embarrassing defeat in the 2015 election. At this point, it is imperative to keep in mind that the USDP had all the necessary "political assets" to secure the votes it needed to stay in power: (a) the 2008 constitution only required the USDP to win a little over 25 per cent of the total contested seats to stay in power, which is not a level playing field for other political parties; (b) the ruling party and the Union Election Commission were perceived to be in alignment with the existing government;[19] (c) it had very good financial resources; (d) the votes of the military and its supporters and dependents were already secured; and (e) some voters favored the USDP to form a new reformist government.

Despite those assets, the USDP failed at the ballot box for a number of reasons. First of all, the USDP could not figure out a way to effectively utilize those important assets, exclusively available for itself. Second, there was a "soft coup" at midnight on 12 August 2015 within the party, just a few weeks prior to the election. A power struggle between the "Thein Sein Camp" and the "Shwe Mann Camp" became very intense, with Shwe Mann finally being purged by force rather than by the party's constitution.[20] That gave the voters the impression that they could not trust the party; how would this party achieve democratic reforms since it did not respect its own "party discipline"?[21] This was definitely a massive failure, making it hard for the party to secure votes even from its own members.[22] Third, despite its supermajority in parliament, resulting from the 2010 election, the USDP did not replace the First-Past-The-Post (FPTP) system with a proportional representation (PR) bill in mid-2014. Hence, under this old system, in the 2015 election, the NLD not only won twice the popular vote of the USDP but ten times the number of seats.[23] Ironically, in a PR system, the USDP would likely have gathered 25 per cent of the seats it needed to keep running the country in collaboration with the military. Fourth, Daw Suu's campaign rhetoric was impressively successful. Throughout her campaign, she kept articulating, "Take whatever they give, but vote for the NLD," which one of the USDP's leading figures admitted had a huge effect on the campaign.[24] The USDP used different campaign methods such as providing assistance (building bridges and roads) to attract votes by showing its ability of delivery. However, it was insufficient to attract votes. In fact, Myanmar voters had high expectations about the election and looked forward to huge change; they did not want to see the same faces in the upcoming government.

Ethnic Parties: An Unexpected Defeat?

The second biggest losers in the 2015 general election were the 55 ethnic parties, arguably suffering far worse than the USDP because they lost within their own ethnic strongholds. Why they suffered such an unexpected defeat is a critical question.

Prior to the election, many analysts argued that the NLD would win a landslide victory but not in the ethnic constituencies, deemed to be strongholds of the ethnic parties. However, the outcome was the opposite, except in the Rakhine and Shan States. There are several reasons why many ethnic parties, like the USDP, did very poorly in the 2015 election. First, many ethnic voters believed that the country's key problems could be better solved from "above" rather than "below." For instance, even if all the ethnic parties united and won all of the 213 seats they contested for both Upper and Lower Houses, they could not establish a new government because, in order to form the government, at least 333 seats must be secured. This is a main weakness of the ethnic parties. The 88 Generation Students leader Ko Ko Gyi argued that "in order to overcome the USDP that had ruled the country for such a long time, many believed that they need to vote for the NLD, and of course there was Daw Aung San Suu Kyi's popularity."[25] Second, there were many more ethnic parties contesting in the elections than expected. For instance, there were 55 ethnic parties (out of 92 registered parties), which illustrated a greater proliferation of ethnic parties in the 2015 election. This caused vote splitting in some ethnic constituencies. Some have argued that the ethnic parties lacked unity among themselves; for instance, in the Shan State, two major Shan parties (SNLD and SNDP) have been fighting against each other, splitting the vote, which favored the NLD in the end, by far the best-known national opposition party.[26] Having learned lessons from the 2015 election, and in preparation for the upcoming 2020 election, many ethnic parties have started talking about merger issues that could avoid the same mistake of "vote splitting." For instance, in the Mon State, two major Mon parties, All Mon Region Democracy Party (AMRDP) and Mon National Party (MNP) started discussing a merger.[27] The third argument is Daw Suu's popularity. Her popularity could not be denied, and it strongly shaped the politics from youth to middle age to elder generations. In addition, some of the ethnic parties that secured ethnic votes are also associated with the NLD.[28] For example, in the Shan State, the SNLD, also known as "NLD-alliance," won a number of seats. The same was true for the Zomi Congress for Democracy (ZCD) in the Chin State.

The Main Opposition: The Tatmadaw, Not the USDP

With the election marginalizing the USDP and the ethnic parties, where would the main opposition to the NLD-led government come from? The obvious answer is: the Tatmadaw, or the army. In this regard, there are some considerable challenges ahead. First, the NLD and the army have little experience working together; indeed, relations between them are usually confrontational. It is highly expected that there will be more intense confrontations especially over 2008 constitutional amendment issues. The NLD-led government and NLD-led parliaments are expected to make concerted efforts to amend the controversial constitution. The army is expected to resist all such efforts to amend it. In this case, the confrontation almost certainly lies ahead, unless the NLD develops the political dexterity to deal with this. It is clear that the army will protect the constitution as its core agenda. This could prompt popular protests against the Tatmadaw. As a result, instability is expected. A prime example already emerged which showed a bitter division between the NLD and the military in April 2016, when the State Counselor Law was enacted, successfully cementing a key executive role for Daw Suu. The military protested against the law during the parliamentary debate.[29] Second, the peace process is critical to the NLD-led government's success. Again, this process demands much stronger cooperation between the NLD and the army. Constitutionally and institutionally, the army does not necessarily need to comply with the government's edicts.[30] Rather, as mentioned earlier, the army exists as a separate autonomous institution. Of course, there was certainly a bridge between the Thein Sein government and the army because the latter simply backed the former's camp.[31] However, it remains to be seen how the NLD-led government will achieve cooperation or a working relationship with the army, which would affect how the peace process works in reality. Overall, national reconciliation is crucial to the success of Myanmar's next step in its democratization; the critical determinant is whether, and how, the NLD and the army can work together. This is definitely a challenge, unless both sides are willing to compromise, seriously commit to working together, and develop strategies to deal with this important reconciliation process. As expected, there have been no significant compromises in many cases between the NLD-led government and the Tatmadaw. On the peace process, for example, under the NLD-led government, there has been almost no progress, demonstrating that there has been very weak coordination between the Tatmadaw and NLD. In fact, for example the two largest ethnic ceasefire Signatories to the Nationwide Ceasefire Agreement (NCA), the Reconciliation Council of Shan State (RCSS) and the Karen National Union (KNU), have withdrew temporarily from the peace process by claiming some frustration on the process, being a blow for the peace agenda.[32] However, there is little exception that shows some coordination between NLD and the Tatmadaw or standing together because of the perceived same views on some issues. For example, the NLD-led government stands with the Tatmadaw on the International Criminal Court's call for prosecution of the Myanmar military leadership over Rakhine atrocities. The State Counselor Office released a statement, rejecting the ICC's call.[33] That demonstrates, the government stands with the Tatmadaw's call "UN has no right to interfere."[34] In fact, when US Vice President pushed her government to take action for those who are responsible over the Rohingya crisis, she responded to him by saying, "We understand our country better than any other country does," not specifically mentioning any accountability actions to pursue.[35]

The Next Government: Could Checks and Balances be Decreased?

Even though the NLD won a landslide in the election, taking control of both executive and legislative branches, the Tatmadaw is still constitutionally granted 25 per cent of the total seats and three executive offices.[36] Constitutionally, the executive and the legislative branches are completely separate. The President and his or her Cabinet Members are not allowed to be involved in party affairs once their appointments are confirmed.[37] It is a key element in the system of checks and balances formulated in the 2008 constitution. Thus, the NLD needs to formulate a pragmatic strategy to play the game within that constitutional mandate. The NLD is expected to play such a game wisely since Daw Suu has control over the party agenda, unlike the split witnessed in the USDP.[38] This could provide "advantages and disadvantages" in the upcoming political landscape, particularly for the NLD. The advantage is that the party's agenda will be implemented quickly. The disadvantage is that checks and balances in the political system will almost certainly be reduced, perhaps in a substantial way. For instance, there are several reports claiming that asking tough questions to the NLD-led government is not allowed in the parliament in order not to make the government look bad.[39] In addition, NLD's internal vetting committee and the two speakers have routinely dismissed draft proposals and motions prepared by individual parliamentarians.[40] Daw Suu alone is expected to largely shape the whole system: party, executive, and legislative jurisdictions. This system could distort democratic standards or norms based on better checks and balances in the system. How to build the democratic institutions while consolidating Myanmar's democratization is important not only for the NLD but also the whole nation.

The new administration is, as the NLD declared, "based on national reconciliation." NLD members and technocrats as well as those from the previous government or the USDP are tasked to accomplish such mission. For instance, the Minister of Religion Affairs came from the USDP while the Minister of Education was from the previous government. While many previous ministries were dissolved, surprisingly the new Ministry of Ethnic Affairs has been created with the appointment of a Mon ethnic leader as its minister. This ministry was established with the specified intention of implementing the law protecting ethnic rights that was enacted in 2015. This law is to promote ethnic culture and languages, as well as to protect the citizen's rights of ethnic populations. The NLD now has an option to shape the next political landscape in a way that benefits the nation at large by installing democratic norms in both principle and institutional practice.

The Governance Challenges

Following the establishment of the NLD-led government, a question stands: Does this mean that the NLD is placed in a crucial power position to run civilian institutions? Because governance arrangements at all levels in Myanmar are complex in nature, this is a very challenging question to answer. To understand this complexity, it is important to analyze how the military as an institution had ruled civilian affairs through the General Administration Department (GAD). The GAD controls overall governance in Myanmar institutionally.

Prior to the 2010 general election, the Tatmadaw stood as the only institution that governed the whole administrative system, ranging from military affairs, business environment, general administration to municipal affairs. Since the new civilian government took power in March 2011 soon after the election, the institutional arrangements in Myanmar have been considerably transformed, with the military institution and civilian institutions technically separated. However, the military institution does not necessarily need to comply with civilian rule; rather it has separate power according to the constitution.[41] The GAD exists under the Ministry of Home Affairs (and the Minister of Home Affairs is constitutionally appointed by the military) as a key department, implementing the day-to-day functions of the civilian government.[42] Therefore, there is a very complex relationship between the civilian institutions and the GAD in terms of separation of power and authority as well as daily public management, including budget allocation issues.[43]

Specifically, at the Union level, the GAD functions in eight key areas: (a) land administration, (b) excise administration, (c) collection of land, excise, mineral, and irrigation taxes, (d) structural settlement of villages and towns, (e) rural development, (f) formation of organizations and associations, (g) conferring honorable titles and medals, and (h) restrictions on transferring immoveable properties.[44] Given the GAD's control of these important functions under the Ministry of Home Affairs (or Tatmadaw), the GAD's administrative power exceeds that of governmental institutions such as the Ministry of Finance (taxation) and the Ministry of Agriculture and Irrigation (land issues).

At the sub-national level, the GAD also plays a very strong role in state and region governance, including the fiscal architecture (budget planning) and financial management. For instance, the GAD controls three key funds: it controls budget preparation for the rural area development of the Ministry of Border Affairs while the Ministry is responsible for implementing the projects; it administers the Poverty Reduction Fund that comes from the Union Budget; and it takes a budget oversight role for the Constituency Development Fund (CDF).[45] While the GAD provides administrative support to the Chief Ministers of the State and Region governments, it controls administrative budget allocation over certain staffing appointments in the Chief Ministers' Cabinet.[46] In the Self-Administered Zones (SAZ) in ethnic regions, the GAD and Chief Executives of the SAZ are very competitive with each other.[47] At the township level, administrative structures have been transformed into a participatory approach in which a few town elders are elected to represent the people on the five committees that give advisory services to the GAD.[48] Overall, the GAD has taken control of those committees, setting their agenda and taking a supervising role, such as the GAD chairing the Township Management Committee (TMC).[49] Even at the village or village tract level, village administrators are controlled by the GAD through the township level. This means that reports usually go to Naypyitaw authorities through the GAD region and state level rather than through the State and Region governments.

Given all this, it appeared to be extremely difficult for the NLD to take a lead in running the civilian institutions well on its own. Since the GAD sets the agenda in day-to-day administration at all levels, the GAD's existing power was definitely a key challenge for the NLD-led administration both at national and sub-national levels (perhaps including village administration affairs). The NLD government has fully been aware of the importance of the GAD functions in its day-to-day administration and took a very bold step in December 2018, announcing that the GAD would be moved under the civilian control that is under the Ministry of the Office of the Union Government, nothing to do with the Ministry of Home Affairs.[50] U Min Thu, 62, with a military background, has been appointed as Union Minister for the Ministry of the Office of the Union Government.[51] Why did NLD took such a bold step three years after the 2015 election? Was there any prior agreement between the Tatmadaw and the NLD government over that move? Those questions remain unanswered. However, the State Media, *The Global New Light of Myanmar*, published the article in April 2019, "Transition Starts with GAD: Securing Rule of Law, Community Peace and Tranquility, Regional Development, Serving Public Interest"—outlining at the very beginning:

> Performing the functions as per the motto "transition starts with GAD", General Administration Department (GAD) aims to provide the people a simple and trouble free administrative and service system that is legal, just, uniform and reduces time and eases the burden.
>
> The General Administration Department under the Ministry of Office of the Union Government provide vital administrative machinery for the country by conducting transition works in an exemplary way for a society free from corruption, self-interest and with good moral character.[52]

This paragraph clearly demonstrates about the aim of the move of the GAD under the civilian control. The next step is to make that aim work in practice—the practical implementation. Minister U Min Thu has toured across the country extensively, explaining three key points to GAD staffs for his ministry's operational works: (a) people-centered approach, prompting public participation, (b) free from corruption, and (c) do reforms bravely.[53] The positive impact of transferring the GAD under the civilian control cannot be seen overnight, however. Instead, it takes much time and effort to earn public trust back in the GAD administrative functions. Without public trust, it is difficult to get public participation in governance decisions made by the GAD. Perhaps, the NLD needs to determine specific scope of works for the GAD, for instance, determining whether some taxation area are still within the GAD's or those of other agencies or ministries such as the Ministry of Planning and Finance and Municipalities. Despite those challenges, the NLD-led government has secured the GAD to make better administrative functions in the near future. Perhaps, this is the biggest achievement so far for the NLD government.

What's Next from 2016 to the Next Election in 2020?

What should the NLD do between 2016 and the next election in 2020? Prior to the 2020 election, there had been two by-elections testing the NLD-led administration. The first by-election was in April 2017 in which the NLD won 9 seats out of the 19 seats contested. The second by-election was in November 2018 in which NLD took 7 seats out of the 13 seats contested.[54] NLD's by-election results were not encouraging as it was in the 2015 general election. That demonstrates, the new government and the ruling party need to do a lot for 2020. Facing many challenges, options, and opportunities, the NLD along with many political stakeholders must take the lead in materializing Myanmar's democratic consolidation in four areas. First, for the NLD and the Tatmadaw: To ensure a peaceful transition, the NLD and the Tatmadaw must find a way to closely cooperate in day-to-day administration (e.g. GAD), the peace process, and national reconciliation. Second, for the Political Parties' Institutionalization: The political parties' agendas and policies will be unable to address the deeply complex political, economic, and social issues Myanmar faces across the country without party institutionalization that would allow them to deliver public goods desperately needed by the Myanmar people. Without party institutionalization, they will not be able to take concrete actions. Though Myanmar has many political parties, they are not yet institutionalized but are "personal-based" rather than based on "institutional practice." Third, for the NLD-led government's capacity: It remains to be seen how the new government can deliver the goods and meet the needs of the public. Of course, to a large extent this will depend on the members of the new NLD government. New blood is needed for the NLD government to initiate new ideas and related reforms. Fourth, for the NLD-led Parliaments: The NLD supermajority in both houses of Parliament must deal with possible constitutional changes, and the main opposition, the Tatmadaw.

Notes

1. Ed Payne, "Aung San Suu Kyi's NLD Wins Historical Majority in Myanmar Elections," *CNN*, 13 November 2015 <http://edition.cnn.com/2015/11/11/asia/myanmar-elections/index.html> [accessed 2 August 2016].
2. "Final Election Reports on Observing Myanmar's 2015 General Elections," Carter Center, 16 August 2016 <https://www.cartercenter.org/news/publications/election_reports.html#myanmar> [accessed 3 August 2016].
3. Aung Tun, *A Report on Youth Participation in the 2015 General Elections*, Danish Institute for Multiparties Democracy (DIPD), 25 November 2015.
4. Twenty-five per cent (110 seats) of the seats are reserved by the constitution for the military; this means that the USDP only had to secure little over 25 per cent of the total contested seats in order to continue running the country.
5. The Lower House has 330 seats in total based on population size while the Upper House has 168 seats composed of 12 seats each from 14 states and regions.
6. Twenty-five per cent (56 seats) of the seats are already reserved by the constitution for the military.
7. For the Kayah State, U Soe Thein, one of President Thein Sein's closest ministers won the seat as an "independent candidate."
8. Union Election Commission (UEC) Myanmar <http://uecmyanmar.org/index.php/election/2016-08-16-10-44-01> [accessed 2 August 2016].
9. Andrew Marshall and Timothy Mclauglin, "Myanmar's Suu Kyi Says will be above the President in New Government," *Reuters News Agency*, 5 November 2015 <http://www.reuters.com/article/us-myanmar-election-idUSKCN0SU0AR20151105> [accessed 5 July 2016].
10. Those laws, including some notorious ones such as articles 18, 19, and 147 as well as 515 (b), are used to arrest activists. Those laws and provisions prevent freedom of assembly, freedom of expression. The successive dictatorial authorities had used those notorious laws in order to arrest political activists and journalists in particular.
11. "Pyithu Hluttaw (Lower House) Repeals Emergency Provisions Act," *Pyithu Hluttaw* <http://www.pyithuhluttaw.gov.mm/?q=eng/bill-repeal-emergency-provisions-act-submitted-pyithu-hluttaw> [accessed 6 August 2016].

12. There are currently nine standing committees composed of *Hluttaw* representatives. Those committees are not designed to debate on any issues arise but they are rather designed to cooperate to address "any affairs" arise. Given this, there would be no parliamentary committee hearings as well, which is understood as "affairs committee" in Myanmar context.
13. President's Office order, 30/2017. Anti-Corruption Commission Reformed <http://www.president-office.gov.mm/en/?q=briefing-room/orders/2017/11/24/id-8026> [accessed 2 March 2018].
14. Htet Kaung Linn, "Myanmar's New President Slashes No. of Ministries from 36 to 21," *Myanmar Now*, 17 March 2016 <http://www.myanmar-now.org/news/i/?id=947fc3ae-c8fd-4735-a0dd-9a840f0cf66b> [accessed 20 June 2016].
15. Neither of the two NLD Presidents, the incumbent, U Win Myint, or his predecessor, U Thin Kyin, held any NDSC meeting.
16. Article 201, 2008 Constitution. Formation of the National Defence and Security Council.
17. This happens unless one or two speakers are elected by the military, which is very unlikely. Apparently, since Daw Suu takes up the Foreign Minister post, she is a member of the Council. In addition, according to the constitution, for her to be a member of the Council, she needs to be either the President or Vice President, which is not possible unless article 59 (f) is amended, or to be a Speaker or a Foreign Minister.
18. Ei Ei Toe Lwin, "Country needs to enact NDSC Law not debate over its power," *Myanmar Times*, 4 September 2017 <https://www.mmtimes.com/news/country-needs-enact-ndsc-law-not-debate-over-its-power.html> [accessed 14 October 2018].
19. According to many media reports, the UEC is thought to be in line with the USDP especially for two reasons: (1) it is appointed by the President (who is the USDP's Chair); and (2) the Chairman himself used to be a key USDP member. In the 2010 elections, there were many examples of electoral irregularities made by the UEC to ensure the USDP won.
20. Min Zin, "In Myanmar, A Soft Coup Ahead of an Election," *New York Times*, 11 September 2015 <http://www.nytimes.com/2015/09/12/opinion/in-myanmar-a-soft-coup-ahead-of-an-election.html?_r=0> [accessed 16 May 2017].
21. U Thura Aung Ko, a USDP leading candidate, gave interview to the BBC Burmese, less than a month after the election, and explained how this coup affected the election results.
22. USDP claims that it has 24 and 25 million voters; given this election outcome (only 43 out of over 500 seats), it is safe to say that the USDP did not even get votes from its party members.
23. Myanmar Elections: Results and Implications, *International Crisis Group*, 9 December 2015 <https://www.crisisgroup.org/asia/south-east-asia/myanmar/myanmar-elections-results-and-implications> [accessed 2 June 2017].

24. USDP's candidate U Khin Swe admitted that in a local media after his defeat. "USDP Candidate Zaygabar U Khin Swe on Election Loss," *Radio Free Asia Burmese*, 11 November 2017 <https://www.youtube.com/watch?v=fHskRm3VWn0> [accessed 2 June 2017].
25. Interview with Ko Ko Gyi, 88 generation student leader, 18 November 2015, Yangon.
26. Interview with Sai Kyaw Nyunt, SNLD Technical Support Director, 15 November 2015, Yangon.
27. Bo Bo Myint, "Two Major Mon Ethnicity Parties Discuss Merger," *Eleven Media*, 1 March 2018 <http://www.elevenmyanmar.com/politics/12995> [accessed 2 March 2018].
28. "The 2015 General Elections in Myanmar: What Now for Ethnic Politics?" Transnational Institute (TNI), 17 December 2015 <https://www.tni.org/files/publication-downloads/bpb17_web_def.pdf> [accessed 3 June 2017].
29. Htoo Thant, "State Counsellor Bill Approved Despite Military Voting Boycott," *Myanmar Times*, 5 April 2016 <http://www.mmtimes.com/index.php/national-news/19844-military-protests-but-parliament-passes-state-counsellor-bill.html> [accessed 15 July 2016].
30. The Tatmadaw stands as one institution that does not need to comply with the government. For instance, when President Thein Sein ordered it not to fight against the Kachin armed groups, the Tatmadaw fought anyway in order to safeguard its own interest. Ba Kaung, "President's Ceasefire Order Fails to Stop Offensive," *The Irrawaddy*, 28 December 2011 <http://www2.irrawaddy.com/article.php?art_id=22741> [accessed 3 June 2017].
31. Thein Sein himself is a former army officer.
32. Ye Mon, "Peace Commission to meet as ceasefire signatories withdraw from peace process," *Frontier Myanmar*, 12 November 2018 <https://frontiermyanmar.net/en/peace-commission-to-meet-as-ceasefire-signatories-withdraw-from-peace-process> [accessed 16 November 2018].
33. The Statement on the International Criminal Court by the State Counselor's Office, 9 August 2018 <http://www.statecounsellor.gov.mm/en/node/2084> [accessed 14 October 2018].
34. "UN should not 'interfere': Myanmar army chief," *Frontier Myanmar/AFP*, 24 September 2018 <https://frontiermyanmar.net/en/un-should-not-interfere-myanmar-army-chief> [accessed 14 October 2018].
35. Shibani Mahtani, "Vice President Pence pushes Myanmar's Suu Kyi on Rohingya and jailed journalists," *Washington Post*, 14 November 2018 <https://www.washingtonpost.com/world/asia_pacific/vice-president-pence-pushes-myanmars-suu-kyi-on-rohingya-jailed-journalists/2018/11/14/f3fca8e8-e73d-11e8-b8dc-66cca409c180_story.html?utm_term=.3aca4ede1a82> [accessed 16 November 2018].
36. Constitutionally, the army is granted three ministries: Home Affairs, Border Affairs, and Defense.

37. This is by the 2008 constitution, prompting the "Shwe Mann camp" to take the Chairmanship of the USDP while Thein Sein became President.
38. As mentioned before, the USDP split into a "Thein Sein Camp" and a "Shwe Mann Camp."
39. Ei Ei Toe Lwin, "Don't Ask Tough Questions: Checks on Power out the Window as NLD Exerts its Majority," *Myanmar Times*, 7 October 2016 <https://www.mmtimes.com/national-news/nay-pyi-taw/22959-don-t-ask-tough-questions-checks-on-power-out-the-window-as-nld-exerts-its-majority.html> [accessed 2 March 2017].
40. Renaud Egreteau, "How Myanmar's Ruling Party Keeps its Lawmakers Under Control," *Tea Circle*, 1 March 2018 <https://teacircleoxford.com/2018/03/01/how-myanmars-ruling-party-keeps-its-lawmakers-under-control/> [accessed 3 March 2018].
41. Article 232 (b, ii) The 2008 Constitution, obtain a list of suitable Defence Services personnel nominated by the Commander-in-Chief of the Defence Services for Ministries of Defence, Home Affairs, and Border Affairs.
42. Mathew Arnold and Kyi Pyar Chit Saw, *Administering the State in Myanmar: Overview of the General Administration Department* (Yangon: The Asia Foundation, 2014), pp. 15–25.
43. Giles Dickenson-Jones, S. Kanay De, and Andrea Smura, *State and Region Public Finances in Myanmar* (Yangon: The Asia Foundation, 2015), pp. 12–21.
44. Mathew Arnold and Kyi Pyar Chit Saw, *Administering the State in Myanmar*, pp. 10–18.
45. *Pyi Htaung Su Hluttaw Order Number* (82/2013), Constituency Development Fund (CDF), Article 7; this fund (approximately US$100,000 equivalent for each MP) is designed to help Member Parliaments assist their respective constituencies, particularly with community development projects.
46. Mathew Arnold and Kyi Pyar Chit Saw, *Administering the State in Myanmar*, pp. 20–8.
47. There are six self-administered zones (five in the Shan State and one in Sagaing Region) in Myanmar, established by the 2008 constitution.
48. There are five semi-elected committees formed for development affairs at township level: township management committee (a critical committee chaired by GAD), township development support committee (GAD supervisory role), township development affairs committee (GAD supervisory role), township farmland management committee (GAD secretarial role), and township planning and implementation committee (GAD secretarial role).
49. Local Governance Mapping, The State of Local Governance Trends (2014), UNDP, Myanmar <http://www.mm.undp.org/content/myanmar/en/home/operations/projects/poverty_reduction/LocalGovernancePillar1/local-governance-mapping.html> [accessed 3 June 2017].

50. "Govt Announces Transfer of Military-Controlled Dept to Civilian Ministry," *The Irrawaddy*, 21 December 2018 <https://www.irrawaddy.com/news/govt-announces-transfer-military-controlled-dept-civilian-ministry.html> [accessed 14 June 2019].
51. Htoo Thant, "Ü Min Thu Nominated to Take Over Ministerial Post," *Myanmar Times,* 27 November 2018 <https://www.mmtimes.com/news/u-min-thu-nominated-take-over-ministerial-post.html> [accessed 14 June 2019].
52. Tahya, "Transition Starts with GAD," Global New Light of Myanmar, 19 April 2019 <http://www.globalnewlightofmyanmar.com/transition-starts-with-gad-securing-rule-of-law-community-peace-and-tranquility-regional-development-serving-the-public-interest/> [accessed 14 June 2019].
53. "Union Minister Min Thu Meets GAD staffs of Shan State (South, North)," Global New Light of Myanmar, 8 February 2019 <https://www.moi.gov.mm/moi:eng/?q=news/8/02/2019/id-16603> [accessed 14 June 2015].
54. By election results of 2017 and 2018, Union Election Commission (UEC) <www.uecmyanmar.org> [accessed 17 November 2018].

References

Arnold, Matthew and Kyi Pyar Chit Saw. 2014. *Administering the State in Myanmar: Overview of the General Administration Department.* Yangon: The Asia Foundation.

Callahan, Mary. 2012. *Drivers of Political Change in Post-Junta, Constitutional Burma*, for USAID projects in Burma.

Carter Center. 2016. "Final Election Reports on Observing Myanmar's 2015 General Elections," 16 August <https://www.cartercenter.org/news/publications/election_reports.html#myanmar> [accessed 3 August 2016].

Chenyang, Li et al., eds. 2016. *Myanmar: Reintegrating into the International Community.* Singapore: World Scientific Publishing.

Constitution. 2008. Burma/Myanmar.

Dickenson-Jones, Giles, S. Kanay De, and Andrea Smura. 2015. *State and Region Public Finances in Myanmar.* Yangon: The Asia Foundation.

International Crisis Group. 2015. Myanmar Elections: Results and Implications, December <https://www.crisisgroup.org/asia/south-east-asia/myanmar/myanmar-elections-results-and-implications> [accessed 2 June 2017].

Markoff, John. 1996. *Waves of Democracy: Social Movement and Political Change.* California: Pine Forge Press.

Local Governance Mapping, 2014. The State of Local Governance Trends, UNDP, Myanmar <http://www.mm.undp.org/content/myanmar/en/home/operations/projects/poverty_reduction/LocalGovernancePillar1/local-governance-mapping.html> [accessed 3 June 2017].

CHAPTER 2

Fragile Balance of Civil-Military Relations in Myanmar

Yoshihiro Nakanishi[1]

On 8 November 2015, the day following the general election in Myanmar, Aung San Suu Kyi delivered a brief speech to her supporters at the headquarters of the National League for Democracy (NLD) at Shwegondine Road in Yangon. While her face suggested her pleasure at the forecasted NLD's electoral win, her speech was far less exciting, even cautionary in tone. In her speech, she urged her supporters to calm down and show respect to those who had lost in the election.[2] She was surely thinking of what had happened after the 1990 election. The military junta (State Law and Order Restoration Council, SLORC) did not accept the NLD's landslide victory despite the fact that, after the coup d'état on 18 September 1988, the junta had promised to transfer state power to the winning party in the general election. Even though the political and social conditions surrounding the 2015 election were markedly different from those in the 1990s, there would be no surprise if Aung San Suu Kyi was worried about the possibility that the government would reject the transfer of power to the NLD.

Contrary to her anxiety, the ruling party, the Union Solidarity and Development Party (USDP), accepted its disastrous loss, and the Tatmadaw (Myanmar's Armed Forces) did not prevent the democratic forces from coming to power. The transition from the Thein Sein government to the NLD's new government was surprisingly peaceful and smooth. This smooth transition suggests something important for a country's political development, since Myanmar has had difficulties in the past creating political rules that would be respected and followed by all stakeholders. The lack of trustable formal institutions was obviously one of the critical obstacles to reconciliation between the military junta and NLD since 1990. SLORC's attempt to include major political parties into the new constitution drafting process of the National Convention in 1993 and 2003, which failed because of the NLD boycott that resulted from SLORC's heavy crackdown on NLD members, shows the state of poor relations between the two institutions. Following the "Seven Step Roadmap to Democracy" between 2003 and 2010, and Thein Sein's liberalization policy after 2011, the Tatmadaw, the Tatmadaw-backed USDP, and the NLD reached agreement on a formal institution which would be the arena for the country's political competition when the NLD decided to participate in the by-election of April 2012.

In this regard, more emphasis should be given to the successful transition in March 2016, even though it was not a transition to the full-fledged democracy that many NLD supporters had hoped for. We could say that the current stage of Myanmar's political development is still in the stage of political institutionalization and liberalization which could be the basis for further developments towards democratization.[3] However, it is rare for a country to follow a linear path of political development. In fact, while accepting the new NLD government, the Commander-in-Chief of the Tatmadaw, Senior Gen. Min Aung Hlaing, did not agree with Aung San Suu Kyi's request to temporally suspend the constitutional article 59 (f) that disqualifies her from the presidency and vice-presidency.[4] He followed instead one of the Tatmadaw's rules laid down in the 2008 Constitution, namely "safeguarding the Constitution" [Article 20 (f)]. Thus, it would be too optimistic to assume that Myanmar would move in a more democratic direction so soon.

Obviously, the Tatmadaw is a key player in determining the future trajectory of Myanmar's politics. Since independence in 1948, the Tatmadaw has been autonomous from political leadership and has also enjoyed reserved formal and informal authority to influence both the administration and the legislative process. This power still remains today, but manifests itself in a different way than before. This chapter will not aim at defining the political character of the Myanmar's military, but will instead discuss how the transition of 2016 could affect its autonomy and political power. It will argue that the political role of the Tatmadaw is facing significant challenges under the new NLD government, even though the constitutional setting is the same as that of the previous USDP government. This chapter will also argue that more attention should be paid to how the transition of 2016 could affect the Tatmadaw's role and function in the state, with a focus on understanding the institutional design behind the 2008 Constitution that was intended to sustain the conventional elite coalition and maintain political stability.

To these ends, this chapter will examine (1) the historical autonomy of Myanmar's military since independence, (2) the new role of the Tatmadaw in the constitutional design after 2011, and (3) the impact of the NLD government on the Tatmadaw and civil-military relations.

Tatmadaw's Autonomy in the Past

The Tatmadaw has served as an organizational backbone for not only national security but also political leadership since independence in 1948. After the Tatmadaw expelled its political rivals such as the various civilian politicians following the coup d'état on 2 March 1962 led by General Ne Win, Myanmar's political development has had a unique trajectory as one of the most durable military rules in the world. Although many contemporary military regimes collapsed in the late 1970s and 1980s, Myanmar's military was able to survive despite its long economic stagnation and the huge anti-government demonstrations of 1988.

Looking at this history, it is no wonder that neither the concept of professionalism nor the institution of civilian control has ever developed in the civil-military relations of the country. When it comes to the concept of professionalism in Myanmar, as Tin Maung Maung Than wrote, "professional army" has been negatively understood to be a mercenary (*kyesar tat*) that hires paid soldiers and fights for personal interests.[5] On the other hand, a positive connotation has often been attributed to the concept of the patriotic army (*myochit tat*), which feeds into a discourse of the nationalists who formed the Burma Independence Army (BIA) in 1941 in Bangkok to fight first against the British Empire, and later against Japan for national liberation.[6] This narrative of the patriotic army has been consistently used by Tatmadaw leaders to justify its institutional autonomy and its political power, and this applies even today. At the same time, however, each historical period has seen somewhat different discourses and institutions employed to protect the Tatmadaw's influence and interests. This section traces the Tatmadaw's organizational autonomy by focusing on the aspects of legitimacy and institution in three eras: the democratic era (1948–61), the socialist era (1962–88), and the military rule era (1988–2010).

The Democratic Era (1948–61)

Even under the parliamentary democracy system, the Tatmadaw had kept its organizational autonomy from the civilian leadership. While it was formally placed under civilian authority especially after the War Office became the Ministry of Defense in 1956, the Tatmadaw's leaders could avoid civilian intervention in military affairs. Since the state was confronting serious domestic insurgencies such as those launched by the Burma Communist Party, Karen National Union, and People's Volunteer Organization in the late 1940s and 1950s, the state leaders needed to prioritize security issues, which included giving the Tatmadaw considerable independence to control security policies. For instance, according to a foreign economic adviser of the government in the 1950s, Louis A. Walinski, the defence budget was separately drafted from other ministries' budgets, despite the fact that it accounted for around one-third of the government's spending and one-fifth of the capital spending every fiscal year. The Prime Minister's Office allowed it to be exempted from the reviews of civilians as well as foreign consultants.[7]

Institutionally speaking, the National Defence Committee headed by the Prime Minister was formed as a sub-committee of the cabinet to handle all defense issues. However, that meeting had been held only 21 times between February 1952 and November 1960, suggesting that the committee was not working well to ensure the civilian control over the Tatmadaw.[8] Meanwhile, the Tatmadaw attempted to formalize its political role through disseminating the military doctrine, resulting in the publication of the "National Ideology and the Role of the Defence Services" in 1958. This doctrine designated three principles which the Tatmadaw should defend: (1) the rule of society by peaceful and lawful means, (2) the development of democracy, and (3) the establishment of a socialist economic system. Although it did not mention anything about the means for defending these three principles, it was apparent that the Tatmadaw's corporate interests were far broader than merely narrowly-defined national security or defense issues at this time.[9]

The Socialist Era (1962–88)

If one takes a comparative perspective on the two coups of the Tatmadaw in 1958 and 1962, one could notice the differences in the mode and the level of political intervention. General Ne Win replaced U Nu as the new prime minister on 28 September 1958, but this coup was accomplished according to a constitutional procedure [the 1947 Constitution,

Article 56 (1)], followed by the promise that state power would return to the civilian leaders selected in the coming general election. In fact, Ne Win, as the head of the caretaker government, repeatedly emphasized the significance of the 1947 Constitution in his speeches to the general public and even to his military men.

Contrary to this "constitutional" political intervention between 1958 and 1960, the second coup on 2 March 1962 triggered a fundamental state reformation based on more radical leftist and nationalistic ideology. After forming the State Revolutionary Council (SRC), Ne Win abolished parliament and other federal institutions through SRC Proclamations soon after the coup. Rejecting the democratic political system for the reason that the "nation's socialist aims cannot be achieved with any assurance by means of the form of parliamentary democracy that we have so far experienced" (Burmese Way to Socialism, Article 14), the SRC established a guiding party, the Burma Socialist Program Party (BSPP), so that it could take leadership of the state by making all other existing parties illegal in 1974. However, leaders seemed to be lacking any concrete ideas for materializing the Burmeseness of their socialism.[10] As a result, the official state structure in the new 1974 constitution was designed to emulate the Marx-Lenin party-state style, although its ideological tone was relatively weak with no reference to well-known international communists and no orientation towards creating a dictator's personal cult.

Under the 1974 Constitution, the BSPP has formal authority over the Tatmadaw, which at the time had another name, "People's Army" (*pyithu tatmadaw*). However, the BSPP's direct control over the Tatmadaw was deliberately avoided so that the Tatmadaw could sustain its organizational autonomy. Most importantly, unlike many contemporary communist countries, the BSPP government did not introduce the political commissar system, in which political officers of a guiding party were sent to supervise each military unit and to participate in the daily decision-making inside the unit.[11] Although the party-organizing committee was formed in each military unit in 1971, no civilian party cadres were appointed as committee members; all were active military officers within that unit, suggesting that the committee had little function to supervise and control the military units. In fact, officers had to be more concerned about surveillance by intelligence agencies like the National Intelligence Bureau headed by General Tin Oo, rather than the BSPP's guiding power. In terms of the BSPP's party leadership, retired and active military commanders predominantly took positions on the Central Executive Committee, and the Tatmadaw appointed active top officers to the Central

Committee as the new committee members at every party convention. Hence, the guiding party's control over the Tatmadaw was limited so that it did not face serious challenges to its organizational autonomy during the era. Rather, most of the party politicians in the democratic era were excluded from the core of the ruling elites under Ne Win's dictatorship, in which he exclusively relied on high-ranking military officers and civilian aides like Dr. Maung Maung.

The Military Rule (1988–2010)

The military coup, which occurred on 18 September 1988, was the third of its kind in Myanmar's history. Facing mass anti-government demonstrations all over the country, General Saw Maung, Chief of General Staff, formed the State Law and Order Restoration Council (SLORC) with 18 other military leaders, and the SLORC issued announcement "No. 1/88," which listed "to restore law, order, peace and tranquility" and "to provide security and to facilitate transport and communications" as the first two duties of the SLORC.[12] Under the SLORC and later State Peace and Development Council (SPDC) (1988–2010) rule, the Tatmadaw leaders thought they had no other choice but to adhere to this security rationale to justify their "provisional" rule with emphasis on the following two aspects.

First, both the SLORC and SPDC consistently claimed that the country faced a crisis of state disintegration, which was enunciated by the state propaganda called the Three National Causes: "non-disintegration of the union," "non-disintegration of national solidarity," and "non-disintegration of perpetuation of sovereignty." Each of them pointed to the Tatmadaw leaders' strong obsession with the integration and order of the state. Confronting the massive anti-government demonstrations by ordinary citizens in 1988 and the international pressure for the country's democratization after the coup, Tatmadaw leaders embraced a paranoid security view, in which even non-violent political movements and the support to them from governmental and non-governmental organizations of Western countries, would have only negative influences on the stability of the nation-state and state sovereignty. In combination with this view on the crisis of state disintegration, the Tatmadaw's paternalistic attitude towards politics had helped it dominate state leadership for more than two decades as an autonomous authoritarian institution. The following 1993 speech of Senior Gen. Than Shwe, Commander-in-Chief and Chairman of the SLORC, is typical of this attitude.

> [T]he Tatmadaw has made preparations to be in the vanguard to work hand in hand with the people and take up appropriate duties in the leading role of national politics in the future.
>
> This actually is an undeniable fact because we are dutifully taking up the task due to the entire people's reliance on the Tatmadaw to defend them and the nation. Therefore, due to the need to respond to the situation when the Tatmadaw must act in defence in consonance with the swiftly changing circumstances to prevent danger befalling the nation and the people, it has become incumbent that the Tatmadaw must participate in the leading role of national politics.[13]

Behind this paternalistic view on politics lies the organizational identity historically constructed in the nationalistic discourse as an army that fought for national independence against the colonialists and the fascists. In addition, since 1962 major rival political forces had been too weak to counter the Tatmadaw or to draw a sort of compromise from it. Most of the political conflict happened only inside the officer corps instead of within a national debate between the state and the society.[14] In terms of the state institution, since administrative authority, legislative authority, and defense authority were concentrated in the SPDC, the officer corps could penetrate further into the civilian sectors of the state, mainly through three avenues: creating dual appointments of high-ranking officers, usually higher than brigadier general, to the positions of minister and vice-minister; establishing the high authority of regional commanders in the local administration in combination with the Ministry of Home Affairs that is under the strong influence of the Tatmadaw; and transferring active military officers, usually middle-ranking officers, to important positions in the civilian ministries. Under such circumstances, one cannot expect any kind of external control over the Tatmadaw, let alone civilian control.

New Roles in a New Setting

This section will discuss the Tatmadaw's new role in politics and the state following the transition in 2011 from direct military rule to a kind of hybrid regime or quasi-democratic regime, positioning that new role in the broader institutional design of the 2008 Constitution.

In his inauguration speech on 30 March 2011, President Thein Sein said, "From now on, Myanmar has initiated democratic transition." This announcement was not a surprise since the junta had been preparing for the establishment of the new political institutions since 2003 through such processes as drafting a new constitution, holding the 2010 general election, and convening the first session of the Union Parliament in 2011. What attracted great attention from observers was whether the president, Thein Sein, could really run the government in a different way and could break the domestic and international political deadlocks. Pessimistic views vis-à-vis the new government were widely shared among observers during the early transition period. Given the fact that Thein Sein was a former general, who had a reputation as a loyalist to his boss, Senior Gen. Than Shwe, and that many of the minister portfolios went to a number of former generals, it seems fairly reasonable that those observers embraced such pessimistic views. However, the Thein Sein government implemented remarkable political and economic reforms in a more comprehensive manner than many expected. Since the Tatmadaw reserves political authority in the formal political institutions, political liberalization rather than democratization must be the more appropriate concept to describe these reforms. In the context of Myanmar's political development, it is not necessarily strange that the transition led by the junta did not remove the Tatmadaw's organizational autonomy and its political leadership from the new constitution. What is of greater importance is how to understand the new roles of the Tatmadaw in the new political setting.

As for the Tatmadaw's legal power, Article 20 of the 2008 Constitution lists the principles in abstract wording, defining the organization as "the sole patriotic defence force" (Article 20a), describing its institutional autonomy from any other institutions, forces and people (Articles 20b & 20c), asserting its responsibility for national security (Articles 20d & 20e), and declaring its duty to safeguard the Constitution (Article 20f). Under these principles, some chapters of the Constitution define the Tatmadaw's concrete legal authority, as can be seen below. While it is true that the legal authorities guarantee the Tatmadaw's power and could hinder further democratization in the future, two new developments should also be noted here.

First, the constitutional institutionalization of the Tatmadaw's political power is novel in Myanmar's constitutional history. Despite the fact that the Tatmadaw has been powerful in politics since independence, no articles to designate its power were evident in either the 1947 Constitution or the 1974 Constitution. The Tatmadaw's political influence had been invisible in formal institutions, making it sometimes difficult for people, including government officers, to know exactly the legal grounds of some decisions made by military leaders.[15] Therefore, this can be regarded as one step forward in the political development of a legal definition of the Tatmadaw's authority, even though the step is just a small one.

Second, the Tatmadaw had stepped back to some degree from politics when compared to the SLORC and SPDC eras when all state powers were under the control of the Commander-in-Chief. The newly-introduced division of power in 2011 reduced the influence of the Tatmadaw over the state, and also created some room for civilian institutions to be proactive. It is imperative to examine how the Tatmadaw's new roles were located within the entire institutional design. Here, the chapter focuses on four basic elements of the new ruling system which the junta put forward, so as to bring about some effective transformation without destabilizing politics and undermining the Tatmadaw's political leadership.

From Dictatorship to Collective Leadership

First, the leadership system has been transformed from a dictatorship to a collective leadership with divisions of authority. Under the SLORC and SPDC, the chairman of both organizations kept dictatorial power in order to influence almost all of the government sectors, which indicates an extremely weak balance of power.[16] The 2011 transition served as an exit policy for Senior Gen. Than Shwe, who had ruled the country since 1992. It is speculated that he decided to withdraw from state leadership sometime in the early 2000s, probably when the "Seven Step Roadmap to Democracy" was announced in 2003, by providing an end to the "provisional" military rule. Alternatively, it would have been impossible for him to have been totally aware of how the new constitution would work after his retirement. But the 2008 Constitution inevitably divided state power into mainly three institutions: the administration, the parliament, and the Tatmadaw.[17]

Although the president is the most powerful authority in the administration, the president is not the supreme commander of the armed forces, which is under the command of the Commander-in-Chief without any kind of effective civilian control. In the legislation process, too, while the president is allowed to send a bill back to parliament with comments within 14 days after being received, this power vis-à-vis the parliament is not particularly strong or effective because the bill can become law with the approval of the majority in the joint parliament (*Pyidaungsu Hluttaw*) even without the president's signature (Article 105).[18] Since the president, vice presidents, and cabinet members are prohibited from taking part in political party activities according to the Constitution [Articles 64 and 232 (k)], the ruling party can move independently of the cabinet in the legislations process. In fact, between the 1st session in 2011 and the 10th session in 2015, the parliament members rejected 68 per cent of the president's comments on bills, suggesting that the parliament members were not necessarily loyal to the president. This division and tension between the administration and the parliament is actually common in the countries that have a presidential system.[19] To the extent that the three institutions work on the principle of balance of power, it is highly difficult for someone to obtain a dictatorial leadership like the chairman of the SLORC and SPDC.

Making a Ruling Party

Second, the state-backed political party, the USDP, was formed to compete in the 2010 election and to become the ruling party through the expected victory of the majority of seats. The predecessor organization of the USDP was the Union Solidarity and Development Association (USDA), which was the junta's sponsored organ designed to mobilize popular support for itself.[20] The USDA announced that it had a membership of more than 20 million people, many of whom were government officers and their family members. It was the only non-military organization which the junta relied upon to win the election. The Tatmadaw carried out a major reshuffling of its top positions in August 2009 with the intent of making the top generals retire and assume high positions in the USDP as "civilians."

Theoretically speaking, a strong ruling party is essential to ensuring the stability of a semi-authoritarian regime, one variation of which is Myanmar's post-2011 ruling system. Under this type of political regime, the ruling party's preference and behavior are different from those in democratic countries. As Levitsky and Way write, "On the one hand, unlike most authoritarian regimes, parties must take seriously elections and other democratic institutions; their ability to gain or maintain power hinges—at least, in part—on their ability to win votes and control legislatures. On the other hand, however, competing on a skewed playing field often requires strategies that have little to do with vote-maximization."[21] The USDP was obviously organized to win votes and control legislatures longer than one term as a ruling party. But an important question here is whether people in the USDP were aware of the necessity of "strategies that have little to do with vote-maximization," which must be carefully handled. Possibly, the party leadership underestimated the importance of such strategies and their essential role for regime maintenance.

Officer Corps Network

Third, the Tatmadaw officer corps network has connected people in power. Twenty-six of the 30 new ministers in March 2011 were active or retired military officers, many of whom were ex-generals. Meanwhile, Shwe Mann, the former No. 3 of the SPDC, controlled the parliament as the Speaker of the Lower House and as the chairman of the ruling party. Both at the federal as well as the regional and state levels, Thein Sein appointed 11 retired military officers and one active brigadier general to the positions of chief minister of regional and state governments. Especially after 2012 when Thein Sein appointed four ex-generals as ministers of the president's office, making them so-called super ministers empowered to manage multiple stakeholder issues within the government, such as Soe Thane for economic issues and Aung Min for ceasefire and border issues, the new administration improved its administrative efficiency by mitigating the negative effect of ministerial sectionalism and rivalries among ex-generals. It is somewhat ironic that the network that was created under the previous military rule functioned as a strong power base for Thein Sein's subsequent path-breaking post-junta reforms.[22]

Military as a Dual Guardian

Fourth, the Tatmadaw is supposed to take two roles: guardian of national security and of the constitution. As mentioned above, the 2008 Constitution guarantees organizational autonomy for the Tatmadaw. One of the crucial institutions for ensuring this autonomy is the National Defence and Security Council (NDSC) (Article 201), which is a consultation organization for decision-making concerning military affairs and security issues. For instance, the president has to co-ordinate with the NDSC when taking military action against aggression aimed at the country. Although the president himself forms the NDSC, at least 6 of the 11 members were active-military men or people whom the military representatives in the parliament had nominated, suggesting that the decisions in the NDSC are under the control of the Commander-in-Chief. Moreover, the appointment of the Commander-in-Chief needs approval from the NDSC.[23] As is well known, the Constitution enables the Tatmadaw to provide some influence over other state organizations. In terms of administration, the President must appoint three ministers (Home Affairs, Border

Affairs, and Defence) from a list of suitable Defence Services personnel who are nominated by the Commander-in-Chief. In the Union Parliament and Regional/State Parliament, one-fourth of the seats are automatically allocated to military representatives, whom the Commander-in-Chief can nominate from active officers. They are expected to represent the military's interests in the legislation process.[24]

Furthermore, the Tatmadaw can exercise substantial veto power over constitutional amendments. According to Article 436 (b) of the 2008 Constitution, the constitution "shall be amended only by a vote of more than seventy-five percent of all the representatives of the Pyidaungsu Hluttaw (the Union Parliament)." This means that constitutional amendments are not expected to happen without the approval of the military representatives under the Commander-in-Chief's control. Significantly, it should be understood that what is represented here is not only the Tatmadaw's material and organizational interests, but also the Tatmadaw's perception of politics, which is often referred as *amyotha nainganyei* (national politics/interest). According to Ino, through the concept of *amyotha nainganyei*, the Tatmadaw presents itself as the guardian of the whole nation's interest, while, by contrast, the political parties represent the interests of a specific group in society (*pati nainganyei*, party politics/ interest).[25] Obviously, this dichotomy of "national politics" versus "party politics" is too simple to fully describe how politics work. At the same time, however, it insinuates that a paternalistic understanding of state leadership and a sense of distrust of political parties have remained in the Tatmadaw since the late 1940s.

The 2015 Election and Beyond

What was at stake in the 2015 general election is not only the mandate to run the next administration and legislatures, but also the stability of the new political system discussed in the previous section. About four and a half years after the USDP came to power, the NLD achieved a landslide victory mainly because of the huge popularity of Aung San Suu Kyi and the widely shared anti-military sentiments even among people in the ethnic minorities states. The Tatmadaw accepted this unfavorable electoral outcome. But, as Croissant rightly suggests, "the stronger the military's position vis-à-vis the civilians at the end of the transition, the more challenging it is for the elected authorities to change the balance of power in their favour."[26]

Since the Constitution guarantees its autonomy and political authority, such as through its veto over constitutional amendments, the Tatmadaw's presence in politics lingers on. By contrast, the USDP's presence depended on the election result. The USDP's defeat in the election has meant it has lost its ability to exercise control over initiatives in the administration and legislatures. Consequently, the conventional elite coalition between the USDP and the Tatmadaw has almost ended only five years after its formation. More importantly, the NLD's toppling of the USDP has fundamentally transformed the informal political system that had linked the government and Tatmadaw. These informal aspects should not be ignored in examining how the 2015 election and NLD's administration could affect civil-military relations in Myanmar. The Tatmadaw's autonomy and power has been shaped by complicated and sometimes conflicting factors around it. This section aims to point out three of the limitations that can be imposed on the Tatmadaw's power.

First, the Tatmadaw's presence in the administration and legislature became weaker due to the fact that it had lost its major ruling partner, the USDP. After the 2015 election, the transition process proceeded relatively smoothly with the notable exception of the three meetings between Aung San Suu Kyi and Senior Gen. Min Aung Hlaing, during which she requested a suspension of Article 59 (f), which would enable her to be president. Ultimately Senior Gen. Min Aung Hlaing refused her request, after which she formed the cabinet, in which her close friend since her high-school days, Htin Kyaw, was nominated and appointed as the new President in the Union Parliament. Aung San Suu Kyi herself took the two ministerial positions in Foreign Affairs and the Presidential Office. The three ministers for Home Affairs, Border Area, and Defence were appointed from the Commander-in-Chief's nominees. The Tatmadaw representatives, who occupy one-fourth of the total seats in parliament, nominated and voted for the ex-military general and former chief minister of the Yangon regional government, Myint Swe, to become a vice president, which ranked second in the votes. Even under the NLD's new government, the Tatmadaw's political presence is apparent because the Constitution legally guarantees its power.

However, the Tatmadaw's actual influence over politics has been undermined because the majority of the executive and parliament members are now NLD members. Without a major partner like the USDP, the Tatmadaw are faced with powerlessness as an opposition group under the principle of majority rule in a democracy. Of course, the Commander-in-Chief was aware of this weakness, and prepared for the new political environment and reality. For instance, he nominated new military representatives for the second term in the Union Parliament, many of whom enjoyed a higher rank than those in the first parliament, probably to endorse more capable officers and to bring more value to the position.[27] Although this sort of minor change is most likely of lesser importance in the legislative process, what is more significant is that the Tatmadaw has lost some of the political leverage necessary to impose its will on the government.

Second, the NLD government could make the Tatmadaw's veto power over the constitutional amendment less effective through the usual lawmaking process, which is now under the control of the NLD. Institutionally speaking, the constitution is the most formal statement of the political rules and norms. However, one should not assume that the 2008 Constitution of Myanmar meets the requirements of popular sovereignty in terms of its drafting process, in which the national referendum to approve the constitution resulted in a doubtfully high approval rate (93.82 per cent) in 2008. In tandem with this weakness of constitutional legitimacy, Aung San Suu Kyi's popularity might help the new government overcome sensitive issues on the bills that could be viewed as in conflict with the Constitution. In fact, when the new Union Parliament passed the State Counsellor Bill, which was drawn to establish a new position for Aung San Suu Kyi allowing her to run the government without holding the presidency in early April 2016, the NLD did not accept the military representatives' argument that the bill could be unconstitutional.[28] While the NLD argued that the bill was constitutional because of Article 217, which says "Nothing in this Section shall prevent the Pyidaunsu Hluttaw [Union Parliament] from conferring functions and powers upon any authoritative body or person," the bill seemed to be contradictive to some articles like Article 232 (k), which prohibits the Union Minister's participation in party activities, since the bill enables the State Counsellor to give suggestions to all the stakeholders, including parliament members.

The Constitutional Tribunal exists for judicial reviews in order to evaluate legal issues in controversial bills. However, there was little hope for the military representatives to get their preferred judgment in the Constitutional Tribunal mainly for two reasons. One is that politicians tend to downplay its importance because the Constitutional Tribunal is new in Myanmar's constitutional history.[29] The other reason is that there is a common perception that all nine judges of the tribunal were under the NLD's influence, because the President, the Speaker of the Lower

House and the Speaker of the Upper House, all of whom belong to the NLD, nominated three judges.[30] Under these circumstances, the constitutional authority to actually reject the constitutional amendment is not as secure as the military men may expect. In this way, the NLD can avoid the constitutional amendment process through normal legislation.

Thirdly, the military's new modernization efforts and its international defense partnerships might create tension between its corporate identity and the international standard of civil-military relations. Since 2011, the Tatmadaw has been under transformation not only as a political force but also as a coercive organization, aiming to develop its defence capability. Senior Gen. Min Aung Hlaing set a new organizational goal using the expression "professional army" or "standard army." The following is a part of his vision for the future Tatmadaw: "Since 2011, we have been doing some reforms to the Tatmadaw with the aim of becoming a professional army, a standard army. The Myanmar army was previously formed to respond to local insurgencies, and based on that experience, it is true the army developed into a force to defend the country.... To conclude, we are building a skillful and a powerful army."[31] What "professional army" and "standard army" mean here is not a non-political army that takes responsibility mainly for national security issues, but a military with a high capability as a defence force.

Fortunately, in recent years, the United States, the United Kingdom, Australia and even Japan are finding greater significance in Myanmar's strategic location in transforming Asia's regional order, leading to an expansion of its range of strategic options to counterbalance China's influence and also to develop its military capability. Although Western countries are aiming at military's operational capabilities and weapon sales in the future, the current focus of the Tatmadaw's military ties with Western countries is still narrow. The main program is officer training that promotes awareness of international legal norms and provides modern military management. Exceptionally, the Myanmar navy's international engagement is slightly ahead of the other two services. While the navy has been establishing ties with the Indian navy, it accepted an Australian warship's port visit to Myanmar in 2015 for the first time since 1959.[32] The expansion of the government budget would help these efforts of the Tatmadaw to develop its military capability. The amount of military expenditure increased from 1,977 billion Kyats to 2,876 billion Kyats between FY2012 and FY2016, while its proportion in the Union Budget fell from 16.5 to 13.5 per cent during the same time period because of the increase in the total budget caused by the economic boom and international aid.[33]

However, the Tatmadaw's defence ambitions face a serious dilemma. On the one hand, the Tatmadaw has now finally obtained more opportunities to develop its military capability with the support of Western countries. On the other hand, this engagement inevitably presents a fundamental challenge to the Tatmadaw's traditional notion of its political leadership role, since the concept of the modern army or military professionalism in the West assumes civilian control over the military in order to prevent its intervention in politics.[34] It is unavoidable that the Tatmadaw will receive external pressure nudging it towards a more democratic rule as its international defence engagement grows. Even though the Tatmadaw leaders maintain a definition of their own professionalism based only on their defence perspective and reasons for taking part in state leadership, it is difficult to convince international society to accept their tradition of political involvement in Myanmar. The Commander-in-Chief has to manage the dilemma between his ambition to develop the country's military capabilities, and the internal and external pressure to introduce international standards of civilian control. We did not have to wait long for this potential contradiction to manifest itself. The United Kingdom and the United States stopped military engagement after the terrorist group called Arakan Rohingya Salvation Army's attacks on 30 Border Guard Police posts and an army base resulted in the army's clearance operations in Northern Rakhine State on 25 August 2017 and the subsequent outflow of more than seven hundred thousand refugees to Bangladesh.[35] If Western governments perceive that the Rohingya Muslim issue is not being adequately addressed by the Tatmadaw, their demand for more Western style civilian control might become higher.[36] As we learnt from the response of the Tatmadaw to international sanctions before 2011, this sort of international pressure could easily stimulate Tatmadaw's nationalistic self-perception and thus have adverse effects on the situation.

Recently, in addition to the "national politics" that ideologically justifies its political role, the Tatmadaw has pointed out the domestic security risk posed by ethnic armed groups and weaknesses in the rule of law in order to claim the necessity of its own political power. Senior Gen. Min Aung Hlaing said in a speech on the 71st Armed Forces Day in 2016, "The two main hindrances in democratization are the lack of abiding by the rule of law, regulations and the presence of armed insurgences. These could lead to chaotic democracy."[37] This logic likely would not convince some who demand a prompt democratization of the country, partly because it gives little explanation of why the civilian government is not able to deal with the rule of law and domestic armed groups, and also because it does not recognize that many people distrust that the Tatmadaw is a player who can bring about peace and the rule of law. Senior Gen. Min Aung Hlaing seems highly aware of this perception. For regaining people's trust and improving the Tatmadaw's public image, he actively accepts interview requests by domestic and international media, in which he clearly articulates the roles of the Tatmadaw in politics and national security. His Facebook page always provides information on his public activities such as attendance at ceremonies, visits to troops and military facilities, and the acceptance of foreign visitors.[38] Such an approach to public relations is totally new in the Tatmadaw's history.

Conclusion

The current civil-military relations in Myanmar are poised in a fragile balance between two different main powers. On the one hand, the NLD runs the government and exercises dominant influence over the administration and legislatures. On the other hand, the Tatmadaw reserves the legal authority to keep its organizational autonomy and can prevent amendments to the Constitution. In other words, while the NLD can dominate the game of politics, the Tatmadaw can control the rules of the game. These distorted power relations are an unintended outcome brought about by the combination of the institutional reform since 2011 and the landslide victory of the NLD in the 2015 election.

When competitive authoritarian regimes in general fail in electoral competitions, countries move towards democratic transition, partly because the electoral failure undermines the legitimacy of the conventional ruling elites and also because the election results pave the way for the rise of new leaders. In Myanmar's case, although the opposition party won in the electoral competition, the armed forces could preserve their autonomy and keep the basic political system from changing towards a more democratic one. In the process of drafting the 2008 Constitution, the junta leaders must have expected the collective leadership to be held by the president, the USDP chairman, and the Commander-in-Chief, thus leading to a long and stable rule by the existing ruling elites. And in fact, their actual political and economic performance over the past five years has not necessarily been disappointing. They set out to drastically alter the preexisting mode of political participation, economic policies, and foreign relations. However, it seemed that they were over-confident to have expected path-breaking reforms. Also, they might have underestimated the challenge caused by Aung San Suu Kyi and the NLD's popularity.

The stability and success of the NLD government in the short term depend on its ability to carefully manage this fragile civil-military balance under the distorted power structure. While some NLD cadres are still expecting more radical reforms reducing the Tatmadaw's political influence, such as replacing the existing constitution with a new one, Aung San Suu Kyi seems to be sufficiently aware of the risk of such an action, which could undermine the Tatmadaw's corporate interest and its paternalistic view of the state leadership. It could be concluded that she has decided to accept the Tatmadaw's institutional power for now, and at the same time to commit to extremely difficult but probably less risky tactics. This is the attempt to achieve a national reconciliation of all the ethnic armed groups in the country through the "Union Peace Conference – 21st Century Panlong." The conference's title is named after the Panlong Conference which in 1947 hosted negotiations between General Aung San and some major ethnic group leaders. While appropriating the name of the historical conference, the aim and structure of the current Panlong takes over from the achievements of the former president's initiative for bilateral ceasefire negotiations and a nationwide ceasefire agreement to establish "a federal union based on ethnic equality, democracy and self-determination."[39] If Aung San Suu Kyi is able to achieve this nationwide ceasefire, it would become another historical Panlong Conference and in the meantime would help to undermine the legitimacy of the Tatmadaw's political role. However, few observers predict that the 18 ethnic armed groups inside the country with different capabilities, interests, and backgrounds would reach a single ceasefire agreement.[40] In fact, only two additional ethnic armed groups have signed the agreement during the first two years of her rule. One of the major reasons for this poor performance is obviously non-coordination between the government and the Tatmadaw. The effect of political negotiation among the stakeholders led by the government has often been undermined by the Tatmadaw's military operations against armed groups. The coordination for security issues between the government and the Tatmadaw is always elusive because of the weak civilian-control and a wide cleavage between the fundamental views on the national interests held by the NLD and the Tatmadaw. The future trajectory of Myanmar politics is still uncertain.

Notes

1. This work was financially supported by JSPS KAKENHI Grant Number JP25285041 and 15KK0085. I would like to thank Prof. Pavin Chachavalpongpun, Prof. Koichi Fujita, Prof. Fumiharu Mieno, Prof. Yoko Hayami, Dr. Adam Simpson, Dr. Matthew Walton, Patrick McCormick, Mr. Aung Tun, Dr. Patrick Strefford, and Mr. Bo Bo Nge for their insightful comments on the original presentation at the international workshop held in Kyoto in February 2016.
2. The part of her speech is as follows: "We will move forward together carefully. I don't think it's appropriate to speak about the election results until the official announcement has been made. But even though I don't speak about it, I believe our people will understand. Just keep calm and remain peaceful" (*Channel News Asia*, 9 November 2015) <http://www.channelnewsasia.com/news/asiapacific/lose-bravely-win-humbly-aung-san-suu-kyi-on-myanmar-elections-8248648> [accessed 9 May 2018].
3. Juan J. Linz and Alfred Stephan, *Problems of Democratic Transition and Consolidation: Southern Europe, South America, and Post-Communist Europe* (Baltimore: The Johns Hopkins University Press, 1996), p. 3.
4. Article 59 (f) says "shall he himself, one of the parents, the spouse, one of the legitimate children or their spouses, not owe allegiance to a foreign power, not be subject of a foreign power or citizen of a foreign country. They shall not be person entitled to enjoy the rights and privileges of a subject of a foreign government or citizen of a foreign country." Since Aung San Suu Kyi's two sons hold UK citizenship, she will never be able to become the president without the amendment of this article. See *Wall Street Journal*, 7 February 2016 <http://www.wsj.com/articles/myanmar-military-defends-against-push-for-suu-kyi-presidency-1454840051> [accessed 9 May 2018].
5. Tin Maung Maung Than, "Burma: The 'New Professionalism' of the Tatmadaw." In *Military Professionalism in Asia: Conceptual and Empirical Perspectives*, ed. Muthiah Alagappa (Honolulu, HI: East-West Center, 2001), pp. 163–79.
6. This narrative is more or less one of the myths in Myanmar politics, resulting from the political struggle inside the military right after the independence. See Maung Maung, *Burma's Constitution* (The Hague: Martinus Nijhoff, 1959), pp. 140–1.
7. Louis J. Walinsky, *Economic Development in Burma, 1951–1960* (New York: Twentieth Century Fund, 1962), p. 436.
8. Mary Callahan, *Making Enemies: War and State Building in Burma* (Ithaca: Cornell University Press, 2003), pp. 162–3.
9. One probably should not overrate this doctrine as something that shaped the Tatmadaw's principle, even though it was one of a few formal doctrines prescribing the Tatmadaw's duty. Actually, the Tatmadaw leaders have rarely referred to this doctrine in its long history of direct political involvement

after 1962. See Yoshihiro Nakanishi, *Strong Soldiers, Failed Revolution: The State and Military in Burma, 1962–1988* (Singapore: NUS Press, 2013), pp. 73–6.

10. The BSPP's formal ideology, which is referred to as "The System of Correlation between Man and His Environment," contains some unique ideas derived from Buddhist thought, but they were probably too abstract for policy makers to obtain practical hints for their original policies.
11. Nakanishi, *Strong Soldiers, Failed Revolution*, pp. 228–32.
12. In the same announcement, SLORC promised "to stage democratic multiparty general elections after fulfilling all the above-stated responsibilities" as the fourth duty. Later this part was replaced by "offering utmost assistance for the emergence of a State Constitution" [Address delivered by Chairman of the State Law and Order Restoration Council, Senior General Saw Maung, Commander-in-Chief of the Defence Services at the 46th Anniversary of the Armed Forces Day (Resistance Day) in 27 March 1997].
13. Address delivered by the Defence Services Commander-in-Chief, General Than Shwe on the 48th Anniversary Armed Forces Day (Resistance Day), 27 March 1993.
14. Kyaw Yin Hlaing, "Factional and Power Struggles in Post-colonial Myanmar," *Journal of Southeast Asian Studies* 39, no. 1 (2008): 149–77.
15. Former Prime Minister Soe Win's memoir tells us his own experience inside the cabinet when he tried to promote legislation. See Myint Thu, *Mahmyawlinthaw Kayishe: Bogyoukgyi Soe Win I Atoukpatti* [Unexpected Long Journey: Memoir of General Soe Win] (Yangon: Myanmar Heritage, 2014), Chapter 8.
16. Myanmar's dictatorship between 1962 and 2010 was based on an interesting mix of personal and institutional dictatorship, in which the dictator respected the formal hierarchy inside the military instead of personalizing the military bureaucracy. At the same time, he could enjoy his power sometimes beyond what was prescribed by the formal institution in order to gain personal benefit.
17. The judiciary can be an independent power in the 2008 Constitution. Yet, it has been powerless in Myanmar because of the long dependency on the junta since 1962. More time is needed before the judiciary can be expected to work a check-and-balance of power. See Nick Cheesman, "What Does the Rule of Law have to do with Democratization (in Myanmar)?" *South East Asia Research* 22, no. 2 (2014): 213–32.
18. The joint parliament (*Pyidaungsu Hluttaw*) is composed of the Lower House (*Pyithu Hluttaw*) and Upper House (*Amyotha Hluttaw*). The role of each house is almost the same in the legislative process, although the electoral process gives some priority to the ethnic minority states in the Upper House by allocating the same number of seats to them as ethnic Burma majority regions.

19. Matthew Soberg Shugart and John M. Carey, *Constitutional Design and Electoral Dynamics* (Cambridge: Cambridge University Press, 1992).
20. Regarding USDA, see Network for Democracy and Development, *The White Shirts: How the USDA Will Become the New Face of Burma's Dictatorship* (Mae Sot: NDD Documentation and Research Department, 2006).
21. Steven Levitsky and Lucan A. Way, *Competitive Authoritarianism: Hybrid Regimes After the Cold War* (New York, NY: Cambridge University Press, 2010), pp. 29–30. As an attempt to explain the transition in 2011 from this perspective, see Adam P. Macdonald, "From Military Rule to Electoral Authoritarianism: The Reconfiguration of Power in Myanmar and its Future," *Asian Affairs: An American Review* 40 (2013): 20–36.
22. An important exception was rivalry between Thein Sein and Shwe Mann that appeared soon after the transition. I think there are two main reasons to explain this rivalry. Firstly it was caused by a typical institutional factor of the presidential system, which could create politics along the division of power between the executive and the parliament. Secondly, we should take Shwe Mann's personal ambition to be the top of the government into consideration. Later Shwe Mann gradually built close ties with Aung San Suu Kyi at the parliament probably because he saw the possibility that her party would come to power in the next administration. His behavior can be regarded as a rational choice of a politician, but it was not acceptable to USDP people, which resulted in his dismissal from the post of party chairman.
23. Maung Aung Myoe, "The Soldier and the State: the Tatmadaw and Political Liberalization in Myanmar since 2011," *South East Asia Research* 22, no. 2 (2014): 239. Even the president and the parliament cannot control the military and defense issues. The only way to influence the military is through budget control. It is probably a "flaw" in the institutional design, but the budget of the Ministry of Defence is proposed to the parliament session as a part of the national budget law. This may become a political minefield in the future.
24. Significantly, those representatives are sometimes reshuffled based on the Commander-in-Chief's order, preventing them from becoming an independent political force in the parliament.
25. Kenji Ino, "Myanma Kokugun no Seiji Kainyu no Ronri – 'Kokumin Seiji' Gainen o Chushin to Shite [Myanmar Military's Logic of Political Intervention – Focusing on the Concept of 'National Politics']," *Tonan Ajia – Rekishi to Bunka*, no. 29 (2000); Renaud Egreteau, *Caretaking Democracy: The Military and Politial Change in Myanmar* (New York: Oxford University Press, 2016), p. 91.
26. Croissant, Aurel, "Civilian Control of the Military in Emerging Democracies: Theory and Empirical Evidence from Asia," *Journal of European Studies* 30, no. 2 (2014): 40.

27. Egreteau, Renaud, "Myanmar Military Chief Revamps his Parliamentary Team," *Nikkei Asia Review*, 27 January 2016 <http://asia.nikkei.com/Viewpoints-archive/Viewpoints/Myanmar-military-chief-revamps-his-parliamentary-team> [accessed 3 June 2017].
28. What the law enables her to do is "to contact government ministries, departments, organisations, associations and individuals and makes her accountable to the Pyidaungsu Hluttaw," *Global New Light of Myanmar*, 6 April 2016.
29. Dominic J. Nardi, Jr. "Finding Justice Scalia in Burma: Constitutional Interpretation and the Impeachment of Myanmar's Constitutional Tribunal," *Pacific Rim Law & Policy Journal* 23, no. 3 (2014): 631–80.
30. Interview with an anonymous judge in Naypyitaw on 22 September 2016.
31. Myawadi, *The Interview with Commander-in-Chief of Defence Services Senior General Min Aung Hlaing and Excerpts from the Interviews with Foreign News Agencies* (Yangon: Myawadi Sapeitaik, 2015), pp. 22–4.
32. *Jane's Defence Weekly* 51, no. 16 (12 March 2014).
33. There is unconfirmed information about the existence of additional funds that the Tatmadaw are allowed to access without other institutions' supervision, *Jane's Defence Weekly* 52, no. 11 (28 January 2015). Same question. On the other hand, institutionally speaking, the parliament could discuss the budget bill to reduce the defence expenditure, and it is not sure yet how NLD deals with this sensitive issue in the discussion of the next fiscal year's budget.
34. For instance, David Steinberg, an experienced Myanmar expert based in Washington DC, gave an interview in September 2016 on the training and democratization of Myanmar: "Democracy is a goal that has never completely been achieved (even in the US); and training should be a means to help the process of democratization along. The Myanmar military must feel comfortable in both its internal political and external relations." In *The Irrawaddy*, 13 September 2016 <http://www.irrawaddy.com/interview/us-training-of-burmas-military-could-help-democratization-david-steinberg.html> [accessed 3 February 2018].
35. "UK to Suspend Training of Burmese Military over Treatment of Rohingya," *The Guardian*, 19 September 2017 <https://www.theguardian.com/world/2017/sep/19/uk-suspend-training-burmese-military-treatment-rohingya> [accessed 3 February 2018], "US Withdraws Assistance from Myanmar Military Amid Rohingya Crisis," *The Guardian*, 24 October 2017 <https://www.theguardian.com/world/2017/oct/24/us-withdraws-assistance-from-myanmar-military-amid-rohingya-crisis> [accessed 3 February 2018].
36. This fragile relationship naturally encourages the Tatmadaw to be closer with other big militaries such as China, India, and Russia.
37. *Global New Light of Myanmar*, 28 March 2016.
38. Win Myat Aung and Yoshihiro Nakanishi, "In Search of Legitimacy: Tatmadaw and New Political Landscape in Myanmar after 2011," unpublished

paper for Southeast Asia Studies in Asia (SEASIA) Conference 2017 held at Chulalongkorn University on 17 December 2017.

39. Nehiginpao Kipgen, "Ethnic Nationalities and the Peace Process in Myanmar," *Social Research* 82, no. 2 (2015): 399–425.
40. International Crisis Group (ICG), "Myanmar's Peace Process: Getting to a Political Dialogue," Crisis Group Asia Briefing, no. 149 (2016).

References

Baraney, Zoltan. 2016. "Armed Forces and Democratization in Myanmar: Why the U.S. Military Should Engage the Tatmadaw." CSIS Report <https://www.csis.org/analysis/armed-forces-and-democratization-myanmar-why-us-military-should-engage-tatmadaw> [accessed 3 February 2018].

Callahan, Mary. 2003. *Making Enemies: War and State Building in Burma*. Ithaca: Cornell University Press.

Cheesman, Nick. 2014. "What does the rule of law have to do with democratization (in Myanmar)?" *South East Asia Research* 22, no. 2: 213–32.

Croissant, Aurel. 2014. "Civilian Control of the Military in Emerging Democracies: Theory and Empirical Evidence from Asia." *Journal of European Studies* 30, no. 2: 23–45.

Desch, Michael C. 2001. *Civilian Control of the Military: The Changing Security Environment*. Baltimore: The Johns Hopkins University Press.

Euro-Burma Office. 2013. "The Tatmadaw: Does the Government Control the Tatmadaw?" Euro-Burma Office Briefing Paper. Brussel: Euro-Burma Office.

Egreteau, Renaud. 2015. "Emerging Patterns of Parliamentary Politics." In *Myanmar: The Dynamics of an Evolving Polity*, ed. David Steinberg. Boulder: Lynne Rienner Publisher.

———. 2016a. "Myanmar Military Chief Revamps his Parliamentary Team." *Nikkei Asia Review*, 27 January.

———. 2016b. *Caretaking Democracy: The Military and Political Change in Myanmar*. New York: Oxford University Press.

Huntington, Samuel. 2001. *The Third Wave: Democratization in the Late Twentieth Century*. Norman: University of Oklahoma Press.

Ino, Kenji. 2000. "Myanma Kokugun no Seiji Kainyu no Ronri – 'Kokumin Seiji' Gainen o Chushin to Shite [Myanmar Military's Logic of Political Intervention – Focusing on the Concept of 'National Politics']." *Tonan Ajia – Rekishi to Bunka*, no. 29: 3–26.

International Crisis Group (ICG). 2016. "Myanmar's Peace Process: Getting to a Political Dialogue." Crisis Group Asia Briefing, no. 149.

Juan J. Linz and Alfred Stepan. 1996. *Problems of Democratic Transition and Consolidation: Southern Europe, South America, and Post-Communist Europe*. Baltimore: The Johns Hopkins University Press.

Kipgen, Nehiginpao. 2015. "Ethnic Nationalities and the Peace Process in Myanmar." *Social Research* 82, no. 2: 399–425.

Kyaw Yin Hlaing. 2008. "Factional and power struggles in post-colonial Myanmar." *Journal of Southeast Asian Studies* 39, no. 1: 149–77.

Levitsky, Steven and Lucan A. Way. 2010. *Competitive Authoritarianism: Hybrid Regimes After the Cold War*. New York: Cambridge University Press.

Macdonald, Adam P. 2013. "From Military Rule to Electoral Authoritarianism: The Reconfiguration of Power in Myanmar and its Future." *Asian Affairs: An American Review* 40: 20–36.

Maung Aung Myoe. 2014. "The Soldier and the State: The Tatmadaw and Political Liberalization in Myanmar since 2011." *South East Asia Research* 22, no. 2: 233–49.

______. 2017. "Emerging Pattern of Civil-Military Relations." *Southeast Asian Affairs*: 259–73.

Maung Maung. 1959. *Burma's Constitution*. The Hague: Martinus Nijhoff.

Myawadi. 2015. *The Interview with Commander-in-Chief of Defence Services Senior General Min Aung Hlaing and Excerpts from the Interviews with Foreign News Agencies*. Yangon: Myawadi Sapeitaik.

Myint Thu. 2014. *Mahmyawlinthaw Kayishe: Bogyoukgyi Soe Win I Atoukpatti* [Unexpected Long Journey: Memoir of General Soe Win]. Yangon: Myanmar Heritage.

Nakanishi, Yoshihiro. 2013. *Strong Soldiers, Failed Revolution: The State and Military in Burma, 1962–1988*. Singapore: NUS Press.

Nardi, Jr., Dominic J. 2014. "Finding Justice Scalia in Burma: Constitutional Interpretation and the Impeachment of Myanmar's Constitutional Tribunal." *Pacific Rim Law & Policy Journal* 23, no. 3: 631–80.

Network for Democracy and Development. 2006. *The White Shirts: How the USDA Will Become the New Face of Burma's Dictatorship*. Mae Sot: NDD Documentation and Research Department.

Selth, Andrew. 2015. "Myanmar's Coercive Apparatus: The Long Road to Reform." In *Myanmar: The Dynamics of an Evolving Polity*, ed. David Steinberg, pp. 13–35. Boulder: Lynne Rienner Publisher.

Shugart, Matthew Soberg and John M. Carey. 1992. *Constitutional Design and Electoral Dynamics*. Cambridge: Cambridge University Press.

Steinberg, David I. 2015. "The Persistence of Military Dominance." In *Myanmar: The Dynamics of an Evolving Polity*, ed. David I. Steinberg, pp. 1–12. London: Lynne Rienner Publishers.

Tin Maung Maung Than. 2001. "Burma: The 'new professionalism' of the Tatmadaw." In *Military Professionalism in Asia: Conceptual and Empirical Perspectives*, ed. Muthiah Alagappa, pp. 390–416. Honolulu, HI: East-West Center.

Walinsky, Louis J. 1962. *Economic Development in Burma, 1951–1960*. New York: Twentieth Century Fund.

CHAPTER 3

Myanmar's Post-2015 Foreign Policy: Prisms of Interpretation

Moe Thuzar and Pavin Chachavalpongpun

Myanmar's Foreign Policy Challenges Today

The country referred to as either Burma or Myanmar in international circles has caught the world's attention yet again on its inability to address human rights violations by the country's military. The criticisms levelled towards Myanmar are, paradoxically, not directed at a military junta in control of the country, but at a democratically elected opposition-turned-ruling party that took over the reins of power in 2016. It should be recognized, however, that the National League for Democracy (NLD) government, led by the country's democracy icon, Daw Aung San Suu Kyi (hereafter referred to as Aung San Suu Kyi), is hobbled constitutionally by a stipulated 25 per cent presence of the military in the country's legislature as well as by the military's continued "national security" role in matters of state. The Commander-in-Chief of the Myanmar Armed Forces (referred to as the Tatmadaw) appoints the defence, home affairs, and border affairs ministers, and rotates the military members of parliament at will.

The conventional narrative that described a largely self-imposed isolation which started barely a decade into Burma's post-1948 independence, and which lasted—in different forms of authoritarian rule—for close to six decades[1] up to 2012, looked set to be replaced by a new narrative after the surprising opening up by a military-backed government led by former generals. The Union Solidarity and Development Party (USDP) came to power via an election in November 2010 that the military insisted was part of its road-map to democracy. But the main opposition party (and indeed the nemesis of the military regime that took power in 1988) the NLD boycotted the 2010 election, and the world at large decried it as sham. The need for legitimacy—domestically and internationally—compelled the USDP government to introduce sweeping political, administrative, and economic reforms, all the more surprising because unexpected. The winds of change, once introduced, took on a force of their own. While giving the USDP credit for starting the process of transition, the world at large and the majority of voters in Myanmar also expected the USDP to be no more than a seat-warmer paving the way for the NLD to take its rightful place denied since the 1990 election which the military junta had annulled.

This helps explain the NLD's overwhelming victory in the 2015 election, which was widely claimed to be as free and fair as possible. There were wide expectations at home and abroad that the NLD, with Aung San Suu Kyi as its public face, would lead the country towards a more active role in foreign relations, engaging with an international community largely sympathetic and supportive to this fledgling democracy. If anything, the "ASEAN-first" foreign policy orientation of the USDP's Thein Sein seemed likely to fade into the shadows of Aung San Suu Kyi's wide international reach and positive image. This certainly seemed to be the case in the early months of the NLD's first year in power, where Aung San Suu Kyi showed an inclination for a continued ASEAN-oriented foreign policy. At the joint press conference following the visit of Thai Foreign Minister Don Pramudwinai to Naypyitaw in May 2016, Aung San Suu Kyi referred to her father's vision of a United States of Indochina as an inspiration for Myanmar's ASEAN directions. For the first time in decades, the precedence of a Burmese leader visiting China as a first stop was broken, when, in her capacity as foreign minister, Aung San Suu Kyi accompanied President Htin Kyaw's maiden visit to neighboring Laos, the ASEAN Chair for 2016 (Laos and Myanmar were admitted to ASEAN together in 1997). She also made her ASEAN debut in that capacity, attending the ASEAN Ministerial Meeting, the annual meeting of the foreign ministers of ASEAN, in July 2016. In her capacity as State Counsellor, Aung San Suu Kyi visited Thailand and China, respectively, the two countries with which Myanmar shares the longest part of its land borders.[2]

But Myanmar now faces a "crisis of community" which affects its foreign policy actions and interpretations. Deep-seated legacy issues have beset the NLD government up to its mid-term mark in 2018 and will possibly even affect the 2020 election. Foremost among these is dealing with ethnic conflict and communal strife, which now define Myanmar's political moment. International attention has been seized by the political and humanitarian implications of the largest exodus to date of Rohingya communities from Rakhine State (UN estimates place it close to 700,000) in the wake of harsh military operations on Rohingya communities in Northern Rakhine, following attacks by the Arakan Rohingya Solidarity Army (ARSA) in August 2017.

Even as the repatriation process is struggling to begin (after months of negotiation, and now with ASEAN-assisted facilitation), Myanmar seems to prefer dealing directly with interlocutors in a bilateral setting.[3] Bilateral channels are certainly important for coordinating with neighbor Bangladesh on the repatriation, but so too are the regional channels facilitated by ASEAN. With Myanmar's dealings with the UN presently at an impasse, ASEAN seems to be the only platform where Myanmar feels comfortable enough to share and brief counterparts on "the situation in Rakhine." At the same time, China's supportive statements advocating for Myanmar to be given the space to deal with the issue[4] have had mixed reception in the country, as well as internationally. All this has added to the international criticism of the NLD government's reluctance to deal with the Rohingya issue in accordance with humanitarian principles and recommendations. The criticism, which continues to mount, has resulted in a solidifying of support for Aung San Suu Kyi, and to a certain extent the military, in Myanmar.

The NLD government's foreign policy actions and pronouncements will now be viewed mainly through the prism of the Rohingya crisis. The crisis has also concentrated attention on the many tensions and conflicts that Myanmar's fragile democracy is trying to manage. Since gaining power, the top priority of the NLD government has been ending the decades-long civil war and restoring peace and stability across the country. But signs of progress towards this are now mixed at best, and the role of the military as the protector of state security has come to the fore.

In their initial assessments of Myanmar's post-2015 foreign policy, two Myanmar experts have highlighted the importance of domestic factors on external projections. Chaw Chaw Sein asserts that while the country's foreign policy remains unchanged in its fundamental principles, the greater attention now required of the NLD government to attend to domestic matters of relevance to foreign policy provides the chance to pursue "several vital issues of considerable domestic sensitivity"[5] which also resonate with regional and international concerns. Maung Aung Myoe posits that Myanmar's foreign policy under the NLD, though not new, will be different in the current directions taken by Aung San Suu Kyi towards a "stronger focus on people-to-people contacts and multi-lateralism."[6] Our own observations and assessment of the country's foreign policy trajectory sees the instinct for survival as a constant link through different iterations of foreign policy over the decades. We argue that this self-preservation instinct may compel the government of Myanmar today towards a new form of neutrality.

Origins and Evolution of Myanmar's Foreign Policy Directions

The importance of being strategic in balancing the different, and often competing, interests among the larger or more powerful of the country's neighbors and partners has been a constant thread in the conduct of foreign policy through the seven decades since Burma became independent. It can be said that Burma pioneered hedging years before the term became a buzzword. Since 1948 Burma has followed a policy of "positive neutrality" and steered away from the East-West bloc confrontation. Foreign policy under then Burmese Prime Minister U Nu was to be on good terms with all, but avoid "entangling alliances" with either East or West. Instead, U Nu sought to play a mediating role between the United States and China. He was one of the key convenors of the 1955 Afro-Asia Conference in Bandung, Indonesia that later led to the Non-Aligned Movement (NAM).[7] General Ne Win, who took over from U Nu in a coup in March 1962 continued the policy of strict neutrality, but nuanced it in 1971 as an "independent" foreign policy. In 1981, this was recast as an "independent and active" foreign policy, to reflect the intent for a more active role in international affairs, although this did not translate to much in practice.

After democracy protests were quelled in a bloody coup in September 1988, the State Law and Order Restoration Council (SLORC) junta portrayed its role more as a guardian of the state in a manner reminiscent of the caretaker role that the armed forces assumed in times of instability. The junta retained the commitment to neutrality and the active and independent stance in foreign policy, but soon found itself seeking closer relations with Asian neighbors, notably China, in the wake of international sanctions that were increasingly imposed with each regressive step taken from the SLORC's stated intentions of restoring democratic rule. Still, under the repressive SLORC regime, Myanmar's foreign ministry undertook important steps towards opening up through greater regional and international interactions. The process started by re-joining the NAM in 1992, followed by application for admission to ASEAN and the Bay of Bengal Initiative for Multi-Sectoral, Technical and Economic Cooperation (BIMSTEC) in 1997. Myanmar's ASEAN membership did not bear much fruit in the way either the hardliners or the diplomats had envisaged: ASEAN did not become a shield in a way that the junta wanted, nor did Myanmar open up through ASEAN membership in the way the technocrats had hoped it would. Myanmar under the military regime did not respond to ASEAN's constructive engagement policy in the way ASEAN had hoped, either.

Yet, the generals bowed to the widespread pressure placed on ASEAN by declining Myanmar's turn to take up the rotational annual chairmanship in 2006. Even so, the military junta showed no signs of relaxing its paranoia. In 2007, the junta's repression of peaceful demonstrations by civilians (later joined by monks),[8] led to a low point in ASEAN's dealings with Myanmar. But in the following year, a small window of hope opened in the wake of Cyclone Nargis, which devastated the country's lower delta areas in May 2008. Over the looming humanitarian crisis in the country, ASEAN brokered what was considered a breakthrough in coordinating the entry and operation of aid workers "regardless of nationality."[9] Still, the path to reform was murky. The seven-step roadmap to democracy that Myanmar announced in 2003 inched at a painstakingly slow pace. Elections were held in November 2010 without the participation of the NLD.[10] The "civilianized" political elite that came into power then sought to shore up its legitimacy deficit domestically and internationally by initiating wide-ranging reforms that eventually saw the NLD taking over responsibilities of the state after its 2015 electoral victory.

The trajectory of Burmese foreign policy thus highlights first a strict neutrality, especially when the military junta was focused on regime survival. A civilianized administration then recognized the strategic interest of gaining legitimacy by opening up to the world. Today, helmed by the NLD government with de facto leader Aung San Suu Kyi in a dual representational role as State Counsellor and Foreign Minister, Myanmar finds itself again at a strategic crossroads of sorts. The transboundary dimension of Myanmar's domestic conflicts or tensions has exposed it to established and rising powers all seeking to assert themselves within respective spheres of influence. At this juncture, the direction of Myanmar's foreign policy as the underlying principle for the conduct of the country's diplomatic/foreign relations, merits deeper examination, particularly with regard to whether the country is returning to a new form of neutralism and non-alignment.

New Neutrality?

Currently, the country's foreign policy does not explicitly state a commitment to neutrality, although non-alignment is mentioned. Myanmar's 2008 Constitution articulates that the "Union practices independent, active and non-aligned foreign policy aimed at world peace and friendly relations with nations and upholds the principles of peaceful co-existence among nations." The foreign policy of a country is invariably based on its national interest and values, marrying domestic needs and external exigencies. The case of Burma is no exception. Frank Trager states this as the outcome of first, the ideological position of the country's leaders and second, the practical necessity of solving its major economic problem: exporting rice, to earn foreign exchange that would enable the implementation of national development plans.[11] Rodolfo Severino also agrees on the dilemma of dependence on a few commodity exports, and adds to that two other factors—national unity and the looming presence of China, the dominant power in the region.[12] More recently, David Steinberg, a consistent and constant analyst of Burma's foreign relations for the past four decades, has suggested the possibility of Myanmar returning to this direction, in discussing the underpinnings of neutralism in Myanmar's interactions with the world.[13]

These assessments also concur largely with the assertions of two senior practitioners of Burma's, later Myanmar's, foreign policy. Daw Than Han, the first female Director-General in Burma's foreign service, listed four conditions accountable for a state's foreign policy in an occasional paper on "Burma's Regional Outlook" authored for Georgetown University's School of Foreign Service in 1988. These conditions are geographical location, the structure of the international system, the state's own domestic economic, social and political needs, and the threat perceptions (to national interest). U Ohn Gyaw, who entered Burma's Foreign Service together with Daw Than Han in 1956, and who later was appointed Foreign Minister by the SLORC, concurs with Daw Than Han's view on the paramountcy of national interest (and domestic factors). He further observed that the exercise of foreign policy is often based on the perceived benefit to one person (usually at the helm of government) who is also the arbiter of policy.[14]

To a large extent, the current situation in Myanmar still fits this broad analysis. However, there are some variables arising from the conduct of Myanmar's foreign relations.

- The determinants of Myanmar's bilateral relations and the extent to which trade, aid and investment now play larger roles in foreign relations;
- The extent to which Myanmar's interests align with those of fellow ASEAN members; and
- The contours—including external influences—that shape the political, economic, and social reforms in Myanmar, which both inform and influence decision-making at domestic (central, local) and regional/international levels.

Throughout the years under the SLORC, and later the State Peace and Development Council (SPDC), there were several moves made by civilian technocrats in the country's foreign ministry to link the conduct of foreign relations to emerging trends shaping the global discourse on inter-state relations, including human rights, environment, and climate change, among others. It is also noteworthy that the push for membership (and in the case of the NAM, rejoining) in regional institutions such as the NAM and ASEAN occurred during the SLORC administration. Myanmar's former foreign minister argues that this was made possible with the personal ties and understanding forged with counterparts at the working level (of senior officials and ministers), through the efforts of diplomacy in a constrained policy environment.[15] Renaud Egreteau and Larry Jagan, in their assessment of Myanmar's diplomatic relations under the military regime, describe the junta's foreign policy actions as "securitization," with the military taking a pre-eminent and dominant role in politics and state structures, and highlight that important elements of continuity underlie Burma's striking postcolonial policy changes and contrasting diplomatic practices.[16] This element of continuity is the role and reach of the Burmese military in retaining their praetorian influence over the country's foreign policy, particularly in the post-junta context of 2011 onwards. Jurgen Haacke also highlights that "Myanmar's threat perceptions vis-à-vis Washington have waned with the shift to the pragmatic, principled and calibrated engagement as favoured by President Obama. The Myanmar government under Thein Sein pursued a non-aligned foreign policy both in declaratory and practical terms."[17] On her part, Aung San Suu Kyi has reiterated continuity with the non-aligned foreign policy, observing that it has been successful since the time of the country's independence.[18]

This has strong implications in terms of the country's foreign policy approach, relevant to international policymakers, potential foreign investors and the country's immediate neighbors, alike. It also leads to a question whether Burma/Myanmar is experimenting with a "new" neutralism, which, in this chapter, is termed "strategic neutrality." This is most evident in the new Myanmar government's nuancing of the strategic pecking order between the US and China.

Balancing Big Power Rivalry

Burma's neutrality has been explained largely as a result of the historical, geographical, and demographic influence of China. John Thomson described this as being "neutral in China's shadow."[19] William Johnstone attempted an empirical approach in assessing the sources and dimensions of neutralism, to test its viability for the newly-independent Burma.[20] Though reaching a similar conclusion that Burma's pursuit of a neutralist foreign policy had brought it "perilously" close to China, and thus, that neutralism lacked viability for Burma, the risks of neutralism have not yet been fully examined. To a certain extent, the strategic alignment practised by the SLORC from 1988 through 2010 can be assessed as running that risk. To this day, China's political and economic footprint entrenched since the SLORC years has led to a legacy of simmering popular resentment against China which the USDP government did not manage to allay, and which has now been inherited by the NLD government. The competing, and often clashing, interests of the US and China in Myanmar has been a phenomenon of Myanmar's relations with both. In the 1950s, Myanmar, then Burma, held to the traditional view that the only conceivable threat to the country was from its largest neighbor China. This led to Burma's opting for China's friendship rather than prepare, with a siege-like mentality, for a Chinese incursion into the country to pursue the remnant Chinese Kuomintang troops (which the US was covertly supporting at the time). The direction of the threat changed, however, with the change in US policy towards Burma post-1988.[21]

Prior to 1988, Burma-US relations were on a relatively even keel, despite the speed-bumps over the Kuomintang issue and the undemocratic nature of the 1962 coup that affected US economic and military cooperation extended to Burma. When the US policy changed, the survival needs of the SLORC pushed Myanmar into a strategic alignment with China. While the SLORC justified this as part of continuing an independent and active foreign policy, in reality the increasing isolation created by international sanctions led the military junta to seek closer relations with East and Southeast Asian nations, and China prominently filled the vacuum left by the US in economic and military cooperation. In fact, in the early part of this century, the Myanmar military increasingly viewed the US as a "foreign threat," as it consistently called for regime change, anathema to Myanmar's military leadership.[22] China's support in countering or vetoing resolutions against Myanmar at the United Nations, and in providing military hardware and training, became necessary—in the military's view—for regime survival and to counter external threats to this survival.

These skewed priorities in the conduct of diplomatic relations has left a bitter legacy. Even after the SLORC had handed over the reins of government to the administration led by the USDP in March 2011, the length of China's shadow continued to be present in Myanmar's foreign policy. President Thein Sein's maiden state visit in May 2011, just two months after taking office, was to China. During this state visit, bilateral relations were elevated to a strategic partnership level. Myanmar supported the One China Policy and China's position in South China Sea. Still, the more strategic need to diversify external relations led to Thein Sein's practically volte-face move in suspending the Myitsone Dam project, and seeking dialogue with then opposition leader Aung San Suu Kyi. The Chinese were caught unaware. This also gives a rare glimpse into a historically pervasive resentment among the Burmese against chauvinistic attitudes from Beijing. Pragmatic alignments notwithstanding, Myanmar's relationship with China was clearly not a strategic zero-sum equation. And, strategic alignments and interests notwithstanding, Myanmar's bilateral relations with China dropped to what can arguably be called its lowest point in at least the past three decades in 2015, especially after the Myanmar military's attempt in February 2015 to retake Kokang from Peng Jiasheng, the leader of the insurgent Kokang and Myanmar National Democratic Alliance (MNDAA), whom the Myanmar military had earlier ousted in 2009.[23] China protested the Myanmar military's airstrikes that bombed areas across the China-Myanmar border in Yunnan.[24] Then, in June 2015, China invited then opposition leader Aung San Suu Kyi to Beijing to meet the highest level of China's leaders, including President Xi Jinping.[25] But the resentment towards what is perceived as Chinese "interference" continues to simmer among populace and armed personnel alike. At the ceasefire negotiations with ethnic armed groups, which the NLD government took over from its predecessor, China participates as an observer, but makes its presence felt nonetheless. For example, China's influence with some of the ethnic armed groups in the ceasefire negotiations has been openly admitted.[26]

Here, China's approach needs to be contrasted with Japan's. Japan has watched with interest China's moves to insinuate itself into the ceasefire negotiations between Myanmar government negotiators and ethnic armed groups operating along the China–Myanmar border, and to mediate the recent flare-up of tensions in Rakhine State. But it has not attempted a similar political assertion, instead seeking to build the necessary economic and social capital in Myanmar's economic hubs as well as in the rural and ethnic minority areas. Japan has appointed a humanitarian envoy and has been providing on-the-ground assistance to communities in need. Japan's Sasakawa Peace Foundation has been implementing school and capacity-building projects in Rakhine since 2012.

As for the US, the differentiation of economic interests from human rights and democracy was most evident under the Obama administration. US–Burma relations have neither improved nor deteriorated since President Trump's inauguration. Even as the Obama administration eased remaining trade sanctions on Myanmar, the arms embargo and other sanctions related to "functional issues" including human and drug trafficking, money laundering, religious freedom, and others were retained.[27] In December 2017, targeted sanctions were imposed against Major-General Maung Maung Soe, the military officer overseeing the military operations in Northern Rakhine.[28] The US has not repealed sanction measures enacted into Federal law. The Obama administration's move was thus limited to trade sanctions, which affected the US investment footprint in Myanmar.[29] President Obama's lifting of remaining trade sanctions restores Myanmar's Generalized System of Preferences (GSP) privileges at the WTO, which had been suspended since 1989, and also raises the reporting threshold for investments to US$5 million. These measures were meant to give a boost to the articulation of policies after the NLD government announced its 12-point economic policy in July 2016. One of the priorities highlights the importance of creating a stable and welcoming environment for foreign direct investment. An unspoken priority is to level the top-heavy dependence on China, which remains the largest investor in Myanmar today. Other investors in the top five positions are Singapore, Thailand, Hong Kong, and the United Kingdom. Meanwhile,

South Korea ranks 6th, Japan 10th, and the US 13th.[30] In terms of new investments, however, the EU was the fourth largest foreign investor behind China, Singapore, and Hong Kong in 2016.[31] A separate Burma Strategy Act 2016 passed by the US Senate with a view to supporting Myanmar's transition will most likely serve as a reference framework for leveraging discussions on human rights issues.

In June 2018, during a visit to Myanmar by Matt Pottinger, Senior Director for Asian Affairs at the White House National Security Council, he confirmed that increasing investment in Myanmar would lead to economic growth which will have the best effect on mitigating the discrimination brought upon different ethnic groups in the country.[32] But, since October 2017, the Trump administration has been considering various forms of "narrow" or targeted sanctions against the Rohingya.

Relations with ASEAN

Former Australian diplomat Trevor Wilson said towards the end of 2006, "It now seemed that a truly satisfactory solution on Myanmar's standing in ASEAN would depend on substantial political changes occurring inside Myanmar."[33] The political opening up of Myanmar has served as a catalyst for an improved relationship it has had with ASEAN. Retrospectively, Myanmar was admitted into the grouping against the view of the international community, which felt that the country was not ready to be recognized as a member of ASEAN when it was still ruled under a firm grip of the military. From this perspective, ASEAN came to play a role as a "legitimacy provider" to Myanmar then, and now too, as the country has undergone political reforms. Meanwhile, Myanmar continues to seek support from ASEAN to legitimize its democratization process. And the search for legitimacy was fulfilled as Myanmar was granted the chairmanship of ASEAN for 2014. So far, ASEAN's chairmanship provided a useful platform for Myanmar to interact with the outside world and, more importantly, to reinvent itself as a responsible member of the international community. On ASEAN's part, awarding Myanmar the regional chairmanship was essentially strategic. It served to vindicate ASEAN's past Myanmar policy, which was criticized of being centred primarily on engagement and not punishment, thus allowing the military to maintain its repressive regime for so long.[34] Myanmar's ASEAN chairmanship also helped strengthen the organization's partnership with the group's dialogue partners—the partnership that had been held hostage by the slow political development in Myanmar.

There was some scepticism that Myanmar, as ASEAN Chair, would be unable to mediate the differences between China and the other ASEAN claimants (Malaysia, Brunei, Vietnam, and the Philippines), particularly on how to come up with acceptable codes of conduct (whereas China preferred to draft individual codes of conduct with each country, the four ASEAN claimants proposed a single code of conduct with China). But Myanmar's ASEAN chairmanship managed to achieve a compromise statement. Myanmar's ASEAN year also set the stage for the ASEAN community's post-2015 vision as well as the work on reviewing and strengthening ASEAN institutions.[35]

It is fair to conclude that Myanmar's ASEAN chairmanship served to render an added legitimacy for Myanmar. This further confirmed the usefulness of ASEAN as a springboard for Myanmar to strengthen its ties with powerful nations outside the Southeast Asian region. To the question of whether the role of ASEAN chairmanship of Myanmar had actually caused an impact on the country's economic development, the answer then was upbeat. It was reported that Myanmar was considered among the top investment destinations in ASEAN for 2015, a year after its ASEAN chairmanship, with growth forecast at 8.5 per cent. Japan's three largest banks—Bank of Tokyo-Mitsubishi UFJ (BTMU), Sumitomo Mitsui Banking Corp, and Mizuho Bank—entered Myanmar since October 2014.[36] Other investments also came from China, the US, Japan, South Korea, Australia, and other Southeast Asian nations, most notably seen in the establishment of the Thilawa Special Economic Zone in south-eastern Yangon in September 2015.[37]

But ASEAN itself has come under fire for its inability to intervene effectively in the Rakhine/Rohingya crisis. Aung San Suu Kyi has sought ASEAN's support, the most recent instance (at the time of writing) being at the ASEAN–Australia Summit in March 2018, to provide help from a humanitarian and capacity-building point of view.[38] Prior to that, Singapore, as Chair of ASEAN, worked with the Jakarta-based Coordinating Centre for Humanitarian Assistance on disaster management (AHA Centre) to facilitate the provision of humanitarian assistance for the displaced communities in Rakhine State.[39] But until now, there have been no concrete solutions from ASEAN in tackling the plight of the Rohingya. ASEAN continues to operate on its traditional basis of non-interference in what it deemed as Myanmar's internal affair, and has not strayed beyond its regional mandate of supporting the humanitarian response to the issue.

Challenges Remain?

For long-time partners, the NLD government's performance thus far, particularly in the economy, and external expectations of Myanmar will all play a part in informing how these countries and their governments formulate their future interactions with Myanmar. The spectre shadowing several newfound freedoms in Myanmar continues to be the military's involvement in the country's administration. There is a mismatch between the huge expectations after the NLD took office, and the reality on the ground. The military's constitutional role in Myanmar's political scene assures it a significant presence (25 per cent) in Myanmar's parliament and in cabinet appointments for defence, home affairs, and border affairs. The long reach of the Ministry of Home Affairs' General Affairs Department countrywide also presents an element of uncertainty over whether Myanmar's de facto leader Aung San Suu Kyi can maintain an equilibrium to achieve her government's policy objectives—ones that range from everyday social welfare needs to nation-wide ceasefire agreements.[40] The uncertainties are compounded by the perceived slowness of the decision-making process, and continued inefficiencies in the bureaucracy which is dominated by military-trained personnel. Although external experts and Myanmar nationals with international expertise and exposure are now advising government policy, the research community's role and inputs in policymaking are still nascent.

A convergence of aspirations, domestically and externally, can be found in the desire to boost Myanmar's economic development and growth. The crackdown on illegal construction, as part of the NLD government's anti-corruption drive, sent shockwaves through the business community. However, the 2016 Myanmar Investment Law, and the 2017 Myanmar Companies Act (entering into force in August 2018), have balanced investor wariness. There is continued interest in Myanmar's untapped economic potential, with China, Singapore, Thailand, South Korea, and the United Kingdom as the top five investors. Japan, which now ranks 10th in the investor stakes, has tried to shore this up with its US$2.72 billion debt relief and a new program of assistance starting 2013.

While China's high-profile infrastructure projects include the controversial Myitsone Dam project which the Thein Sein government suspended, and the Shwe oil and gas project in southern Rakhine State with an attendant deep-sea port and special economic zone (SEZ) at Kyaukphyu, Japan's investments are focused more pragmatically on boosting the port capacity of Myanmar's economic hub Yangon via the Thilawa

Port and SEZ project. The SEZ has many still-vacant sites, indicating a lack of economic dynamism, and lending credence to Thilawa being labelled a "showcase."

Meanwhile, nationalist sentiments seem to be influencing views on foreign investment. This is not exactly a new phenomenon, as strong public criticism and petitions had influenced the USDP government to cancel controversial real-estate development projects in Yangon.[41] Opinion pieces in local newspapers have floated views that express perceptions or attitudes towards external interest—or lack thereof—to invest more in Myanmar similar to other Southeast Asian markets.[42] External investors' experience in Myanmar's economic scene, however, make them more concerned with the country's manufacturing capacity, technology needs, and the continued shortage of skilled workers. Low wages in Myanmar pushed many workers to seek opportunities abroad, prompting the government to hike minimum wages for garment workers from MMK3600 (US$2.66) to MMK4800 (US$3.55). This had an adverse effect of making investors wary as it affected their (already low) profit margins, while labor unions in Myanmar are imploring the government to consider the actual cost of living, which continues to be affected by high prices of basic food commodities.

Conclusion

The best option for Myanmar's foreign policy might still be to continue with the balancing act between US and China. ASEAN's policy of not taking sides as well as Myanmar's own historical experience of being friends with all and an enemy to none serve as good references. Another reference point is in focusing on development towards change, most strikingly evidenced in the fallout over—and subsequent responses to—Cyclone Nargis in 2008. The Nargis response model has been brought up in the context of dealing with the fallout from the Rakhine/Rohingya crisis, and ASEAN's role has once again been deemed useful, although the issue has tested ASEAN's centrality and credibility severely. Ultimately, it is still about Myanmar's survival needs. Up to now, Myanmar has been preoccupied with its own domestic issues and concerns; national security and stability overrode all else in relations with neighbors and in the country's position in ASEAN and other multilateral processes. Yet, as the transition to democracy takes root, the country's foreign policy should also evolve to a more proactive stance, integrating economic, environmental, and social priorities. Lessons from past experience in history may induce the NLD administration to consider a return to the natural cornerstone of the country's survival over the past decades: strategic neutrality with pragmatic considerations and affiliations.

Indications of this potential return to neutrality with a strategic nuance could be seen as early as the USDP administration. In his annual new year "state of the union" address to the nation via radio on 1 January 2015, President Thein Sein touched on the country's foreign policy, stating that "We are also on the path of a much more dynamic and multi-aligned foreign policy"[43] and that "Unlike what we have done in the past, we should actively seek the strongest possible relations with all countries and all powers."[44] Although on the surface, this seemed a departure from the 2008 Constitution's statement of the country's foreign policy principles as being non-aligned, independent, and active, it was actually a simple oversight in translation from the expression in Burmese which would connote more a foreign policy that is "dynamic and multi-partner."

Still, the future direction of Myanmar's foreign policy will depend on decisions taken by the NLD government to address the following realities:

1. Myanmar looks set to return to a strategic neutralism in foreign policy, but in a way that seems different from the neutralist policies of the past. Past experience has highlighted the practicality of following a realpolitik approach to engaging with external partners, the benefits of belonging to a regional organization, and the dangers of depending too heavily on one dominant power for economic and political survival.
2. This return to a more neutralist stance in foreign relations will see more reactive than proactive measures, mainly due to the current dichotomy between domestic and international attitudes towards the Rakhine/Rohingya crisis. Thus, Myanmar's actions on the diplomacy front will not only have to balance between competing external interests but also reflect security- and proaction-seeking behaviors to manage (and protect) diverse domestic interests that are often competing (and conflicting) for priority attention.[45]
3. The key player in setting foreign policy directions in 21st-century Myanmar is Aung San Suu Kyi. How her approach differs from those of Nu, Ne Win, the SLORC/SPDC generals, and Thein Sein's USDP administration will be a reflection of the extent to which Myanmar's internal politics limits the country's "freedom of choice" in its foreign relations.

4. The choices open to Myanmar will also be affected by the state of the economy (including the new economic reforms that the NLD government hopes to institute with the newly-launched Myanmar Sustainable Development Plan), external expectations juxtaposed against public sentiments in the country towards the NLD's performance thus far, and internal power dynamics including how the ceasefire negotiations progress. The addition of two ethnic groups—New Mon State Party and the Lahu Democratic Union—to the nationwide ceasefire agreement is seen as a plus point for the NLD's performance in the peace process.[46]
5. Myanmar's geopolitical relevance to the US and China, mainly for its strategic location and unique opportunity to access resources, can be both an asset or a drawback in Aung San Suu Kyi's efforts to negotiate with the remaining ceasefire groups. Moving the country towards a federal structure of government requires pragmatic compromises on power- and resource-sharing among the administrative states and regions of Myanmar. Engaging with foreign interlocutors on different aspects or stages of the peace process requires skilful balancing (and maneuvering) of domestic developments to match external and multilateral interests.

Notes

1. Following David Steinberg's practice, the authors use "Burma" when referring to the country before 1989 when the State Law and Order Restoration Council changed the country's official name to "Myanmar."
2. Moe Thuzar, *Myanmar and ASEAN: New Beginnings, New Directions*, Myanmar Institute for Strategic and International Studies (MISIS) and Norwegian Institute of International Affairs (NUPI) Research Capacity-Building Project, November 2016.
3. The Secretary-General of ASEAN visited Myanmar in December 2018 and May 2019 to discuss "practical measures to alleviate the situation in Rakhine," and on 27 May 2019, ASEAN entered into an agreement with the Myanmar Government to commence these measures. The ASEAN Coordinating Centre for Humanitarian Assistance on Disaster Management (AHA) Centre was tasked to conduct a preliminary needs assessment for the repatriation process. A draft report leaked to the press raised an outcry over its forecasting of a "smooth return" of the Rohingya to Myanmar, amidst concerns that conditions in Rakhine were not conducive to ensure a safe return. See <https://www.straitstimes.com/asia/se-asia/outcry-as-an-asean-report-predicts-smooth-return-of-rohingya-to-myanmar>.

4. China and Russia resist voting on or supporting international calls for increasing pressure on the Myanmar government, giving reasons of not upsetting the country's efforts to restore or maintain internal stability. Of the many analyses of this aspect, the Council on Foreign Relations' backgrounder on the Rohingya crisis, https://www.cfr.org/backgrounder/rohingya-crisis, which is periodically updated, and the International Crisis Group reports on the Rohingya crisis, as well as the ongoing ceasefire negotiations in Myanmar <https://www.crisisgroup.org/asia/south-east-asia/myanmar> are useful references.
5. Chaw Chaw Sein, *Myanmar's Post-election Foreign Policy*, Myanmar Institute for Strategic and International Studies (MISIS) and Norwegian Institute of International Affairs (NUPI) Research Capacity-Building Project, June 2016.
6. Maung Aung Myoe, "The NLD and Myanmar's Foreign Policy: Not New, But Different," *Journal of Current Southeast Asian Affairs* 36, no. 1 (2017): 89–121.
7. The then Prime Minister of Indonesia invited his counterparts from Sri Lanka (then called Ceylon), Burma, India, and Pakistan to discuss the organization of the conference. That meeting, which took place in Bogor, Indonesia on 28–29 December 1954, was the inception of the Afro-Asian Conference the following year, in <http://asianafricanmuseum.org/en/sejarah-konferensi-asia-afrika/> [accessed 10 April 2017].
8. These protests, which caught more media attention when the monks joined, have been popularly dubbed Saffron Revolution. In actual fact, the 88 Generation Students' group first held protests against the fuel price hikes when these were announced on 15 August 2007, well before monks joined in September 2007. See <http://factsanddetails.com/southeast-asia/Myanmar/sub5_5b/entry-3024.html>.
9. Myanmar's military supremo, Senior General Than Shwe, agreed on 23 May 2008, to allow all humanitarian workers into the country, regardless of nationality, in response to diplomacy efforts by the UN and ASEAN Secretaries-General. See "Burma Grants all UN Visa Requests," in <http://news.bbc.co.uk/2/hi/asia-pacific/7425130.stm> [accessed 29 May 2008].
10. Moe Thuzar, "Myanmar and the 2014 ASEAN Chairmanship," *ISEAS Perspective* 14, no. 18 (March 2013).
11. See Frank N. Trager, ed., "The Labour Movement," *Burma* (New Haven: Human Relations Area Files Inc, 1956).
12. Rodolfo Severino Jr., "The Pressures on Burma's Foreign Policy: A Case Study," *Philippines Studies* 16, no. 3 (July 1968): 460–86.
13. David Steinberg, "Neutralism as Nexus," *Handbook of Contemporary Myanmar* (London: Routledge, 2014), pp. 374–83.
14. Personal interviews from 2011 to 2014.
15. Personal interviews from 2011 to 2016.

16. Renaud Egreteau and Larry Jagan, *Soldiers and Diplomacy in Burma: Understanding the Foreign Relations of the Burmese Praetorian State* (Singapore: NUS Press, 2013).
17. Jurgen Haacke, "Myanmar's Foreign Policy under President U Thein Sein: Non-aligned and Diversified," *Trends in Southeast Asia, TRS*, no. 4 (Singapore: ISEAS Publishing, 2016).
18. Her statement is here <https://www.youtube.com/watch?v=yBIJ7ugDn6Y> [accessed 25 April 2018].
19. See John Seabury Thomson, "Burma: A Neutral in China's Shadow," *The Review of Politics* 19, no. 3 (July 1957): 330–50.
20. See William Crane Johnstone, *Burma's Foreign Policy: A Study in Neutralism* (Cambridge: Harvard University Press, 1963).
21. Moe Thuzar, "Engaging Two Giants: Myanmar's Relations with the US and China in the ASEAN Context," in *New Dynamics in US-China Relations*, ed. Li Mingjiang and Kalyan Kemburi (London: Routledge, 2015), pp. 260–1.
22. David I. Steinberg, "The US, China, and Burma/Myanmar: Reconsidering the Siege of an Outpost of Tyranny?", *Myanmar: Prospect for Change*, ed. Li Chenyang and Wilhelm Hofmeister (Singapore: Select Publishing; Konrad Adenauer Stiftung; Yunnan University, 2010), pp. 331–58.
23. Haacke, "Myanmar's Foreign Policy under President U Thein Sein," pp. 5–11.
24. "China Protests over Deadly Myanmar Border Raid," *BBC*, 14 March 2015 <https://www.bbc.com/news/world-asia-31885318> [accessed 15 June 2018].
25. Jurgen Haacke, "Why Did Myanmar's Opposition Leader Just Visit China?", *The Diplomat*, 15 June 2015 <http://thediplomat.com/2015/06/why-did-myanmars-opposition-leader-just-visit-china/> [accessed 10 April 2017].
26. "Mixed Results at Latest Panglong Peace Conference," *Frontier Myanmar*, 30 May 2017 <http://frontiermyanmar.net/en/mixed-results-at-latest-panglong-peace-conference> [accessed 18 June 2017].
27. "President Obama lifts Myanmar Trade Sanctions," *BBC*, 17 October 2016 <http://www.bbc.com/news/world-asia-37592380> [accessed 17 October 2016].
28. See <http://www.bbc.com/news/world-asia-42447510> [accessed 25 April 2018].
29. Moe Thuzar, "US Sanctions on Myanmar: An Economic Equation," *ISEAS Commentary* 60 (15 September 2016) <https://www.iseas.edu.sg/medias/commentaries/item/3991-us-sanctions-on-myanmar--an-economic-equation-a-commentary-by-moe-thuzar> [accessed 10 April 2017].
30. Directorate of Investment and Company Administration (DICA), Myanmar. List of Foreign Investment by Permitted Enterprises (by country) as of 31 May 2018 <http://www.dica.gov.mm/sites/dica.gov.mm/files/document-files/fdi_country_permitted.pdf> [accessed 19 June 2017].
31. See <http://www.worldbank.org/en/country/myanmar/overview> [accessed 25 April 2018].

32. Oliver Slow, "US to Continue support for Myanmar: Senior Official," *Frontier Myanmar*, 15 June 2018 <https://frontiermyanmar.net/en/us-to-continue-support-for-myanmar-senior-official#.WyQQ2p04dQs.twitter> [accessed 18 June 2018].
33. Trevor Wilson, "Foreign Policy as a Political Tool: Myanmar 2003–2006," in *Myanmar: The State, Community and Environment*, ed. Monique Skidmore and Trevor Wilson (Canberra: Asia Pacific Press, 2007), p. 87.
34. Pavin Chachavalpongpun, "The Vexing Strategic Tug-of-War over Naypyidaw: ASEAN's View of the Sino-Burmese Ties," *Journal of Current Southeast Asian Affairs* 31, no. 1 (2012): 103.
35. See Chairman's Statement of the 25th ASEAN Summit: "Moving Forward in Unity to a Peaceful and Prosperous Community," Nay Pyi Taw, 12 November 2014 <http://www.eria.org/Chairman%20Statement%20of%20the%20 25th%20ASEAN%20Summit.pdf> [accessed 24 January 2016].
36. Shiwen Yap, "Myanmar Tops 2015 Investment Markets," *Deal Street Asia*, 6 April 2015 <http://www.dealstreetasia.com/stories/myanmar-tops-2015-investment-markets-4787/> [accessed 15 January 2016].
37. In "Business and Investment," *Network Myanmar*, 18 November 2015 <http://www.networkmyanmar.org/index.php/business-and-investment> [accessed 15 January 2016].
38. See <https://www.theguardian.com/world/2018/mar/18/aung-san-suu-kyi-asks-australia-and-asean-for-help-with-rohingya-crisis> [accessed 25 April 2018].
39. See <https://ahacentre.org/press-release/press-release-aha-centre-facilitates-humanitarian-assistance-between-singapore-and-myanmar-for-displaced-communities-in-rakhine-state/> [accessed 25 April 2018].
40. The Ministry of Home Affairs, had, in August 2018, decentralized the management of General Affairs Department, together with Prisons, Special Investigations, Police, and Fire Services, but later backpedalled this by stating that it was "wrongly misinterpreted." See <https://www.mmtimes.com/national-news/22773-ministry-of-home-affairs-retracts-offer-of-civilian-controlled-departments.html>.
41. See <https://www.irrawaddy.com/news/burma/govt-cancels-controversial-development-near-shwedagon.html>.
42. An article in *Myanmar Times* (English edition) of 22 December 2017 caused considerable comment and discussion among the Japanese business community in Myanmar. See Aye Nyein Win's "Toyota Should Reconsider Myanmar Growth Strategy" <https://www.mmtimes.com/news/toyota-should-reconsider-myanmar-growth-strategy.html>.
43. Haacke, "Myanmar's Foreign Policy under President U Thein Sein," p. 1.
44. English text (translation) of President Thein Sein's radio speech of 1 January 2015 <http://www.mofa.gov.mm/wpcontent/uploads/2015/04/RadioSpeechin Janineng.pdf> [accessed 1 July 2015].

45. T. Clifton Morgan and Glenn Palmer, "A Two-good Theory of Foreign Policy: An Application to Dispute Initiation and Reciprocation," *International Interactions* 22, no. 3 (1997): 225–44.
46. "EU Witnesses Two More Parties to Sign Myanmar's Nationwide Ceasefire Agreement," news report on European External Action Service homepage shared by the Delegation of the European Union to Myanmar <https://eeas.europa.eu/delegations/myanmar-burma/39939/eu-witnesses-two-more-parties-sign-myanmar%E2%80%99s-nationwide-ceasefire-agreement_en> [accessed 16 June 2018].

References

Chaw Chaw Sein. 2016. *Myanmar's Post-election Foreign Policy*. Myanmar Institute for Strategic and International Studies (MISIS) and Norwegian Institute of International Affairs (NUPI) Research Capacity-Building Project, June.

Egreteau, Renaud and Larry Jagan. 2013. *Soldiers and Diplomacy in Burma: Understanding the Foreign Relations of the Burmese Praetorian State*. Singapore: NUS Press.

Haacke, Jurgen. 2015. "Why Did Myanmar's Opposition Leader Just Visit China?", *The Diplomat*, 15 June <http://thediplomat.com/2015/06/why-did-myanmars-opposition-leader-just-visit-china/> [accessed 10 April 2017].

______. 2016. "Myanmar's Foreign Policy under President U Thein Sein: Non-aligned and Diversified," *Trends in Southeast Asia, TRS*, no. 4. Singapore: ISEAS Publishing.

Johnstone, William Crane. 1963. *Burma's Foreign Policy: A Study in Neutralism*. Cambridge: Harvard University Press.

Maung Aung Myoe. 2017. "The NLD and Myanmar's Foreign Policy: Not New, But Different," *Journal of Current Southeast Asian Affairs* 36, no. 1.

Morgan, T. Clifton and Palmer, Glenn. 1997. "A Two-good Theory of Foreign Policy: An Application to Dispute Initiation and Reciprocation," *International Interactions* 22, no. 3.

Pavin Chachavalpongpun. 2012. "The Vexing Strategic Tug-of-War over Naypyidaw: ASEAN's View of the Sino-Burmese Ties," *Journal of Current Southeast Asian Affairs* 31, no. 1.

Seabury Thomson, John. 1957. "Burma: A Neutral in China's Shadow," *The Review of Politics* 19, no. 3 (July).

Severino Jr., Rodolfo. 1968. "The Pressures on Burma's Foreign Policy: A Case Study," *Philippines Studies* 16, no. 3 (July).

Slow, Oliver. 2018. "US to Continue support for Myanmar: Senior Official," *Frontier Myanmar*, 15 June <https://frontiermyanmar.net/en/us-to-continue-support-for-myanmar-senior-official#.WyQQ2p04dQs.twitter> [accessed 18 June 2018].

Steinberg, David I. 2010. "The US, China, and Burma/Myanmar: Reconsidering the Siege of an Outpost of Tyranny?". In *Myanmar: Prospect for Change*, ed. Li Chenyang and Wilhelm Hofmeister. Singapore: Select Publishing; Konrad Adenauer Stiftung; Yunnan University.

Thuzar, Moe. 2013. "Myanmar and the 2014 ASEAN Chairmanship," *ISEAS Perspective* 14, no. 18 (March).

———. 2015. "Engaging Two Giants: Myanmar's Relations with the US and China in the ASEAN context." In *New Dynamics in US-China Relations*, ed. Li Mingjiang and Kalyan Kemburi. London: Routledge.

———. 2016a. "US Sanctions on Myanmar: An Economic Equation," *ISEAS Commentary*, vol. 60, 15 September <https://www.iseas.edu.sg/medias/commentaries/item/3991-us-sanctions-on-myanmar--an-economic-equation-a-commentary-by-moe-thuzar> [accessed 10 April 2017].

———. 2016b. *Myanmar and ASEAN: New Beginnings, New Directions*. Myanmar Institute for Strategic and International Studies (MISIS) and Norwegian Institute of International Affairs (NUPI) Research Capacity-Building Project, November.

Trager, Frank N. ed. 1956. "The Labour Movement," *Burma*. New Haven: Human Relations Area Files Inc.

Wilson, Trevor. 2007. "Foreign Policy as a Political Tool: Myanmar 2003–2006." In *Myanmar: The State, Community and Environment*, ed. Monique Skidmore and Trevor Wilson. Canberra: Asia Pacific Press.

Yap, Shiwen. 2015. "Myanmar Tops 2015 Investment Markets," *Deal Street Asia*, 6 April <http://www.dealstreetasia.com/stories/myanmar-tops-2015-investment-markets-4787/> [accessed 15 January 2016].

SECTION TWO

The Challenge of the Political Economy

CHAPTER 4

The Structure of Myanmar's Corporate and Financial System: Growth Challenges since the 1990s[1]

Fumiharu Mieno

It is imperative to identify the outcomes of some of the economic reforms implemented in Myanmar since 2010, the year which saw the first election since 1990. Foreign direct investment (FDI) has increased, and many official development aid (ODA) projects in infrastructure construction have begun. There has been a dramatic resurgence in urban consumption. Exports of agricultural products have also continued to increase. The basic structure of the economic system, however, barely changed from the one that existed during the two decades of the junta rule and thus serious challenges remain. To achieve long-term economic growth through industrialization, it is necessary to rearrange the fundamental structure in the following aspects of the economic system: state ownership, fiscal policy, the labor market, corporate governance, and education. Among them, one of the most important policy issues is the system for channeling resources into industrialization.

The purpose of this chapter is to investigate the long-inherited structure of economic growth and capital accumulation in Myanmar, focusing on its central elements, the financial and corporate systems. After outlining the fundamental facts of the economy (such as growth rate, trade structure, and foreign investment), the chapter examines the country's economic regime that dictates the flow of capital and investment. In fact, most parts of the economic system associated with this financial channel have their origins in the system in operation during the period of the military rule in the 1990s–2000s. Some were newly established while others were inherited from the pre-1980s socialist regimes or even from the colonial period.[2] Tracing the process by which the economic systems and entities were formed, this chapter identifies the persisting structure, which existed over the last two decades. It explains what is being changed, what should be further changed, and discusses how they can be changed.

A part of the argument in the chapter relies on macroeconomic statistics. It is well known that some official statistics are unreliable in Myanmar. This study carefully examines the possibility of misguidance and attempts to demonstrate the comparison of multiple statistical sources including international estimations (on GDP growth rate for example), or to estimate values based on informally collected information (on trade value). The other part of the discussion is based on qualitative information from existing studies or my own surveys.

The chapter as a whole focuses on three factors: (1) the financial system, (2) the corporate system, and (3) the supply channel for long-term capital. Usually, at the early stage of industrialization under developing market economies, the issue of long-term capital market occurs as a crucial and uneasy challenge. For one thing, the demand for long-term capital explosively increases as the industrialization process begins to require resources for constructing equipment (called capital goods). Meanwhile, the infant banking system, mostly holding short-term deposits, lacks the capability of providing this necessary long-term funding. Moreover, the weak corporate system means that equity and bond markets are nonexistent, duly depriving the sector of long-term capital sources. Thus, factor (3) is located within the policy agenda regarding how to overcome market failure as derived from factors (1) and (2).

The issue of establishing a financial system is associated with the enhancement of financial intermediation between savings and investments by financial institutions. A successful financial institution minimizes the social costs of such intermediation through information processing, and loosens credit rationing, which is regarded as a market failure associated with the problem of information asymmetry (specifically meaning that when those with capital lack sufficient information about investment opportunities, they incorporate their perceived risk into the price of borrowing, often creating a price to capital so high that many productive endeavors are precluded). When the economy is in the early stages of development, however, so too are the financial institutions, so the capacity for financial intermediation is generally limited. Given this, discussions need to start by establishing an agenda for overcoming the incompleteness of the current financial system and widespread credit rationing.

Meanwhile, the issue of establishing a corporate system is associated with the enhancement of corporate governance. Like the financial system, the corporate system is less organized during the early stages of economic development. Generally, the growth of firms tends to be extremely unbalanced, meaning that a limited number of firms accumulate a large amount of assets under certain favorable conditions, which are often related to their connections to government. Some entrepreneurs expand and diversify their businesses to form business groups under pyramid or cross-holding ownership structures. In transitional economies, state-owned enterprises (SOEs) usually continue to act as major players. A capital market does not exist—or if it does, it remains very primitive—in the initial steps of economic development. In addition, ownership of firms tends to be highly concentrated, and transparency is limited.

Since corporate governance is usually weak at this stage, corruption and the illegal transfers of corporate assets are widespread. This, in turn, leads to very high agency costs due to the existence of information asymmetries between the corporation and its creditors (or investors), which prevents financial institutions from fully functioning as financial intermediaries in the market. Credit rationing is defined by banks tending to behave as credit suppliers within the inner circle of their own business groups, while many potential borrowers remain unable to access credit. In fact, banks are usually established within growing business groups, and behave as one of the group's core firms. Given this, it is natural, in a sense, for banks to provide loans to firms with which they have a connection, defined as "connected lending" during the early period of economic development.

The issue of establishing a channel for long-term capital is an important objective as it is necessary for the formulation of policies for a country's growth strategy. In the process of industrialization, demand for long-term capital increases at an accelerating rate, as investment in infrastructure is required and larger, longer-term investments are crucial in upgrading the export manufacturing process from a labor-intensive to a capital-intensive one. Therefore, the formulation of a system for supplying long-term capital becomes a key policy concern at a relatively early stage. Long-term capital can be provided in the form of ODA (particularly for activities in the quasi-public sector such as infrastructure building in the earliest stage of development) and, to a degree, FDI into private businesses. This does not mean, however, that a system for long-term capital is unnecessary. Without an appropriate channel for long-term capital, the private sector will remain dependent on short-term borrowing or self-financing, which could become a serious bottleneck for growth. There are multiple policy options to address this issue. Developing a capital market (for both bonds and equity) is the most common practice. Nonetheless, a lesson seen in many countries is that a securities market is not equipped to function very smoothly during the economic development process. In some countries, long-term capital is supplied through policy-based finance that is usually provided by what is known as a "development bank," which either takes the form of a state bank or a specially licensed private bank.

The rest of this chapter is organized as follows. The next section provides an overview of the characteristics of Myanmar's economic structure during the 20 years of the military rule. This is to be followed by case studies on SOEs, private capital, and the financial sector in modern-day Myanmar, and a discussion of the policy problem with regard to the supply system for long-term capital.

Economic Structure During Junta Period

Reforms since the Early 1990s and Economic Trends

The reforms enacted by the military in the early 1990s can be seen as an important benchmark when examining the process of transformation through which the Myanmar economy has undergone. In September 1988, the military declared its intention to abolish what was known as the Burmese Way of Socialism, and attempted to introduce economic reforms to strengthen the market economy. The military government started its reforms by separating the fiscal and financial sectors. The mono-bank system employed by Myanmar's socialist government was broken up into a central bank and a number of other state banks established to provide specific services, such as commercial banking, foreign exchange, or agricultural finance. The banking sector was opened up to private capital under license, with many private banks being established in quick succession until the mid-1990s. Unlike the financial sector, however, the reform of the fiscal sector did not progress very smoothly. SOEs got stuck in an immature state. Although some small factories and retail shops were privatized, most SOEs remained in the government's hands. In fact, the SOE integrated accounting system introduced in 1990 directly weakened their managerial autonomy.

In another aspect of the reforms, Myanmar's economic relationships with other countries were largely liberalized. Foreign trade, previously strictly limited under the Burmese Way of Socialism, was completely liberalized through the introduction of an import license system both at its ports and borders. "Authorizing" overseas trade in this way resulted in a fundamental change to the economy. The institutional entities associated with foreign investment were gradually set up, the Foreign Investment Law (1988) and the Myanmar Citizen Investment Law (1994) enacted, and the Myanmar Industrial Development Committee established in 1995. In contrast, the government's attitude towards reforms aimed at macroeconomic stabilization was largely passive. The establishment of a financial sector, the deregulation of trade, and the increase in capital flow through FDI inevitably stimulated the flow of money and foreign exchange. The monetary control system, meanwhile, remained unchanged, as demonstrated by the fact that the exchange rate continued to be pegged to the Special Drawing Right (SDR) of the IMF, essentially fixed at 5–6 per cent against the US dollar; the private sector was not allowed to hold foreign exchange; all exporters were obligated to deposit their export revenue in foreign exchange at a state bank [the Myanmar Investment and Commercial Bank (MICB) or the Myanmar Foreign Trade Bank (MFTB)].

Although they were inconsistent in those respects just mentioned, the reforms resulted in substantial economic growth in the 1990s. The upsurge in trade generated a vast trade surplus, particularly from primary sector goods such as agricultural products, marine products, and precious metals. This, in turn, accelerated capital accumulation in the private sector. Expanding exports triggered a diversification in the crops cultivated in the agricultural sector.[3] FDI was directed mainly into the construction, tourism, and mining sectors. Due to the growing number of local businesses, more and more private banks were established and emerged into key players in the financial system.

At the same time, however, inconsistency in the reforms led to serious macroeconomic instability. The most significant confusion concerned the foreign exchange system. The official exchange rate was preserved at an unrealistic level, resulting in a huge expansion of the black market. Between 1997 and 2001, the government did attempt to unify the various exchange rate systems to form a managed float system that converged on the market rate by manipulating a Foreign Exchange Certificate (FEC).[4] After this attempt failed, the gap between the official rate and the market rate widened increasingly to the point where it became uncontrollable. The markets were essentially divided into public and private sectors, and inefficient SOEs continued to be subsidized through applying the official foreign exchange rate (that is, by means of a vastly appreciated kyat). This subsidization of SOEs become a major cause of the worsening fiscal deficit, which in turn accelerated inflation and produced a further depreciation of the kyat on the black market, thereby worsening the problem by enlarging the gap between the official and market exchange rates.

The government basically remained stuck with this system until 2011, but minor changes were made at particular times. The Asian Financial Crisis (AFC) of 1997–98 brought about a sudden drop in exports and FDI inflow, making foreign exchange control much more difficult. Facing a serious shortage of foreign reserves, the government implemented direct restrictions on imports and strict controls on foreign exchange in the private sector. This was done with a view to maintaining foreign exchange controls and separating the foreign exchange markets between the public and private sectors. In the midst of the macroeconomic instability brought about by the AFC, a bank run on a private bank occurred in 2003, triggering a serious economic recession. Since 2006, a different change in circumstances occurred, following a rapid expansion in the export of natural gas reserves that had been under development since the early 1990s. This helped to refloat the economy and reduce the shortage of foreign reserves and fiscal revenue. When the Thein Sein government introduced its reforms in early 2011, the problematic economic structure was persistent, but the climate had recovered sufficiently to produce relatively favorable conditions for the reforms.

Growth Performance

Although the performance during the last 20 years could not be described as a success, the economy was not always in a poor state. It actually performed quite well at times. Figure 4.1 shows the real economic growth rate for Myanmar over this period. As the official GDP estimates for 1989–2012 are generally considered to be unreliable, it is important to include alternative estimates produced by the International Monetary Fund (IMF) and the Economist Intelligence Unit (EIU). While the alternative estimates vary substantially, one can quickly identify a few common trends and it is clear that Myanmar's economic transformation over the last two decades before the 2011 reform can be divided into three distinct periods.

During the first period from 1988 to 1996, the government implemented reforms to transform the economy from a socialist system to a market-based one. During the second period from 1997 to 2003, the economy experienced a significant external shock from the AFC. After 1998, export growth slowed and FDI declined sharply. The country's

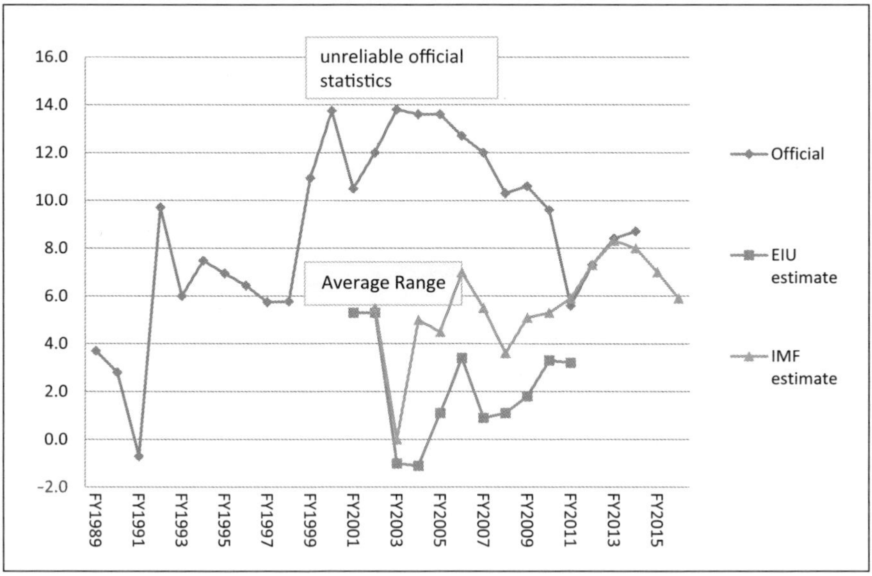

Note: FY2013 figures are estimates, FY2014 figures are projections.

Sources:

Official: 1993–94: Key Indicators 2003, Asian Development Bank; 1995–2007: Statistical Yearbook (SY) 2008, Central Statistical Organization; 2008–19: SY 2012; 2010–14: SY 2015.

EIU: Economist Intelligence Unit, 1999–2001: ver. Nov. 2002–05, ver. Sept. 2005, 2006–07: ver. April 2009, 2008–11: Regional Outlook, ISEAS, 2012–13, p. 171.

IMF: IMF Country Report.

Figure 4.1 Various Estimates for Real Growth Rate, 1989–2012

expanding current account deficit and the disappearance of foreign capital inflow led to a serious shortage of foreign reserves, and thus resulting in harmful macroeconomic instability. Despite this, however, growth was sustained for a short while due to the domestic service sector enjoying a real estate and construction boom and the emergence of an export market for the garment industry. The booming domestic economy ended when the private banking sector, which was still in its infancy, suffered a bank run in 2003, leading to a widespread economic depression.

According to the official statistics, the growth rate had declined slightly in 1997 and 1998 before rising significantly from 1999 onwards. But this did not appear to be consistent with actual events. The EIU and IMF started using their own alternative estimates in about 2001 or 2002. Yet, even these alternative GDP estimates show moderate growth around 5 per cent until 2003. It was presumed that the economy continued to exhibit moderate growth driven by the domestic service sector until the end of 2002. It then came to a standstill as a result of the bank run in 2003. As some of the alternative GDP estimates (EIU and IMF) indicated, the economic growth rate in 2003 could be considered negative. During the third period from 2005 onwards, the economy was transformed in an unexpected way. The natural gas industry, which had been developed by the junta with the assistance of FDI during the first period, entered into a stable production in 2003–04, serving as a significant source of export revenue. Owing to these natural gas exports, the current account recorded a surplus after 2002, and the foreign reserve shortage was eliminated. As a result, the economy recovered to register a growth rate of 2–6 per cent and the macro economy returned to a position of stability.

As a result of these reforms and driven by commodity exports and FDI, the Myanmar economy has attained a reasonable level of economic growth of about 6–8 per cent annually since 2012. The elected Thein Sein government was able to commence its reforms in 2011 under these favorable economic and fiscal conditions. The reform in 2011 once accelerated the growth pace to over 8 per cent under the optimistic sentiment, but the economy has shown slight setback in the confusion and delay of economic policy under the NLD government since 2015.

Table 4.1 Sectoral Composition of GDP (%)

	Agriculture	*Mining*	*Electricity, gas, and water*	*Manufacturing*	*Construction*	*Trade*	*Others*
1988	57.4	0.7	0.4	7.5	1.1	20.8	12.2
1992	60.5	0.5	0.2	6.9	1.8	22.6	7.4
1996	60.1	0.6	0.3	7.1	2.4	22.6	6.8
2000	57.2	0.6	0.1	7.2	1.8	24.0	9.0
2004	48.2	0.6	0.2	11.6	3.9	22.3	13.2
2008	40.3	0.9	0.7	16.8	4.2	21.1	15.9
2009	38.1	1.0	1.0	18.1	4.5	20.3	17.0
2010	36.4	0.9	1.0	19.5	4.5	19.8	17.8
2012	30.6	6.2	1.2	20.1	4.9	19.0	18.0
2014	27.8	7.4	1.4	19.9	5.8	18.7	19.0
2015	26.8	6.1	1.4	20.8	6.1	18.9	19.8
2016	25.5	4.4	1.4	22.8	6.4	19.7	19.8

Source: Statistical Database System, Asian Development Bank, downloaded at 21 May 2017 for 1988–2014, and 26 April 2018 for 2015–16.

Sectoral Structure

Generally speaking, macroeconomic growth is a result of sectoral development. In the case of Myanmar in the 1990s to 2000s, it was based on changes in the country's external economic relationships; that is, trade and FDI. Table 4.1 and Figure 4.2 show the composition of GDP and FDI inflow by sector since the 1980s. Figure 4.3 details trends in trade broken down by export products and the trade balance (in Myanmar kyat). These three illustrations provide us with an overview of the nature of economic growth in Myanmar since the 1990s. When the Myanmar economy grew rapidly during the early 1990s (the first period), the largest industry in terms of value added was agriculture (representing about 50–60 per cent of total GDP) followed by trade, which was gradually increasing its value added (some 20 per cent of total GDP). In contrast, the manufacturing sector had only a 6.8 per cent share of economic activity in 1993, and this increased only slightly during the 1990s.

Figure 4.2 indicates that while Myanmar's FDI inflow was accelerated by the relevant legal arrangements, it was mostly directed towards service sector businesses and extractives—such as hotels, real estate, and mining—with very little finding their way into the manufacturing sector. Economic growth in Myanmar in the first period was mostly driven by trade and domestic service sectors. The prevailing trade structure confirms this feature. As shown in Figure 4.3, Myanmar's main exports were primary sector goods such as agricultural and marine products, and others, which presumably include precious gems and noble metals. Such facts suggest that growth during the first period was mainly driven by an expansion in commodity exports as a result of trade having been opened up and foreign investment being directed towards the service sector. The degree of industrialization at this time remained small.

An economy that is dependent on commodity exports and foreign investment, and is not in the process of industrializing, is frequently vulnerable. Myanmar's vulnerability was revealed by the external shock it suffered from the onset of the AFC during the second period. Since the early days of the country's reforms, the trade balance had worsened and the trade deficit expanded. When the AFC struck, it brought FDI inflow to a sudden halt in 1998 and led to a foreign reserves shortage. Coping with a further decline in the market exchange rate, the government strengthened its foreign exchange controls so as to preserve the system for transferring foreign exchange from the private sector to the public sector under an extremely appreciated value. The government even imposed

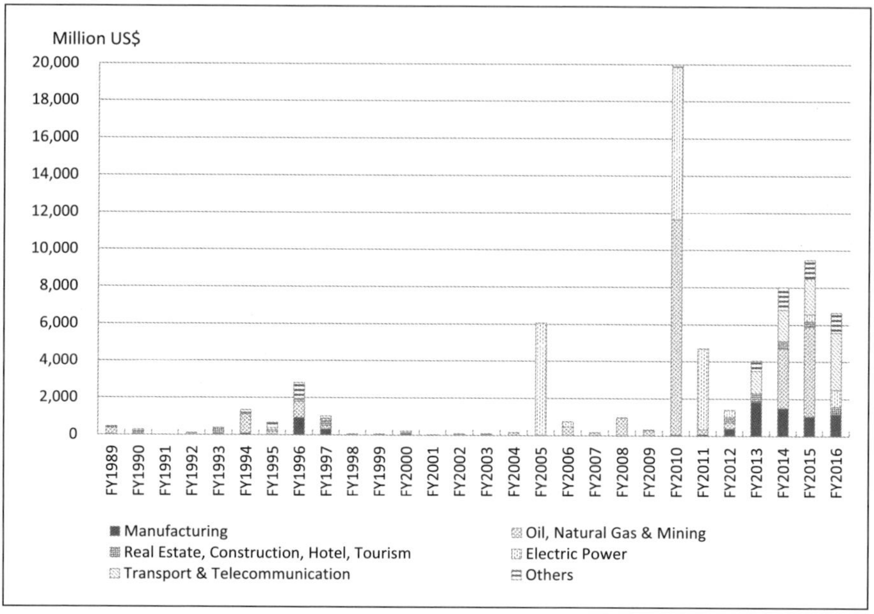

Source: Selected Monthly Indicators, CSO, various years.

Figure 4.2 FDI Inflow (Approval Base)

direct restrictions on imports from 1999 onwards to restrict foreign exchange outflow. As can be seen in Figure 4.3, any increase in imports was limited from 1999 to 2005.

It is worth noting that even in an environment such as this, the export sector evolved remarkably. In fact, the garment sector emerged as a major exporter, leading to increased exports until 2002. Table 4.1 shows that manufacturing's share of GDP increased slightly in the 2000–02 period, from the 6 per cent level to around 7 per cent. This means that, in the late 1990s to the early 2000s, the Myanmar economy showed signs of shifting towards industrialization based on labor-intensive sectors until US sanctions were introduced in 2002.

As mentioned above, although the FDI inflow slowed down dramatically from the late 1990s through the early 2000s (the second period), domestic service sectors (for example, real estate, construction, and hotels) appeared to be active during and after the AFC. Real estate development continued to flourish in the Yangon area. Most private banks were erected as part of business groups in domestic service sectors, and the credit they offered was mostly directed toward their own business groups. The real

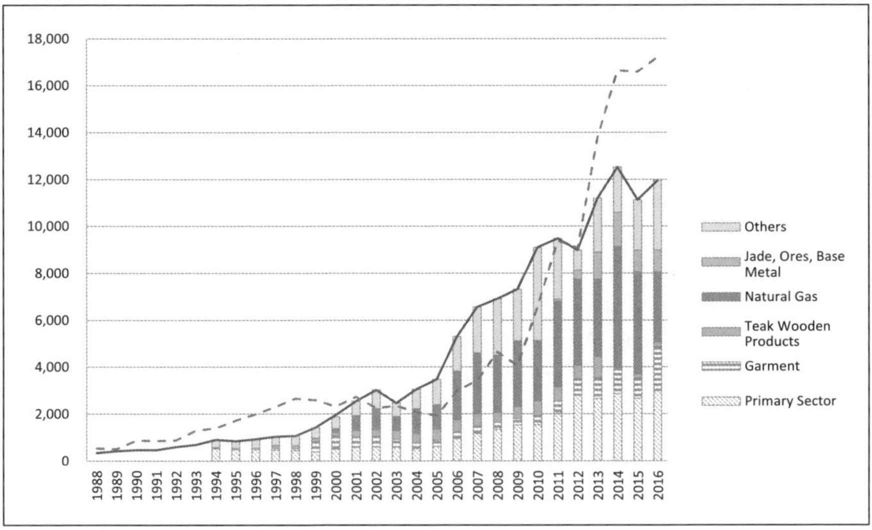

Note: Million US$. For the volumes of each commodity before FY2011, they are reported in kyat based. US$ value is calculated based on official exchange rate at each period. "Jade, Ores, Base Metal" is available only after FY2012. It is presumed to be included in "Others" before FY2011.

Source: Statistical Yearbook, CSO.

Figure 4.3 Trend in Export Commodities and Trade Account

estate boom continued through to the end of 2002, when it came to a sudden end in early 2003 due to runs on several private banks resulting in a serious recession. During the third period (2004 onwards), however, the economy exhibited yet another upswing in activity. The development of natural gas fields in Myanmar was completed and production began. Natural gas exports from Myanmar, which started in 2000, have exhibited a stable upward trend since 2004, bringing about a dramatic surge in total exports. The total value of exports tripled over the period from 2004 to 2010, with natural gas exports accounting for between 30 and 39 per cent of this value (see Figure 4.3). This development can be interpreted as a fruitful outcome of strong foreign investment in the sector during the first period. Figure 4.2 reveals that the share of total GDP accounted for by other services increased after 2004 as well. Responding to the economy's recovery, the FDI inflow into Myanmar increased after 2005, mainly in the electricity and natural gas sectors, and this further accelerated the development of these sectors. By end 2000, the Myanmar economy had retrogressed from a nascent industrializer in late 1990s–early 2000s (the second period) to a commodity-exporting economy.

The US and the European Union had imposed economic sanctions on Myanmar's trade and investment. The United States banned new investment by US companies in 1997 in response to the junta's house arrest of Aung San Suu Kyi. In 2003, the US government introduced comprehensive sanctions to ban the import of all commodities and remittances, and to freeze the asset of Myanmar high ranking officers. The EU also strengthened the sanctions in 2004 and 2007 to ban financial transactions and freeze assets.

The effect of the sanctions by the western countries, however, seems to have remained partial. Although Figure 4.2 shows the apparent decline of FDI inflow in 1997, a large part of this is perhaps reflected by the decline of the inflow from Asian neighbors due to the AFC. The US sanctions in 2003 substantially damaged Myanmar's economy since the majority of the exports from the then-infant garment industry were directed at the US market. The growth of the industry temporarily slowed down. While Canada and Australia followed the sanctions, most Asian countries took a wait-and-see attitude or even ignored them. In particular, during the 2000s, China expanded its economic commitment to Myanmar, which minimized the damage, and generated the country's high dependence on its giant neighbor. Consequently, Myanmar's economic development could continue. Since the middle of the 2000s, the growth became driven by the construction and mining sectors rather than the industrial sector. The sectoral structure has been slow to change after the Thein Sein government. Although the trend of FDI inflow shows the increasing investment of manufacturing sectors since 2012 (Figure 4.2), the components of manufacturing production in GDP (Table 4.1) and products in export (Figure 4.3) indicate only a slight increase. Industrialization is still in a sprout stage in Myanmar, and the economy has not gotten out of the structure formed in the military period.

In summary, since the reforms initiated by the junta in the early 1990s, Myanmar's economic growth had been driven by exports of primary products and investment in the non-manufacturing sector. The AFC worsened the country's trade deficit and created a foreign reserves shortage. At the same time, it had a minimal effect on the export sector due to the substantial emergence of a garment sector and the rewards of natural resource development. In the post-2004 economic recovery in particular, the latter factor played an overwhelmingly significant role. Myanmar under the new NLD government inherited such an economic structure and is forced to rely on it for now.

Table 4.2 Share of Value Added to GDP by Sector

	Sectoral Share to GDP in 2007	*FY1986*			*FY1996*			*FY2007*		
		State	*Cooperative*	*Private*	*State*	*Cooperative*	*Private*	*State*	*Cooperative*	*Private*
Agriculture	35.6	0.1	6.4	93.4	0.2	1.9	97.9	0.4	2.4	97.2
Energy	0.2	99.9	0.1	0.0	76.3	9.3	14.4			
Mining	0.5	89.8	2.2	8.0	10.8	1.0	88.2	2.9	0.2	96.9
Manufacturing	15.0	41.6	4.2	8.0	28.2	0.9	70.8	9.2	0.2	90.6
Service	14.8	60.7	2.5	36.9	54.5	2.6	43.0	14.8	0.1	85.0
Commerce	36.5	44.6	9.1	46.3	37.2	2.5	60.3			
Total GDP	100.0	24.6	6.8	68.6	21.8	1.9	76.3	7.8	1.5	90.7

Source: Reprinted from Kudo 2012: 173. (Original source: *Review*, MNPED.)

Corporate and Financial Systems

SOEs in Myanmar

Many SOEs have survived and operated in Myanmar because the country's reforms were ended prematurely in the early 1990s. The SOE sector has continued to be based on the light and heavy industry sectors while enjoying some government privileges.

Although information on SOEs in Myanmar is generally scarce, the share of value added to GDP that is attributable to SOEs is fairly well reported. As shown in Table 4.2, it was 7.8 per cent for total GDP in 2007, down from 21.8 per cent in 1996 and 24.6 per cent in 1986. For the manufacturing sector, the share of value added that is attributable to SOEs was 7.8 per cent in 2007. In contrast, the share of value added by SOEs for particular sectors remains very high. Factually, it was 76.3 per cent for the energy sector in 2007. Although the shares of value added by SOEs probably increased for particular sectors in the 2000s, the number of SOEs in the Myanmar economy is not especially large, despite the strong protection they have received from the government.

The subsidy provision system that makes use of a foreign exchange quota with an appreciated exchange rate is said to have been gradually loosened and approaching full abolition since April 2012. It seems certain that the privatization of SOEs has been undertaken as part of the current economic reform process.[5]

Private Capital: The Emergence of Conglomerates

Private business capital has increased during the economic growth experienced over the last 20 years. In the early 1990s, private businesses grew by adapting to the changing economic structure. Several large business conglomerates were formed to serve as bases for operations in service sector industries such as trade, construction, and real estate. Some of these groups initially relied on and have continued to develop close relationships with the military government.

The profiles of several business groups established by the late 1990s were revealed by recent researches based on interview-cum-research.[6] One example of those profiled is the FMI–SPA Group, which was founded by a Myanmar businessman of Chinese descent after he had succeeded in business in Hong Kong and Thailand. Starting out as an importer of cosmetics, this group subsequently grew to include over 40 subsidiaries and various affiliates by 2003. In 2004, the core businesses of its 51 affiliated firms included finance, real estate, services (hotels, golf courses, and hospitals), and commerce. It is however worth noting that their presence in the manufacturing sector appeared to be minimal. Another recent example is the Kanbawza Bank Group, which was founded by a ruby trader in Shan State in 1994 and is known for its conservative management. Kanbawza had been a relatively small bank in the first decade, but it subsequently grew rapidly by absorbing the outflow of deposits from troubled banks and has now become Myanmar's largest private-sector bank. After the post-2005 economic recovery, the group diversified its businesses into modern service sector industries, such as domestic airlines.

Even during the 2000s, an already huge amount of private capital thrived further. For example, the Asia World Group was established by a well-known rebel leader from the Kokang area of Shan State. Previously known to have been a drug lord, he expanded his legal business into the construction and real estate sectors after his surrender. This group, a typical junta crony, thrived rapidly under the leadership of the founder's son during the country's post-2005 economic recovery, and it is now heavily involved in the construction of infrastructure for the new capital city, Naypyitaw. The group is also currently involved in the construction of roads in Yangon in partnership with the Yangon City Development Committee, as well as jetties at Yangon Port and Thilawa Port.

The Htoo Group is another example of a business group that flourished rapidly after the 2003 recession, rather than during the early period of the junta's reforms in the 1990s. With its humble origin as a rice mill leasing business in the late 1980s, the group expanded to encompass agriculture and timber businesses. Since the mid-2000s, the group has further grown into various service sector industries, including aviation, hotels, and construction. In 2010, the group entered banking. The Max Myanmar Group was founded in the early 1990s as an import agent for buses from Japan, and expanded its business to cover timber, gems, construction, hotels, and transportation. The group moved quickly in response to changes in the political and economic climate in the late 2000s. It acquired gas stations under the privatization scheme launched by the junta, and a banking license in 2010. The Htoo Group and the Max Myanmar Group tried to set up a capital channel in Singapore by attempting to take over a business group and establishing fundraising companies there. Asia World, Htoo, and Max Myanmar have all been subject to sanctions by the US Department of Treasury.[7]

As these examples illustrate, the growth of big business conglomerates went hand-in-hand with the growth in the trade and service sectors over the last two decades. They typically started to build up their capital by exporting primary goods—such as gems, drugs, or agricultural products—before reinvesting them in the service sectors. Recently, they have moved into modern service sector industries, such as aviation.

In terms of the problems faced with regard to the corporate system and corporate governance, post-reform Myanmar seems to find itself in the "confused infant" stage. The rapid process of capital accumulation experienced by Myanmar can be seen as similar to that experienced by its ASEAN neighbors in the early stages of their development. While private capital provides its economy with vitality, Myanmar's corporate system is far from ideal, suffering as it does from continued cronyism, lack of transparency, and an extreme concentration of businesses. And although some conglomerates are already intent on modernizing their management, a fundamental requirement is a mechanism for corporate governance and a regulatory framework for the financial system. The country continues to face huge policy challenges in terms of introducing a legal framework through the enactment of basic and functioning company laws, as well as installing a well-functioning financial system.

Banking Sector and Private Banks

The banking sector in Myanmar is characterized by its slow transition away from the dominance of the state banks and the rapid but less orderly development of its private banks. Although its private banks have been expanding fast since the introduction of the recent reforms, the financial system in Myanmar is still in its embryonic stage in terms of performing the function of financial intermediation. Most state banks were created by dividing in 1976 the monolithic socialist regime People's Bank of Myanmar; the banks that emerged from this division have had little experience functioning as financial intermediaries. The Myanmar Economic Bank (MEB) is by far the largest entity in the banking sector, accounting for 4 per cent of the sector's total assets in 2007. It is also worth noting that 8 per cent of the other state banks account for 55 per cent of the total assets of all financial institutions. This share has gradually declined since the reforms, but still accounted for 35.5 per cent in March 2012.

Many private banks were formed by major business groups, while some were originally established by particular branches of the government. As of April 2015, the banking system consisted of 4 state-owned banks and 22 private banks. Of the latter, 15 were founded between 1993 and 1996 following the 1990 enactment of the Financial Institutions Law allowing the private sector to enter the banking sector, four were new entrants licensed by the junta in 2010, and the remaining three were newly established in 2013 to fulfill specific purposes under the current government. Many banks are subsidiaries of large business conglomerates that operate in the service sector. In particular, the four banks newly established in 2010 belong to the major business groups that have grown rapidly since the 2000s: Htoo, Max Myanmar, IGE, and Eden. Several banks have been launched as branches of the government, such as the Ministry of Industry or the Myanmar Army, so these are regarded as "semi-government" banks.

The private banking sector has experienced both strong expansions and contractions since the mid-1990s. The explosive growth of the banking sector in the 1990s was largely due to the absorption of public deposits. Together with the flourishing real estate sector, Myanmar's banks continued to expand even after the AFC. In light of this situation, informal financial institutions—then known as General (Financial) Service Companies—began issuing deposit-like certificates and flourished from around 2000 to 2002. These institutions are said to have promised their depositors high interest rates (2–6 per cent monthly), and they were involved in various types of speculation. In late 2002, they suddenly stopped paying any interest and went into liquidation one after the other. This incident triggered a run on three private sector banks in February 2003: the Asian Wealth Bank, the May Flower Bank, and the Yoma Bank. Following this run, the first two banks ended up going out of business and were liquidated. The Asian Wealth Bank and the May Flower Bank were then rumored to have been involved in the drug business and money laundering, so they subsequently faced serious deposit outflows.[8] The government froze their operations under the control of the Money Laundering Law, and later they were ordered by the authority to shutter. As a result, other banks with healthier finances and management reputations, such as the Kanbawza Bank and the Myawaddy Bank, have emerged as major players in the banking sector. Facing the bank run, the government urgently introduced new regulations to restrict bank deposits to ten times the equity value of the bank. This regulation has become a major impediment to the collection of deposits by Myanmar's banks.

The Thein Sein government has worked to reform the financial system since 2011. The unification of the foreign exchange rate in April 2012 brought about a reconsideration of the role of state banks, particularly in the case of the MICB and the MFTB. The government enacted the Central Bank of Myanmar Law in August 2013, which strengthened the central bank's independence with regards to the setting of monetary policy and its power to regulate private banks. The regulation over the deposit-equity ratio was abolished. A new financial institution law upgrading the country's financial regulations to better reflect standard practice was enacted in January 2016. In light of these developments, private banks have undertaken remarkable changes recently. Some major banks, such as the Kanbawza Bank and the CB Bank, have rapidly expanded their assets by extending their branch networks. The speed at which their deposits is growing is much higher than that of the MEB, suggesting the possibility that private banks may in the near future catch up with the state banks presently dominating the banking sector in terms of size. Some "semi-government" banks have "normalized" their management and ownership to become purely private commercial banks, while others have strengthened their positions as policy-based banks.[9]

Table 4.3 illustrates trends in terms of the financial assets and operations of private sector banks in Myanmar. The assets and deposits of private sector banks speedily grew following the establishment of such banks after 1992 until the bank run of 2003. However, the ratio of M2[10] to GDP has remained very low at around 30 per cent, and has even declined recently. This figure suggests that the lending operations of these banks have not yet caught up to the mounting level of their deposits. This increase in deposits was accompanied by a continual decline in the loan-to-deposit ratio between 1992 and 2000. Despite this dramatic expansion of private-sector banks in Myanmar, they still tend to act as private asset managers to particular conglomerates, and not yet appear to be fully functioning as effective financial intermediaries in the national economy.[11] From the view of the role of financial institutions, the private bank sector emerged under the junta's reforms in the early 1990s and which extensively transformed during the reforms being enacted in the 2010s has only partially enhanced the bank sector's capacity of financial intermediation in the economy. Meanwhile, another wave for transforming the banking sector is expected. Table 4.3 shows that since 2012 the asset of private banks have been explosively increasing. Ratios of M2, Loan and TB holding have also been drastically changing recently.

Supply System for Long-term Capital

Capital Market Development in Myanmar

The Yangon Stock Exchange was inaugurated in October 2015, established in cooperation with Japan Exchange Group (JEG), Daiwa Securities Co.,

Table 4.3 Financial Position of Private Banks

	(1)	(2)	(3)	(4)	(5)	(6)	(7)	(8)
	Total Asset	Deposit	Total Asset/ GDP	Deposit/ GDP	M2/ GDP	Loan/ Deposit	TB/ Deposit	(6)+(7)
1992	522	230	0.2	0.1	31.2	78.1	0.0	78.1
1993	2,400	1,578	0.7	0.4	27.4	82.0	2.5	84.5
1994	6,676	4,840	1.4	1.0	27.9	72.6	0.8	73.5
1995	20,231	15,705	3.3	2.6	30.7	61.9	3.2	65.0
1996	48,966	37,014	6.2	4.7	32.5	70.8	3.1	73.9
1997	85,062	58,156	7.6	5.2	29.7	86.8	7.7	94.5
1998	139,849	110,784	8.7	6.9	28.2	54.9	8.3	63.3
1999	230,588	186,169	10.5	8.5	26.8	52.1	31.8	83.9
2000	384,101	324,580	15.0	12.7	32.7	49.2	31.1	80.4
2001	597,174	487,101	16.9	13.8	34.3	63.6	22.0	85.5
2002	846,215	644,692	15.0	11.5	28.9	72.3	15.8	88.1
2003	439,204	215,579	5.7	2.8	21.1	85.9	37.0	122.9
2004	531,387	346,245	5.9	3.8	24.1	60.2	31.0	91.2
2005	514,981	364,559	4.2	3.0	22.1	68.5	19.5	88.0
2006	711,435	519,366	4.3	3.1	20.2	62.6	20.7	83.3
2007	948,189	689,449	4.1	3.0	18.8	68.6	23.7	92.3
2008	1,331,262	928,091	4.6	3.2	17.2	63.2	28.8	91.9
2010	6,079,494	4,911,005	15.3	12.3	23.6	39.2	26.3	65.5
2012	22,977,110	11,310,631	44.8	22.1	30.3	46.8	0.7	47.5
2014	33,611,205	20,847,517	51.5	31.9	30.3	54.4	0.1	54.5

Note: unit for (1) and (2): million kyat, unit for (3)–(8): percentage.

Source: Statistical Yearbook 2002 and 2007, ADB Key Indicators, and Annual Report, Central Bank of Myanmar 2015–16.

Ltd. of Japan, and the government of Japan, with 49 per cent of its share owned by JEG and Daiwa. As of January 2018, the shares of four companies were listed and traded. A month earlier, a new company law was enacted, updating the old colonial period laws, and clarifying the role of board of management and shareholders, which is expected to accelerate foreign investment.

The capital market is expected to play a key role in providing the economy with relatively large amounts of capital over the long term. It is generally expected to play a complementary role to the commercial banking sector, whose main role is to provide short-term credit. However, the greatest difficulty in setting up a capital market in a developing country is that it usually takes a substantial amount of time before it is able to fully function following its physical establishment. The historical experience of Myanmar's neighboring ASEAN countries teaches us that it may take a decade or more for the market to begin its operation as a tool for resource allocation. For a securities market to become fully operational, the government must first take steps to lay out the necessary legal systems, protect investors' rights, and provide incentives that will encourage firms to participate in it. Once the government fulfills these steps, the market should provide a vital platform for further governmental and corporate reform in terms of government bond absorption, SOE privatization, and transparency in the management of private corporations, including banks. Particularly regarding the enhancement of the financial system, private banks need to be more transparent and public, and to operate independently of any particular business group. The securities market can play a vital role in imposing discipline on banks with a view to improving the quality of the financial system in the future.[12]

Development Bank System in Myanmar

While capital market development is a standard means of providing long-term capital, some countries in East Asia have adopted an alternative means, known as the development bank system, during their high-growth stages. These development banks were normally created within the banking system in the form of a policy-based financial institution specializing in long-term credit. The fundraising side of their operations is designed to ease the long-term finances through fiscal sources, privileged bonds, or compulsive deposits from private banks for development banks to sustain resources of long-term lending. They could be found in Japan during its high-growth era—both in the form of state-run banks (Japan Development Bank) and special private banks (Long-term Credit Banks)—and in Korea even today in the form of a state-run bank (Korea Development Bank). Recently, some ASEAN countries have attempted to establish state-run banks specializing in the provision of credit for infrastructure.

It should be noted that there is essentially a fundamental trade-off between the capital market and the development bank system. The creation of a development bank amounts to a sort of government intervention in the financial market designed to mitigate a certain market failure. In the early stages of development, the market sometimes fails to create enough long-term credit due to severe information asymmetry or as a result of risk arising from inadequate information processing capabilities. In some situations, loan coordination by the government or the provision of interest subsidies can prove effective. Such policy interventions, however, generally impede capital market development in the long run. For example, during Japan's high-growth era (1960s–1970s), the system for providing long-term credit employed by the Japan Development Bank and Long-term Credit Banks was only made possible through the repression of equity and bond issues by corporations and the imposition of partial restrictions on the operation of commercial banks.[13]

The debate concerning the introduction of a development bank system in Myanmar is intimately related to the reform policy for state banks, particularly the MEB. While the MEB seems to provide a great source for fundraising, its capacity for financial intermediation as a bank appears to be insufficient. The possibility of introducing a development bank system should be carefully examined with consideration given not only to the capacity of existing state and private banks, but also to its effect on capital market development.

Conclusion

This chapter looks back at the process by which Myanmar's economy had changed and developed over the last two decades, with its focus on the emergence of the private sector during the period of the military rule in the 1990s. Myanmar's economy exhibited the substantial private sector-led growth, and the development of the trade, construction, and banking industries that was supported by the growth of primary sector exports during the early stages of the reforms enacted by the junta in the 1990s. Furthermore, while a sprout of industrialization by the labor-intensive garment sector was shown in the late 1990s, due to the economic turmoil caused by the AFC, signs of a downturn in the industrialization driven by the private sector began to appear in 2003, and since its recovery, the economy has become characterized by commodity (natural gas) exports in the government sector, and domestic service industries, such as construction, in the private sector. This transformation has certainly contributed to the recovery and rescued the government from a fiscal and foreign reserve crisis, but it may also have made the economy more vulnerable to external conditions, such as variations in international commodity prices. The current reforms, executed in 2011, are still built upon this fundamental principle.

The dissolution of major SOEs was limited, and this policy was later suspended under the junta's reforms. The private sector, on the other hand, has grown to emerge as another major entity. Most large private corporations, however, expanded their businesses into the service sector and formed business groups, some of which developed intimate ties with the government. These crony relationships have essentially remained unchanged, even since the new government took power. Myanmar's corporate system is still in the primitive stages of its development. Established during the military rule, Myanmar's private banks have grown quickly during the current reforms, even replacing the state banks within the financial system. This notwithstanding, most of these banks were created by private business groups and still behave as the financial departments of these groups, rather than as public corporations. As a result, their performance of financial intermediation is not yet sophisticated. In terms of the provision of long-term capital, the establishment of a capital market remains at its preparatory stage.

It is important that the reforms should be designed to deliver corporate and financial systems that are suited to the industrialization process. Construction of a financial channel for supporting growth in the manufacturing sector should be the country's first priority, and this can be broken down into three criteria. Firstly, the existence of well-functioning private commercial banks that are managerially independent is a prerequisite. To this end, a legal framework and regulatory practices for the banking sector are crucial. Secondly, discussions must be encouraged with regards to the design of a system for creating a financial channel for long-term capital, which is of immense importance for achieving widespread industrialization. Discussions concerning a system for channeling credit to small and medium enterprises and agricultural production are also important. Lastly, a policy regarding the creation of a fair corporate system—including the issue of SOE privatization as well as corporate ownership and governance—will become a vital part of plans for achieving long-term sustainable growth in Myanmar.

Notes

1. This chapter is the revised version of a part of a policy paper written as the final report of the JICA Myanmar Economic Development Program <http://libopac.jica.go.jp/images/report/P1000023158.html>, and is largely based on the author's previous articles. See F. Mieno, "Toward Myanmar's New Stage of Development: Transition from Military Rule to the Market," *Asian Economic Policy Review* 8, no. 1 (June 2013), and F. Mieno and K. Kubo, "Growth Structure and Macro-economy under 20 Years Junta Regime," in *Myanmar in the 21st Century: An Economy in Transition*, ed. F. Odaka (Tokyo: Springer, 2015).

2. The Burma Company Act, for example, has not been revised since it was enacted in 1914, when the country was still a British colony.
3. Fujita, K. and I. Okamoto, "Overview of Agricultural Policies and the Development in Myanmar," in *Economic Transition in Myanmar after 1988: Market Economy versus State Control*, ed. K. Fujita, F. Mieno, and I. Okamoto (Singapore and Japan: NUS Press and Kyoto University Press, 2009), pp. 169–215.
4. FEC system was introduced in 1993 for limiting direct foreign currency circulation.
5. In an interview with the author in March 2012 at the Ministry of Commerce, a high level official in charge stated, "[With] 140 SOEs, mainly in the heavy industry sector, now being privatized, the number of SOEs will fall to 63. [The] Public Private Partnership (PPP) method is being actively utilized."
6. F. Mieno, "Characteristics of Capital Accumulation in Myanmar, 1988–2003," in *Economic Transition in Myanmar after 1988*, ed. Fujita, Mieno, and Okamoto, pp. 48–50, and F. Mieno, "Toward Myanmar's New Stage of Development: Transition from Military Rule to the Market," *Asian Economic Policy Review* 8, no. 1 (June 2013): 109–11.
7. For the case study on Htoo Group and Asia World Group, see Aung Min and T. Kudo, "Business Conglomerates in the Context of Myanmar's Economic Reform," in *Myanmar's Integration with Global Economy Outlook and Opportunities*, ed. Lim H. and Y. Yamada, Chapter 6 (BRC Research Report, Bangkok, 2014), pp. 143–8. It summarized the profiles of representative business groups in Myanmar based on information from newspapers and other publications, covering 11 groups, including ones under the control of the army (Myanmar Economic Corporation and Union of Myanmar Economic Holdings Ltd.).
8. See F. Kubo et al., "The Financial Sector during the Transition to a Market Economy in Myanmar," in *Economic Transition in Myanmar after 1988*, ed. Fujita, Mieno, and Okamoto, pp. 128–65; and S. Turnell, *Fiery Dragons: Banks, Moneylenders and Microfinance in Burma* (Copenhagen: NIAS Press, 2009).
9. F. Mieno, "Some Perspectives on the Banking Sector in Myanmar: Based on the Banking Sector Survey," *The Program for Economic Development in Myanmar*, Final Report, 2015 <http://libopac.jica.go.jp/images/report/P1000023158.html> [accessed 1 June 2017].
10. M2 is essentially a metric of liquid or near-liquid money supply, including cash, checking deposits, and savings deposits.
11. Mieno and Kubo 2015.
12. When Thailand established its stock exchange in the late 1970s, for example, all its commercial banks were compelled to become public companies and listed on the exchange.
13. T. Hoshi and A. Kashyap, *Corporate Financing and Governance in Japan: The Road to the Future* (Cambridge, MA: The MIT Press, 2000).

References

Asian Development Bank. 2012. *Myanmar in Transition: Opportunities and Challenger*. Manila: Asian Development Bank.

Fujita, K., F. Mieno, and I. Okamoto. 2009. *Economic Transition in Myanmar after 1988: Market Economy versus State Control*. Singapore and Japan: NUS Press and Kyoto University Press.

Fujita, K. and I. Okamoto. 2009. "Overview of Agricultural Policies and the Development in Myanmar." In *Economic Transition in Myanmar after 1988: Market Economy versus State Control*, ed. K. Fujita, F. Mieno, and I. Okamoto. Singapore and Japan: NUS Press and Kyoto University Press.

Hoshi, T. and A. Kashyap. 2000. *Corporate Financing and Governance in Japan: The Road to the Future*. Cambridge, MA: The MIT Press.

Kubo, K., R. Fukui, and F. Mieno. 2009. "The Financial Sector during the Transition to a Market Economy in Myanmar." In *Economic Transition in Myanmar after 1988*, ed. Fujita, Mieno, and Okamoto. Singapore and Japan: NUS Press and Kyoto University Press.

Aung Min and T. Kudo. 2014. "Business Conglomerates in the Context of Myanmar's Economic Reform." In *Myanmar's Integration with Global Economy Outlook and Opportunities*, ed. Lim H. and Y. Yamada. BRC Research Report, Bangkok.

Mieno, F. 2009. "Characteristics of Capital Accumulation in Myanmar, 1988–2003." In *Economic Transition in Myanmar after 1988*, ed. Fujita, Mieno, and Okamoto. Singapore and Japan: NUS Press and Kyoto University Press.

———. 2013. "Toward Myanmar's New Stage of Development: Transition from Military Rule to the Market." *Asian Economic Policy Review* 8, no. 1 (June).

Mieno, F. and K. Kubo. 2015. "Growth Structure and Macroeconomy under 20 Years Junta Regime". In *Myanmar in the 21st Century: An Economy in Transition*, ed. Konosuke Odaka. Tokyo: Springer.

Mya Than and Myat Thein. 2000. *Financial Resources for Development in Myanmar: Lessons from Asia*. Singapore: Institute of Southeast Asian Studies.

Myat Thein. 2004. *Economic Development of Myanmar*. Singapore: Institute of Southeast Asian Studies.

Turnell, S. 2009. *Fiery Dragons: Banks, Moneylenders and Microfinance in Burma*. Copenhagen: NIAS Press.

Turnell, Sean. 2011. "Fundamentals of Myanmar's Macroeconomy: A Political Economy Perspective." *Asian Economic Policy Review* 6, no. 1: 136–53.

Wang, S. 2004. "Private Banks in Myanmar (1990–2003)." In *Myanmar under Transition to Market Economy*, ed. K. Fujita. Chiba: Institute of Development Economies.

CHAPTER 5

Urban Real Estate and the Financial System in Myanmar

Bo Bo Nge

This chapter reviews the boom in real estate in Myanmar in the ten-year period preceding 2015, which left the country uncompetitive due to high rental costs for land. The potential causes of the boom during the opening up of Myanmar are diagnosed, and the relationship of real estate prices and stability of financial system is examined. The chapter presents how high valuation in real estate properties occasioned domestic credit expansion and discusses the potential consequences of heavy reliance on urban real estate to provide security to loans extended by financial institutions.

Land Value as Economic Heritage and Major Obstacle for Myanmar

Major cities in Myanmar, especially Yangon, experienced a dramatic rise in prime office rents since 2012, as more foreign businesses attempted to get a foothold in the country that previously lacked world-class properties. By the end of 2014, Yangon stood only second to Hong Kong in the level of office rents in the region. Table 5.1 describes Yangon prime office market vis-à-vis those of other major Asian metropolises.

Although prime office space commanded high rental income, it was highly questionable whether the real estate prices were connected to economic fundamentals in any meaningful way.

Price-to-Rent Ratios

Price-to-rent ratio[1] measures the number of years it takes to pay down the value of a property using only its rental income. High (or low) price-to-rent

Table 5.1 Office Rent in Major Cities (Second Half of 2014)

Cities	*Prime Office Rent in Central Business District (US$/sq. ft./annum)*	*Vacancy Rate Forecast 2015 (%)*	*Supply Forecast 2015 (million sq. ft.)*	*Supply Forecast 2016 (million sq. ft.)*
Singapore	84.10	4.60	0.53	3.58
Jakarta	41.40	10.30	6.49	6.10
Ho Chi Minh	44.50	9.00	1.00	1.50
Bangkok	29.70	5.00	0.41	0.52
Hong Kong	120.00	4.80	1.33	1.04
Tokyo	82.20	6.00	5.02	6.60
Kuala Lumpur	22.20	12.10	2.33	0.19
Yangon	93.00	12.30	0.26	0.59

Source: Colliers International.

ratios might suggest a divergence of price levels from what is suggested by rent levels and expectations about future property prices. Internationally, the rule of thumb is that the property markets with price-to-rent ratio above 30 are considered vulnerable to sharp corrections triggered by events such as a change (rise) in interest rates. Conversely, values below 20 are considered low and are also susceptible to changes in macroeconomic conditions.

Primary price and rent data were collected in order to calculate price-to-rent ratio for years 2006 through 2014 for Yangon.

Take note that the data for Yangon was for the outer city areas whereas the data for other countries (produced by Global Property Guide) represented "properties ... located in premier city centers." We could hence consider the estimates for Yangon as conservative ones in this comparison exercise: if the sample data sufficiently covered Yangon's central city area, the line presenting Yangon would likely be higher than what was plotted in Figure 5.1. The ratio for Yangon came in well above 30 in all observations. Its average (38.77) over the period approximated values for Hong Kong and Singapore (second half of 2014). Among the countries where property statistics existed, Yangon had the highest price-to-rent ratio (or, conversely, lowest yielding real properties) than all other developing countries in the region except India. If the sample data covered Yangon's central city area, it would potentially surpass price-to-rent ratios in both Hong Kong and Singapore.

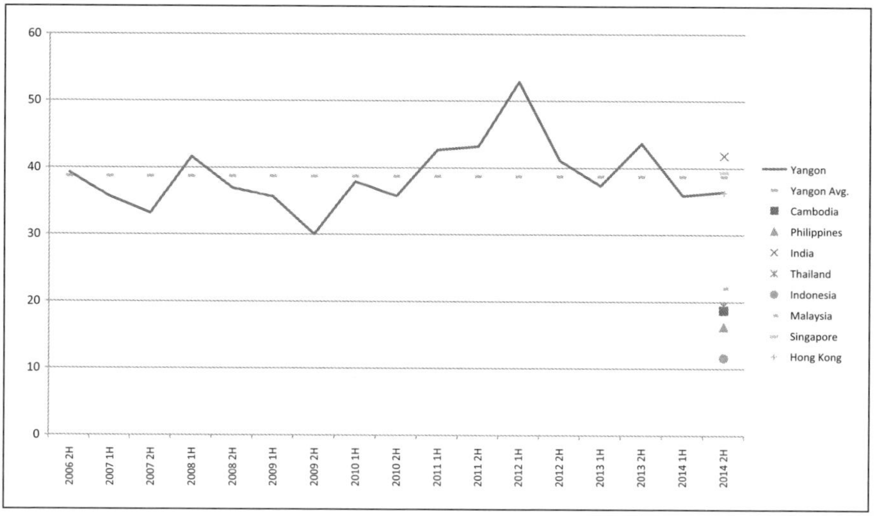

Source: For data on Myanmar: calculations based on data collected from *A-Kyo-Saung* Journal and *Zaykwet* Journal (multiple issues); for other countries: Global Property Guide.[2]

Figure 5.1 Price-to-Rent Ratios: Yangon Outer City Areas vs Central City Areas in Other Countries

Price-to-Income Ratios

Price-to-income ratios provide a comparison of the real estate values vis-à-vis economic fundamentals for each locale. The Geneva-based Bank for International Settlement (BIS) regularly publishes nominal residential property prices collected in 58 countries. I utilized residential prices for five countries in the neighboring regions covered in the BIS property price data set, and calculated price-to-income ratios for all available years.

Home price data for Myanmar was from appraisal values from a private assessor office covering properties in the whole of Myanmar. For all countries income was represented by nominal GDP per capita and calculations were carried out in local currency units. For some countries in Figure 5.2 (China and Thailand), the price-to-income ratios revealed that home prices and average income rose in comparable proportions. Other countries (Malaysia and India) saw home prices increased by more than income in recent years. The contrast was between Myanmar and Indonesia. While this ratio was halved in Indonesia, Myanmar experienced doubling of the ratio in the same number of years. It means income increased twice as fast as home prices in Indonesia while home prices rose twice as fast as income increases in Myanmar.

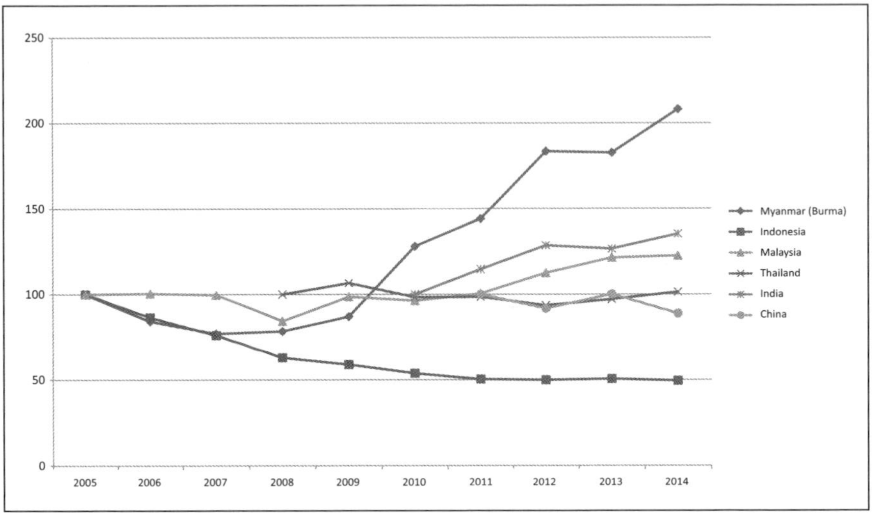

Source: For other countries, BIS Property Price Statistics and World Economic Outlook Database.

Figure 5.2 Price-to-Income Ratios (all available data)

The two ratios presented above describe a state of high valuations for real property in Myanmar. Though we cannot rule out the possibility that the real asset value could rise again, it is highly doubtful that real estate values can rise much further beyond their current levels.

How Did It Get Here?

The state of Myanmar lacked a modern taxation and public finance system to provide for the state expenditures. Its budget was chronically cash-constrained due to widespread tax-evasion and avoidance by potential taxpayers. The taxes collected as per cent of GDP for Myanmar were in low single digits until 2011–12 and were still in the single digit range in

Table 5.2 Selected Sources of State Revenue and the Size of Budget Deficits

	Tax Revenues and Budget Deficit (as % of GDP)							
	2000–01	*2005–06*	*2010–11*	*2011–12*	*2012–13*	*2013–14*	*2014–15*	*2015–16*
Tax Revenues	2.97	3.88	3.36	3.61	6.59	7.53	9.84	8.71
Budget Deficit	8.41	3.31	4.75	3.66	2.69	1.27	1.18	4.99

Source: Budget Department, Ministry of Planning and Finance.

2015–16, though they crept up to high single digits in the last four years of available data.

The country's tax revenues did not compare well to an average of other developing countries in the Southeast Asia region.[3]

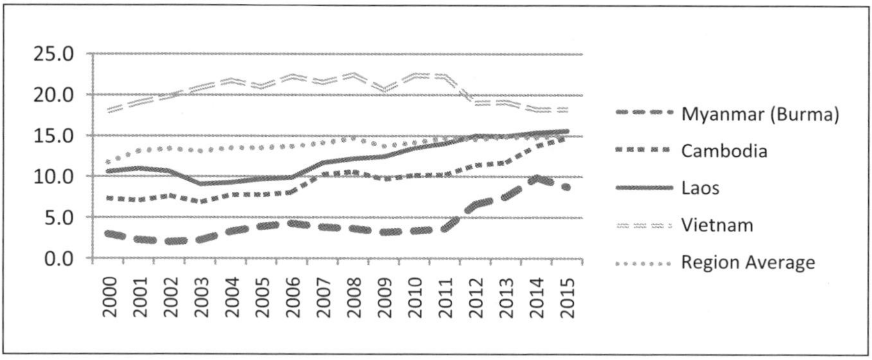

Source: Data for Myanmar (Budget Department, MOPF); data for other countries: ADB, Key Economic Indicators for Asia and Pacific, 2016, Country Tables. Regional average calculation includes Thailand, Malaysia, and Indonesia in addition to the countries in the figure.

Figure 5.3 Tax Revenue Comparison (as per cent of GDP)

The Myanmar state, lacking public political support to collect taxes from a wider public until recently, relied a great deal on the imposition of a de facto "inflation tax," with the average inflation tax equivalent to around 2.7 per cent of the country's annual GDP during the period (1992–2016).[4] In this environment, keeping any available form of monetary asset with predetermined nominal values—cash, bank deposit accounts, government bonds—presented a loss in real value to the holder, given that bank deposit rates and bond coupon rates were fixed or capped. As available financial assets could not be counted upon as a store of value, the need for the citizenry to store savings (and maintain savings' real value) meant that savings and wealth were kept as real assets rather than financial assets.

Real Estate as a Shelter from Inflation Taxes

The land taxation system in Myanmar must be first presented in order to discuss its impact on the investments in real properties. During the British colonial era, revenue from land taxation was a major source of income for the state: more than half of the total revenue of the Government of Burma was attributable to land revenue. The convention in the tax assessment of real estate since the colonial times has been to denominate the tax in fixed absolute nominal amounts rather than as a fixed proportion of market or assessed values. The disadvantage of this system is that it requires the tax authorities to re-state (fixed) tax amounts payable periodically after observed changes in the market value of properties while fixed-proportion tax systems just need periodic reassessments of land values. If the assessed (nominal) value, as well as the tax amount due, is not reviewed, the real value of the tax amounts becomes more and more insignificant as time elapses, even in a low inflationary environment. This scenario did take place in the land taxation in Myanmar, and by a large degree: the last revision of land revenue (tax) rates was in 1938–40, just prior to the Second World War. There were several reviews of land tax rates in the 1951–63 period, but the land tax amounts were not revised upward to keep them in line with prevailing prices. Ultimately, as they had not been adjusted for over seven decades, tax rates on land were unreasonably low. This contributed to land speculation, since the cost of holding a property became minuscule.

Although the state was generally ineffective in collecting taxes, there were occasions in which exacting tax on real estate holdings was convenient for the state. If the parties to a real estate transaction needed to transfer legal title, they must have their contract registered with the state. On such occasions when a property changes hands, the state could assess two kinds of taxes: property transaction fees and stamp duties. Critically, a property transaction fee was imposed only if a buyer could not prove the legality of his or her income. If a buyer could prove that the funds used for purchasing property were of legal origin and that the taxes due on these funds had been duly paid, then only stamp duty fee on the transaction value was collected.

Role of Tax and Subsidies in Valuing Real Estate

Tax Amnesty (2007–12)

Prior to 2007, the transaction fee imposed on property title transfers was 50 per cent if the source of income could not be proven as legal. However, in August 2007, the state lavishly bestowed a special tax treatment on those acquiring real estate properties without funds of legal origin. The government cut the transaction fee payable on real property purchases from

50 per cent to 8 per cent.[5] This special tax relief was maintained until 2012 when the state's levy on funds without legal origin went up to 30 per cent. After a year and half, in March 2015, the levy on these funds was lowered again to a tiered range of 3 to 30 per cent. By 2015–16, the highest rate for the income without legal origin remained capped at 30 per cent. The changes in fees and taxes related to real estate transactions are summarized in Table 5.3.

Table 5.3 Change in Government Levies in Chronological Order (2007–Dec. 2016)

Period	*Transaction Fee (without proof of legal income)*	*Stamp Duty*
Prior to 11 Aug. 2007	50%	?
11 Aug. 2007 to 10 Aug. 2012	8%	7%
11 Aug. 2012 to 31 Mar. 2014	30%	7%
1 Apr. 2014 to 31 Mar. 2015	3% to 30% (Tiered Rates)[6]	7%
1 Apr. 2015 to 31 Mar. 2016	3% to 30% (Tiered Rates)[7] 5% (3 major cities)[8]	3% (outside 3 major cities)

Source: *Myanmar Times*, multiple issues.

The preferential tax treatment was conditional upon the funds documented[9] to have been invested in the real estate sector. The 8 per cent fee levied during the five-year period (2007–12) was a token measure for legitimizing any income. In 2015–16, 30 per cent levies on funds without a proof of legal origin were even less than normal corporate income tax rates in a number of countries.[10] No other economic sector in Myanmar could offer such a preferential treatment to those aspiring to bring illicit funds into the legal fold. In reality, it implied a real estate sector-specific tax amnesty for those with black or grey sources of income. This unprecedented favor turned real properties into a distinctive investment vehicle with special tax advantages, a repertoire for capital gains, national savings, and all sources of income. This act predictably opened floodgates of money into real estate sector. The consequential impact on property valuations was indeed profound, as described below.

As for the market's reaction to the tax amnesty, it was obvious that tax treatment on property and property sales were quite generous for those with unaccounted wealth. In 2014–15, if one paid 20 per cent on MMK 1.5 billion (then equivalent to about US$1.5 million), 100 per cent of his or her income (US$1.5 million) became legal. The cost of legalizing illicit funds therefore would be even less than 20 per cent (it is only 20/120 = 16.67 per cent in this case). There were no limits on the number of transactions an individual could be involved in, nor a total ceiling amount of deals in a year, as long as the transactions involved real estate properties. Regardless of the legality of income sources, any buyer who paid the transaction fee (plus stamp duties due) on the transacted value to the state received a clean title to the property and his or her money was officially made legal. The relief was in fact an official pardon with a slap on the wrist of those with illicit money. The property transaction fee and stamp duties were a one-time levy collected only when the transaction was reported to the authorities so that title transfers could be issued and the sale (and the riches involved) legalized. After the acquisition was formally completed, real estate owners need not pay any more: there was effectively no periodically-assessed property tax on holdings that did not change hands.

As such, landed properties became a preferred investment vehicle—an official whitewashing privilege—vis-à-vis other real assets such as gold or automobiles. In response to this decree, the investments in real estate sector increased. Real estate dealers and agents all over the country started lobbying for the extension of preferential tax treatment year after year as the continuation of such policy guaranteed the inflow of more money. The five-year period with the lowest tax rate (August 2007 to August 2012) especially provided significant momentum to real estate markets and laid favorable conditions for property speculation.

Real Estate as Legitimizing Medium

It is worth further analyzing the lure of the special tax relief to discern how it might have impacted investors' micro behavior in the acquisition of properties. In this analysis, the effect of stamp duties on the investors' property acquisition decisions are ignored as they were uniformly levied on all property at any point in time as shown in Table 5.3. In some fiscal years (2007 through 2013, and 2016), the transaction fees were also uniform and hence differentiation of their effects in investment decisions would not be palpable. However, there were tiered rates in the 24-month period starting April 2014 (through March 2016) and the role played by the tiered rates in the acquisition of properties can be analyzed.

Given that differentiated tiered rates apply to properties of different value brackets, sensible investors would come up with a strategy to determine the optimal value of the property to minimize the cost of acquisition. In order to do this, we need to make an assumption about the miscellaneous fees (information costs, lawyer fees, broker commissions, etc.) involved in transacting one property. This cost was fixed at MMK 5 million to be realistically close to actual practice in the market. Since an investor without a legal source of income was required to pay 3 to 30 per cent to the state to legalize the funds equivalent to 100 per cent of the transaction value, his legalizing cost is: $[x/(1+x)]$, where x is the percentage on the value of the property required to pay into the state. Table 5.4 shows the estimation of the investor's total cost derived as the percentage of property value.

It could be readily identified that in the first period (April 2014 through March 2015), the properties worth between MMK 100 to 150 million offered the least costly option for an investor. In fact if one could get as close as possible to MMK 150 million (the ceiling of the bracket), the more tax-efficient this transaction would be. In the same way, in the second period (April 2015 to March 2016), properties worth between MMK 500 million and MMK 1 billion offered the best tax trade off. The best value options were those properties as close as possible to MMK

Table 5.4 Hypothetical Costs Involved in Property Acquisition

	Property Value (MMK million)	*Transaction (legalizing) Fee (payable to the State) (%)*	*Legalizing Cost (as % of property value)*	*Legal Fees Assumption (MMK million)*	*Legal Fees (as % of property value)*	*Total Cost (as % of property value)*
1 Apr. 2014 to 31 Mar. 2015	50	3	2.91	5	10.00	12.91
	100	5	4.76	5	5.00	9.76
	150	10	9.09	5	3.33	12.42
	300	20	16.67	5	1.67	18.33
	400	30	23.08	5	1.25	24.33
1 Apr. 2015 to 31 Mar. 2016	100	3	2.91	5	5.00	7.91
	500	5	4.76	5	1.00	5.76
	1,000	10	9.09	5	0.50	9.59
	1,500	20	16.67	5	0.33	17.00
	2,000	30	23.08	5	0.25	23.33

1 billion. If we take a property with the sale value close to upper limit of 1 billion, say 950 million (about US$0.8 million, using the average exchange rate for the period), the cost to legalize that much illegal income would be only 5.3 per cent.[11] At this rate, it might be even cheaper to declare legal income as illegal and pay less tax by acquiring real estate properties than to pay the standard income tax.[12] It was the reason property market attracted so much cash inflow from all sources.

Potential Capital Inflows into Real Estate: Illicit Funds

Attraction of property investment alone was not a sufficient explanation for the rise of property values. There had to be some sources of funds to flow into the property sector. The purpose of the discussion on potential sources of funds is not to pinpoint their origin—that task would require an investigative bureau with multiple staff. Rather the purpose in the section below is to highlight that there *were* illicit fund flows that might end up in the real estate sector. This section draws on the work of Dev Kar and Joseph Spanjers who studied capital and illicit financial flows to and from Myanmar for a period spanning over five decades (1960–2013).[13] Employing the two-step approach first implemented in 1974 by Jagdish Bhagwati, they compared annual trade data reported by all Myanmar's trading partners with the data reported by Burmese authorities. Their analysis focused on mis-invoicing in foreign trade transactions in order to back out the data on capital inflows and outflows to and from the country. They then supplemented the results with the estimates of the gap between source of funds and use of funds utilizing the World Bank Residual Method and IMF's balance of payments statistics. Interestingly, they found total inward illicit capital flows into Myanmar in this period (US$82.7 billion) were more than two times larger than total outward illicit capital flows (US$35.8 billion).

Kar and Spanjers suggested drug trafficking as the potential reason for net inflows given Myanmar's standing as a top-ranking drug producing country in their study period. A distinct characteristic of countries with significant drug trafficking was that illicit inflows were much larger than illicit outflows. To finance the drug business, the authors reasoned, there was a need to bring in significant capital through export over-invoicing or import under-invoicing. Their study covered up to 2013. Table 5.5 draws from their annual capital inflow and outflow data for selected years. For 2014, the year not covered by their study, I calculated the illicit capital flows data for only one export commodity, jade, since it was likely to be the top export commodity by value for the country, based on comparison of Chinese import data[14] extracted from UN Comtrade Database and export statistics on jade reported by Burmese Central Statistical Organization.

Table 5.5 Union of Myanmar: Capital Inflow and Outflow Estimates

	Amount of Net Inflow (US$ million)	*Net Inflow/ GDP (%)*	*Total Inflow*	*Total Outflow*
2005	1,477	5.40	2,219	742
2006	1,167	3.77	1,796	629
2007	3,881	11.20	4,240	359
2008	1,529	4.26	3,434	1,905
2009	2,796	7.40	3,904	1,108
2010	4,897	12.31	7,377	2,480
2011	5,356	12.75	5,356	–
2012	14,009	31.08	14,009	–
2013	10,323	21.12	10,323	–
2014*	9,638	18.14	N/A	N/A

Note: *For 2014 the inflow estimates are only for one export item: Jade.

Source: IMF World Economic Outlook Database (1980–2021); Kar and Spanjers 2015, Table Three; UN Comtrade Database.

The estimates by Kar and Spanjers were less sensitive to illegal activities on the ground, as the illegal businesses were hard to quantify. They did not include smuggling of timber, precious stones, drugs and other goods transported across the various porous overland borders. The addition of cash flow estimates from these activities might have added more to inflows. At the same time, being reliant on officially reported figures, their study's estimation methods could not incorporate observed practices among Burmese importers making partial payments for their imports through unofficial remittance channels of money lenders. Nor were the remittances made by millions of Burmese migrants working in neighboring countries included. If estimates were available for the outward remittance to pay for imports and inward remittance by Burmese migrant workers abroad, we could better analyze the situation.

The analysis of available cash flow data showed that the annual net inflows as a per cent of GDP were in double digits except in the years 2008 and 2009 (the years when global financial crisis was severe).

Given the data limitations, we could not conduct formal tests in order to draw definite conclusions on the influence of tax favors bestowed on real estate sector in pulling the capital in. However, it was probable that the substantial amount of the funds from abroad poured in to real estate sector, given the lack of investment opportunities for estimated billions of dollars that flowed in to the country each year and the observed rise in real estate values.

Other Potential Capital Inflows and Their Impact on Rents and Prices

Local Burmese business reports indicated that foreign investors' involvement in property and rental markets was observed in the post-2010 period in Yangon, and in Mandalay, the second largest commercial city, during the opening-up process of the previously closed economy. As the country's perceived investment opportunities started enticing outsiders, these commercial cities attracted a sizable wave of foreign investors who flocked to major economic hubs and sought rental office and residential space[15] in order to establish their presence.

Capital Inflows and Real Estate Boom: Impact on Construction Industry

The phenomenal rise of rents from a low base prompted a strong response from the construction industry. Building permits issuances more than tripled in the four-year period since 2010. Property acquisition activities intensified since 2010[16] and seemed to have reached a plateau in 2014–15,[17] according to local reports[18] on the real estate transactions.

New building developments and investments were a significant, concentrated capital injection, which could create significant momentum and sustain a real estate boom for a period. The momentum created brought in its wake such economic aspects commonly observed in real estate surges: multiplier effects of construction spending, higher creditworthiness of landowners and consequential additional credit expansion, and the entry of new participants enticed by higher returns into real estate market.

Lenders' Total Reliance on Collateral Requirements

In selecting good credit among potential borrowers, increasing interest rates on loan would cause adverse selection problems (that is, attracting only high-risky borrowers and projects).[20] High interest rates on loans also

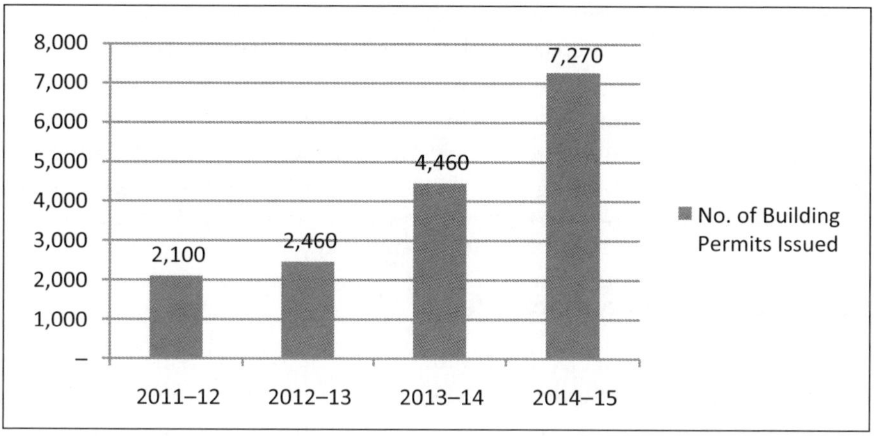

Source: Yangon City Development Committee.[19]

Figure 5.4 Increase in the Number of Building Permits

mean any surplus the borrowing businesses managed to bring forth would be appropriated by the lenders. Increasing collateral requirements on the other hand puts financial pressure on borrowers to perform. A collateral requirement over 100 per cent of loan value also allows a lender to shield himself from the consequences of moral hazard after a loan is approved. As such, collateral requirements could be helpful in safeguarding the banks' loan exposure. Collateral requirements are a pervasive practice in the financial sector in both developed and developing countries. The Burmese banking system has greatly relied on collateralized lending to generate income. Since their formation in the early to mid-1990s, the commercial banks were required to take collateral well in excess of 200 per cent of the loan amount to safeguard themselves against potential defaults. Urban land and landed buildings which are protected with strong rights have been used as collateral for almost all of the loans made by both private and public deposit-taking institutions.

The collateral requirements were quite severe: two to four times the size of loan. This requirement compels the borrowers to bear effectively all credit risk, operational risk, and other risks associated with doing business. For the lenders, the regulatory guidance to solely rely on the value of collateral precluded standard due diligence practices to seek more information from loan applicants, to understand the borrower's business, and to conduct a proper credit analysis. In addition to stifling credit analysis skills in the local banks, the exclusive reliance on collateral created incentives for private borrowers aspiring to borrow from banking system to get hold of real properties as their first move. Existing borrowers also aspired to acquire more real estate as more collateral led to more credit from domestic banking system. Hence, this intention to protect lenders from the dominant systemic risk in the Burmese domestic commercial banking sector by requiring real estate collateral meant the exposure of banks to high valuations of real estate properties around the country.

Real Estate Boom and Its Effects

On Borrowers' Behavior: Market value of collateral real estate being the determinant of the loan amount, the owners of collateral properties became increasingly creditworthy as the valuations of urban real estate rose over time and with increased demand. An existing borrower with growing creditworthiness would refinance with another lender in the domestic banking system. He or she could pay back the primary loan (plus cumulated interest) from lender A with a new larger second loan from lender B (with the same interest rate) and repeat the same process every few years, or even in a single year if there was a sufficient increase during that period in the value of real properties pledged as collateral. This ride atop the rising waves of real estate boom could foster among borrowers the practice of "letting the property pay for the loan by itself" and not by the cash flows generated by a functioning business. As valuations kept rising, both borrowers and lenders tended to get more complacent with such practice of pay-as-valuation-grows (PAVG) borrowing.

On Lending Practices and Loan Accounting: The practice of refinancing loans should not be disparaged. It is normal in healthy financial systems. Business models of lenders may shift over time as they refocus their resources in the areas of their strength. Such shifts might necessitate the removal of particular business segments and assets. Other lenders would take up these assets if they consider them to be complementary to their core business. Refinancing of loans based solely on the property valuations is different, however, from a healthy intermediation practice. A bank's refinancing decision oblivious of underlying business reasons in the origination of a particular loan could not be considered a sound practice. However, in the context of the Burmese system, as long as a borrower refinances with different lenders, such transaction was only half as bad for the well-being of the system. Assume realistically a borrower repays lender A the full outstanding amount of the loan plus any interest (though it may be possibly overdue amount that the lender A has been recording and reporting as income) with the funds borrowed from lender B, then lender A can claim that he or she has done proper accounting of its loan and can wash his or her hands off the loan. However, this does not absolve the issue of the deteriorated quality of assets, nor the banking system's underlying exposure to the volatility of real estate values. Over time, this issue could become convoluted and breed more problematic offspring. If lenders get frustrated with losing customers to their competitors, they might as a consequence decide to internalize the refinancing process. If lender A monetizes interest [that is, it makes a decision to make a larger loan to the same borrower who owes him over-due interest payments and who would like to borrow using the same but reassessed (higher value) property as collateral], the quality of the bank's assets would have become more and more questionable each time the loan is rolled over.

In the refinancing process, the decision by lender B to refinance the loan to enable the borrower to repay to lender A at least represents some confirmation of the reappraised value by another market participant, though they both may suffer a value illusion. When the refinancing process is internalized in a single institution that originated the loan in the first place, the market (or regulators) could not verify that the appraised value of collateral is within a reasonable range vis-à-vis the economic fundamentals and the market conditions. Larger and larger credit granted on the same piece of property can carry the market farther and farther away from what is warranted by economic fundamentals.

On Domestic Credit Expansion: Supported by high valuations of real estate, credit extended by domestic banks would grow over time. Indeed, domestic credit expanded by slightly over 50 per cent in two consecutive years 2012–13 and 2013–14. The IMF projected that the expansion in domestic credit would continue.

One can observe that the behavior of both borrowers and lenders adjusted to the real estate boom. Urban real estate markets tend to be cyclical in nature, and the financial factors can be pro-cyclical. Previous studies identified these financial factors as related to monetary policy and banking system's credit. Capital flows associated with expansion or contraction of bank credit may impact real estate prices. Incentives and disincentives of holding real estate instigated by a taxation system are also found to have caused swings in real estate prices. Regulatory or deregulatory changes may cause the emergence, or the entry, of new players and trigger changes in corporate and banking strategy, which can spill over into property and rental markets.

Table 5.6 Domestic Private Sector Credit Growth

	2006	*2007*	*2008*	*2009*	*2010*	*2011*	*2012*	*2013*	*2014*
Credit to private sector (billion kyat)	653.00	799.00	912.00	1,177.00	1,896.00	3,124.00	4,772.00	7,448.00	10,140.00
Of Domestic Credit (% of private sector)	18.16	16.95	16.87	16.41	18.90	24.43	40.98	47.99	53.69
Domestic Credit (% change)	26.99	30.98	14.73	32.63	39.84	27.48	–8.92	33.26	21.69
Credit to private sector (% change)	14.19	22.28	14.20	28.98	61.12	64.77	52.75	56.06	36.15

Source: IMF Article IV publications.

Total reliance on the value of the collateral can also make loans risky as the amount a client could borrow may not be related to his or her funding needs or to the size of the cash flows of the business. Some borrowers with high-value collateral may get more funding than they need while the others without pricey property but with a good business case may get less. The borrowers who get larger-than-needed loans might divert funds away from the projects approved by the lender, while the projects of the borrowers with smaller-than-necessary loan might not be implemented at all.

If the lenders in an economy rely largely on the value of collateral real estate in lending decisions and determination of loan amounts, it would create incentives for borrowers to become more creditworthy by acquiring more property. In addition, even without acquisition of more properties, as real estate prices move further up, lenders have more reason to lend to those recently-made "high net worth" individuals. This incentive for acquisition of collateral-eligible real estate is stronger in upward trending markets as buyers anticipate capital gains in addition to potential higher rental income (implicit or explicit) accruing to property owners.

Volatility in Real Estate Prices and the Banking System

In later (speculative) stages of the boom, valuation is no longer dependent on magnitude of income streams from real estate assets, but rather on expected capital gains. The valuations are likely to become divergent from the economic fundamentals, and thus set a stage for later declines as the balance sheet of the lenders become overstretched during the boom. In the case of Myanmar, the indicators that connect real estate prices to economic fundamentals (price-to-rent ratio and price-to-income ratio above) strongly indicate that real estate prices were already very high compared with what they could command in the rental market and prevailing level of individual income.

The credit and real estate nexus needs to be explained. Real estate has a dual function. The first is as a physical input in the production process in an economy. Land has historically been a primary input along with capital and labor in production. The second (additional and optional) use is as a real (physical) backup for bank loans.

Of the two uses, the expedient use of real estate at different times relates to their valuations at a particular time. In normal economic times, a property can be put to dual uses by the owner: as a physical real input (by renting it out to producers) and/or as a physical backup (collateral) to secure financing. When times are not "normal," when real properties are highly valued regardless of how much they can earn, they become less attractive as a real economic input. Consider a situation in which an asset is highly priced compared to the level of income it generates. Its dividend yield would be low. If it is a standalone asset, such as an equity share of a corporation with regular dividend payouts, the investors looking for income would bypass a lower yielding asset and invest in other (higher yielding) assets. This is true especially when the growth rates of income streams are expected to be equalized across the economy over the long term. Land, however, is an essential and finitely supplied input in the production process of goods and services, including housing services. If the price level of land is high, a larger proportion of the revenue generated from production business would have to be spent on paying rent. If the market value of land and real estate keeps rising, less and less return will be available to the owners of other inputs such as capital and labor.

Putting real estate to dual uses in the normal times, that is when valuation are not exorbitant, serves the interests of agents involved in production process: landlords, renters (producers), and financiers. When valuations of real estate are too high compared to its earning power (not "normal"), these real assets serve the interest of landlords, but are not as beneficial to both producers and their financiers as they are in normal times. In such a time, however, the owners of real estate can still put it advantageously to the second use.

Real Estate in the Lending Process

Inherent Risk in Banking: In banking, equity capital is routinely put up by a bank's shareholders in securing a bank charter from monetary authorities. The equity amount is normally insufficient to fully fund the loan amount that borrowers demand from the bank. As such, banks normally attract depositors' money and in the process they create liquid claims (checking and savings deposits) on them on one side of their balance sheets. When banks provide loans based on the value of collateral real estate for long-term investment projects, they create real estate-backed assets on the other side of their balance sheets. These assets are highly illiquid as selling them before maturity to another lender involves thorough evaluation by potential buyers, if any exist, and lengthy negotiations between the parties involved. By juxtaposing such illiquid assets and liquid liabilities on banks' balance sheets, banking system "monetize" illiquid collateral real estate and introduce[21] or supplement liquidity in the economy and thus perform their social function. This liquidity and credit creation process can be greatly accelerated during economic expansions.

Inherent Risk in Property Investments: Business cycles are observed in urban real estate markets and such price instability undermines eligibility of urban real estate as collateral for loans. The general real estate sector model described by DiPasquale and Wheaton[22] incorporated markets for property and assets. They explain how rent levels jointly determined in the property market by the demand for property (space) and existing stock of space (housing supply) in turn establish price levels for properties.[23] Price levels again dictate the supply response of construction and land development industry, which brings new additions to the existing stock of properties. In stylized urban building and development cycles, the demand for property stimulated by an exogenous factor first pushes up the rental rates in the central business district (CBD). Lucrative rent levels (high yield for owners' capital) would entice investors into the property market and lift up the prices of properties. The construction activities incited by high prices tend to aggravate prices of land located not only in the CBD, but also in the other business zones as well. The construction cycle created by this initial shock tends to reverberate for several years until a new (over)supply of housing units suppresses rental income. Lower rental income hence suppresses property prices in order to keep the yield of real estate competitive to other sectors in the long run.

Some of the property cycles are endogenous in their nature: property cycles might be started by non-financial, real economic factors such as increase or decrease in income, discovery, or depletion of natural resources, and growth or decline in jobs creation. A positive demand shock causes prices to rise, and vice versa. DiPasquale and Wheaton showed that households formed future price expectations by observed trend in past prices. Prices could continue to rise even in the face of new construction activities since expectations were already formed by past experiences. In most cases, the principal factor that causes a turn in price movements to the opposite direction is the arrival of new supply. Prices tend to peak as new supply of properties is being developed and brought to market. The supply tends to dwarf demand as many uncoordinated construction projects are completed about the same time. Then, prices start to decline. These phases —initial price increase, followed by a flurry of start-ups in land development and construction, and overstock of new properties, resulting in eventual price declines—comprise real, endogenous cycles of urban real estate market.[24]

Risks in Combining Real Estate and Banking: Given the potential fickleness of real estate values, their acceptance by banks as loan collateral is objectionable. Compared with the practice in which lending decisions are based solely on the value of collateral, some banks, especially those in advanced economies, also incorporate business prospects such as recent past and future cash flows, soundness of a business and its profitability in the loan allocation process. However, borrowers universally have information advantages over lenders about the business for which the loans are made. As much as information asymmetry exists between borrowers and lenders, the value of the collateral is a significant factor that lenders take into account in making loan decisions, especially for less established borrowers.

Raising loan interest rates instead of taking collateral might be an alternative way to overcome the information disadvantage, but it attracts those willing borrowers with high risk projects—the adverse selection problem identified by Stiglitz and Weiss[25]—creating challenges for a lender unable to fully differentiate the level of riskiness in all loan applications. Furthermore, after a loan is approved and funds are disbursed, borrowers may divert the loans to other uses (moral hazard) even though loan contracts might contain restrictive covenants. In addition, monitoring capabilities of lenders are always limited. When lending is undertaken in such circumstances of imperfect information and insufficient monitoring, keeping the collateral of a borrower safeguards a lender to a reliable degree from these two common perils. Studies in other markets have suggested that collateral requirements slightly enhance the borrower firm's productivity by increasing the financial pressure on managers. For all these reasons, collateral remains an important element in credit approval process. When real estate properties are accepted as collateral by banks, an exogenous factor might have been added to sometimes endogenous real estate cycles. As described above, when banks make loans based on the collateral value of the properties, an upward property cycle could have been inadvertently lengthened and/or intensified as high collateral value support higher loan amounts which can in turn support even higher collateral values as more credit is injected into the economy.

Gaffney takes the analysis on the dynamics of interaction between asset prices and bank credit to a structural level.[26] He explains that when real estate values become truly high, economic contraction is bound to follow since high price of this essential input in productive process would choke the economic growth by lowering the expected return to other factors of production. The banks' loan amounts, based on collateral value, tend to be the highest at this point too, with potential adversities for the banking system. The logic of economic contraction is built into the cycle from the start. There is direct conflict between the high land values of the boom phase and the rate of return on productive, job-making real investments. High land values may mean low rates of return on new investments. The high land values are supported by siphoning off part of cash flow to income payments to those who own the land, or to those who lend entrepreneurs funds to buy it. The combination of high credit-worthiness with low returns on newly-created capital can only spell trouble: banks expand as real investment falls. Gaffney reasons that when the borrowers (businesses) hampered by low profits could not repay the loans as a consequence, banks could become illiquid. If banks become seized by panic and stop issuing new loans, the capital returned to banks from matured loans would become locked up in the banks and economic growth would further suffer.

In addition to the indirect exposure to real estate cycle through collateral to loans as described above, commercial banks can have direct exposure to the real estate sector. This direct exposure comes from their own holdings of real estate assets. The higher the proportion of physical real estate assets in banks' equity capital, the more severe the illiquidity issue would be, if and when this issue arises, for the banking system.

The analysis of Myanmar real estate sector in the ten-year period prior to 2015 revealed that the policies prevailed in this era induced the inflow of capital with questionable origins into real estate properties. The inflated price of Myanmar real estate properties was further aggravated by collateral requirements for loans. If this property bubble conditions could not be contained and gradually deflated in the subsequent period, the broader economy might be at risk for a significant contraction in the years that followed.

Notes

1. Price-to-rent ratio is somewhat akin to price-to-earnings ratio (PE ratio, the reverse of EP ratio) in equity investment and gauge the attractiveness of renting vs. owning the property. The difference is that annual earnings, not annual dividend, of the equity-issuing company is in the denominator of PE ratio, whereas the rental income is in the denominator for price-to-rent ratio. Rental income has certainty with respect to its amount and timing: Rental income is directly pocketed by property owner like a monthly dividend received. Earnings are much less certain: earnings might or might not be distributed as dividend to shareholders, and if they do, all periodic earnings

or only a fraction of periodic earnings might get paid out. The decision is up to the company's management and its board of directors. Frequency of rental income payments is monthly whereas frequency of dividend payments tends to be quarterly or for a longer period. Thus, price-to-rent ratio has more direct relationship to property's value than PE ratio has to an equity share's value.

2. Global Property Guide calculated property statistics for the countries based on the data published by the countries' central banks or central statistical bureaus. For individual country data sources, please see <http://www.globalpropertyguide.com/template/assets/Yields-Brochure.pdf> [accessed 7 February 2017]. Historical data for rent were not available for other countries.
3. Data is for 14 developing countries in the region, except Brunei. Source: ADB Key Indicators.
4. For the fiscal years starting in April and ending in March; annual inflation tax is derived as: Inflation $Tax_{(t)}$ = Monetary $Base_{(t-1)} \times Inflation_{(t)}$
5. Buyers were required to pay a separate stamp duty of 7 per cent on transaction value.
6. Three per cent for transaction value up to MMK 50 million; 5 per cent up to MMK 100 million; 10 per cent up to MMK 150 million; 20 per cent up to MMK 300 million; 30 per cent above MMK 300 million.
7. Three per cent for transaction value up to MMK 100 million; 5 per cent up to MMK 500 million; 10 per cent up to MMK 1 billion; 20 per cent up to MMK 1.5 billion; 30 per cent above MMK 1.5 billion.
8. Yangon, Mandalay, and Naypyidaw were designated as major cities.
9. The fact that funds were destined for real estate sector was documented by the sale deeds submitted for the issuance of a conveyance.
10. This tax treatment might have rendered Burmese real estate sector a little-noticed semi-tax haven. Illicit capital inflows are discussed in the article.
11. However, the investor had to pay separate stamp duties ranging from 3 to 5 per cent, as described above. As those properties lying outside three major cities were required to pay only 3 per cent stamp duties (vis-à-vis 5 per cent in the three cities), this tax treatment might have contributed to spreading property boom to second and third tier cities across the country.
12. The government announced the floor price of the sale value in 2013 to clamp down those who attempted to evade this small tax. However, the enforcement of such floor sale prices was not effective, as revealed by above-the-floor ask-prices in the classifieds of local publications in the post-2013 period.
13. Dev Kar and Joseph Spanjers, *Flight Capital and Illicit Financial Flows to and from Myanmar: 1960–2013* (Washington DC: Global Financial Integrity, 2015). <https://www.researchgate.net/profile/Dev_Kar3/publication/283090940_Flight_Capital_and_Illicit_Financial_Flows_to_and_from_Myanmar_1960-2013/links/562a8f3708aef25a2440251e.pdf>.

14. Since Chinese import values are reported to UN Comtrade Database on c.i.f basis, they are converted to f.o.b basis with insurance and freight cost factor of 10 per cent in line with standard factor used in the IMF's Direction of Trade Statistics. The difference between the resulting value and reported Burmese export value for the same year is reported as illicit flow for 2014.
15. See Htar Htar Khin, "Foreign Interest Sparks Office Rental Surge: Agents," *Myanmar Times*, 30 May 2011 <http://www.mmtimes.com/index.php/business/property-news/2670-foreign-interest-sparks-office-rental-surge-agents.html>.
16. A substantial portion of the borrowed funds from the banking system might have been diverted to real estate sector. Among the Burmese citizens' investments authorized by Myanmar Investment Commission, sectors that used real estate as the major input (construction, hotel and tourism, property development, industrial estate) attracted the majority (59%) of investments in over ten years (Feb. 2004 through Apr. 2015) period.
17. The highest 2015 vacancy rate forecast by Colliers International for Yangon among the regional cities in Table 5.1 also possibly reflected a slowdown in the market by 2014–15.
18. This boom apparently came to a virtual standstill since the end of the second quarter of the 2014–15 fiscal year. There were reports of far fewer transactions completed in the real estate sector in major cities. See Myat Nyein Aye 2014, Toe Wai Aung 2014, Carlisle 2015, and Zay Yar Lin 2016.
19. Quoted in Myat Nyein Aye, "Large Increase in Building Permits," *Myanmar Times*, 2 March 2015 <http://www.mmtimes.com/index.php/business/property-news/13309-large-increase-in-building-permits.html>.
20. See Mieno's contribution to this volume.
21. In early American banking, "bank notes" issued by individual banks were used as currency. As these bank notes were linked to real assets which the banks accepted as collateral from borrowers, they represented ownership interest on a fraction of collateral real estate. See Mason Gaffney, "3. Money, Credit, and Crisis," *American Journal of Economics and Sociology* 68, no. 4 (2009): 983–1038.
22. Denise DiPasquale and William C. Wheaton, *Urban Economics and Real Estate Markets* (Englewood Cliffs, NJ: Prentice Hall, 1995).
23. The price = rental income/interest rates. The relationship between rent and price is akin to Earnings to Price ratio (EP ratio) in equity investment. Yield of real estate investments is calculated as (rent/price) for the investors. The yield is taken as exogenously determined as it depends on the level of interest rates and returns to other assets in the broader economy.
24. The rise of urban land prices in Japan triggered by the need for office space in central business district, as described by Mera in Mera and Renaud 2000, has similarities with urban real estate cycles in other countries. For cities in Canada, see Buckley 1952. For construction cycles, see Solow 1962 and

Grebler and Burns 1982; for housing market stock and flow models, see Maisel 1963, Kearl 1979, and Smith 1969.

25. Joseph E. Stiglitz and Andrew Weiss, "Credit Rationing in Markets with Imperfect Information," *American Economic Review* 71, no. 3 (1981): 393.
26. Mason Gaffney, "3. Money, Credit, and Crisis," *American Journal of Economics and Sociology* 68, no. 4 (2009): 983–1038.

References

Buckley, K.A.H. 1952. "Urban Building and Real Estate Fluctuations in Canada." *The Canadian Journal of Economics and Political Science* 18, no. 1: 41 <https://doi.org/10.2307/138533>.

Carlisle, Peter. 2015. "Construction Slows down in Yangon." 24 December <http://www.thailand-construction.com/construction-slows-down-in-yangon/> [accessed 16 January 2017].

DiPasquale, Denise and William C. Wheaton. 1995. *Urban Economics and Real Estate Markets*. Englewood Cliffs, NJ: Prentice Hall.

Gaffney, Mason. 2009. "3. Money, Credit, and Crisis." *American Journal of Economics and Sociology* 68, no. 4: 983–1038.

Grebler, Leo and Leland S. Burns. 1982. "Construction Cycles in the United States Since World War II." *Journal of the American Real Estate and Urban Economics Association* 10, no. 2: 123–51.

Htar Htar Khin. 2011. "Foreign Interest Sparks Office Rental Surge: Agents." *Myanmar Times*. 30 May <http://www.mmtimes.com/index.php/business/property-news/2670-foreign-interest-sparks-office-rental-surge-agents.html> [accessed 11 May 2016].

Kar, Dev and Joseph Spanjers. 2015. *Flight Capital and Illicit Financial Flows to and from Myanmar: 1960–2013*. Washington DC: Global Financial Integrity <https://www.researchgate.net/profile/Dev_Kar3/publication/283090940_Flight_Capital_and_Illicit_Financial_Flows_to_and_from_Myanmar_1960-2013/links/562a8f3708aef25a2440251e.pdf> [accessed 2 December 2017].

Kearl, J.R. 1979. "Inflation, Mortgage, and Housing." *Journal of Political Economy* 8, no. 5: 1115–38.

Mera, Koichi. 2000. "Land Price Ascent and Government Response in Japan." In *Asia's Financial Crisis and the Role of Real Estate*, ed. Koichi Mera and Bertrand Renaud, pp. 27–63. Armonk, NY: M.E. Sharpe.

Mera, Koichi and Bertrand Renaud, eds. 2000. *Asia's Financial Crisis and the Role of Real Estate*. Armonk, NY: M.E. Sharpe.

Myat Nyein Aye. 2014. "Yangon Market Losing Its Steam." *Myanmar Times*. 18 May <http://www.mmtimes.com/index.php/business/property-news/10396-yangon-market-losing-its-steam.html> [accessed 4 November 2016].

_____. 2015. "Large Increase in Building Permits." *Myanmar Times*. 2 March <http://www.mmtimes.com/index.php/business/property-news/13309-large-increase-in-building-permits.html> [accessed 3 November 2016].

Nickell, Stephen and Daphne Nicolitsas. 1999. "How Does Financial Pressure Affect Firms?" *European Economic Review*, no. 8: 1435.

Sherman J. Maisel. 1963. "A Theory of Fluctuations in Residential Construction Starts." *The American Economic Review*, no. 3: 359.

Smith, Lawrence B. 1969. "A Model of the Canadian Housing and Mortgage Markets." *Journal of Political Economy*, no. 5: 795.

Solow, Robert M. 1962. "Technical Progress, Capital Formation, and Economic Growth." *The American Economic Review*, no. 2: 76.

Stiglitz, Joseph E. and Andrew Weiss. 1981. "Credit Rationing in Markets with Imperfect Information." *American Economic Review* 71, no. 3: 393.

Toe Wai Aung. 2014. "Sales Sluggish in Yangon." *Myanmar Times*. 10 November <http://www.mmtimes.com/index.php/special-features/200-property-2014/12241-sales-sluggish-in-yangon.html> [accessed 4 February 2017].

Zay Yar Lin. 2016. "Construction Industry Calls for Tax Change." *Myanmar Times*. 4 November <http://www.mmtimes.com/index.php/business/property-news/23488-construction-industry-calls-for-tax-change.html> [accessed 5 November 2016].

CHAPTER 6

Myanmar's Environmental Governance in Transition: The Case of the Extractive Industries Transparency Initiative

*Marjanneke J. Vijge and Adam Simpson**

Introduction

Though still one of the least developed countries in the world, Myanmar is undergoing rapid economic transformations as it opens up its borders to trade with regional and global markets.[1] While the country's social and economic activity is dominated by agriculture, the largest source of economic growth and foreign exchange is the extractive industries sector. Myanmar is rich in natural resources, particularly gas, oil, timber, gemstones and minerals, which form the main source of revenue for the Myanmar government.[2]

Despite the resultant opportunities for Myanmar's economic development, its wealth in natural resources and the resulting influx of Foreign Direct Investment also pose significant challenges. Historically, the exploitation of natural resources in Myanmar has been prioritized over environmental protection. In the past decades, Myanmar has seen a steady shift from small-scale and relatively low-impact extractive industries, towards large-scale and more environmentally damaging projects. The main environmental problems caused by extractive industries are air, water and soil pollution, soil erosion, deforestation, and the destruction of watersheds. These problems particularly affect poor and marginalized communities that are often based in ethnic minority regions. These areas have been subjected to extensive resource exploitation, sometimes as a result of ceasefires between ethnic armed groups and the military.[3] Many parts of the extractive industries sector are characterized by militarization and/or ethnic conflict, resulting in widespread displacement and severe human rights abuses.[4]

The transition, therefore, towards coherent and effective environmental governance is crucial to Myanmar's national development. An important part of this transition is the implementation of the Extractive Industries Transparency Initiative (EITI) in Myanmar. The EITI is an international standard to promote open and accountable governance of the extractive industries sector through enhanced transparency and multi-stakeholder dialogue. Launched in 2002, the EITI standard is currently implemented by over 50 countries around the world. The EITI in Myanmar has provided a stimulus for both civil society engagement as well as more awareness of the social and environmental impacts of extractive industries in the country. We therefore employ the EITI as a prism to assess Myanmar's environmental governance transition and its impact on both these areas.

This chapter proceeds in four main sections. The first section sets out our research questions and describes natural resource governance in Myanmar and the associated environmental governance transition. The second and third sections assess whether the EITI in Myanmar (MEITI) can stimulate more sustainable governance of the extractive industries sector, using the empowerment of civil society organizations (CSOs) and the management of social and environmental impacts as key indicators. The fourth section considers the EITI within Myanmar's wider regulatory reform process. The conclusion reflects on the conditions under which the MEITI might result in more sustainable governance of the extractive industries sector.

Environmental Governance and the EITI in Myanmar

One of the main challenges in sustainably managing Myanmar's extractive industries sector is the lack of government capacity, combined with high levels of secrecy and corruption.[5] In 2018 Myanmar ranked 132nd of the 180 countries on Transparency International's Corruption Perception Index.[6] In 2017 Myanmar scored 83rd of the 89 evaluated countries on the Resource Governance Index, a measure of transparency and accountability in the oil, gas, and mining sector.[7] Until Myanmar's political and economic reform process commenced, no legal provisions existed for information disclosure, revenue reporting, public participation, or the right to review or appeal in the extractive industries sector.[8] Historically, the governance of this sector has been characterized by poor coordination between the different ministries, with no policy framework or vision for the development of the sector.[9] In areas with high levels of militarization, alternative forms of natural resource governance sometimes co-exist, conflict or overlap with governance systems developed by the line ministries.[10]

Myanmar's capacity to manage the adverse environmental and social impacts of the extractive industries sector is also very low.[11] Before the reform process, very few regulations existed to control the environmental and social impacts of the extractive industries sector, resulting in large information gaps regarding the actual impacts of the extractive industries sector.[12] The governance of natural resources at the sub-national level is severely limited. According to the 2008 Constitution, state and regional governments are merely authorized to enact national laws, and can only collect an insignificant portion of the taxes from extractive industries.[13]

Given these conditions, many have argued that Myanmar exemplifies the condition known as the "resource curse": the apparent paradox that countries rich in oil, gas, and minerals have lower human development rates, as well as poorly developed institutional and regulatory frameworks to govern extractives, resulting in low levels of accountability and high levels of corruption and conflict.[14]

Apart from increased economic development and its associated environmental, social, and governance challenges, the recent reform process in Myanmar is accompanied by a transition in Myanmar's environmental governance. In 2011 the Ministry of Environmental Conservation and Forestry was established, which the National League for Democracy (NLD) government merged with the Ministry of Mines in 2016 to form the Ministry of Natural Resources and Environmental Conservation. In 2012 an Environmental Conservation Law was adopted, which, for the first time, provided an overarching environmental law in the country that regulates new investment projects.[15] Nevertheless, it was only in January 2016, after several years of drafting, that Myanmar launched its first Environmental (and Social) Impact Assessment procedures along with Environmental Quality Standards that aim to assess and limit the adverse environmental and social impacts of investment projects.[16]

An important part of Myanmar's environmental governance transition is the implementation of the Extractive Industries Transparency Initiative (EITI). Countries that are candidate or compliant to the EITI are required to disclose information about payments, production, export, licenses, license allocations, and contracts between oil, gas, and mining companies and government agencies. EITI-implementing countries are also required to collaborate with civil society and extractive companies by establishing a multi-stakeholder group (MSG) that oversees the implementation of the EITI in the country. Transparency is often seen as a key solution to corruption, particularly in the natural resources sector.[17] Though the EITI's narrow mandate is to enhance transparency of revenue flows in the extractive industries sector, its broader vision is to help countries prevent the resource curse by guaranteeing that their abundance in natural resources leads to "sustainable economic growth that contributes to sustainable development and poverty reduction."[18]

Myanmar became candidate to the EITI in July 2014. The EITI process was seen as a "central part" of Myanmar's democratic reform process.[19] The vision of the EITI in Myanmar is "to realise the good governance and sustainable development of the extractive industries for the long-term interest of the people and nation."[20] After relatively quick progress in establishing a functional MSG and in data collection and consolidation, Myanmar managed to produce its first EITI report in January 2016. Its second report was due in March 2017, but because of the governmental transition in early 2016, the MSG was disbanded for more than a year.[21] However, Myanmar successfully applied for an extension, and made quick progress again since the MSG was re-established in April 2017. Myanmar's 2nd and 3rd EITI reports were published in March 2018, and its 4th report followed in March 2019. Myanmar's validation commenced in July 2018 and has been finalized in October 2019, resulting in the decision that Myanmar has made "meaningful progress" in the overall implementation of the EITI.

The MEITI process has created high expectations, not only among some of the highest levels of government, but also among many CSOs. Due to a lack of grievance mechanisms and regulatory frameworks to address adverse social and environmental impacts in extractive industries, many CSOs view the EITI as a tool to enhance transparency and accountability through the entire extractive industry value chain, address environmental problems and human rights abuses, and enhance stakeholder participation in decision-making regarding extractive industries.[22] The MEITI is also expected to stimulate wider regulatory reforms, such as amendments to laws related to the sharing of information and the mitigation of adverse environmental and social impacts of the extractive industries sector.[23]

A key question for Myanmar's future is, however, whether the environmental governance transition of which the MEITI is part will be comprehensive enough to ameliorate the deleterious effects of natural resource extraction that are drastically increased by the far-reaching and rapid economic transformations. Will this environmental governance transition enable Myanmar to prevent the resource curse and to sustainably govern its rapidly growing extractive industries sector? Considering the MEITI as a central component of the environmental governance transition, we assess whether, how and under what conditions the MEITI can stimulate a more sustainable governance of the extractive industries sector with due consideration of its environmental and social impacts.

In doing so, we focus on two key aspects in the governance of extractive industries: first, the empowerment of civil society organizations (CSOs); and, second, the management of social and environmental impacts of extractive industries. Regarding the first aspect, the EITI requires countries to realise a "full, independent, active and effective participation of civil society."[24] The EITI is expected to lead to the empowerment of citizens, not only through enhanced political space of CSOs to contribute to the EITI process, but also through enhanced technical, financial, and institutional capacity of CSOs.[25] We assess the levels of involvement of CSOs in the on-going MEITI process at national and sub-national levels. Since the MSG is appointed by the government, CSOs that are more independent on or more critical of the government may be excluded from and undermined in the EITI MSG.[26] Apart from CSOs' participation in the MEITI MSG, we also assess the effects of the MEITI on the ability of CSOs to build their knowledge and capacity to organize themselves and influence the governance of the extractive industries sector. The questions addressed in this chapter are how, under what conditions, and to what varying degrees the MEITI empowers (or disempowers) different types of CSOs at the national and sub-national level.

Regarding the second aspect—the management of environmental and social impacts of extractive industries—according to former President U Thein Sein, one of MEITI's aims was to prevent the extractive industry from having negative social and environmental impacts.[27] Since the EITI is meant to enhance transparency rather than directly address the adverse impacts of the extractive industries sector, we study the indirect ways in which the MEITI influences the management of such impacts. We focus on whether and how the MEITI might stimulate (discussion of) broader regulatory reform of the extractive industries sector, as well as whether and how it enhances opportunities to hold extractive industries accountable for their actions.

The chapter directly and indirectly draws on over 80 face-to-face and Skype interviews with representatives of CSOs, extractive industry companies, and national and sub-national government agencies, both in

Myanmar and elsewhere, gathered since Myanmar's decision to join the EITI in 2012.

MEITI: Empowering CSOs?

Historically, civil society and community organizations in Myanmar have had very little to no involvement in governmental decision-making processes or politically sensitive topics, instead focusing on the provision of social services at the village level.[28] The Myanmar EITI process was the first formal process that resulted in dialogues between government agencies, companies, and civil society. That natural resource governance is now openly discussed between these three stakeholder groups was previously unthinkable within the Myanmar context.[29] A Myanmar delegation which attended the 2013 Global EITI Conference in Sydney and associated Australian mine visits, for example, established the first meaningful interactions between environmental activists and government representatives in the country's history. As it was held outside the country, it forced these groups to interact in meeting rooms and small buses for the duration of the visit. Initially, representatives of the Myanmar Centre for Economic and Social Development (CESD)—a national think tank which became Myanmar's in-country MEITI secretariat—struggled to bring both government representatives and civil society representatives together: meeting rooms would initially be split with each group talking amongst themselves.[30] The 2013 trip therefore became a key trust-building exercise for hitherto estranged communities within Myanmar's society, as did the MEITI more generally.[31] Eventually, the persistent close proximity throughout the excursion, along with the efforts by CESD members, resulted in a relative thaw in relations between the various groups, establishing a limited rapport that, despite regular ructions, provided the basis for future negotiations. This trip—and the MEITI more generally—can therefore be considered a key moment in the recent development of state-civil society relations in Myanmar.

Throughout the rest of 2013, the MEITI MSG was gradually established and it met for the first time in February 2014. The role of the MSG is to make key decisions regarding the implementation of the MEITI. Discussions about MEITI implementation provided CSOs with unprecedented opportunities to be involved in the governance of natural resources and to empower themselves in broader EITI-related debates, awareness-raising activities, as well as monitoring of environmental and social impacts of extractive industries. The MEITI process has helped

CSOs to more effectively select, demand, check, and collect information with which they can hold actors to account, though limited accountability mechanisms still restrict the extent to which CSOs can evoke action from responsible actors (see below).[32] Besides national level MSG discussions, multi-stakeholder discussions related to the MEITI—and natural resource governance more broadly—also take place in some state levels, organized under the so-called EITI sub-national coordination units.[33,34] Though notifications have been issued for the establishment of such units in all states and regions of Myanmar, five units were operational at the time of writing.[35] Vijge et al. 2019[36] showed that in Magway and Mandalay—the early adopters of the sub-national coordination units—CSO involvement in multi-stakeholder discussions has significantly enhanced self-organization and empowerment of CSOs, and increased trust and understanding between governmental, civil society, and private sector actors.

Overall, the MEITI has resulted in enhanced opportunities for civil society to voice their opinion on natural resource governance issues in Myanmar, with CSOs involved in the MSG generally stating satisfaction with their role in the MEITI process at both national and sub-national levels.[37] Despite the very active role of CSOs in the MEITI process, however, not all CSOs are equally represented in the MSG. Those CSOs that have previously been in exile and are still operating from neighboring countries such as Thailand, for example, did not always participate in MSG meetings.[38] Some of these organizations are of the opinion that the MEITI process is a form of window dressing rather than a way to address the core issues related to natural resource governance in Myanmar.[39] Adding to the inequalities between CSOs is that those operating in Nay Pyi Taw or Yangon are often privileged over CSOs operating in rural areas and (post-)conflict zones, a result replicated in other environmental areas.[40,41] In these latter areas, militias often dominate mining projects, and regional civil society groups do not yet have the freedom of speech that Nay Pyi Taw- or Yangon-based, often Burmese, groups have started to gain.[42] Within the national MEITI MSG, CSOs with an ethnic minority background are relatively disadvantaged over Burmese CSOs.[43]

Notwithstanding the previously mentioned high expectations among many CSOs of the MEITI process, not all CSOs are equally positive about the process, mainly due to a lack of trust in the government. Though the MEITI process has significantly contributed to building trust between government, civil society actors, and companies, mistrust between those stakeholders has not yet disappeared.[44] Myanmar has a long history of civil society oppression and domination by the central state, its army, and local state and non-state militias. For decades, grievances in the extractive industries sector have been resolved using force rather than political dialogue.[45] Border-based and ethnic groups tend to be much more critical of the EITI process than those based in Yangon. Some argue that Yangon-based CSOs, driven by funding opportunities from international donors and soothed by promises of governmental reform processes, have reduced their criticism of the government's actions.[46] In 2014 and 2015, negotiations between government and civil society representatives at times resulted in threats by civil society representatives to walk away from the MEITI process, even as those within the MSG tend to be less radical.[47] Relations between communities and the business sector have commonly been poor or even hostile in Myanmar. Until 2012, no legal provisions existed for the participation or consultation of local communities in investment projects, and extractive industry companies rarely consult, let alone involve, local communities before starting their investments.[48]

Apart from initiating civil society involvement in governmental decision-making processes, the MEITI process has also resulted in the establishment of Myanmar's first ever CSO umbrella organization: the Myanmar Alliance for Transparency and Accountability (MATA). MATA was established in April 2014 to facilitate CSOs' engagement in the MEITI process and demand transparency and accountability in the natural resource sector. Through an election process, CSO members are selected from all states and regions in Myanmar to represent CSOs in the national MEITI MSG. MATA has brought various opportunities for CSOs to be involved in multi-stakeholder processes related to, in particular, the governance of natural resources. MATA regularly holds workshops and trainings for its members on natural resource governance and related topics. Apart from being involved in the national MSG, MATA members also operate at sub-national levels, for example in the earlier-mentioned sub-national coordination units. Such enhanced civil society action and empowerment, as well as the resulting (improved) relations with governmental and private sector representatives are often more important than the disclosure of information from the MEITI reports alone.[49]

Despite this, inequality between CSOs persists. Partly due to ethnic tensions, not all CSOs want to be members of MATA. This has resulted in disagreement among CSOs over whether or not CSO representatives in the MSG are required to be members of MATA.[50] In addition, some CSOs that were originally part of MATA and represented in the MSG have left the organization. Reasons to leave included the marginalization of ethnic and border-based civil society groups by Burmese CSOs, and personal and political conflicts within MATA, which also cut across the ethnic and non-ethnic divide.[51] While MATA significantly improved coordination amongst CSOs and strengthened their position within the MSG, the above provides a cautionary tale on attempts to homogenize civil society representation in formal governance fora such as the MEITI MSG.

MEITI: Addressing Environmental and Social Impacts?

Citizens and CSOs in Myanmar often lack basic information such as who owns extractive industry companies that operate in their region—whether private companies, state- or military-owned companies, or non-state militias—what the costs and benefits of such extractive industries are, and who bears or receives these costs and benefits. This severely limits the ability of citizens and CSOs to hold extractive industries to account for their social and environmental impacts.[52] The MEITI reports that have been published so far provided crucial information on, among others, the production, export, licenses, legal ownership, and revenues from the oil and gas sector and—though to a much lesser extent—the mining sector. The fourth report consists of almost 400 pages of information about Myanmar's extractive industries, in addition to an equally lengthy supplementary report. However, the MEITI reports have some crucial omissions. For example, they cover only a small fraction of the jade and gemstone sector—much of which consists of sales outside the so-called Emporium, including illegal trade—did not report on beneficial ownership (disclosure is mandatory from 2020) and export data, and did not disclose the terms and allocation procedures of contracts and licenses of extractive industries (the fourth EITI report recommends disclosure from 2021). There were also concerns regarding the reliability of data in the MEITI reports, which, according to the latest report, have only partially been addressed.[53] Myanmar has long had no reporting procedures, and there has not been a culture of information disclosure within the government of Myanmar. The MEITI process stimulated information disclosure by some of the highest ministerial levels and companies, but it takes time and strong political commitment for this to become common practice among all ministries and companies, as well as the lower and sub-national levels of government and state- or military-owned companies.[54,55]

Though the EITI can provide crucial information about resource extraction, the EITI does not require countries to include information about environmental and social impacts, and create complaint or grievance mechanisms for citizens to use the information and hold industries to account for their adverse impacts. During MSG meetings in Myanmar, CSOs repeatedly demanded action of government agencies and companies to address the environmental and social impacts and include impact assessments in the MEITI report. The government's recurrent response was that the MEITI MSG was not the right venue to discuss these issues, and that EITI reporting should be kept within its narrow scope and not cover environmental and social impact assessments of extractive industries.[56] As a result, CSOs' demands to incorporate such assessments have not yet been met in the MEITI reports.

However, with conflicts over natural resources openly discussed among government, CSO and company representatives in both national and sub-national multi-stakeholder discussion groups, it seems that repeated demands to address the adverse impacts of extractive industries can no longer be ignored.[57] In 2014, for example, in a highly unusual process within the EITI, MATA was able to request a special meeting of the EITI secretariat with the Myanmar government to discuss the adverse social and environmental impacts of the notorious Letpadaung copper mine in Monywa.[58] MATA threatened to withdraw from the national MEITI process if the government failed to address the adverse environmental and social impacts of the mine, accusing it of breaching its EITI commitments.[59] Although no decisions were taken during the special meeting, the meeting did trigger media attention and increased pressure on responsible actors to address the mine's impacts.[60] Partially as a response to this, MATA, in collaboration with international non-governmental organizations (the Natural Resource Governance Institute, Publish What You Pay and Global Witness) helped to develop and pilot a reporting template that can be used worldwide as a tool to document potential breaches of the EITI Civil Society Protocol related to not only the EITI process but also natural resource governance more broadly.[61] This tool could help enhance the opportunities for civil society to address the social and environmental impacts of extractive industries.[62]

Another example of how the MEITI increases pressure on government officials to address the adverse consequences of resource extraction are the so-called "road shows" that CSOs in Magway, sometimes joined by a regional director from the EITI international secretariat, organize to create awareness around the EITI. These road shows help to put pressure on government officials to be accountable to their constituencies at the sub-national level.[63]

A final example of how the MEITI process has provided platforms to discuss broader natural resource governance issues is the earlier-mentioned

EITI sub-national coordination units.[64] The MEITI facilitated discussions of environmental and social impacts of extractive industries in Magway and Mandalay, the early adopters of these units. These discussions are important in improving (accountability) relations between the stakeholder groups. As a result, CSOs—sometimes together with government and company representatives—monitor and demand accountability for the impacts of resource extraction in their region. So far, however, the units have resulted in little concrete decisions or actions taken on natural reource governance in these regions.[65] It is important to note that the subnational coordination units have mostly been established in the seemingly less problematic Burmese regions of Myanmar, and not yet, for example, in the ethnic state of Kachin, where many of the ethnic conflicts around illegal mining take place.[66] Even so, the (future) establishment of these sub-national units, initiated as a result of the MEITI process, clearly shows that Myanmar is taking efforts to go beyond the narrow scope of the EITI to discuss (though not yet address) environmental and social impacts of extractive industries at the sub-national level. Full establishment of these units may eventually lead to effective use of the publication of sub-national level data, which is a requirement of the EITI standard since 2016.[67]

While, clearly, the MEITI has stimulated discussions of environmental and social impacts of extractive industries, some CSOs have criticized the government's focus on improving Myanmar's international business reputation to attract Foreign Direct Investment without due consideration of the potential adverse impacts.[68] The business environment in Myanmar is one of the worst in the world,[69] and the EITI is expected to improve this and thereby significantly increase the rapidly growing influx of Foreign Direct Investment into Myanmar.[70] Though this brings economic opportunities, many Myanmar citizens are of the opinion that such foreign investment should not be stimulated without first establishing a sound environmental and social safeguards framework for such investments.[71] Some CSOs warn that if the EITI is implemented in its most narrow form without consideration of how it might be integrated with the broader institutional and regulatory framework for the extractive industries sector, the EITI's impacts may be very limited.[72] Crucially, some of the more radical civil society groups, particularly those based in ethnic states and on the border, assert that the EITI process takes away attention and funding—both among government agencies and among civil society groups—from the more significant problems such as human rights abuses and militarization resulting from natural resource extraction in, among others, the ethnic minority areas of Myanmar.[73]

MEITI and Wider Regulatory Reform

For the EITI in Myanmar to achieve its aim of realising "good governance and sustainable development of the extractive industries,"[74] it is necessary for the governance norms associated with the EITI to be taken up by various arms of the government so that the EITI does not operate in isolation. This is particularly difficult to achieve in Myanmar because, historically, the Myanmar government has been characterized by line ministries operating in relative isolation from one another with very little fiscal, administrative, legal, or political decentralization to sub-national government agencies. One of the challenges to implementing the EITI in Myanmar are conflicting interests between different ministries.[75] It remains unclear to date whether the MEITI process has, or will have, significant effects on the coordination between line ministries and any (future) decentralization process.[76] The MEITI process seems to have done more to facilitate interactions between civil society and the government than to facilitate coordination between different government departments.[77] The EITI process is carried by a small number of ministers. The Ministry of Planning and Finance (formerly the Ministry of Finance and the Ministry of National Planning) is assigned to lead the process, but has historically been weak relative to other ministries, and does not yet have full capacity to lead the process. Among lower placed government officials, there seems to be much less enthusiasm to implement the EITI and disclose information.[78]

Overall, the EITI process has not been a priority issue for the NLD government.[79] One small success that could (at least partially) be attributed to the MEITI is the inter-ministerial working committee to discuss natural resource governance issues in Myanmar. The establishment of this committee in 2015/16 was likely stimulated by the MEITI process.[80] Other examples of a potential spill-over effect of the EITI on wider regulatory reform processes are the side-meetings among civil society, company, and government representatives to discuss the amendments of the mines and forest law. The EITI process has likely set the stage for these three stakeholders to meet, not only within the MEITI MSG, but also in other fora.[81]

A parallel development to the EITI within Myanmar's environmental governance transition is the publication of the Environmental Impact

Assessment (EIA) procedures to assess and limit the adverse environmental and social impacts of both domestic and foreign investment projects.[82] Since their effective implementation is still limited, it is too early to assess their impact on the broader environmental governance system. EIA reports have been required for Foreign Direct Investment projects ever since the Foreign Investment Law—now superseded by the Myanmar Investment Law—was promulgated in late 2012. As a result, a burgeoning environmental consultancy industry is producing the mandatory environmental and social impact assessment reports, though the quality of these assessments varies significantly.[83] The main challenges for the government are to establish rigorous processes to facilitate and review companies' EIAs and enforce the environmental quality guidelines. Some international organizations, such as the Asian Development Bank and the Norwegian Environment Agency, which were absent during military rule,[84] now provide support on this. The EIA procedures require companies and responsible governmental departments to disclose the EIA reports to the public, though this is only done to a limited extent.

As the EIA assessment and reporting capacity improves, both within the Myanmar government and the private sector, it should not only create crucial information about the social and environmental impacts of extractive industries, but also make such information widely accessible. Combined with data from the MEITI report regarding, for example, legal and (in future) beneficial ownership of extractive industry operators, the information disclosed via EIA reports will be crucial for CSOs to demand accountability of these operators for the adverse impacts citizens experience from extractive industries. Whether this also leads to enhanced answerability depends on parallel reform processes, as we argue in the conclusion.

Conclusion

This chapter discussed whether the environmental governance transition in Myanmar will be robust enough to ensure sustainability in Myanmar's rapidly growing extractive industries sector. Considering the Myanmar Extractive Industries Transparency Initiative (MEITI) as a key component of this transition, we assessed whether, how, and under what conditions the MEITI might stimulate civil society empowerment and the management of adverse impacts of extractive industries. We argued that the MEITI has increased the empowerment of civil society and stimulated discussions of environmental and social impacts of the extractive industries in Myanmar. The MEITI process has created unique opportunities for

CSOs, government, and companies to discuss not only the implementation of the EITI, but also natural resource governance more broadly, though ethnic and Burmese CSOs do not have equal opportunities for involvement. The MEITI also resulted in the establishment of the first ever civil society network in Myanmar, which greatly enhanced CSOs' opportunities to build their capacity and interact with government and private sector representatives, even though some (perhaps unavoidable) conflicts between CSOs persist. Such conflicts also show that any attempt to homogenize civil society representation within the national MEITI MSG is bound to be problematic.

For enhanced civil society empowerment and participation to be meaningful and equitable, discussions around natural resource governance need to take place at both the national and the sub-national levels, and include a fair representation of Burmese and ethnic organizations. Since ethnic organizations are often based in their own region, sub-national coordination units need to be established and replicated in all states and regions, as per Myanmar's current plans. Though such coordination units go beyond the mandate of the EITI standard—which requires sub-national reporting but not the establishment of sub-national MSGs—research has shown that these are important for CSOs to voice their opinion and for natural resource governance issues to be discussed within the region. While the discussions in the coordination units have been useful to exchange information and views and for civil society to put pressure on government and extractive industry representatives to address adverse impacts, these units generally lack the mandate to make decisions or take action.[85] This inhibits CSOs from truly influencing natural resource governance and addressing the social and environmental impacts of extractive industries. Any form of political decentralization that could address this would require amendments to the 2008 Constitution as part of a broader federalization process, which would require the support of the military in parliament.[86]

The MEITI reports fill important gaps of information about the extractive industries sector. For the EITI to be effective, however, information disclosure needs to become common practice among different arms of the government, including higher- and lower-placed union level ministries and departments, sub-national government agencies, and military- and state-owned companies. This cultural shift is essential in order to avoid the mismanagement associated with the resource curse. Such a shift was also recommended in the fourth EITI report, calling for the "institutionalization of EITI policies and legislation."[87]

For the EITI to become meaningful, it also needs to coincide with wider regulatory reform processes. Transparency is often associated with more accountable governance. In order for transparency to enhance accountability, however, actors need both complete information and the ability to use this information to hold others accountable.[88] At present, information on the environmental and social impacts of extractive industries is not required in EITI reports, though some countries—such as the Philippines—voluntarily include it in their report. In order for the EITI to help address these impacts, information on such impacts needs to be publicly available. The launch of the Environmental Impact Assessment procedures in Myanmar should help create such information sources and make it more accessible. Hence, ongoing efforts to improve EIA reporting by companies and to advance the review process by the responsible government departments could increase the effectiveness of the EITI in stimulating the sustainable governance of the extractive industries sector. However, the disclosure of information alone does not help to improve natural resource governance in Myanmar, shown by the limited use and uptake of information from the first MEITI report by CSOs. What is needed in addition to information disclosure are complaint and grievance mechanisms for citizens and civil society actors to hold extractive industries to account for any adverse environmental and social consequences.[89] Repeated demands by CSOs for grievance mechanisms to be established and attempts to discuss and address such consequences during MSG meetings—which are not primarily designed for this—are indicative of the lack of such mechanisms.

While the MEITI reports contain crucial information that, given the right conditions, might enhance the ability of CSOs to hold extractive industries accountable, they avoided many of the most troublesome areas of natural resource extraction in Myanmar, which often harbor the most severe social and environmental impacts. The reports did not, for example, cover the bulk of the extremely opaque jade and gemstone sector, nor did they report on illegal or unlicensed, artisanal, and small-scale natural resource extraction. The EITI requires that subsequent reports go beyond the scope of earlier reports and implement their recommendations. Notwithstanding the huge challenges, therefore, for the MEITI to become effective in promoting the sustainable governance of the extractive industries sector, future reports need to include Myanmar's more opaque sectors, a recommendation that was already included in the first MEITI report. As natural resource extraction in Myanmar is inextricably linked with conflicts between ethnic groups and the Myanmar military, enhancing transparency through the MEITI will only have limited effect without an ongoing peace process in the country. Though natural resource extraction is being examined in discussions around the ceasefire agreement, such discussions do not yet do justice to the crucial role natural resources play in the continuation of civil conflicts in Myanmar.

In short, the MEITI has created unique opportunities for civil society to become involved in and organize themselves around natural resource governance issues in Myanmar, including in discussions of the social and environmental impacts of extractive industries. It also provides crucial information that actors may use to hold extractive industries to account for adverse impacts. We argue, however, that for the MEITI to stimulate the sustainable governance of extractive industries, it needs to cover the more problematic and opaque areas of natural resource extraction, be mainstreamed in the work of different national and sub-national government agencies, and be accompanied by parallel governmental reform processes. Thus, whether or not Myanmar's environmental governance transition is robust enough to ensure sustainability in Myanmar's rapidly growing extractive industries sector still remains to be seen.

Notes

* Marjanneke J. Vijge wrote this chapter as part of her postdoctoral research, which was funded by the Niels Stensen Fellowship. She would like to thank the Niels Stensen Fellowship, without which her research would not have been possible. Adam Simpson wrote much of his contribution to this chapter during a 6-month Research Fellowship at the Centre for Southeast Asian Studies (CSEAS), Kyoto University. He would like to thank Pavin Chachavalpongpun, Yoshihiro Nakanishi and then-Centre Director, Yasuyuki Kono, for making the Fellowship possible. Finally, the authors would like to heartily thank all the interviewees for their time and the invaluable information they provided about the EITI in Myanmar.

1. Asian Development Outlook, "Financing Asia's Future Growth" (Mandaluyong City, Philippines, 2015); Adam Simpson, Nicholas Farrelly, and Ian Holliday, eds., *Routledge Handbook of Contemporary Myanmar* (London and New York: Routledge, 2018).
2. Thet Aung Lynn and Mari Oye, "Natural Resources and Subnational Governments in Myanmar: Key Considerations for Wealth Sharing," 2014, <http://www.theigc.org/wp-content/uploads/2014/06/Lynn-Oye-2014-Working-Paper.pdf>; Adam Smith International, "Institutional and Regulatory Assessment of the Extractive Industries in Myanmar," 2015, <http://documents.

worldbank.org/curated/en/504691467992478731/Main-report; John Buchanan, Tom Kramer, and Kevin Woods, "Developing Disparity: Regional Investment in Burma's Borderlands," 2013, http://www.burmalibrary.org/docs14/Burmasborderlands-red.pdf>.

3. Kevin Woods, "Ceasefire capitalism: Military–private partnerships, resource concessions and military-state building in the Burma–China borderlands," *The Journal of Peasant Studies* 38, no. 4 (2011): 747–70.
4. Adam Smith International, "Institutional and Regulatory Assessment of the Extractive Industries in Myanmar."
5. Adam Simpson, "Natural Resources: Wealth and Conflict," in *Myanmar: Politics, Economy and Society*, ed. Adam Simpson and N. Farrelly (London and New York: Routledge, 2020).
6. Transparency International, "Corruption Perception Index," 2018, <http://www.transparency.org/cpi2018/>.
7. Natural Resource Governance Institute, "Resource Governance Index," 2017, <www.resourcegovernanceindex.org>.
8. Global Witness, "The Shell Starts to Crack? Real Owners of Myanmar's Oil and Gas Blocks Come Forward," 2014, <https://www.globalwitness.org/reports/shell-starts-crack/>; Ken Maclean, "Counter-Accounting with Invisible Data: The Struggle for Transparency in Myanmar's Energy Sector," *Political and Legal Anthropology Review* 37, no. 1 (2014): 10–28, doi: 10.1111/plar.12048.
9. Benjamin K. Sovacool, "Environmental Conservation Problems and Possible Solutions in Myanmar," *Contemporary Southeast Asia* 34, no. 2 (2012): 217–48, doi: 10.1355/cs34-2d; European Union, "The Extractive Industries Transparency Initiative (EITI) Options Study: MEITI Guidebook, Proposed Action under Development Cooperation Instrument Strengthening Policy Development to Meet MDGs in Burma/Myanmar," 2013, <http://myanmareiti.org/download/file/fid/102>.
10. Thet Aung Lynn and Mari Oye, "Natural Resources and Subnational Governments in Myanmar: Key Considerations for Wealth Sharing."
11. World Bank, "Myanmar: Ending Poverty and Boosting Shared Prosperity in a Time of Transition. A Systematic Country Diagnostic" (Yangon, Myanmar, 2014), <http://www.worldbank.org/en/news/press-release/2014/12/15/ending-poverty-and-boosting-shared-prosperity-in-myanmar>; Buchanan, Kramer, and Woods, "Developing Disparity: Regional Investment in Burma's Borderlands."
12. Edward L. Webb et al., "Deforestation in the Ayeyarwady Delta and the Conservation Implications of an Internationally-Engaged Myanmar," *Global Environmental Change* 25 (2014): 321–33, doi: 10.1016/j.gloenvcha.2013.10.007; Matthew Smith, "Environmental Governance of Mining in Burma," in *Myanmar: The State, Community and the Environment*, ed. Monique Skidmore and Trevor Wilson (ANU E Press, 2007), pp. 218–45; European Union, "The

Extractive Industries Transparency Initiative (EITI) Options Study: MEITI Guidebook, Proposed Action under Development Cooperation Instrument Strengthening Policy Development to Meet MDGs in Burma/Myanmar."

13. Adam Smith International, "Institutional and Regulatory Assessment of the Extractive Industries in Myanmar"; Thet Aung Lynn and Mari Oye, "Natural Resources and Subnational Governments in Myanmar: Key Considerations for Wealth Sharing."
14. Cullen S. Hendrix and Marcus Noland, "Managing Myanmar's Resource Boom to Lock in Reforms," 2014; David Pick and Htwe Htwe Thein, "Development Failure and the Resource Curse: The Case of Myanmar," *International Journal of Sociology and Social Policy* 30, no. 5/6 (2010): 267–79, doi: 10.1108/01443331011054235; Helen James, "Resources, Rent-Seeking, and Reform in Thailand and Myanmar (Burma): The Economics-Politics Nexus," *Asian Survey* 50, no. 2 (2010): 426–48, doi: 10.1525/as.2010.50.2.426; Peter J. Perry, *Myanmar (Burma) Since 1962: The Failure of Development* (Aldershot: Ashgate, 2007).
15. Adam Simpson, "Starting from Year Zero Environmental Governance in Myanmar," in *Environmental Challenges and Governance: Diverse Perspectives from Asia*, ed. S. Mukherjee and D. Chakraborty (Hoboken: Taylor and Francis, 2015), pp. 152–65, doi: 10.4324/9781315717081.
16. GMS, "Launch Ceremony: EIA Procedure and Environmental Quality Guidelines," *Greater Mekong Subregion Core Environment Program*, 2016, <http://www.gms-eoc.org/events/launch-ceremony-eia-procedure-and-environmental-quality-guidelines>; Adam Simpson, "Environment and Natural Resources," in *Routledge Handbook of Contemporary Myanmar*, ed. Adam Simpson, Nicholas Farrelly, and Ian Holliday (London and New York: Routledge, 2018).
17. Adam Simpson, "Corruption, Investment and Natural Resources," in *International Natural Resources Law, Investment and Sustainability*, ed. Shawkat Alam, Jahid Bhuiyan, and Jona Razzaque (London and New York: Routledge, 2018); Marjanneke J. Vijge, Robin Metcalfe, Linda Wallbott, and Christoph Oberlack, "Governance Transformations to Reverse the Resource Curse? The Extractive Industries Transparency Initiative in Myanmar," *Resources Policy* 61 (2019), doi: 10.1016/j.resourpol.2019.02.006.
18. EITI, "The EITI Standard 2016," Report, p. 11 (Oslo: The EITI International Secretariat, 2016).
19. MEITI, "Myanmar EITI," 2017, <https://eiti.org/Myanmar>.
20. MEITI, "MEITI Candidacy Application Annexes," in *Myanmar Extractive Industries Transparency Initiative (MEITI) Multi-Stakeholder Group (MEITI-MSG) Draft Terms of Reference*, 2014, 1, <https://eiti.org/files/Annex_07052014_op.pdf>.
21. Paul Rogers, Marjanneke J. Vijge, and Min Zar Ni Lin, "Institutionalising the Extractive Industries Transparency Initiative: Lessons Learned from Myanmar's Democratic Transition." Unpublished manuscript, n.d.

22. Interviews with strategic advisor of CSO, 20 September 2016, Yangon; EITI senior technical and policy analyst, 13 September 2016, Yangon; former coordinator of CSOs, 22 September 2016, Yangon; former visiting fellow of national think tank, 1 September 2016, London; and Myanmar focal point of international NGO, 31 August 2016, London.
23. European Union, "The Extractive Industries Transparency Initiative (EITI) Options Study: MEITI Guidebook, Proposed Action under Development Cooperation Instrument Strengthening Policy Development to Meet MDGs in Burma/Myanmar."
24. EITI, "The EITI Standard 2016," Report (Oslo: EITI secretariat, 2016).
25. EITI, "G20 Leaders Confirm Support of the EITI," 2011, <https://eiti.org/news-events/g20-leaders-confirm-support-eiti>; EITI, "The EITI Standard 2016," 2016.
26. Ivar Kolstad and Arne Wiig, "Is Transparency the Key to Reducing Corruption in Resource-Rich Countries?," *World Development* 37, no. 3 (2009): 521–32, doi: 10.1016/j.worlddev.2008.07.002; Susan Ariel Aaronson, "Limited Partnership: Business, Government, Civil Society, and the Public in the Extractive Industries Transparency Initiative (EITI)," *Public Administration and Development* 31, no. 1 (February 2011): 50–63, doi: 10.1002/pad.588; Saule Ospanova, Ingilab Ahmadov, and Emma Wilson, "EITI and Sustainable Development: Lessons and New Challenges for the Caspian Region" (London: IIED, 2013), <https://eiti.org/files/EITI IIED paper.pdf>; Emma Wilson and James Van Alstine, "Localising Transparency: Exploring EITI's Contribution to Sustainable Development" (London, 2014), <http://pubs.iied.org/16555IIED.html>.
27. U Thein Sein, "Speech during the 3rd Anniversary of the President's 'Assumption of Duty', at the Pyidaungsu Hluttaw (Parliament), 26 March 2014," 2014, <http://www.myanmarpresidentoffice.gov.mm/2015en/?q=briefing-room/2014/03/26/id-3496>.
28. Tom Kramer, *Civil Society Gaining Ground: Opportunities for Change and Development in Burma* (Amsterdam: Transnational Institute, Burma Center Netherlands, 2011).
29. Christina Fink and Adam Simpson, "Civil Society," in *Routledge Handbook of Contemporary Myanmar*, ed. Adam Simpson, Nicholas Farrelly, and Ian Holliday (London and New York: Routledge, 2018); Adam Simpson, "Challenging Hydropower Development in Myanmar (Burma): Cross-Border Activism under a Regime in Transition," *Pacific Review* 26, no. 2 (2013): 129–52, doi: 10.1080/09512748.2012.759264; Adam Simpson, *Energy, Governance and Security in Thailand and Myanmar (Burma): A Critical Approach to Environmental Politics in the South* (Copenhagen: NIAS Press, 2017); Adam Simpson and Mattijs Smits, "Transitions to Energy and Climate Security in Southeast Asia: Civil Society Encounters with Illiberalism in

Thailand and Myanmar," *Society and Natural Resources* 31, no. 5 (2018), doi: 10.1080/08941920.2017.1413720.

30. Interview with EITI senior technical and policy analyst, 23 May 2013, Sydney, Australia.
31. Interview with director of think tank, 23 May 2013, Sydney, Australia.
32. Marjanneke J. Vijge, "The (Dis)empowering Effects of Transparency Beyond Information Disclosure: The Extractive Industries Transparency Initiative in Myanmar," *Global Environmental Politics* 18, no. 1 (2018), doi: 10.1162/GLEP_a_00442; Marjanneke J. Vijge, Robin Metcalfe, Linda Wallbott, and Christoph Oberlack, "Governance Transformations to Reverse the Resource Curse? The Extractive Industries Transparency Initiative in Myanmar," *Resources Policy* 61 (2019), doi: 10.1016/j.resourpol.2019.02.006.
33. For an analysis of the MEITI's impacts at the sub-national level, see Marjanneke J. Vijge, Robin Metcalfe, Linda Wallbott, and Christoph Oberlack, "Governance Transformations to Reverse the Resource Curse? The Extractive Industries Transparency Initiative in Myanmar," *Resources Policy* 61 (2019), doi: 10.1016/j.resourpol.2019.02.006.
34. Interviews with strategic advisor of CSO, 20 September 2016, Yangon; and former coordinator of CSOs, 22 September 2016, Yangon.
35. MEITI, "Myanmar EITI Annual Progress Report 2018–2019," June 2019. <https://eiti.org/sites/default/files/documents/apr_2018-2019_final_30-6-2019.pdf>.
36. Marjanneke J. Vijge, Robin Metcalfe, Linda Wallbott, and Christoph Oberlack, "Governance Transformations to Reverse the Resource Curse? The Extractive Industries Transparency Initiative in Myanmar," *Resources Policy* 61 (2019), doi: 10.1016/j.resourpol.2019.02.006.
37. For a full assessment of the effects of the EITI on civil society empowerment in Myanmar, see Marjanneke J. Vijge, "The (Dis)empowering Effects of Transparency Beyond Information Disclosure: The Extractive Industries Transparency Initiative in Myanmar," *Global Environmental Politics* 18, no. 1 (2018), doi: 10.1162/GLEP_a_00442.
38. Interviews with EITI support coordinator of multilateral organization, 6 September 2016, Yangon; and Myanmar focal point of international NGO, 31 August 2016, London.
39. Interviews with Myanmar focal point of international NGO, 31 August 2016, London; and representative of border-based CSO #1, 4 October 2016, Chiang Mai.
40. Adam Simpson and Mattijs Smits, "Transitions to Energy and Climate Security in Southeast Asia: Civil Society Encounters with Illiberalism in Thailand and Myanmar," *Society and Natural Resources* 31, no. 5 (2018), doi: 10.1080/08941920.2017.1413720.
41. Interview with representative of oil company, 17 November 2016, Yangon.

42. Myanmar Centre for Responsible Business, "Civil Society Organisations and the Extractives Industries in Myanmar – A Brief Overview," 2014, <http://myanmar-responsiblebusiness.org/pdf/2014-10-11-Briefing-Paper-CSOs-and-Extractives-Industries-Myanmar.pdf>.
43. Interviews with former director of ethnic CSO, 25 March 2014, Yangon; and EITI senior technical and policy analyst, 7 December 2016, Nay Pyi Taw.
44. Interviews with former director of ethnic CSO, 5 October 2016, Chiang Mai; EITI support coordinator of multilateral organization, 6 September 2016, Yangon; and strategic advisor of CSO, 20 September 2016, Yangon.
45. Adam Smith International, "Institutional and Regulatory Assessment of the Extractive Industries in Myanmar."
46. Interviews with representatives of border-based CSOs #1 and #2, 4 October 2016, Chiang Mai.
47. Adam Simpson, "The Extractive Industries Transparency Initiative: New Openings for Civil Society in Myanmar," in *The Business of Transition: Law Reform, Development and Economics in Myanmar*, ed. Melissa Crouch (Melbourne: Cambridge University Press, 2017); Marjanneke J. Vijge, "The (Dis)empowering Effects of Transparency Beyond Information Disclosure: The Extractive Industries Transparency Initiative in Myanmar," *Global Environmental Politics* 18, no. 1 (2018), doi: 10.1162/GLEP_a_00442.
48. Gillian Cornish and Vlado Vivoda, "Myanmar's Extractive Industries: An Institutional and Regulatory Assessment," *The Extractive Industries and Society*, 2016, doi: 10.1016/j.exis.2016.08.002.
49. Marjanneke J. Vijge, "The (Dis)empowering Effects of Transparency Beyond Information Disclosure: The Extractive Industries Transparency Initiative in Myanmar," *Global Environmental Politics* 18, no. 1 (2018), doi: 10.1162/GLEP_a_00442; Marjanneke J. Vijge, Robin Metcalfe, Linda Wallbott, and Christoph Oberlack, "Governance Transformations to Reverse the Resource Curse? The Extractive Industries Transparency Initiative in Myanmar," *Resources Policy* 61 (2019), doi: 10.1016/j.resourpol.2019.02.006.
50. Interview with strategic advisor of CSO, 20 August 2016, Yangon.
51. Interviews with EITI senior technical and policy analyst, 5 September 2016, Yangon; strategic advisor of CSO, 20 September 2016, Yangon; and former director of ethnic CSO, 5 October 2016, Chiang Mai.
52. Pick and Htwe Htwe Thein, "Development Failure and the Resource Curse: The Case of Myanmar."
53. MEITI, "Myanmar 2016-2017 EITI Report," March 2019. <https://eiti.org/document/myanmar-20162017-eiti-report-0>.
54. Marco Bünte, "Building Governance from Scratch: Myanmar and the Extractive Industry Transparency Initiative," *Journal of Contemporary Asia* 48, no. 2 (2017), doi: 10.1080/00472336.2017.1416153.

55. Interview with former coordinator of CSOs, 22 September 2016, Yangon; and EITI senior technical and policy analyst, 13 September 2016, Yangon.
56. Interviews with regional coordinator of international standard, 18 September 2016, Nay Pyi Taw/Magway; former visiting fellow of national think tank, 1 September 2016, London; and strategic advisor of CSO, 20 September 2016, Yangon.
57. Interview with regional coordinator of international standard, 17 September 2016, Magway.
58. Alex Gordy, "Jumping in the Deep End," 2015, <https://eiti.org/blog/jumping-deep-end>.
59. Eleven, "Civic Coalition for EITI to Discuss Letpadaungtaung Conflict," 2015, <http://www.elevenmyanmar.com/local/civic-coalition-eiti-discuss-letpadaungtaung-conflict>.
60. Interview with EITI senior technical and policy analyst, 17 September 2016, Magway.
61. EITI, "Reporting Template on Civic Space and the EITI Process: An Independent Tool to Document Potential Breaches of the EITI Civil Society Protocol," Version of 12 April 2016.
62. Interview with EITI program officer of international NGO, 31 August 2016, London.
63. Interview with regional coordinator of international standard, 17 September 2016, Magway.
64. Interviews with member of EITI watch group, 18 September 2016, Magway; senior technical and policy analyst, 5 September 2016 and 30 January 2018, Yangon/Skype; strategic advisor of CSO, 20 September 2016, Yangon; and former coordinator of CSOs, 22 September 2016, Yangon.
65. Marjanneke J. Vijge, Robin Metcalfe, Linda Wallbott, and Christoph Oberlack, "Governance Transformations to Reverse the Resource Curse? The Extractive Industries Transparency Initiative in Myanmar," *Resources Policy* 61 (2019), doi: 10.1016/j.resourpol.2019.02.006.
66. MEITI, "Myanmar EITI Annual Progress Report 2018–2019," June 2019. <https://eiti.org/sites/default/files/documents/apr_2018-2019_final_30-6-2019.pdf>.
67. EITI, "The EITI Standard 2016," 2016.
68. Paul Vrieze, "Burma Accepted for EITI Scheme, But NGOs Remain Concerned," *The Irawaddy*, 2014, <http://www.irrawaddy.org/business/burma-accepted-eiti-scheme-ngos-remain-concerned.html>.
69. World Bank, "Ease of Doing Business in Myanmar," 2015, <http://www.doingbusiness.org/data/exploreeconomies/myanmar>; Adam Smith International, "Institutional and Regulatory Assessment of the Extractive Industries in Myanmar."
70. U Thein Sein, "Speech at Chatham House in London," 2013, <http://www.myanmargeneva.org/pressrelease/President's speech at chatham house 16 July

2013.pdf>; Maya Schmaljohann, "Enhancing Foreign Direct Investment via Transparency? Evaluating the Effects of the EITI on FDI," 2013.

71. World Bank, "Overview World Bank Group Country Partnership Framework Consultations in Myanmar," 2014, <https://consultations.worldbank.org/Data/hub/files/consultation-template/world-bank-group-holds-consultations-inform-its-partnership-framework/phases/myanmar_cpf_consultations_2nd_round_summary_oct_17.pdf>; Marco Bünte, "Building Governance from Scratch: Myanmar and the Extractive Industry Transparency Initiative," *Journal of Contemporary Asia* 48, no. 2 (2017), doi: 10.1080/00472336.2017.1416153.
72. Shwe Gas Movement, "Good Governance and the Extractive Industry in Burma: Complications of Burma's Regulatory Framework," 2013, <http://www.burmalibrary.org/docs15/SGM-%0DGovernance-2013-06-en-red.pdf>; Vrieze, "Burma Accepted for EITI Scheme, But NGOs Remain Concerned."
73. Interview with representative of border-based CSO #1, 4 Oct. 2016, Chiang Mai.
74. MEITI, "MEITI Candidacy Application Annexes," 1.
75. Marco Bünte, "Building Governance from Scratch: Myanmar and the Extractive Industry Transparency Initiative," *Journal of Contemporary Asia* 48, no. 2 (2017), doi: 10.1080/00472336.2017.1416153.
76. Interview with regional coordinator of international standard, 17 September 2016, Magway.
77. Interviews with Myanmar country manager of NGO, 6 September 2016; and former director of ethnic CSO, 5 October 2016, Chiang Mai.
78. Interviews with former coordinator of CSOs, 22 September 2016, Yangon; Myanmar country manager of NGO, 6 September 2016; and EITI support coordinator of multilateral organization, 6 September 2016, Yangon.
79. Interviews with former director of ethnic CSO, 5 October 2016, Chiang Mai; executive program manager of corporate organization, 7 September 2016, Yangon; EITI support coordinator of multilateral organization, 6 September 2016, Yangon; and EITI senior technical and policy analyst, 5 September 2016, Yangon.
80. Interviews with senior technical and policy analyst, 17 September 2016, Magway; and regional coordinator of international standard, 17 September 2016, Magway.
81. Interviews with former coordinator of CSOs, 22 September 2016, Yangon; and Myanmar associate of NGO, 20 September 2016.
82. GMS, "Launch Ceremony: EIA Procedure and Environmental Quality Guidelines."
83. Interview with extractive industries manager of corporate organization, 7 September 2016, Yangon.
84. Adam Simpson and Susan Park, "The Asian Development Bank as a global risk regulator in Myanmar," *Third World Quarterly* 34, no. 10 (2013), doi: 10.1080/01436597.2013.851911.

85. Marjanneke J. Vijge, Robin Metcalfe, Linda Wallbott, and Christoph Oberlack, "Governance Transformations to Reverse the Resource Curse? The Extractive Industries Transparency Initiative in Myanmar," *Resources Policy* 61 (2019), doi: 10.1016/j.resourpol.2019.02.006.
86. Adam Simpson and Nicholas Farrelly, eds., *Myanmar: Politics, Economy and Society* (London and New York: Routledge, 2020).
87. MEITI, "Myanmar 2016-2017 EITI Report," March 2019, p. 238, <https://eiti.org/document/myanmar-20162017-eiti-report-0>.
88. See Marjanneke J. Vijge, "The (Dis)empowering Effects of Transparency Beyond Information Disclosure: The Extractive Industries Transparency Initiative in Myanmar," *Global Environmental Politics* 18, no. 1 (2018), doi: 10.1162/GLEP_a_00442; Marjanneke J. Vijge, Robin Metcalfe, Linda Wallbott, and Christoph Oberlack, "Governance Transformations to Reverse the Resource Curse? The Extractive Industries Transparency Initiative in Myanmar," *Resources Policy* 61 (2019), doi: 10.1016/j.resourpol.2019.02.006.
89. Marjanneke J. Vijge, "The (Dis)empowering Effects of Transparency Beyond Information Disclosure: The Extractive Industries Transparency Initiative in Myanmar," *Global Environmental Politics* 18, no. 1 (2018), doi: 10.1162/GLEP_a_00442.

References

Aaronson, Susan Ariel. 2011. "Limited Partnership: Business, Government, Civil Society, and the Public in the Extractive Industries Transparency Initiative (EITI)." *Public Administration and Development* 31, no. 1: 50–63. doi: 10.1002/pad.588.

Adam Smith International. 2015. "Institutional and Regulatory Assessment of the Extractive Industries in Myanmar." Adam Smith International and MDRI-CESD. <http://documents.worldbank.org/curated/en/504691467992478731/Main-report> [accessed 30 August 2017].

Asian Development Outlook. 2015. "Financing Asia's Future Growth." Mandaluyong City, Philippines: Asian Development Bank.

Buchanan, John, Tom Kramer, and Kevin Woods. 2013. "Developing Disparity: Regional Investment in Burma's Borderlands." Amsterdam: Burma Center Netherlands. <http://www.burmalibrary.org/docs14/Burmasborderlands-red.pdf> [accessed 25 September 2019].

Bünte, Marco. 2017. "Building Governance from Scratch: Myanmar and the Extractive Industry Transparency Initiative." *Journal of Contemporary Asia* 48, no. 2: 230–51. doi: 10.1080/00472336.2017.1416153.

Cornish, Gillian and Vlado Vivoda. 2016. "Myanmar's Extractive Industries: An Institutional and Regulatory Assessment." *The Extractive Industries and Society* 3, no. 4: 1075–3. doi: 10.1016/j.exis.2016.08.002.

EITI. 2011. "G20 Leaders Confirm Support of the EITI." <https://eiti.org/news-events/g20-leaders-confirm-support-eiti> [accessed 30 August 2017].

———. 2016a. "Reporting Template on Civic Space and the EITI Process: An Independent Tool to Document Potential Breaches of the EITI Civil Society Protocol." Version of 12 April.

———. 2016b. "The EITI Standard 2016." Report. Oslo: The EITI International Secretariat.

Eleven. 2015. "Civic Coalition for EITI to Discuss Letpadaungtaung Conflict." <http://www.elevenmyanmar.com/local/civic-coalition-eiti-discuss-letpadaung taung-conflict> [accessed 20 May 2015].

European Union. 2013. "The Extractive Industries Transparency Initiative (EITI) Options Study: MEITI Guidebook, Proposed Action under Development Cooperation Instrument Strengthening Policy Development to Meet MDGs in Burma/Myanmar." European Union, MDRI-CESD and International Management Group. <http://myanmareiti.org/download/file/fid/102> [accessed 29 August 2017].

Fink, Christina and Adam Simpson. 2018. "Civil Society." In *Routledge Handbook of Contemporary Myanmar*, ed. Adam Simpson, Nicholas Farrelly, and Ian Holliday. London and New York.

Global Witness. 2014. "The Shell Starts to Crack? Real Owners of Myanmar's Oil and Gas Blocks Come Forward." <https://www.globalwitness.org/reports/shell-starts-crack/ [accessed 18 May 2015].

GMS. 2016. "Launch Ceremony: EIA Procedure and Environmental Quality Guidelines." *Greater Mekong Subregion Core Environment Program*. <http://www.gms-eoc.org/events/launch-ceremony-eia-procedure-and-environmental-quality-guidelines> [accessed 16 May 2016].

Gordy, Alex. 2015. "Jumping in the Deep End." <https://eiti.org/blog/jumping-deep-end> [accessed 8 October 2016].

Hendrix, Cullen S. and Marcus Noland. 2014. "Managing Myanmar's Resource Boom to Lock in Reforms." Working paper No. PB14-11. Washington DC: Peterson Institute for International Economics.

James, Helen. 2010. "Resources, Rent-Seeking, and Reform in Thailand and Myanmar (Burma): The Economics-Politics Nexus." *Asian Survey* 50, no. 2: 426–48. doi: 10.1525/as.2010.50.2.426.

Kolstad, Ivar and Arne Wiig. 2009. "Is Transparency the Key to Reducing Corruption in Resource-Rich Countries?" *World Development* 37, no. 3: 521–32. doi: 10.1016/j.worlddev.2008.07.002.

Kramer, Tom. 2011. "Civil Society Gaining Ground: Opportunities for Change and Development in Burma." Amsterdam: Transnational Institute, Burma Center Netherlands.

Maclean, Ken. 2014. "Counter-Accounting with Invisible Data: The Struggle for Transparency in Myanmar's Energy Sector." *Political and Legal Anthropology Review* 37, no. 1: 10–28. doi: 10.1111/plar.12048.

MEITI. 2014. "MEITI Candidacy Application Annexes." In *Myanmar Extractive Industries Transparency Initiative (MEITI) Multi-Stakeholder Group (MEITI-*

MSG) Draft Terms of Reference, 2014. <https://eiti.org/files/Annex_07052014_op.pdf> [accessed 5 June 2015].

______. 2017. "Myanmar EITI." <https://eiti.org/Myanmar> [accessed 9 September 2017].

______. 2019a. "Myanmar 2016-2017 EITI Report." March. <https://eiti.org/document/myanmar-20162017-eiti-report-0> [accessed 9 September 2019].

______. 2019b. "Myanmar EITI Annual Progress Report 2018–2019." June. <https://eiti.org/sites/default/files/documents/apr_2018-2019_final_30-6-2019.pdf> [accessed 9 September 2019].

Myanmar Centre for Responsible Business. 2014. "Civil Society Organisations and the Extractives Industries in Myanmar – A Brief Overview." <http://myanmar-responsiblebusiness.org/pdf/2014-10-11-Briefing-Paper-CSOs-and-Extractives-Industries-Myanmar.pdf> [accessed 20 May 2015].

Natural Resource Governance Institute. 2017. "Resource Governance Index." <www.resourcegovernanceindex.org [accessed 25 September 2019].

Ospanova, Saule, Ingilab Ahmadov, and Emma Wilson. 2013. "EITI and Sustainable Development: Lessons and New Challenges for the Caspian Region." London: IIED. <https://eiti.org/files/EITI IIED paper.pdf [accessed 9 June 2015].

Perry, Peter J. 2007. *Myanmar (Burma) Since 1962: The Failure of Development.* Aldershot: Ashgate.

Pick, David and Htwe Htwe Thein. 2010. "Development Failure and the Resource Curse: The Case of Myanmar." *International Journal of Sociology and Social Policy* 30, no. 5/6: 267–79. doi: 10.1108/01443331011054235.

Rogers, Paul, Vijge, Marjanneke J., and Min Zar Ni Lin. n.d. *Institutionalising the Extractive Industries Transparency Initiative: Lessons Learned from Myanmar's Democratic Transition*. Unpublished manuscript.

Schmaljohann, Maya. 2013. "Enhancing Foreign Direct Investment via Transparency? Evaluating the Effects of the EITI on FDI." Discussion paper series, no. 538. University of Heidelberg, Department of Economics.

Shwe Gas Movement. 2013. "Good Governance and the Extractive Industry in Burma: Complications of Burma's Regulatory Framework." <http://www.burmalibrary.org/docs15/SGM-%0DGovernance-2013-06-en-red.pdf> [accessed 9 June 2015].

Simpson, Adam. 2013. "Challenging Hydropower Development in Myanmar (Burma): Cross-Border Activism under a Regime in Transition." *Pacific Review* 26, no. 2: 129–52. doi: 10.1080/09512748.2012.759264.

______. 2015. "Starting from Year Zero Environmental Governance in Myanmar." In *Environmental Challenges and Governance: Diverse Perspectives from Asia*, ed. S. Mukherjee and D. Chakraborty, pp. 152–65. Hoboken: Taylor and Francis. doi: 10.4324/9781315717081.

______. 2017a. *Energy, Governance and Security in Thailand and Myanmar (Burma): A Critical Approach to Environmental Politics in the South*. Copenhagen: NIAS Press.

———. 2017b. “The Extractive Industries Transparency Initiative: New Openings for Civil Society in Myanmar.” In *The Business of Transition: Law Reform, Development and Economics in Myanmar*, ed. Melissa Crouch, pp. 32–54. Melbourne: Cambridge University Press.

———. 2018a. “Corruption, Investment and Natural Resources.” In *International Natural Resources Law, Investment and Sustainability*, ed. Shawkat Alam, Jahid Bhuiyan, and Jona Razzaque. London and New York: Routledge.

———. 2018b. “Environment and Natural Resources.” In *Routledge Handbook of Contemporary Myanmar*, ed. Adam Simpson, Nicholas Farrelly, and Ian Holliday. London and New York.

———. 2020. “Natural Resources: Wealth and Conflict.” In *Myanmar: Politics, Economy and Society*, ed. Adam Simpson and Nicholas Farrelly. London and New York: Routledge.

Simpson, Adam and Susan Park. 2013. “The Asian Development Bank as a global risk regulator in Myanmar.” *Third World Quarterly* 34, no. 10: 1858–71. doi 10.1080/01436597.2013.851911.

Simpson, Adam, Nicholas Farrelly, and Ian Holliday, eds. 2018. *Routledge Handbook of Contemporary Myanmar*. London and New York: Routledge.

Simpson, Adam and Mattijs Smits. 2018. “Transitions to Energy and Climate Security in Southeast Asia: Civil Society Encounters with Illiberalism in Thailand and Myanmar.” *Society and Natural Resources* 31, no. 5: 580–98. doi 10.1080/08941920.2017.1413720.

Simpson, Adam and Nicholas Farrelly, eds. 2020. *Myanmar: Politics, Economy and Society*. London and New York: Routledge.

Smith, Matthew. 2007. “Environmental Governance of Mining in Burma.” In *Myanmar: The State, Community and the Environment*, ed. Monique Skidmore and Trevor Wilson, pp. 218–45. ANU E Press.

Sovacool, Benjamin K. 2012. “Environmental Conservation Problems and Possible Solutions in Myanmar.” *Contemporary Southeast Asia* 34, no. 2: 217–48. doi: 10.1355/cs34-2d.

Thet Aung Lynn, and Mari Oye. 2014. “Natural Resources and Subnational Governments in Myanmar: Key Considerations for Wealth Sharing.” Subnational governance in Myanmar discussion paper series, no. 4. International Growth Centre, MDRI-CESD and Asia Foundation. <http://www.theigc.org/wp-content/uploads/2014/06/Lynn-Oye-2014-Working-Paper.pdf> [accessed 29 August 2017].

Transparency International. 2018. “Corruption Perception Index.” <http://www.transparency.org/cpi2018/> [accessed 9 September 2019].

U Thein Sein. 2013. “Speech at Chatham House in London.” <http://www.myanmargeneva.org/pressrelease/President’s speech at chatham house 16 July 2013.pdf> [accessed 9 October 2016].

———. 2014. "Speech during the 3rd Anniversary of the President's 'Assumption of Duty', at the Pyidaungsu Hluttaw (Parliament), 26 March 2014." <http://www.myanmarpresidentoffice.gov.mm/2015en/?q=briefing-room/2014/03/26/id-3496 [accessed 9 October 2016].

Vijge, Marjanneke J. 2018. "The (Dis)empowering Effects of Transparency Beyond Information Disclosure: The Extractive Industries Transparency Initiative in Myanmar." *Global Environmental Politics* 18, no. 1: 13–32. doi: 10.1162/GLEP_a_00442.

Vijge, Marjanneke J., Robin Metcalfe, Linda Wallbott, and Christoph Oberlack. 2019. "Transforming institutional quality in resource curse contexts: The Extractive Industries Transparency Initiative in Myanmar." *Resources Policy* 61: 200–9. doi: 10.1016/j.resourpol.2019.02.006.

Vrieze, Paul. 2014. "Burma Accepted for EITI Scheme, But NGOs Remain Concerned." *The Irawaddy*. <http://www.irrawaddy.org/business/burma-accepted-eiti-scheme-ngos-remain-concerned.html> [accessed 9 October 2016].

Webb, Edward L., Nicholas R.A. Jachowski, Jacob Phelps, Daniel A. Friess, Maung Maung Than, and Alan D. Ziegler. 2014. "Deforestation in the Ayeyarwady Delta and the Conservation Implications of an Internationally-Engaged Myanmar." *Global Environmental Change* 25: 321–33. doi: 10.1016/j.gloenvcha.2013.10.007.

Wilson, Emma and James Van Alstine. 2014. "Localising Transparency: Exploring EITI's Contribution to Sustainable Development." London: IIED. <http://pubs.iied.org/16555IIED.html> [accessed 9 June 2015].

Woods, Kevin. 2011. "Ceasefire capitalism: Military–private partnerships, resource concessions and military–state building in the Burma–China borderlands." *The Journal of Peasant Studies* 38, no. 4: 747–70.

World Bank. 2014a. "Myanmar: Ending Poverty and Boosting Shared Prosperity in a Time of Transition. A Systematic Country Diagnostic." Yangon, Myanmar: World Bank Group. <http://www.worldbank.org/en/news/press-release/2014/12/15/ending-poverty-and-boosting-shared-prosperity-in-myanmar> [accessed 20 May 2015].

———. 2014b. "Overview World Bank Group Country Partnership Framework Consultations in Myanmar." <https://consultations.worldbank.org/Data/hub/files/consultation-template/world-bank-group-holds-consultations-inform-its-partnership-framework/phases/myanmar_cpf_consultations_2nd_round_summary_oct_17.pdf> [accessed 20 May 2015].

———. 2015. "Ease of Doing Business in Myanmar." <http://www.doingbusiness.org/data/exploreeconomies/myanmar> [accessed 20 May 2015].

SECTION THREE

The Socio-cultural Issues

CHAPTER 7

The Post-2011 Transition in Myanmar: Donor-driven Aid and Donor Capacity Deficit

Patrick Strefford

In late 2015, the people of Myanmar were able to vote in their freest general election since 1990. At that time, the opposition National League for Democracy (NLD) won a resounding victory, but was prevented from forming a new government by the Tatmadaw (Burmese military), who governed directly by decree until 2010, when the first general election was held under the new constitution that had been written by the Tatmadaw. The NLD boycotted the 2010 election, and as a result, the Tatmadaw-backed Union Solidarity and Development Party (USDP) won just under 60 per cent of the seats in both houses. With 25 per cent of seats reserved for military appointees and thus uncontested, the Tatmadaw/USDP won a resounding victory. While the NLD did win 43 out of the 45 seats contested in the by-election of 2012, it was the general election of 2015, which saw the finally completed full cycle. The NLD won 60 per cent of seats, while the USDP won only 5 per cent. With the military appointees still counting for 25 per cent, the elections can hardly be called completely free and fair, but it seems safe to conclude that the NLD does indeed enjoy a popular mandate.

While the current transition in Myanmar is often described as beginning in 2011, it should perhaps really be framed as the latest set of developments within a much longer time frame. In this way, the current transition began with the economic collapse and political upheavals of the late 1980s that resulted internally from the long-term underdevelopment of then-Burma, and externally from the structural shifts connected to the end of the Cold War. In 1988, the Tatmadaw took direct control of the state (as it had done in 1958 and 1962), although it announced at the time that it was "transitory."[1] As previously done so, therefore, the Tatmadaw had always planned to withdraw from politics, and the second decade of the 21st century was deemed to be the right time. In this way, the sanctions period of the 1990s and 2000s are also included within the transition that has been thus running for 25 years or so.

The perceived triumph of democracy and capitalism, and the removal of the Cold War balance of power imperative allowed the victors of the Cold War to raise in foreign policy priority certain ethical/moral considerations that were paid mere lip-service during the Cold War. Whilst during the Cold War, the democracies of the West courted and allied with a multitude of authoritarian governments around the world, after the Cold War, such behavior was restricted to only key allies. The triumph of democracy allowed, indeed decreed, the prioritizing of democratization in non-democracies. It could be said that the end of the Cold War allowed the Western democracies to mount their moral "high horse" and preach, or champion, democratization around the world. In the late 1980s/early 1990s, just as the West was re-formulating its foreign policy agenda, then-Burma became entangled in its own democratization struggle. Burma became the "poster-child" for those within the Western democracies most assertively advocating democratic transition overseas. When Western democracies spoke of the need for democracy and human rights in developing countries, Burma would inevitably be one of the examples. This research will not delve into the empirical case for the Democratic Peace Theory, which has been used as the rationale for democracies to foster, or force, democratic transition in another state. Simply put though, this theory asserts that democracies are more peaceful members of the international community than non-democracies, and that democracies do not fight with other democracies. Regardless of whether this is true, it has provided an attractive ideology for certain actors to advocate for the foreign policy imperative of fostering democratic transition in other countries.

Regardless of the rationale, in the case of Burma/Myanmar, the democracies of the West put into place sanctions that were ostensibly intended to modify government behavior in favor of improving human rights and democratic transition. Through the 1990s and 2000s, these sanctions became both broader and deeper. The primary architects of the sanctions were the US, the EU, and certain European governments.

Whilst there were many components to the sanctions, this chapter focuses only on the restriction of development aid, or Official Development Assistance (ODA), meaning that foreign aid disbursed by (the democratic) OECD member states for development in the recipient/partner country. This chapter will focus on one core *modality* of development aid, "technical assistance." It will also further focus on one core *concept* of development, "capacity," and on one key *principle* of development assistance, "ownership." Using technical assistance to improve capacity in developing countries has become a major component of ODA, and of international development in general. Likewise, ownership (a country's control over its own development policies and programs) is accepted to be a fundamental principle of development and development assistance. Even a cursory look at the international proclamations on development cooperation will uncover the dominant positions of capacity and ownership. Auspiciously perhaps, the 2011-initiated transition in Myanmar coincided with the latest round of international declarations for improving the effectiveness of ODA. The Busan Partnership for Effective Development was an international agreement, signed in 2011. Senior members of the newly-installed Government of Myanmar (GoM) attended the Busan meetings in 2011, and used the Busan Partnership as the primary template for the Naypyitaw Accord for Effective Development Cooperation, which is a set of commitments to which both the GoM and donors agreed in January 2013.

Within the international development aid discourse, capacity and Capacity Development (CD) are almost always used in reference to the recipient country, the developing country. It is typically used to frame the underdeveloped status of the recipient: capacity is lacking. However, this chapter will instead focus on the capacity of the donors. It will argue that, while not discounting the capacity deficit in Myanmar, there also exists a capacity deficit within the donor community, and this deficit stems from the reality that much aid is still donor-driven. This limits the ability of donors to provide effective development assistance that is required by the government and the peoples of Myanmar.

Response of Donors to Myanmar's Transition

Whilst this chapter will attempt to outline the transition as being a longer-term phenomenon than merely since 2011, it is during this period that we have seen a dramatic impact. Figure 7.1 shows total net ODA to

Myanmar, of about US$6 billion, between 1986 and 2016. We can easily see the result of the sanctions that began at the end of the Cold War. We can also see easily the consequence of the dramatic easing of sanctions that resulted from the 2012 by-election and the success of the NLD. It was not until 2013 that ODA dramatically increased and this represents the lag time between the decision to ease sanctions and provide considerable aid, and the implementation of such policies.

Figure 7.1 uses data from the OECD, meaning data that is given to the OECD by the member states, the ODA donors. However, we could also use data from the recipient/partner country, and in the case of Myanmar, there is a website called *Mohinga*, which has been established by the Foreign Economic Relations Department (FERD) of the Ministry of National Planning and Economic Development (MNPED) and the Development Partners Working Committee (DPWC). It is remarkable how different the data is. According to the Mohinga database, between January 2012 and December 2017, US$2.3 billion was disbursed (more on the reasons behind this discrepancy below).

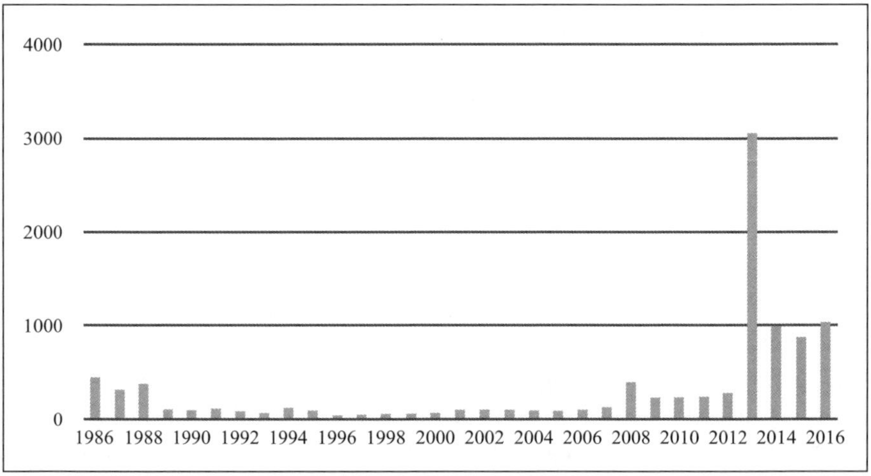

Source: Compiled from OECD.Stat by the author.

Figure 7.1 Net ODA to Myanmar, US$ millions, 2015 Constant Prices

Regardless of the differences in data, it seems self-evident that the easing of sanctions that resulted from the 2012 by-election caused a dramatic increase in ODA disbursals and commitments to Myanmar. However, if we look more closely at this data, we will be able to discern other events that had significant impacts on ODA disbursals to Myanmar even before the post-2011 transition. Cyclone Nargis in 2008 is such a case in point. We can also see that ODA began to increase at the turn of the century and this was in response to the public health crisis that was arguably exacerbated by the sanctions. The UK's Department for International Development (DFID) and the United Nations were notably increasing their aid at this time. In this way, while accepting that the increase in ODA has indeed been dramatic since 2013, it would be imprudent to ignore those increases that occurred prior to the post-2011 transition. These increases do look minor compared to the jump in 2013 but they are significant in that they were in contrast to the trend of that time, which was one of increasing sanctions. These sanctions, to be discussed briefly below, had resulted in Myanmar receiving significantly less development aid than its peers in the region. In 2007, for example, Myanmar received just US$4 per person in ODA, and this compared with US$67.19 for Lao PDR, US$46.70 for Cambodia, and US$29.34 for the comparatively well-off Vietnam.[2]

In 2003, the same year that the US expanded its sanctions against Myanmar through the Burma Freedom and Democracy Act, the UN Joint Program for HIV/AIDS in Myanmar and the Fund for HIV/AIDS in Myanmar were also established. It received finance from the governments of UK, Sweden, Norway, and the Netherlands. The 2004 DFID Burma Country Plan cited the Joint Program as a success saying,

> Policy change is possible: Patient advocacy by NGOs and the UN on specific issues such as voluntary HIV/AIDS testing has been successful at changing SPDC policy. Change is achievable in the medium to long term if the case for change is presented in a way that both demonstrates the benefits for the people and does not challenge the SPDC.[3]

At the same time as this, in 2004, the EU Common Position on Burma/Myanmar was extended. The Common Position outlined EU sanctions against Myanmar. Because of the increase in aid from donors such as the UK, as Figure 7.1 shows, it was after 2001 that ODA increased beyond the US$150 million mark. However, we should also say that the US Congress forced the Global Fund on HIV/AIDS to cease activities in Myanmar in 2005. The next notable increase came in 2008, in response to Cyclone Nargis that devastated the Irrawaddy delta area of Myanmar. Providing humanitarian aid to the victims of the cyclone became a highly contentious issue, with the GoM being slow both in its domestic response and in accepting international assistance. Remarks by international figures such as First Lady Laura Bush inflamed the issue, by offering scathing criticism—up to the point of even encouraging regime change—of the GoM.[4] However, ASEAN members persuaded the GoM to allow international aid to flow in, and the Myanmar-ASEAN-UN Tripartite Core Group was created as a cooperative mechanism to facilitate the disbursal of aid and the reconstruction of the delta region. In some ways, the standoff between the GoM and the international community was a vivid indicator of just how bad Myanmar's international relations had become. Indeed, it could be said that it was evidence of the failure of the sanctions policy towards Myanmar. However, regardless of this, in 2008 over US$500 million was disbursed in ODA to Myanmar, and importantly, levels of aid would never again reach the lows of the mid-1990s.

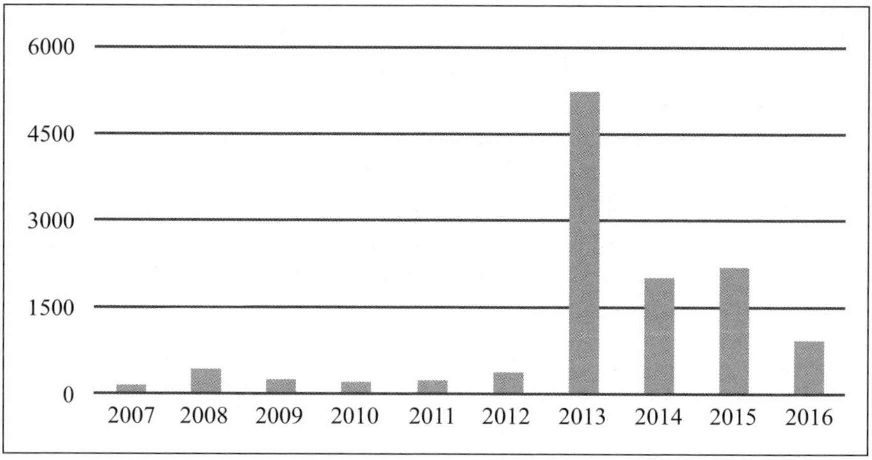

Source: Compiled from OECD.Stat by the author.

Figure 7.2 ODA Commitments to Myanmar, US$ millions, 2015 Constant Prices

Returning to the post-2011 transition, the decision to provide aid to Myanmar's transition can perhaps be more vividly illustrated in Figure 7.2, which shows ODA commitments, and not actual disbursals, as are shown in Figure 7.1. ODA commitments represent those agreements that have been signed. In this way, Figure 7.2 shows the upwelling of international support, backed by promises of aid, which followed the by-election results. Data from the GoM, whilst being different regarding actual disbursements, supports this. According to the Mohinga database, a total of US$9.41 billion was committed in ODA to Myanmar in the 2012–15 period.

It is also necessary to take another important factor into account when analyzing the data on ODA to Myanmar during this period. Figure 7.3 shows total net ODA to Myanmar while excluding debt relief, which allows us to highlight the importance of debt relief, especially in the 2013–14 period. According to the OECD, Myanmar received US$3.555 billion in debt relief grants from OECD donors in 2013, and US$851 million in 2014. Such debt relief was a necessary step in enabling both bilateral donors and international financial institutions to reengage with the GoM. Bilateral donors such as Japan, and international financial institutions such as the World Bank, are unable to offer new development loans if the recipient is in arrears, and so it was necessary to clear those arrears before new loans could be offered. In this way, the clearing of Myanmar's arrears was as important as the removal of sanctions.[5]

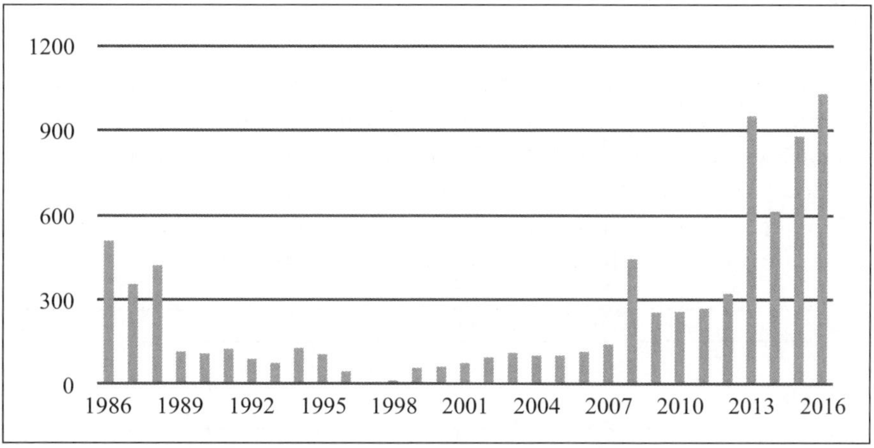

Source: Compiled from OECD.Stat by the author.

Figure 7.3 ODA to Myanmar, excluding Debt Relief, US$ millions, 2015 Constant Prices

If we now turn our attention to the data on the topic of this chapter, we can see from Figure 7.4 that ODA for Technical Cooperation in Myanmar also began to rise to pre-sanction level at the same time as sanctions were being expanded. While the rate dropped off somewhat after 2002, it began to increase again after Cyclone Nargis in 2008. Of course, this longer-term view does not deny the considerable expansion in technical cooperation in the 2013–16 period.

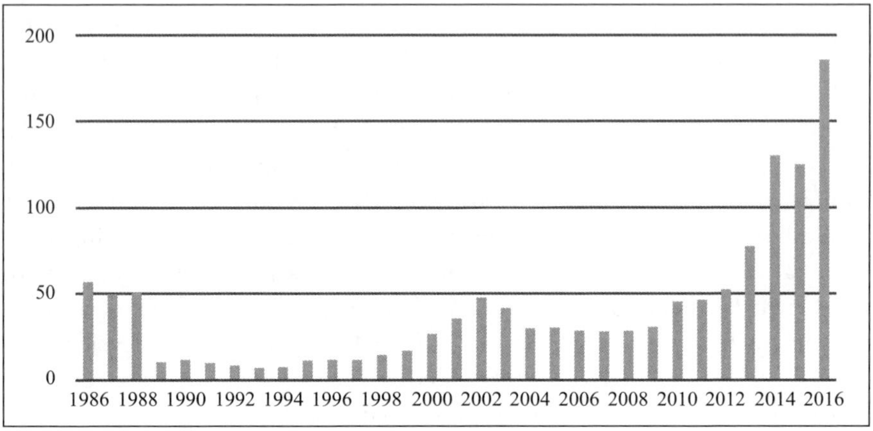

Source: Compiled from OECD.Stat by the author.

Figure 7.4 ODA Technical Assistance to Myanmar, US$ millions, 2015 Constant Prices

Looking more closely at these data, we find that the majority of the technical assistance came from just one bilateral donor, Japan. Figure 7.5 overlays the data for ODA for Technical Cooperation from Japan only. It shows the traditionally dominant position of Japan with regards to ODA for Technical Cooperation in Myanmar. While this dominance has gone down dramatically since 2011, it is still considerable.

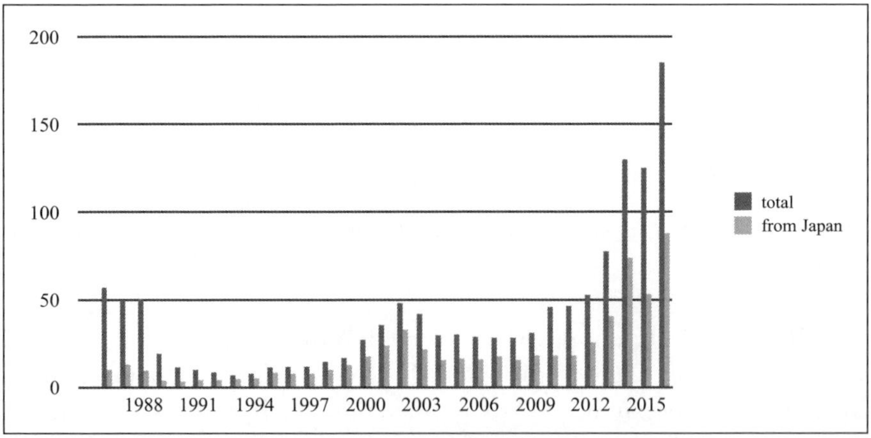

Source: Compiled from OECD.Stat by the author.

Figure 7.5 ODA Technical Cooperation to Myanmar, US$ millions, 2015 Constant Prices

Before dealing with the international discourse on ODA and international development as outlined in the Busan Partnership and Naypyidaw Accords, it is necessary to link the modality of technical cooperation with the concepts of capacity and ownership, and it is therefore necessary to discuss and clarify these concepts first.

Capacity and Ownership

In the simplest sense, capacity means ability, or capability. This was how Amartya Sen used the concept when he described the purpose of development to be enabling individuals to increase their capabilities, their potential and hence increase their freedom/independence. In this way, capacity is the ability of individuals to choose the way of life that has value for them.[6] It is connected to freedom and independence because this capacity is within the agent, and so the agent is free from excessive dependence. In ODA terminology this is ownership, meaning "empowering communities to collaborate in addressing the challenges they face. By implementing development strategies themselves, they're able to take control of their own destiny."[7]

The ability or capability to achieve a desired outcome means then that capacity is the ability to identify, plan for, and achieve goals. Indeed, the United Nations Development Program (UNDP) defines CD as "the process through which individuals, organizations, and societies obtain, strengthen, and maintain the capabilities to set and achieve their own development objectives over time" (UNDP 2009). The UNDP here is alluding to the interdependence between the concept of capacity and the principle of ownership. The World Bank too defines capacity as, "the ability to solve problems, make informed choices, define priorities and plan futures."[8] If we look, for example, at capacity in the public sector, then capacity refers to the ability or capability of the public sector to provide services to citizens. In principle, these public services must be distributed in a fair manner according to need, and perhaps more importantly, citizens must perceive it to be the case that public services are distributed fairly and according to need. Because of this, capacity and capacity building are essential to the effective running of the state, the economy, and for smooth, peaceful relations within society. The concept of capacity is inextricably linked to the principle of ownership. Indeed, ownership for the state is sovereignty. It means that the state has ownership over its development policies and their implementation. To achieve this, capacity is necessary. The state is also responsible for setting the rules and regulations, which are one factor that determines the capacity of private sector actors to achieve something that has value. Of course there are other external factors that determine an actor's ability to realize his/her goals. There are also internal factors, such as motivation, intelligence, skills, and knowledge. If the state is to set the stage, as it were, for private activities, and if the public sector is to provide services that citizens need, it is essential for the state and the public sector to be aware of the needs and goals of private citizens. In this way, it is important for the state to respond to the needs of the citizens, as though it were the "servant of the people."

Capacity Development (CD) is therefore the process of enhancing abilities and capabilities through the acquisition of skills, techniques, and knowledge. Needless to say, tools and technologies are often an indispensable component of capacity development. In this way, CD is part of a broad definition of education that includes formal and non-formal, academic, technical, and vocational training. Whilst this is no doubt a natural phenomenon that occurs during development, in terms of ODA and technical cooperation, external support is being provided to foster domestic CD. According to the OECD, "CD has been at the center of the international aid debate" since the 2005 Paris Declaration on Aid Effectiveness.[9] According to the World Bank, "the objective of aid assistance is to help developing countries build their capacities, that is, boost their ability to achieve development goals."[10] We can see therefore, that not only is CD a specific goal of ODA, it is also a necessary condition for success in development in general, and in development cooperation, or ODA, in particular. If we now consider the principle of ownership, then capacity is a necessary condition for achieving ownership, which is a necessary principle for effective development. Within the ODA discourse, this is somewhat of a paradoxical relationship. Whilst accepting that ownership is a necessary condition for effective development, donors undertake interventions to improve capacity, for the purpose of ownership.

Within the international development community, capacity is perceived as being directed at recipient countries in the form of capacity building assistance programs, from donors who are presumed to have the capacity to provide effective aid that enables effective development. Therefore, capacity and CD are framed as parts of a technical process, whereby developing countries are "backward," and in need of raising their capacity to meet that of the donors. This externally-defined condition then requires external intervention, which raises serious doubts about sovereignty, even though the goal of (and principle underpinning) intervention is ownership (for the developing country). Capacity and CD in the recipient country are therefore essential components of both effective aid and effective development. Within this paradigm, donors transfer skills, techniques, knowledge, and technology to the recipient predominantly through a modality referred to as Technical Assistance/Cooperation.

However, importantly, while the purpose of CD is to improve the ability of actors within developing countries to realize the goal of development, or in the case of public sector CD, to improve the ability to provide the services needed by citizens, it does not include the ability of donors to provide the aid that is needed. Whilst it should be the case that this is what donors do, and certainly it is a principle enshrined in the Busan Partnership, it may not necessarily be the reality. It seems that the reality is that CD is often a one-way street, with technocrats transferring generic skills, techniques, knowledge, and technology, without tailoring that to local conditions so as to provide the most effective aid. Hence, donor-driven aid undermines the principle of ownership, which is anyway predicated on the delicate relationship between it and capacity.

There is one final crucial issue with the concept of capacity, and the modality of capacity building. This concerns the method of measurement. How do we measure improvements in capacity? We could measure the increase in public services to determine improvements in capacity, although there are a number of other important factors that would likely affect this. We could use GDP growth rates to measure improvements in the capacity of private sector actors, although, again, there are countless other important factors. Before we turn our attention to the improvements in capacity we have seen in the public sector in Myanmar over the last five years, let us very briefly discuss the international and domestic frameworks that have been codified for regulating interactions between development partners.

Frameworks for Cooperation

As previously outlined, the Busan Partnership for Effective Development Cooperation was the result of the 2011 Fourth High Level Forum on Aid Effectiveness. It was the latest in a series of international agreements on development and development assistance. The Busan Partnership however, has been proclaimed to be more inclusive than previous agreements, in that developing countries, civil society, as well as OECD donors reached a consensus on a set of principles, commitments, and actions. According to the Busan Partnership, the following principles, "underpin all forms of development cooperation":

- Ownership of development priorities by developing countries, with approaches to development that are tailored to the country.
- A focus on results—eradicating poverty, reducing inequality, achieving sustainable development and enhancing capacities—that, importantly, is also aligned with the priorities and policies of the developing country.
- Inclusive development partnerships.
- Transparency and accountability between the Development Partners (DPs)/donors and the recipient country.
- The use of country systems (as the default approach), to the extent possible.

Capacity and CD are mentioned throughout the document, and particularly important for this study is the following passage, "institutions fulfilling core state functions should, where necessary, be further strengthened, alongside the policies and practices of providers of development co-operation, to facilitate the leveraging of resources by developing countries." Of course this is recognition of the need, not only for CD in the public sector of the recipient country, but also for CD in DPs/donors.

Importantly, as previously outlined, senior officials from the Thein Sein administration attended the Busan meetings, and so were well aware of the international development discourse, as outlined at that meeting. It was used to frame the Naypyitaw Accord (NPTA), which would be the primary reference point for the burgeoning interactions between the GoM and DPs. Indeed, it could be said that in many ways, the NPTA is a carbon copy of the Busan Partnership. Alternatively, it is "the localization of global development effectiveness principles in Myanmar."[11] Either way, it seems that the government of Thein Sein accepted the contents of the Busan Partnership as legitimate and applicable to the development realities of Myanmar.

According to the NPTA, "it has been informed by deliberations at the Fourth High Level Forum on Aid Effectiveness and takes forward the principles of ownership, focus on results, inclusive development partnerships, and transparency and accountability, embodied in the Busan partnership for Effective Development Cooperation."[12] In the NPTA, the GoM commit to participatory development, the creation of an aid management system, capacity building in public institutions, and transparency. The DPs commit to taking the local context as the starting point, aligning aid with local priorities, adhering to a country-led process, etc.

Capacity on the Recipients Gide: GoM

In a 2012 speech President Thein Sein remarked that, "while undertaking political and democratic reforms, we must wholeheartedly try to improve the capacity and performance of both individual public servants and the entire bureaucracy as a whole."[13] This can be interpreted as a very public recognition of what was, and still is to a lesser extent, a serious problem in Myanmar. Years of underdevelopment and military rule had resulted in a dramatic capacity deficit. Underdevelopment had squeezed resources and limited opportunities, and military rule had prioritized military prerogatives and institutions over all others.

However, there is now considerable evidence to support the view that capacity has dramatically increased in the GoM. Of course, this is not denying the difficulties in measuring capacity. This assessment is based on a number of factors. Firstly, based on interviews with development practitioners in Yangon and Naypyitaw in the years 2013–16,[14] it seems to be a dominant perspective within the development community in Yangon. Secondly, as previously shown there has been a dramatic increase in the amount of aid flowing into Myanmar. Thirdly, there has been a dramatic increase in government development-related activity in recent years. In 2013, for example, there were 100 government development projects. In 2015, this had risen to 800. While many of these may be financed externally, government capacity is necessary to implement such projects. Finally, the successfully held general elections in late 2015, and the relatively smooth transition of power to the new government in January 2016 is perhaps the best evidence of positive CD.

By 2015 it seemed to be a prevalent attitude with the community of development partners that the GoM and the donors were talking the same language.[15] This may seem somewhat strange, considering that the NPTA is a virtual carbon copy of the Busan Partnership. It may be the case that knowledge of ODA/development-related language and concepts took time to filter through the state bureaucracy. Having said that, even though it is also widely recognized that the quality of data has improved dramatically in Myanmar (which must also be assumed to be accompanied by at least some level of increased capacity), it seems to be a pervasive attitude within the community of development partners in Yangon, that the GoM capacity to analyze data is still lacking. This means that capacity in terms of conceptual understanding is an area that needs further development. It seems then that according to the externally-defined conditions for effective capacity, the GoM still does not have the capacity to formulate policy according to data.

There also seems to be a widespread attitude that capacity has increased to a level where it is possible to utilize government systems, a key principle of the Busan partnership. This is a key condition for the principle of ownership, as well as a key methodology for further increasing capacity in the public sector. However, there is still poor coordination between different government departments. For example, the FERD of the MNPED does not have access to all the data regarding ODA disbursals and projects, even though it is supposed to be the window through which aid passes. We should note, of course, that bureaucratic politics is a tendency in all large institutions, and so poor coordination between different organs is a pervasive problem in many states.

Donor-Driven: Structural/Attitudinal Limits on Effective Aid in Myanmar

It is perhaps the widely-held perception within the development community that, in line with classic modernization theory, there exist within developing countries traditional values, methods, and structures that must be overcome in order to allow the country to develop. Mosse and Lewis summarize the manifestation of this as an aid partnership that, "is a moralizing process expressed through an ideology of 'capacity' (a will to modernize) which is both personal and has an 'ordering power' which creates its own hierarchy of authority and expertise."[16] In this way, CD is part of the process of modernizing. The adoption of new techniques, technologies and processes, transferred through technical assistance, enables a society to overcome the barriers to development that are traditional values, systems, and approaches. In this way, capacity building is about adopting international development standards that have been set by the economically-advanced (modernized) donors, so that a developing country can follow the same path that other developed states have already trod. In this way, we can see how ODA is donor-driven, meaning the aid is largely not given according to needs of the recipient, but given according to the priorities of the donors. There are a number of examples, or on-the-ground results, of this.

As previously discussed, the Mohinga database is provided through a joint effort by the Foreign Economic Relations Department (FERD) of the Ministry of National Planning and Economic Development (MNPED) and the Development Partners Working Committee (DPWC). It is funded by the EU, presumably meaning this donor supports and endorses the idea. It began in early 2015 as an aid database to encourage transparency and effective aid. This chapter used the data from the Mohinga database to compare with the OECD data. We found that there were considerable differences between the two data sets. It is possible that the Mohinga database is less than complete. Indeed, according to the officials who were responsible, the donor agencies were less than forthcoming in providing their data to this database. It took pressure from civil society actors to nudge donors into providing their data.[17] Such transparency in aid data is obviously essential, and is recognized as such within the development discourse (as indicated within the Busan Partnership). The reluctance of donors to provide data is evidence of the insufficient efforts to abide by the principles that they have themselves set. It is plausible to speculate that donors are reluctant to provide data that may differ from GoM data. It may also be the case that donors think is not necessary because all data is already submitted to the OECD.

As previously outlined, technical assistance is a core modality of ODA, and a primary method of CD. It has been criticized for decades, even while it has become more widespread. For example, a comprehensive World Bank review of TA concluded that, "the efficacy and effectiveness of TA had been disappointing."[18] Likewise the UNDP concluded that TA "was expensive, donor-driven, often served to heighten dependence on foreign experts, and distorted national priorities."[19] Being aware of this, the GoM initiated the creation of Code of Conduct (COC) for TA in Myanmar. The purpose of this COC is to ensure high quality technical assistance that can increase capacity and lead to effective development. Such a COC is in line with the principles of the Busan Partnership, which requires donors to align their aid to recipient needs, and make their aid accountable. Presumably, an effective COC for TA would minimize the negative impacts that result from the previously discussed problematic relationship between CD and ownership. The COC, although it was supposed to be released at the end of 2015, has yet to be made public. However, according to officials involved in the creation of the Code of Conduct, it is so "full of holes," and has been so "watered down" by the DPs that it is "unworkable."[20] It seems that this is a direct result of the intransigence on behalf of the DPs with regards to aligning their systems of TA to the requirements of the GoM. In this way, the systems of TA are donor-driven and not aligned to the needs of the recipient. This can be interpreted as a lack of capacity on the part of the DPs. In the same way that the inability of the public sector in a developing country to provide the required services to its citizens is classified as a lack of capacity, so too should the inability of the DPs to provide the required aid be likewise classified as a lack of capacity. Even if this inability stems from an unwillingness that stems from a lack of trust, the end result is less effective development assistance. Whilst the DP would cite the lack of capacity in the recipient, this can also be interpreted to result from a lack of capacity on behalf of the DP.

The inability of the DPs to agree to a Code of Conduct for TAs that is requested and required by the recipient, and is also in accordance with the proclamations of the international donor community, is a sign of the national interest and domestic political economy (in the donor country) that are still driving factors behind much aid allocation, policy, and practice. It is an example of the lack of DP accountability to the recipient, and instead highlights the dominant role of donor capital cities in the aid process, and this is despite the attempts to reduce this role. It need not be said that this seriously undermines the principle of ownership as enshrined in all international development proclamations. This type of approach is donor-, or supply-driven, not demand-driven, meeting the needs of recipients. In this way, capacity is lacking within the DPs. Daw Aung San Suu Kyi, as Chairperson of the Development Assistance Coordination Unit (DACU), is heavily involved in GoM-DP interactions and, in her opening address at the 1st Meeting of DACU in December 2016, she criticized the system of international consultants, saying that "many consultants have minimal country knowledge," and "some try to impose pre-conceived ideas and templates onto the Myanmar context." In the same speech she referred to international consultants as an "expensive resource," expressing her desire to see consultants salaries lowered.[21] It seems clear that there is some frustration within the GoM at the perceived donor-driven aid to Myanmar. However, as with the COC for TA, donors are unwilling to change their donor-driven systems.

While interviewing senior officials in the FERD of the MNPED, the author was surprised to hear the perspective that DPs often come just for "window-shopping," meaning that they are browsing to see if anything "takes their fancy." Whilst window-shopping, the customer (for a window shopper is a customer and not a partner) may not be seriously considering purchasing anything at all, and may merely be passing time. If the customer does in fact find something of interest, the shop worker will try to persuade the customer to buy. If we transplant the interactions in this scenario, then it does not cast a favorable light on the interactions between DPs and the GoM. Whilst window-shopping, the concept of domestic state ownership is irrelevant, as is accountability. From one viewpoint, this is merely anecdotal evidence for the claim that much aid to Myanmar is donor-driven, and it was certainly the case that this comment was initially made in a somewhat lighthearted manner. Alternatively, it may be that DPs are less than persuasive in demonstrating their commitment to providing development assistance to Myanmar. Upon further investigation it became clear that this was a substantive perception based on experience. That officials within the FERD, which is the window through which the GoM interacts with the DPs, have such a perception is significant. It indicates that the principle of ownership can be perceived to be weak within the structure of interactions between the GoM and DPs.[22]

As previously discussed, the public sector is crucial for development. If we take just a cursory look around Myanmar's neighborhood, we can see that the successfully developing countries all have a strong and active public sector. This means that capacity within the public sector is necessary to provide the infrastructure and regulatory framework for private actors to invest. If we accept this assumption, then aid to the public sector is one of the most important components of any foreign assistance to a country in transition. As can be seen from Table 7.1, a relatively small amount of aid is flowing through/into public institutions. When compared with two similar countries, Cambodia and Afghanistan, it is obvious that aid to the public sector is relatively low, and this is evident even after the massive increase in aid following the start of the transition. While ODA to the public sector and civil society averaged over 40 per cent (of total ODA) for Afghanistan for the 2007–16 period, and 7.5 per cent for Cambodia, for Myanmar it was just 1 per cent. Of course, as previously discussed, total ODA in 2013 was extremely high because of the considerable debt relief, but between 2012 and 2016, just 1 per cent of foreign assistance was going into the public sector of Myanmar.

Prior to the initiation of reforms by President Thein Sein, Myanmar was under sizable sanctions, which severely limited both the amount of total ODA flowing into the country, and also the amount of ODA going into the public sector. However, as can be seen from the above data, this continued into 2014, although there were signs of change. In the initial year or two of the transition, it was widely accepted that the public sector

Table 7.1 ODA to the Public Sector, Current Prices, US$ millions

	ODA flowing through the public sector for government and civil society									
	2007	*2008*	*2009*	*2010*	*2011*	*2012*	*2013*	*2014*	*2015*	*2016*
Cambodia	26	38	26	19	46	11	25	19	24	39
Afghanistan	719	1,461	1,619	1,396	815	804	553	780	426	422
Myanmar	1	3	4	1	1	12	16	11	13	31
	ODA total									
	2007	*2008*	*2009*	*2010*	*2011*	*2012*	*2013*	*2014*	*2015*	*2016*
Cambodia	181	379	373	306	316	247	378	449	456	526
Afghanistan	2,784	4,067	3,543	2,295	1,892	1,595	1,634	1,479	1,086	784
Myanmar	15	88	60	36	50	133	4806	1563	1683	447

Source: Compiled from OECD.Stat by the author.

of Myanmar was not able to absorb high levels of ODA. However, by 2015, it seems to have been recognized by much of the DP community in Yangon that country systems were of sufficient level to be utilized by donors. A reflection of this was the suggestion by the World Bank and the EU that the time was right to begin budget support, meaning direct injections of finance into the government budget. Apparently, this was overruled by both the US and the UK. Indeed, DFID still proclaim that they do not provide any aid directly to the GoM.[23] According to the OECD, in the 2015–16 period, just less than US$0.5 million was provided as direct budget support.[24] This means that while some donors have judged that the time is right to provide more direct and effective development aid, others have judged this not to be the case. This is another example of the donor-driven nature of aid to Myanmar that can be interpreted as a lack of capacity on behalf of donors to provide effective development aid. In one way, this deep reluctance to provide aid direct to the public sector in Myanmar is a remnant of the sanctions era. The sanctions were accompanied by an often-vitriolic demonization of the GoM, and civil society actors in many Western countries remain vehemently opposed to providing aid direct to the GoM. Certainly, the FCO and DFID in the UK have to be sensitive to the very forceful and seemingly inflexible civil society actors.[25] Alternatively, DPs are still wary of the military's role in the "new" quasi-democratic Myanmar. It was expected that aid to the public sector would increase dramatically after the NLD government took over in 2016. However, given the crisis in Rakhine State, and the criticisms raised against the NLD government, a dramatic increase in direct support to the public sector is now deemed extremely difficult. Indeed, according to the OECD, in 2016 only US$24.616 million in ODA was committed to use the public sector as the channel for the "Government and Civil Society" sector, much of which was for "donor country personnel," "scholarships/training in donor country" or "other technical assistance."[26]

Conclusion

So, within the long time frame of Myanmar's transition (from 1988 to the present), how do we evaluate the technical cooperation activities of ODA donors in Myanmar with regards to capacity and ownership?

Whilst it is self-evident that capacity in the public sector in Myanmar has improved significantly in the post-2011 transition, challenges still remain. That this improvement is self-evident can be based purely on the fact that the election of 2015 were reasonably free and fair (within a constraining constitution), and that the transfer of power to the new government was reasonably smooth. Challenges regarding domestic capacity are typical of any developing country transitioning from authoritarian to democratic rule. However, externally, it is evident that capacity within the donor community is lacking. Donor-driven aid is one of the reasons for this lack of capacity. This chapter has highlighted some examples where the priorities of the donor override the development needs of the recipient, and this results in donors not being able to provide the assistance required by the developing country. Specifically, donors are not able to comprehensively change their method of technical cooperation, which is only supplied according to donor needs. The attempts by the GoM to formulate a Code of Conduct for technical cooperation have been thwarted by donors who want to maintain the current system. It seems that elements within the GoM perceive ODA to be donor driven in many respects, and this obviously undermines the principle of ownership.

Our examples seem to support the delicate theoretical relationship between the concepts of capacity and ownership. Whilst ownership over national development is a fundamental imperative for the GoM, that same government has accepted the dominant role of the concept of capacity within international development, and this is regardless of the accompanying hierarchical power relations, and underdeveloped/backward status thus attached to Myanmar. In this way, the GoM is in the same position as other developing countries who are walking the tightrope of maintaining sovereignty/ownership over the development process, whilst accepting ODA for that development.

It is perhaps natural, considering Myanmar's previous pariah status that in the immediate post-2011 transition, there existed a strong desire to avoid providing aid directly to the GoM. This is shown in the data for ODA to the public sector, where Myanmar received very little, despite the upwelling of international support for the transition. It seemed likely that this would change dramatically with the coming to power of the NLD and Daw Aung San Suu Kyi in 2015. The moral authority that Daw Aung San Suu Kyi had built up during the sanctions period provided a considerable obligation within the international community to provide as much assistance as possible. However, the deepening crisis in Rakhine State and the one million Rohingya refugees stranded in Bangladesh has resulted in the virtual evaporation of international goodwill towards the government of Myanmar. Moreover, the crisis has seriously damaged the status of Daw Aung San Suu Kyi, and the international obligation to assist seems to be evaporating too. In 2018, it is very difficult for donor agencies to push their respective governments and citizens to provide aid to the public sector of a state that is carrying out acts of genocide, as claimed by Zeid Ra'ad al-Hussein, the United Nations High Commissioner for Human Rights, in December 2017.

The transition in Myanmar will take at least a generation. It will take at least that time to completely remove the military from politics. Creating a sustainable peace for the border regions could also take that long. A key factor in both these two will be sustained and inclusive economic development, which will depend to a large extent on capacity in the public sector. International cooperation will be necessary for pursuing and sustaining economic development in all corners of Myanmar. After the election results of 2015, it seemed to the donor community that they had finally got something like the politics that they had long demanded. However, the current crisis in Rakhine State has highlighted yet again the extreme challenges facing the government of Myanmar.

Appendix Table Breakdown of Interviews Conducted

	Summer 2013	*Spring 2014*	*Summer 2014*	*Summer 2015*	*Spring 2016*
DP-bilateral (Japan, Germany, Norway, UK, USA)	4	3	2	2	1
DP-multilateral (ADB, EU, ILO, WB, UN)	1	3	1	5	
GoM					1
Independent Consultants	1	2	2	1	2
Yangon-based academics/researchers	1		1		
NGO/CSOs	2		1	2	2

Notes

1. Robert H. Taylor, *The Armed Forces in Myanmar's Politics: A Terminating Role?* Trends No. 2 (Singapore: Institute of Southeast Asian Studies, 2015), p. 5.
2. Elliott Prasse-Freeman, "Power, Protest, Inchoate Politics of the Daily in B/M," *Journal of Asian Studies* 71, no. 2 (2012): 372.
3. DFID, *Burma Country Plan*, October 2004, p. 8.
4. Violet Cho, "Laura Bush Comments 'Inappropriate' Says Analyst," *The Irrawaddy*, 6 May 2008.
5. For a discussion of this, see Patrick Strefford, "Overcoming Bottlenecks: Japan-led Support for Myanmar's Transition," *The Bulletin of the Institute of World Affairs*, no. 29 (March 2014).
6. Amartya Sen, *Development as Freedom* (Oxford: Oxford University Press, 1999), pp. 24–5.
7. Les Roopanarine, "Development Jargon Decoded: Local Ownership," *The Guardian*, 19 August 2013.
8. World Bank, "Dimensions: Capacity Development in Practice," 2011 <http://go.worldbank.org/O1RMGUIXX0> [accessed 24 June 2018].
9. OECD, *Capacity Development: A DAC Priority*, November 2010 <https://www.oecd.org/dac/governance-peace/governance/docs/46682429.pdf> [accessed 24 June 2018].
10. World Bank, "Dimensions: Capacity Development in Practice," 2011 <http://go.worldbank.org/O1RMGUIXX0> [accessed 24 June 2018].
11. "The Outcomes of 3rd MDCF and New Resolution: towards Sustainable Development Goals after Millennium Development Goals," *The Global New Light of Myanmar*, 15 February 2015.

12. *Naypyitaw Accord for Effective Development Cooperation*, 2013 <https://mohinga.info/static/docs/NPTA_Effective_Development_Cooperation.pdf> [accessed 24 June 2018].
13. "President U Thein Sein Calls for Cutting 'Red Tape'," *The New Light of Myanmar*, 27 December 2012.
14. For this research, the author conducted interviews with open-ended questions in Yangon and Naypyitaw in the 2013–16 period. See Appendix Table for a breakdown of interviews conducted.
15. Interviews with officials conducted in Yangon, September 2015 and February/March 2016.
16. David Mosse and David Lewis, eds., *The Aid Effect: Giving and Governing in International Development* (London: Pluto Press, 2005), p. 20.
17. Interview with Yangon-based international consultant, Yangon, February 2016.
18. Roger C. Riddell, *Does Foreign Aid Really Work?* (Oxford: Oxford University Press, 2007), p. 206.
19. Sakiko Fukuda-Parr, Carlos Lopes, and Khalid Malik, eds., *Capacity for Development: New Solutions to Old Problems* (New York: Earthscan and UNDP, 2002), p. 4.
20. Interview with Yangon-based international consultant, Yangon, February 2016.
21. The Global New Light of Myanmar, "Development Assistance Coordination Group holds first meeting with Cooperation Partners Group," 13 December 2016.
22. Interview with GoM officials, Naypyitaw, September 2015.
23. DFID, "Operational Plan 2011–2016 DFID BURMA Updated December 2014," <https://assets.publishing.service.gov.uk/government/uploads/system/uploads/attachm ent_data/file/401505/Burma1.pdf> [accessed 24 June 2018].
24. In 2015, the French government provided a grant of US$277,000 to support the elections, and in 2016, the French government provided two grants totaling US$220,000 as Emergency Food Aid.
25. Interview with FCO official, London, March 2014.
26. OECD.Stat, Creditor Reporting System.

References

Cho, Violet. 2008. "Laura Bush Comments 'Inappropriate' Says Analyst." *The Irrawaddy*, 6 May <http://www.irrawaddy.org/article.php?art_id=11794>.

Fukuda-Parr, Sakiko, Lopes, Carlos, and Malik, Khalid, eds. 2002. *Capacity for Development: New Solutions to Old Problems*. New York: Earthscan and UNDP.

Gasper, D. 1999. "Ethics and the Conduct of International Development Aid: Charity or Obligation." *Forum for Development Studies* 1: 23–57.

Mosse, David and Lewis, David, eds. 2005. *The Aid Effect: Giving and Governing in International Development*. London: Pluto Press.

OECD. 2010. *Capacity Development: A DAC Priority*. November <https://www.oecd.org/dac/governance-peace/governance/docs/46682429.pdf>.

Riddell, Roger C. 2007. *Does Foreign Aid Really Work?* Oxford: Oxford University Press.

Sen, Amartya. 1999. *Development as Freedom*. Oxford: Oxford University Press.

Taylor, Robert H. 2015. *The Armed Forces in Myanmar's Politics: A Terminating Role?* Singapore: ISEAS Trends No. 2.

UNDP. 2009. "Capacity Development: A UNDP Primer." <http://www.undp.org/content/undp/en/home/librarypage/capacity-building/capacity-development-a-undp-primer/>.

World Bank. 2011. "Dimensions: Capacity Development in Practice." <http://go.worldbank.org/O1RMGUIXX0>.

CHAPTER 8

Ethnic Education Systems in Burma: Possibilities for Harmonization and Integration[1]

Patrick McCormick

In a context of great ethnolinguistic diversity and armed conflict with the army of the central government, a number of "ethnic education systems" have arisen in various places in Burma.[2] In many of the areas which have been outside of the control of the central government, ethnic-minority actors have set up administration systems, including schools. Many of these schools provide "mother tongue education," using an ethnic-minority language as the medium of instruction while also teaching content related to their history and culture. In the past, the ethnic education systems provided education in areas which were geographically and politically beyond the reach of the central government, in for example border regions where the state was unable or unwilling to reach. Burma has entered a time of transition, one in which the current government has the burden to deal with decades of mismanagement, poor decisions, poor governance, and chronic under- and de-funding across all sectors.

In education, the ethnic education systems continue to function in their previous roles, but now within an emergent environment. Recent national governments have increased their funding for education dramatically and have embarked on a number of ambitious reforms, including working towards decentralization and allowing languages other than Burmese to be used in school.[3] In 2016, the Ministry of Education released a "National Language Policy" which affirms the central role of Burmese as the medium of instruction, but which supports ethnic and indigenous communities to transmit their languages.[4] There is little funding for these efforts and minority languages are usually taught outside school hours.[5]

At the same time, however, the ethnic education systems are deeply imbricated in on-going political processes of negotiating and renegotiating ceasefires and ·peace agreements between the various non-state armed actors and the central government. This chapter is a snapshot of three major ethnic education systems in Burma—the Mon, Karen, and Kachin—and provides an analysis of the overall situation in which these systems operate, including aspects of ideology.

Current Context

In Burma, education, politics, conflict, language, and ethnicity are tightly interwoven. Philosophies towards education and visions for the future of the country also differ significantly among the various actors. Some ethnic armed groups see integration of their territory with the central government —in other words, with Burma—as a long-term possibility and desirable. In the short term, some groups recognize their own limitations and may be willing to harmonize or accommodate the provision of education. In other cases, ethnic armed actors, in reaction to violence and armed conflict with the Tatmadaw or Burmese army, have not seen harmonization, much less integration, as desirable, and may seek independence. All groups want to retain some autonomy in education, and some actively seek official recognition. In a context of decades of endemic warfare, many ethnic armed actors are slow to trust the central government. The recent political environment and changes have raised expectations for growth and change, but such hopes are tempered by the breakdown and renegotiation of existing ceasefires.

Since the first change of government away from a wholly military-run system in 2010, the central government has begun to change some of its long-term stances in relation to minority affairs and towards education more specifically. The state of ceasefire agreements and relations with both the Burmese army and the central government inform the ethnic education systems, how they operate, their reach, and their vision of association with Burma and Burmese institutions. With the formal accession to power of the new government led by the National League for Democracy in February 2016, hopes have been running high for change and reform. The previous government, for example, stated its intention to promote greater decentralization in governance.[6] If understood as allowing greater autonomy and local decision-making power, decentralization could accommodate established ethnic education systems, but also more widely allow the possibility for greater local autonomy in educational matters. Widespread interest in providing "mother tongue education," or using languages other than Burmese as a medium of instruction, is a major point of intersection with some of the interest in ethnic education systems.

Historical Context of Education in Burma

Burma is a country of great ethno-linguistic diversity. Government figures put the number of "national races" at 135, while linguistic classifications state there are around 117 languages spoken in the country.[7] Government classification schemes tend to put the 135 races under eight large umbrella ethnic labels: Burman (Bamar), Mon, Kachin, Chin, Rakhaing, Kayah, Karen, and Shan. These labels reflect history and politics as much as they reflect linguistic and cultural difference. Under some categories, such as the Kachin, exist great differences in language, not just dialect. Other groups, such as the Mon, form a fairly cohesive unit. The Burman (Bamar) majority makes up some 60 per cent of the population of 52 million people, whereas the various ethnic groups form the remaining 40 per cent. Although widely spoken as a second language, the degree of exposure to Burmese and opportunities for education in the government schools vary widely. Large sections of the population do not speak Burmese at all, or at least not well. Nevertheless, most groups recognize the role of Burmese as a lingua franca and the benefits of being able to speak the language.[8]

Ethnic diversity is a feature of society throughout the country, but it is often associated with the border areas. This idea of "the border," however, is a hazy concept and can potentially include areas deep inside the internationally recognized boundaries. A useful way to understand "the border" can be in terms of those areas outside of government control. Not all members of an ethnic category live on "the border" nor do they live in the state bearing an ethnic name. The population of Kayin (Karen) State, for example, contains only a minority of the Karen-speaking population, which is spread between Bago Region, Ayeyarwady Region, Mon State, and Tanintharyi Region. This disjuncture reveals a potential pitfall in federalist models of government which depend on an association of ethnicity with territory. While some ethnic groups do tend to live in clearly demarcated areas, in many cases settlement patterns tend to be far more mixed. Burma's major cities host sizeable populations of various ethnic groups, especially Yangon and Mandalay.

The country's shape, borders, and the mix of ethnic groups living there are the result of Burma's pre-colonial past and the contingencies of colonialism. Under the British, peoples and political entities which had been only loosely associated with the Burmese court were brought much more directly under central state authority. This process is an important underlying reason for the armed conflict against the central Burmese government and army. Said another way, the central government has never been wholly sovereign throughout the internationally demarcated borders of the country and has always been concerned with preventing the country from breaking up, especially as valuable resources are located in various "ethnic" areas. Central governmental and military control in many areas has only ever been weak, contested, or non-existent. Government services, including education, have been sporadic or non-existent. An aim of many ceasefire agreements at least from the perspective of the central government, is to bring more people and resources under central government control.

Successive regimes since independence in 1948 have viewed ethnicity with suspicion. Many have tried to carefully control expressions of cultural identity or history, and have been chary of promoting indigenous languages through the government education system. Many Burmans, who form the majority of the government and military, genuinely do not understand the situation in ethnic and border areas, and so do not understand the extent to which the Burmese language is not spoken, or the resentment that many members of minority groups feel towards the central government.[9]

Immediately after independence, the new government allowed teaching in some minority languages and translated government textbooks into ethnic languages. Because of the weakness of the central government and a fear of chaos and disintegration, General Ne Win took control of the county in 1962. The new government soon made Burmese the sole official language and medium of instruction in government schools.[10] This change created great resentment, while also putting ethnic minority children at a disadvantage in the school system.

Against these long-term trends, the educational context in Burma has begun to change rapidly in the past few years. The changes in government have also meant changes in educational policy, including increases in spending. Until the change in government, Burma had had some of the lowest expenditures on education of any country in the region.[11] Another year has been added to schooling, expanding it from the "ten standard" system in place for decades. Myanmar has signed onto the Millennium Development Goals, which include improving educational outcomes. Common is rhetoric to promote greater accommodation, as in the ethnic rights for the transmission of language and culture in the 2016 National Language Policy. In the background, for many years, foreign donors and ethnic minority groups have been using mother tongue education, and more recently, have brought the issue to the greater attention of the government, which has garnered a limited response, as noted above. The government has been slow and reluctant to make concessions on this point, but there have been a few important signs that a shift may be underway.

There is a deep connection between the operation of the various ethnic education systems on the one hand, and the long-term maintenance of peace between armed groups, ceasefire groups, and the central government on the other. In 2011, the newly-elected USDP government nullified all ceasefires negotiated under previous regimes and said they would have to be renegotiated bilaterally. In 2015, eight major groups had signed the nation-wide ceasefire, although several, such as the Kachin Independence Organization, have not and have been at war with the Tatmadaw.[12]

The Government Education System

A brief discussion of government schools will throw into relief aspects of education in general. The government and ethnic systems face many of the same difficulties. The chief education provider are the government schools, from primary through the tertiary level, which are under the Ministry of Education. A parallel system is the monastic schools, which often operate in areas where families cannot afford to send their children to the government schools. The monastic schools, a system in place since before colonization, largely follow the government curriculum, although there is greater room for autonomy or for running local programs. These monastic schools fall under various ministries, including the Ministry for Religious Affairs. Because of this greater freedom and because restrictions which had been in place until quite recently on working in government schools, foreign non-governmental organizations and donors have been more active in the monastic school system than in the government system. There are also private schools, such as the international schools primarily in Yangon, which are legally businesses and so do not follow the government curriculum. The term "government schools" is useful for describing the situation of institutions run by various government ministries following the same basic curriculum.

Overall, outcomes are generally poor and fail to meet the needs of society. Schools emphasize rote learning, are under-funded, and use corporal punishment. Dropout rates are high, especially in the transition between middle and high school.[13] Matriculation rates in the final year of high school are less than half of the students. Reflecting societal preferences and economic calculations, families often pull girls out of school in order to work or take care of younger siblings, especially when the girls are teenagers. Yet girls tend to perform better than boys when they have the opportunity. Official statistics often do not reveal the extent to which children do not actually attend school—there are various incentives for registering children who may not actually attend school. Access to school is uneven and unequal, with rural and ethnic areas generally more poorly served, while affluent, urban areas getting higher quality teachers and infrastructure. One recent study revealed that less than one half of school age children in Shan State received any schooling at all.[14]

Government schools are often overcrowded and noisy because of the preference for children learning by recitation together in a loud voice.[15] Class sizes tend to be quite large. Teachers may have inadequate training or education themselves. In many places, government schools are either far away or non-existent. High schools, for example, may be too far away to serve local populations. Although technically education is provided free of charge, there are numerous, often burdensome informal fees associated with schooling. Most notoriously is the common practice of "tuition," in which teachers do not teach the answers to tests during school hours, but only in paid "tutoring" classes. Students who do complete a government education are often ill-equipped to find work or carry on further education. The emphasis on rote learning and memorization in order to pass tests means that students do not develop critical and analytical skills.

Adequate salaries for teachers is a perennial problem throughout all systems, although the government system has recently increased spending on education, including pay raises for teachers. Problems with training and pay equity have become more acute in recent years as the government has embarked on an ambitious plan of expanding the reach of government education. In addition to adding another year of education and constructing numerous new schools, the government has started hiring "daily wage teachers" as a way to provide five teachers in each primary school. These teachers are not civil servants and have not undergone the same training at teachers' colleges as the regular teachers. A disproportionate number have been sent to remote schools, including in ethnic minority areas, and have been associated with an increase in dropouts there.[16] School teachers are posted following a centralized process, meaning that the teachers in many peripheral areas are not from local communities, but rather Burman Buddhists. Many teachers posted to remote ethnic areas are underpaid, find the work or lifestyle unsatisfying, and are often called away to distant towns to receive pay and fill out paperwork, leading to high levels of absenteeism and turnover.[17] These teachers do not know local languages, so that teaching becomes ineffective or worse, leaving many children effectively uneducated.

Whatever the shortcomings of the school system, Burmese society places a high value on education. Parents tend to do whatever they can to have their children educated, and teachers and administrators do their best, according to their understanding, to provide an education. Burmese society has not clearly articulated the purpose of education, nor what it means to be educated. For many, being educated means to speak English. Around the world, many other societies view education as a way to create citizens able to participate in civic life, or to prepare citizens for the workforce. In Burma, however, the educational rhetoric takes the form of vague aspirations, such as the large signboards around schools which declare, "towards a modern and developed nation through discipline." What it means to be "developed" is also left unspecified. It is easy to think about what the education system lacks, but it does in fact suit a particular vision of society, in which young people do what their elders and superiors tell them. The problem is that the skills and attitudes which serve an agrarian, monarchical, hierarchical society are not the same as those of capitalist markets, which demand higher overall educational abilities, if indeed becoming a capitalist society is a societal goal.

Ethnic Education Systems

The ethnic education systems are key to providing education to more of the citizens of the country, especially in hard-to-reach places. As one recent report observes, the government system will not be able to expand their provision of education across the country, even under their ambitious new plan. Recent years have seen increasing interactions between the government and ethnic systems, sometimes welcome, sometimes contested. Ethnic systems tend to be funded by local communities, although foreign donors often provide substantial amounts of money, as has been the case with the Mon system in which foreign donors were subsidizing a significant amount of teachers' salaries.[18] A difficulty, however, is that foreign donors typically provide only short-term funding and are not interested in providing money for a public good which they see as the responsibility of the central government.[19] Teachers in some ethnic systems tend to be young, often working as much as volunteers as regularly paid teachers.[20] Common to all of the ethnic systems are outmoded pedagogy, curriculum, and textbooks, even as each group has made efforts to update them.

Strictly speaking, the three ethnic education systems are not comparable. There is no one "ethnic education" model representative of the experience as a whole. These systems are still "in process," still emerging, in that their fates depend on interactions between changes of thinking and legislation in the central government, and on the resolution of complex political and military events. The Mon system stands on one end of the spectrum, in that it is fairly coherent and represents a single entity. The "Karen System" actually encompasses a variety of arrangements and accommodations. Differences among the systems represent the particularities of history and relationships with the central government and the military and their experience with armed conflict. Ideological, religious, and cultural diversity also factor into the variation. When discussing these systems, questions emerge about who operates them, how these people represent their ethnic group, and how they are accountable to students, teachers, and communities. Many international donors and governments are keen to work with ceasefire groups and support ethnic minorities. All education systems in Burma have their origins in hierarchical social structures and do not involve elected officials. The ethnic minority systems have developed under their respective militaries, so that it is not clear to what extent ethnic education systems represent the views and interests of the people, or to what extent they reflect elite ideologies. Starting in 2012, foreign donors encouraged the New Mon State Party (NMSP) to hold a series of on-going consultations with the Mon public to address precisely the ambiguity of the NMSP's position and their ability to represent the people they claim to govern.

Today the three ethnic education systems considered here operate not only in territory which ethnic armed actors—the New Mon State Party (NMSP), the Karen National (KNU), and the Kachin Independence Organization (KIO)—control, but also in areas under overlapping control with the central government. In these areas, the ethnic schools may complement the government system, or work together with the government system in various local accommodations, often called "mixed schools." Increasingly, as the central government has sought to expand its reach into new areas, they have opened new schools in areas which previously did not have them. At times local ethnic communities have accepted or even asked for these schools because they can provide education beyond what has been available locally, or because the costs of supporting teachers are lower. Where these schools are built, there is usually already a community school, whose administration the government then takes over, thus creating a mixed school.[21] Where there are two competing schools, parents often face difficult choices of which school to send their children to. Mixed schools, however, can present opportunities for fruitful accommodation: teachers may "teach" in Burmese but "explain" the lessons in a local language. This practice can potentially benefit children whose first language is not Burmese. A difficulty is that although the National Language Policy of 2016 supports the transmission of ethnic languages and an amendment to the National Education Law in 2015 allows "local languages" to be used along with Burmese as necessary at the basic level as noted above, the practice is highly contingent upon local head teachers and administrators, in addition to the presence of teachers who know the local language. In areas where teachers cannot speak the local language, however, morale among both students and teachers is often low, with many students leaving school.

Mon National Schools

The Mon-speaking population of Burma is around 800,000. The largest Mon armed ethnic group, the New Mon State Party, started the "Mon National Schools" with the founding of the Mon National Education Committee in 1972.[22] The New Mon State Party had been in armed conflict with the central government since independence until 1995, when the two sides signed a ceasefire agreement. In the mid-1990s, there were 76 Mon national schools in the Mon-majority areas of Mon and Karen States.[23] The original site of the schools was areas the New Mon State Party held, but since the ceasefires, various strategies and accommodation have allowed Mon-medium and Mon-content education to spread through Mon-majority areas of Mon and Karen States, although there are also populations of Mon speakers in adjacent Bago and Tanintharyi Regions, and significant clusters of Mon speakers in and around Yangon.

Typically, Mon schools use Mon as the sole medium of instruction through primary school. Burmese and English are taught as subjects, as is Mon history. In middle school, they switch to Burmese as the medium of instruction, with Mon history and language taught as subjects. Through local, unofficial agreements, students from the Mon schools have been able to take the examinations to enter government high schools. None of these agreements are the result of official legislation (even if, as noted above, some new legislation raises the possibility), but rather depend on the attitudes and inclinations of local government officials. The possibility of students transferring into government schools from the ethnic schools is critical to many students and parents. For many parents, teachers and students, it is of critical importance that students who go through ethnic systems can take the entrance examinations to be admitted to government high schools, which are also the gateway to universities.

There are also a number of government schools where varying degrees of accommodation are made to the local Mon community, called here and elsewhere as "mixed schools." Accommodations typically include allowing Mon teachers to use government school buildings after school hours, or providing actual Mon-speaking teachers to either "teach" or "explain" in Mon following the practice outlined above, or actually using Mon-language textbooks and teaching Mon-relevant content such as history and language.[24] The Burmese government allowed the teaching of minority languages beginning in 2014, although it appears that how local officials interpret this permission and how it plays out in schools varies.[25] Monastic schools have been a site of expansion of Mon-medium and Mon-content instruction throughout Mon-speaking areas.

The ease (in theory) of transferring from the Mon system into the government system is one of the most distinctive features of this system. Many international donors and experts have seen the Mon system as ideal because it allows for the preservation and transmission of the ethnic language and ethnic history, while also fostering integration into national life. The length of the ceasefire between the New Mon State Party and the Burmese military, recent good relations with the central government, together with close historical, cultural, and religious links between the Mons and Burmans, have worked in favor of the system. At the same time, however, as will become clear in the discussion of the Kachin systems, the lack of significant natural resources in Mon-speaking areas has precluded the possibility of the New Mon State Party from holding out and funding a parallel administration through other means.

Karen Systems

Similar to the Mon situation, a network of schools providing education to members of Karen ethnic groups has arisen out of political and military organizations. The Karen National Association (KNA) was founded in 1881 before developing into the Karen National Union (KNU) in 1947. Fighting broke out between the central government and the KNU in 1949 and persisted until the signing of a ceasefire in 2012. The KNU set up administrative structures, including the Karen Education Department (KED), formerly the Karen Education and Culture Department. The KED is largely active in areas which the KNU hold, particularly areas closer to the Thai-Burma border, meaning that many areas where Karens live are not served by the KED. Additionally, the Democratic Karen Benevolent Army and the Democratic Karen Buddhist Army (the former a splinter group of the latter) also run about 100 schools. Another place providing education to Karen children are the several Karen and Karenni (Kayah) refugee camps along the Thai-Burma border. Some 30,000 children were attending school in these camps in 2015.[26] As is the case of the Mons, large numbers of Karens live in government-controlled areas. In the past 15 years, the Karen Teachers' Working Group (KTWG) has been active in improving the quality of teachers, curriculum, textbooks, and pedagogy in Karen schools.[27]

Unlike the situation of the Mons, who encompass one group speaking one language, Karens speak a variety of languages and dialects which are not mutually intelligible. The Karen population is scattered through parts of Karen and Mon States, eastern Bago Region, Tanintharyi Region, and Ayeyarwady Region. Not all of these areas are Karen majority, nor are they geographically contiguous. About 20 per cent of the 5–7 million Karens living in Burma are Christian, especially Baptist, and represent the majority of actors involved in Karen education. The remainder of the non-Christian population is at least nominal Buddhist.

After the suppression of Karen-language education in the 1960s, many local churches and monasteries continued to provide informal instruction in the two major Karen languages, Sgaw and Pwo (Phloun).[28] Most Karen schooling is organized and controlled by local communities and must seek funding from the community, meaning that securing adequate funding for the teachers and schools is a perennial problem. Truly reliable data are hard to come by, but government statistics suggest that in at least one Karen area, Kayin (Karen) State, literacy rates (presumably in Burmese) are low, at 75 per cent, and out of a population of around 580,000 children, around 70,000 may not be registered. Only 24 per cent of 5-year-old children are in school, and as in other systems, promotion rates between primary and middle, and between middle and high school, are low, as are high school matriculation rates.[29]

As described above, under the government expansion of the education system, new government schools have opened in areas held by the KNU, and in the process, the new government officials often try to bring the local Karen community schools under their control. Karen students appear to have been particularly affected by this development, in that over 1,000 of the daily-wage teachers in Karen areas have been reported as absent from the schools for more than a month. The fact that these teachers cannot speak a Karen language has also had a severe impact on the education of the children in these areas.[30]

The KTWG has been making great efforts in strained circumstances to improve the quality of teaching in Karen schools, and has been instrumental in providing education in hard-to-reach places. For teachers, their efforts have focused on training teachers before they start work and also while they are working, often through "mobile training." The KTWG also supports mother tongue-based teaching and local curriculum. Nevertheless, significant challenges remain. The KED curriculum diverges significantly from that of the government, mostly in the promotion of Karen language instruction and content, and with its limited study of the Burmese language. Unlike in the Mon systems, where some local officials have made accommodations so that students from the Mon national schools can transfer into government schools, no such accommodation is possible for KED schools.[31] There is an acute shortage of Karen teachers, and the curriculum, textbooks, and pedagogy are all outdated.

Many teachers, students, parents, and donors would like to see the possibility of greater harmonization with the government system. This harmonization might look like the Mon system, with instruction in a Karen language with Karen content, but with the gradual introduction of Burmese so that students would have the option of switching into government schools if they chose. In addition to legal barriers—Burmese law does not recognize any ethnic education system—in light of decades of civil war and violence, many Karens are wary of closer integration into the government system. Particular education situations at particular times, for example among refugees on the Thai border, may be less interested in teaching Burmese and focus instead on English in anticipation of resettlement in an English-speaking third country.

Kachin Systems

"Kachin" is actually an umbrella term encompassing linguistically-diverse people who have come to participate, in varying degrees, in a cultural, religious, and political system centered historically on clans and a system of exchanging wives between them.[32] While all the languages falling under the rubric of Kachin are from the same Tibeto-Burman language family, they are from rather different branches and are not mutually intelligible.

Jinghpaw is the majority language with around 630,000 speakers and often serves as the lingua franca. Other languages include Maru (Lhaovo), Zaiwa (Atsi), Lachik, Rawang, and some Lisu, although their participation in the Kachin complex is more recent and contested. As with the Karen, Kachins live throughout a wide region of Upper Burma, not only in Kachin State, but also in many parts of Shan State and, as is the case with most large ethnic groups, in the major cities of Mandalay and Yangon.

The Kachin education system shows most clearly the influence of political developments on education. Key to the current situation is the breakdown of the ceasefire between the Burmese army and the Kachin Independence Organization in June 2011. The Kachin Independence Organization took up arms against the central government in 1961. In 1994, the Kachin Independence Organization signed a ceasefire. Over the decades since its founding, the Kachin Independence Organization and other Kachin organizations have been able to build up a variety of administrative functions and bureaucracy, such as for education, health, and agriculture. KIO-controlled areas have built their own state apparatus.

There are some crucial structural differences between the situation among the Kachin in opposition to the Karen and Mon systems. Thailand, and therefore the Thai-Burma border, served as a haven for refugees and also an access point for international aid and support. This was much less the case along the Burma-China border, and far fewer NGOs have been able to work with the Kachins. On the other hand, the Kachins have been able to rely on revenue from natural resources such as the jade trade with China, which has allowed not only the building up of infrastructure but also acts as a disincentive to signing a ceasefire. Indeed, some Kachin want outright independence, although given the geopolitical context, such an aspiration is likely to prove difficult.

The Education Department of the Kachin Independence Organization, established in 1978, operated 180 schools in 2016 with about 30,000 students. Notably, this system teaches the government curriculum with additions for Jinghpaw language and culture—similar to the Mon model. Unlike the Mon system, however, the Kachin system had used Burmese as the medium of instruction more than Jinghpaw (or other Kachin languages). Textbooks are all in Burmese, even in places where teachers and students have little Burmese ability, a situation resulting in much hardship.

The resumption of fighting since 2011 has had deep impacts on the Kachin society, including on the education system, not least of which is the large number of internally-displaced persons. First, graduates of the

Kachin system are no longer allowed to transfer into government schools, effectively curtailing their education and career choices. Second, there is much greater antagonism—at least among elites—towards the idea of being part of Burma, and therefore many schools are using less Burmese and more Jinghpaw and English. The switch to English is part of creating a curriculum aimed at sending students abroad to study, and thus represents a wider trend of creating a separate system altogether.

The Future of the Ethnic Education Systems: Opportunities and Constraints

This brief overview of the three systems highlights their great diversity in their development and their relations with the government system. In considering the future, the most important question is, what do the various parties concerned want? There are two parts to this question: relations of each of the armed ethnic groups to the central government and military; and more widely, respective ideas about being part of the Republic of the Union of Myanmar. The answers to these questions are key to understanding the futures of ethnic education systems. Groups like the Mon, which see themselves as part of Burma and which have stable ceasefires, would likely move towards integration and accommodation. Even with a ceasefire between the Burmese military and Kachin groups, it is still likely that anti-Burmese sentiment will linger for some time, and in any case, most ethnic minorities are wary of the central government. It will take time to build trust, especially when there are recent memories of conflict, or in places where interactions with the Tatmadaw remain frequent and tense. In certain situations, as seems to be the case with the Kachin and in refugee communities, some groups will prefer not to teach Burmese and use English or another local language instead, and focus on maintaining a separate education system that would not prepare graduates for life in Burma. It is likely that even if association with, or eventual integration into, the central government system is the goal, it will be a long time coming.

Second, there is crossover between discussions of ethnic education systems and mother tongue education. It is important to note briefly that not every ethnic group that speaks a language other than Burmese, or would like to transmit a language other than Burmese, has their own ethnic education system, or is connected with an armed group. Continuing debates about the desirability and possibilities for mother tongue instruction may lead to ethnic education systems changing in the coming years.

At the same time that the Kachin system disfavors Burmese, it may increase the use of English and the various Kachin languages, while the Karen, Mon, and even government systems may reconsider their heavy emphasis on English. Such rethinking of the role of English reflects global shifts away from introducing English as a subject early into formal education, because children are unable to absorb it and tend to create negative associations with it. These questions of language use and attitudes are central to larger questions of federalism, local autonomy, and the integration into the country of areas held by ceasefire groups. Perhaps a federalist model based on territory, as usually understood in Burma, has to be rethought: the ethnic states do not encompass all the members of the ethnicity after which they are named, and large numbers of other ethnic groups live within these territories. For example, some groups in Shan State feel oppressed by Shan elites, language, and culture, and do not want to have to learn Shan.

A third consideration is the legal and constitutional framework. It is not clear to what extent minority issues will garner the attention of the new government. Before the 2015 election, there was a widespread expectation that ethnic minority parties would be elected, but this was largely not the case with a few exceptions. Perhaps as ethnic minority education systems are tied into larger developments in the education system, such as the recent Comprehensive Education Sector Review, some changes may start to take place.

A central constraint is the possibility for the devolution of power, at least within the government system. One way to approach the accommodation of the ethnic education systems is through decentralization. Some might see association with ethnic education systems as a way to devolve power to local levels and to recognize areas of local autonomy. From a strictly legal perspective, however, according to the constitution, matters related to education in terms of policy and curriculum are decided at the national level. Devolution of control would necessitate a constitutional amendment.

Relatedly, decentralization may seem like a logical way to approach addressing change throughout the education system, especially if understood as giving people lower down in the bureaucracy decision-making power. There are few signs that this is happening, or indeed, that many people lower down in the bureaucracy see this as desirable. Even assuming that some kind of legal change could be enacted to allow a devolution in policy making, the Ministry of Education as a whole would have to foster new practices encouraging local initiatives. The evidence of governance suggests a continued preference for decision and responsibility to stay at the highest levels.

Fourth, technical challenges having to do with training, recognition, and equity remain. As discussed above, all education systems throughout the country are under-funded, teachers are not necessarily properly trained, and there is a widespread recognition that curriculum, teaching methods, and textbooks are all in need of an overhaul. Assuming that closer association or harmonization with the central government system is desirable, how exactly the teachers of the ethnic schools will be recognized remains to be negotiated. The solution revolves around training: teachers in the ethnic education systems cannot be recognized by the central government if they have not had formal government training as teachers and civil servants. As described above, sending Burman teachers into ethnic areas, where they will be unable to communicate with local students, serves no one's interests. Yet to not address these questions means undermining equity in terms of all students, whatever their linguistic background, being able to go to school with the same relative advantages.

The possibilities for integrating—or better, harmonizing—the ethnic education systems with the government system, will depend on politics, both in the sense of formal legislation, and in the sense of negotiations. Recognizing the ethnic systems in the short term, allowing transfer between the ethnic and government system, and making provisions for long-term harmonization of qualifications, may all be feasible short-term solutions. If integration or accommodation are not the goals, then education will form a central part of whatever agreements are made between ethnic armed groups and the central government. In the long term, it is likely that ethnic education systems narrowly, and mother tongue education more widely, will be accommodated. The changes in legislation and attitudes in the past several years are reasons to feel optimistic in the long run. In the short term, the future of the ethnic education systems will likely be decided by high-level political negotiation rather than legislation.

A final point is that the ethnic education systems are crucial partners for spreading education throughout the country. Ethnic education systems cannot and do not serve all the students of any given ethnic group because of geographical and political constraints. The government system, even under its current expansion, cannot provide education to everyone, nor will it be able to in the near future. The ethnic education systems are well poised to provide an education in hard-to-reach areas, such as along the Thai-Burma or Thai-China borders. Ethnic education systems, such as the KED, have been in a position to pioneer new practices to improve the quality of education.

Notes

1. I wish to thank Catherine Johnston for her generous time and assistance with revising this chapter and to an anonymous reviewer. All the opinions herein are my own.
2. The term "Myanmar" is unwieldy because it refers to language, people, country, citizenship, and often ethnic majority. Instead of resorting to non-native sounding locutions such as "Myanmar people" or "Myanmar language," I use "Burma" for the country, "Burmese" for the language and citizenship, and "Burman" for the ethnic majority.
3. For an in-depth discussion of decentralization, see Brooke Zobrist and Patrick McCormick, "A Preliminary Assessment of Decentralization in Education: Experiences in Mon State and Yangon Region" (Yangon: Asia Foundation, 2013), pp. 15–24.
4. Kim Jolliffe and Emily Speers Mears, "Strength in Diversity: Towards Universal Education in Myanmar's Ethnic Areas" (Yangon: Asia Foundation, 2016), pp. 37, 109 for the National Language Policy.
5. A 2015 amendment to the National Education Law does permit teachers to use an ethnic language in addition to Burmese at the basic level. The government has paid for classroom assistants who speak local languages to be present in the primary classrooms.
6. See Zobrist and McCormick 2013: 5–6.
7. Figures related to languages and speakers are taken from <www.ethnologue.org> [accessed June 2018].
8. Some Christian minority groups have called for using English as the national language. Unlike former British colonies like India or Malaysia, which have no clear ethnic majority but do have significant numbers of English-speaking elites, Burma has a clear numerical majority, but high levels of English-language proficiency have only been achieved among very small elites.
9. This is an observation based on my 14 years' experience living, working, and conducting research in Burma. A senior Burmese academic researcher I worked with expressed their surprise that members of ethnic minority whose village we were in would want to keep their language since they already have their "ethnic dress" and culture.
10. Jolliffe and Speers Mears (p. 8) note that many think that the Ne Win government immediately outlawed the use of other languages, but it appears that by 1964–65, the nationalization of religious and private schools and the instituting of a national curriculum effectively ended the earlier practice of teaching minority languages.

11. Zobrist and McCormick, pp. 14–15. Spending as a proportion of GDP fell from 0.4 per cent in 2002 to 0.1 per cent in 2007, before rising to 0.7 per cent by 2010. In 2006, Burma's proportion was five times lower than the regional average of 3.6 per cent of GDP. In 2013, spending was raised to 5.8 per cent of the national budget, but inaccuracy dogs government data in Burma.
12. It is not always clear what a "ceasefire" means because skirmishes sometimes break out between the Tatmadaw and signatories. The Tatmadaw is not, after all, under the control of the central government.
13. Brooke Zobrist, "Mapping Teaching-Learning and Operational Experiences in Fifty Monastery Schools Across Myanmar" (Yangon: Pyoe Pin Programme, 2010).
14. Cited in Jolliffe and Speers Mears, p. 22. This is based on Ministry of Immigration data, and like all government data, must be treated with caution.
15. This picture of the government schools is based on Zobrist and McCormick 2013; Jolliffe and Speers Mears 2016; and Zobrist 2010.
16. See Jolliffe and Speers Mears, p. 30 and Catherine Johnston, "A Model of Education in Hard-to-Reach Areas: The KTWF Model" (Yangon: Save the Children, 2016), pp. 43–5.
17. Discussed in Zobrist and McCormick, Jolliffe and Speers Mears, and Johnston, pp. 43–5.
18. The Mon National Education Committee receives most of its funding from foreign donors. See Patrick McCormick, "NPA and the MNEC: Considerations for the Future, an Internal Review" (Yangon: Norwegian People's Aid, 2017).
19. Funding cycles for the MNEC, for example, were typically limited to a year. See McCormick 2017.
20. This is the observation of Zobrist and McCormick after visiting several MNEC-run Mon National Schools in 2013, and McCormick in 2012.
21. Jolliffe and Speers Mears describe this process, pp. 14–16.
22. My discussion of the Mon sector is based on Zobrist and McCormick 2013; Ashley South and Marie Lall, "Schooling and Conflict: Ethnic Education and Mother Tongue-Based Teaching in Myanmar" (Yangon: Asia Foundation, 2016), and McCormick 2017. My thanks to Ashley South for sharing his report.
23. There is also a sizeable Mon-speaking community in Yangon and some around Bago (Pegu).
24. Jolliffe and Speers Mears note that in some ethnic systems, students, at least at higher levels, often do not take these classes seriously because they are not part of the official government exams. To what extent this applies to the Mon system merits further investigation.
25. See Lawi Weng, "Lawmakers Highlight Shortcomings in Ethnic Language Teaching," in *The Irrawaddy*, 10 June 2016.
26. South and Lall 2017.

27. Johnston, p. 13.
28. In the past, Pwo parents often sent their children to nearby Mon monasteries to be educated, hence the old term "Mon Karen" for Pwo speakers.
29. Johnston, pp. 16–17, who is quoting Department of Population figures, and KTWG information for promotion and matriculation rates.
30. Johnston, p. 7.
31. South and Lall 2016.
32. See for example Mandy Sadan, *Being and Becoming Kachin: Histories Beyond the State in the Borderworlds of Burma* (London: The British Academy, 2013).

References

British Academy and the École française d'Extrême-Orient. 2015. *Language Choice in Higher Education: Challenges and Opportunities*. Yangon.

Callahan, Mary. 2004. *Making Enemies: War and State Building in Burma*. Singapore: NUS Press.

Ha, Phan Le, Joyce Kho, and Brendan Chang. 2013. "Nation Building, English as an International Language, and Language Debate: Malaysia and Possible Ways Forward." *Journal of International and Comparative Education* 2, no. 2: 58–71.

Jacquet, Carine. 2015. "The Kachin Conflict: Testing the Limits of the Political Transition of Myanmar." *IRASEC Occasional Paper Series 2*.

Lall, Marie and Ashley South. 2013. "Comparing Models of Non-state Ethnic Education in Myanmar: The Mon and Karen National Education Regimes." *Journal of Contemporary Asia* 44, no. 2: 298–321.

Mandy, Sadan. 2013. *Being and Becoming Kachin: Histories Beyond the State in the Borderworlds of Burma*. London: The British Academy.

Paauw, Scott. 2009. "One Land, One Nation, One Language: An Analysis of Indonesia's National Language Policy." *University of Rochester Working Papers in the Language Sciences* 5, no. 1: 2–16.

Romaine, Suzanne. 2002. "The Impact of Language Policy on Endangered Languages." *International Journal on Multicultural Societies* 4, no. 2: 194–212.

South, Ashley and Marie Lall. 2016. *Schooling and Conflict: Ethnic Education and Mother Tongue-Based Teaching in Myanmar*. Yangon: Asia Foundation.

Steinberg, David. 2001. *Burma: The State of Myanmar*. Washington DC: Georgetown University Press.

Taylor, Robert. 2009. *The State in Myanmar* (Second Edition). Singapore: NUS Press.

Zobrist, Brooke. 2010. *Mapping Teaching-Learning and Operational Experiences in Fifty Monastery Schools Across Myanmar*. Yangon: Pyoe Pin Programme.

Zobrist, Brooke and Patrick McCormick. 2013. *A Preliminary Assessment of Decentralization in Education: Experiences in Mon State and Yangon Region*. Yangon: Asia Foundation.

CHAPTER 9

Myanmar's Political Transition and Its Effects on the Buddhist Religio-Political Landscape

Matthew J. Walton

Introduction

After almost five decades of international isolation and repressive rule by a succession of military governments, Myanmar began a gradual political transition in March 2011, with the partial handover of power to a quasi-civilian government. Defying expectations, then-President Thein Sein, a former military general himself, initiated a series of reforms that opened up significant space for political participation and economic development. However, each of the encouraging reforms has carried with it a sobering counterpart that serves not only as a reminder that the military still maintains significant formal and informal power and influence in Myanmar, but that any one of the country's many domestic conflicts could serve to undermine the promise of democratization. These challenges have translated into ongoing feelings of anxiety, cynicism, and uncertainty for many in the population. Anxiety related to the perpetuation of the Buddhist religion, and specifically of a Burmese Buddhist identity, in the face of so many outside influences has been particularly strong and often directed towards non-Buddhist communities, specifically Muslims.

Buddhist influences seemed subdued during the first year of Myanmar's current political transition. However, starting from the violence between Buddhists and Muslims in June 2012, continuing through the resurgence of Buddhist activism and anti-Muslim violence and sentiment since that time, and culminating in the massive wave of violence against, and the ethnic, national and religious exclusion of, the Rohingya in the most recent re-ignition of that conflict since August 2016, it is apparent that religion remains an important factor in Burmese politics. The current political transition has undoubtedly provided additional political space for the expression of Buddhist perspectives and concerns in the public sphere, some of which support democratic reform and some of which express a more anti-democratic or exclusionary agenda. Additionally, political, economic, and social changes have created an environment of uncertainty in which both Buddhism and the dominant sense of Burmese national identity as Buddhist have been portrayed as under threat. This chapter explores some of the aspects of Myanmar's political transition that seem to have enabled or supported the rise of Buddhist activist groups, especially those that have taken a leading role in anti-Muslim protests and violence. It lays out the general religious landscape in contemporary Myanmar and looks at the rise of several influential Buddhist activist organizations since 2012. It then considers several different factors that may have promoted the rise of these groups or conditioned the dynamics of Buddhist-Muslim conflict, including changing communication practices and technologies, the influence of global anti-Muslim discourse and sentiment, the reorganization of democratic space (including lifting restrictions on speech and expression), anxieties about Buddhism, and perceived threats to monks' authority and role in society. Finally, it considers whether and how these dynamics have changed since the former democratic opposition National League for Democracy (NLD) assumed control of the government in early 2016.

Religious Landscape

Myanmar is a religiously plural state, with a clear Buddhist majority, but not much clarity beyond that. The general stance of scholars and analysts has been to treat demographic figures with scepticism, mostly because state record-keeping has tended to mis-categorize any member of ethnic groups with majority Buddhist populations (including the Burmans, Mons, Rakhine, and Shans) as Buddhist. But even within the category of "Buddhists," state categorization does not meaningfully reflect the adherence to both Buddhist and animist (or pre-Buddhist) practices that is widespread among much of the population.[1] With UN assistance and funding from multiple Western countries, Myanmar held a census in 2014 (the first in over 30 years) that was also the subject of widespread criticism because of alleged mis-categorization of ethnic groups and the last minute exclusion of the Rohingya Muslim population.[2] Due to the sensitivity of religious issues since inter-religious conflict broke out in 2012, a breakdown of census data according to religious categories was not released until July 2016. According to those figures, of Myanmar's approximately 51.5 million population, 87.9 per cent are Buddhists, 6.2 per cent are Christians, 4.3 per cent are Muslims, with the remaining population consisting of Hindus, animists, and other religions.[3]

It has also been common for people to mention the *sangha* (Buddhist monkhood) as the only institution that can rival the Burmese military, in terms of both size and influence. We can only guess at the numerical accuracy of this claim, since a significant proportion of Myanmar's monastic population is transient. While some "career" monks take robes at an early age and see the monkhood as a lifelong vocation, many others move in and out of the order. It has been common in Myanmar (as in other Theravada Buddhist countries in Southeast Asia) for men to ritually enter the monkhood for short periods at certain times in their lives. And of course, only a small percentage of the large novice population will go on to take their full vows. This practice of temporary ordination also results in closer relationships between monastics and the laity, as many who are laypeople have had (however brief) experience of the life of the monk. However, it also reflects a situation of uncertainty and even anxiety regarding the perpetuation of the institution, which itself is seen as necessary for the perpetuation of the religion. If young men are not repopulating the *sangha*, Buddhism itself could be seen as endangered. It is difficult to know the real extent of any given perception of threat to the monkhood due to a younger generation's unwillingness to take robes, since these concerns recur throughout Myanmar's history, but the widespread perception and sincere concern certainly does animate movements designed to protect the religion, as will be demonstrated below.

Because of their vows of renunciation, their (idealized) detachment from worldly concerns, and their orientation towards spiritual matters, monks possess a high degree of moral authority. Even monks whose conduct does not always accord with this ideal are generally respected because of their association with the institution of the *sangha*, the Buddhist monkhood. However, it is this ideal of detachment that complicates monastic intervention into areas of lay life, including politics. Numerous rules in the *vinaya* (the monastic code of conduct) prohibit a range of common worldly activities, but monks have commonly gotten involved in the realm of the mundane and have developed complex justifications for their actions, some of which are considered below as part of their actions on behalf of democratization or nationalism.

The Buddhist *sangha* is deeply rooted in Myanmar's society and there is a strong cultural reverence attached to the vocation of a Buddhist monk that amplifies the power of monks' pronouncements.[4] The words of monks are almost always accepted without argument or question by the laity or by more junior monks, at least publicly. Monks are assumed to be better acquainted with the Buddha's teachings and to have spent time contemplating them and their implications for the laity's daily conduct. Monastic authority also derives (both collectively and for individual monks) from the practice or perception of renunciation. As evidenced in the seemingly widespread and persistent support for the monk-led association MaBaTha (described in more detail below),[5] monks are particularly able to rally and guide the laity in matters connected to Buddhism.

The relationship between Buddhist authorities and Burmese state authorities has been complex, as is the case in other Theravada Buddhist countries where the cultural norm is usually for monks to remain detached from political life but practically monks engage in politics in a number of ways. The state has sought to regulate the monkhood's potential as a political (and oppositional) actor but also to draw on the legitimation that religious endorsement can provide. Technically the monkhood is completely dependent financially, not on the state necessarily, but on the lay community more generally. Monks rely on the laity for donations of all of their basic needs, including food, clothing, and shelter. In practice, this is a well-institutionalized process and there are many rich monasteries. Monks, monasteries, and religious organizations receive donations from individuals connected to the Burmese government and from the government itself; this is a historically-rooted practice that mirrors the ways in which Buddhist kings would have been expected to materially support the *sangha*. Monasteries also rely on state authorities to continue to honor certain economic privileges, including tax-exempt status. Scholars have documented the ways in which successive governments in Myanmar have attempted to assert their control over the projects of monks through offering religious titles and material support.[6]

Despite being relatively decentralized, the *sangha* has retained and developed a strong communications network that has only been bolstered by technological advances. Accounts from monks and nuns involved in organizing the 2007, so-called "Saffron Revolution," demonstrations reveal the continued use of traditional forms of communication between religious institutions, augmented by the targeted use of email and limited social media (which were still not widespread in the country at the time). These networks have also been used since 2012 by the 969 Movement and MaBaTha to convene large numbers of monks and lay supporters in short amounts of time, with social media usage now being commonplace.

Buddhist Activism Since 2012

While the aim of this chapter is to explore the conditions that facilitated the rise of religious actors in Myanmar's current transition period, it is necessary to include at least a brief overview of some of the key events and dynamics that have characterized the past few years. In June 2012, after the rape and murder of a Buddhist girl by three Muslim men in Myanmar's western Rakhine State, ethnic Rakhine Buddhists retaliated by killing ten Muslims in an attack on a bus. The fighting quickly escalated and, although conflict was primarily between Rakhine Buddhists and Rohingya Muslims, other Muslim groups were also victims. Both Buddhists and Muslims suffered casualties and displacement, although most accounts of the conflict agree that Rohingya suffered a disproportionately greater loss of life and property. In October 2012, violence again broke out across Rakhine State, bringing the death toll to at least 200 with more than 100,000 displaced.[7]

Riots soon flared in other parts of the country, mostly directed at Muslim communities. In March 2013, the central Myanmar town of Meikhtila was rocked by several days of riots that resulted in dozens of deaths.[8] The Shan State city of Lashio also saw anti-Muslim violence in May 2013, as did Thandwe in Rakhine State, in October of the same year. The final instance of riotous violence in that period occurred at the beginning of July 2014 in Mandalay, the second largest city in the country, and resulted in the deaths of two people, one Buddhist and one Muslim.

Organized Buddhist groups, led by monks, have been at the center of anti-Muslim activities in the country since 2012. The first to emerge was the 969 Movement, a decentralized, loose grouping of monks and laypeople. While many commentators have portrayed U Wirathu and other prominent monks as "leaders" of the movement, this is an incorrect characterization, as even the monks who have claimed credit for the contemporary revival of the symbol have emphasized its leaderless nature and the availability of the 969 logo to anyone seeking to defend and promote Buddhism. The movement rose to prominence in 2012 and its supporters have claimed that their movement is intended solely for the protection of Buddhism and not as an anti-Muslim crusade. However, some of its leading monastic members regularly preach sermons in which they spread rumors, denigrate Islam and Muslims, and the main activity of 969 when it emerged into the public was an economic boycott of Muslim businesses. The movement has also employed social media (especially Facebook) and mass distribution of sermons and anti-Muslim tracts to disseminate its message. Despite the tendency for analysts to overstate both its coherence and its unity, 969 has always been a decentralized movement held together by a common symbol and some roughly defined common tenets. It has become a relatively minor player, having been surpassed in organizational capacity, public prominence, and influence by MaBaTha.

The Organization for the Protection of Race and Religion (known more commonly by its Burmese language acronym MaBaTha) was officially founded in 2013 but was publicly unveiled at a large conference of monks convened in Mandalay in January 2014. The formation of this group may have initially been a response to a ban on the political use of the 969 symbol in September 2013 by the State Sangha Maha Nayaka Council, the highest religious authority in the country.[9] However, it also displayed a tactical shift, working more closely with political parties and other actors inside the system, through channels unavailable to Myanmar's civil society actors under previous authoritarian governments, including championing four controversial pieces of religious legislation that are analyzed in more detail below. The 969-allied monks such as U Wirathu have also held prominent and visible positions within MaBaTha, although these relationships and overlapping memberships have shifted over time, with Wirathu resigning his official position in MaBaTha in early 2018. These changing configurations of alliances and cooperation, along with the shift in tactics indicate that Buddhist nationalism in contemporary Myanmar is both dynamic and responsive to changing political opportunities. The ways in which Muslims have been portrayed by Buddhists have also been somewhat dynamic, although one element that has remained consistent since 2012 is the view that Muslims and Islam pose an existential threat to Buddhists and to Buddhism in a range of different ways.[10]

MaBaTha was most widely known in association with the four "laws for the protection of race and religion" that it helped to write and promote. The first of the laws, which sought to restrict inter-religious marriage, was introduced to the public in June 2013, with the others (related, respectively, to population control, religious conversion, and polygamy) unveiled the following month. They received strong support from a wide range of political actors, including members of the then-ruling USDP (Union Solidarity and Development Party) government, and were passed in mid-2015, in the months leading up to the November elections, although with vocal dissent from NLD MPs and many civil society groups.

In addition to these bills, MaBaTha has launched campaigns to restrict and even prohibit cattle slaughter by Muslims for economic or ritual purposes, effectively destroying livelihoods.[11] During the 2015 election campaign prominent MaBaTha monks endorsed President Thein Sein and the ruling USDP while painting the opposition NLD as the "party of Islamists" and weak on the protection of Buddhism.[12] Although the NLD's sweeping victory was certainly evidence that voters rejected that characterization of the country's main democratic opposition party, the monk-led campaign against the NLD had additional effects that will resonate through the political system in the coming years. Cowed by criticism from MaBaTha, the democratic opposition party declined to run a single Muslim candidate, out of over 1,100 seats that it contested (the USDP also had no Muslim candidates). This monk-led anti-Muslim sentiment has led to the complete formal political exclusion of Muslim representation in Myanmar's Parliament, for the first time in history.

Since the NLD took control of the government in 2016, its officials have conducted a sporadic campaign against MaBaTha and individual monks connected with nationalist and anti-Islamic activities. Many observers saw a July 2016 statement by the State Sangha Maha Nayaka Committee (MaHaNa), the official national Buddhist authority in Myanmar, as a sign of the beginning of the end of MaBaTha. In fact, although it came in the context of denunciations of MaBaTha from other leading monks and government officials[13] and a renewed push to pass an anti-hate speech law that had been stalled in Myanmar's Parliament,[14] the statement was not a rejection of MaBaTha's aims, necessarily, but just an attempt by the Buddhist authorities to distance themselves from criticism of the group's more extreme activities.[15] Similarly, a more targeted disciplining statement in May 2017, that barred the group from using the Burmese term "*a-myo batha thathana*" in its name was equally not a "ban" on the group, as widely understood and celebrated by foreign and domestic media,[16] but yet another move to insulate "Buddhism" writ large from criticisms directed at MaBaTha and its more extreme elements, while avoiding any direct confrontation with the organization.

Since the NLD took over the government, MaBaTha in 2016 experienced the high-profile defection of several leading members of the group,[17] saw the formation of an allied lay organization in May 2017,[18] and, ultimately, accepted the MaHaNa ruling and officially changed its name to the Buddha Dhamma Parahita Foundation (although at least two MaBaTha chapters, in Mandalay and Karen State, are resisting the name change). But whatever name it is using, and facilitated by its sophisticated utilization of social media, MaBaTha remains a popular organization in Myanmar, with aims (not just anti-Muslim sentiments, but pro-Buddhist intentions as well) that are widely endorsed by a broad section of the Buddhist population.[19]

Transitional Factors and Dynamics Affecting the Religious Landscape

Changing Communication Practices and Technologies

An incredibly important and influential trend in Buddhist communication practice in Myanmar has been the growing production and expanding availability of videos of monks preaching. This is a significant development that has had an enormous impact on the ways in which Buddhists share information about their religion, the ways they treat popular monks, and the ways in which certain interpretations of Buddhist teachings and Buddhist identity spread more rapidly in Myanmar today. Even a decade ago, there was a limited season within which it was common for a small population of monks to travel to different places to give sermons. One might hear a teaching from a local monk on the occasion of a festival day, but opportunities to hear other monks were relatively rare. Cassette recordings of some more famous monks circulated, but not widely. With the advent of cheaper video production capabilities, however, the sermon a monk gives in a relatively isolated part of the country can be turned into a DVD and within a week, be available for purchase on the streets of Yangon, or be uploaded to YouTube almost instantaneously. When a community sponsors a monk to give a sermon, they can make and distribute videos as a form of merit-making, making the teachings available to those who weren't able to attend the actual event.

These videos are shared among friends and family (and they are relatively affordable in DVD copy and increasingly freely available online) and discussed and circulated around neighborhoods. They have also produced super-star monks, who are known widely for their insightful or at least entertaining sermons. And, they have proven to be an effective vehicle for the spread of nationalist and anti-Muslim views. In addition to the videos spreading a message rapidly to a large audience, 969, MaBaTha, and other groups have developed extensive and increasingly sophisticated online presences, with leading monks having tens of thousands of followers on social media sites. They are also complemented by a more difficult to track network of profiles that "like," retweet, or otherwise circulate and reinforce their messages.[20]

At the same time, we should be very careful in assessing the causal effects of either new social media or expanded internet access. With very limited empirical data that would help us understand exactly how online communication possibilities support or interact with more traditional, offline modes of communication, we must rely primarily on anecdotal accounts. What does seem clear is that these new modes of communication and dissemination have sped up the sharing of information and have expanded audiences, in a relatively short amount of time, allowing for the popular rise of individual monks and of particular groups such as MaBaTha. What remains to be seen, however, is whether these new possibilities have fundamentally changed Burmese practices of evaluating information or the prevailing dynamics of networks of trust and legitimation. We should also be wary of blanket statements that relate to the sharing of false information or the naiveté of Burmese information consumers, since these are based on false assumptions, negatively contributing to an understanding of present dynamics.[21]

Global Anti-Muslim Discourse and Sentiment

Anti-Muslim sentiment is not new in Myanmar. Although the circumstances differed in very important ways, riots in the 1930s variously targeted Indians, Muslims, or those with darker skin who looked to be from South Asia. In part, sentiment against these groups was the result of their privileged position (or perceived privileged position) under the British colonial government, and the sheer changes in demographics in certain parts of the country in the early decades of British rule were enough to animate majority Burman and Buddhist fears. One of the most influential organizations of the nationalist movement was the *Dobama Asiayone* (We, the Burmese Association). While it made its name advocating for Burmese causes before and after the 1930 riots, its boundaries of national inclusion were actually both broad and malleable, at times allowing space for non-Buddhists, non-Burmans, and even non-Burmese nationals within the national community.[22] After the military takeover in 1962, the government regularly and strategically used, or at least allowed, anti-Muslim sentiment and violence to take place at times.

But the present moment seems particularly ripe for the kind of anti-Muslim discrimination and violence that we have seen in Myanmar since 2012. Islamophobia existed prior to the attacks on the United States on 11 September 2001, but since that time, the expansion of a "global war on terror" (GWOT) has affected media, communications, and people's perceptions of Muslims.[23] One scholar has referred to this as an "industry of Islamophobia."[24] It is certainly the case that those who have encouraged Myanmar's anti-Muslim movements have benefitted from the near-continuous reinforcement of GWOT images of Muslims as violent, expansionist, and singular and unitary in form. But we cannot forget that those actors themselves, whether monks, military officials, or members of the democratic opposition, have also been influenced by the circulation of these images.[25] As Matt Schissler puts it, "The construction of anti-Muslim narratives circulating *within* Myanmar draws on arguments that are not spatially limited to *inside* Myanmar."[26] Myanmar's print media, whether government-controlled or privately owned, rarely—if ever—run positive stories about Muslims or Islamic countries; in fact, most depictions simply reinforce the stereotypical associations with violence.

Reorganization of Democratic Space

Myanmar's transition has certainly been guided and circumscribed by the military, in accordance with its philosophy of "discipline-flourishing democracy." Yet, despite the fact that the 2008 Constitution legitimizes and institutionalizes various direct roles for the military in politics, it also lays out key rights and freedoms, including broad freedom of speech and expression. Monks and religious organizations have made effective use of that space, even testing its limits in the early years of the transition. Both individual monks and monastic and lay groups have moved into social media spaces in significant ways in the past five years, using Facebook and other sites to share information, including both verified news and unsubstantiated rumors. Until early 2016, they rarely received any sanction, even when they have been implicated in contributing to violence, such as in 2014, when many people believed that U Wirathu's sharing of an untrue rumor about Muslims in Mandalay was responsible for the outbreak of riots in that city.[27] That dynamic has changed somewhat under the NLD, as described above, although the NLD's antagonistic attitude towards MaBaTha sits uncomfortably alongside the party's general embrace of an anti-Rohingya sentiment and staunch support for the military's operations in Rakhine State.

Public protests against Muslims and allegedly in defense of Buddhism have also been a common sight in the past few years, in cities and towns across the country. In the months leading up to the elections in November 2015, MaBaTha held numerous rallies ostensibly in support or celebration of its four religious protection laws. NLD party members and activists supporting other causes complained that gatherings of as few as five people for issues such as interfaith peace or student rights received harsh responses from authorities, while in some cases, MaBaTha events were allowed to continue even without official permission.[28] Apparently former President U Thein Sein was enlisted to intervene personally to secure permission for MaBaTha to hold its largest rally at Thuwunna Stadium in Yangon in October 2015.[29]

It can be difficult to know whether a lack of official response or sanction represents a general unwillingness on the part of public officials to criticize or punish a monk, or whether it reflects tacit support of the rhetoric and activities of these monks. Certainly some monastic leaders believe it is the latter, as one told Reuters in 2013: "By letting us give speeches to protect our religion and race, I assume they are supporting us."[30] However, under the USDP government, while officials were reluctant to comment negatively on even the most virulent and incendiary anti-Muslim speech of monks and other religious leaders, they did selectively target pro-NLD monks. Prominent and outspoken monk Shwe Nya Wa Sayadaw was evicted from his monastery in 2012 after hosting political events and also received a one-year ban on public speaking in 2015.[31]

It is not only the expansion of space for free expression that has altered the dynamics of the religious sphere, the implementation of a system of elected government, organized largely along democratic lines has also created new dynamics in the relationships between religious and political actors, as well as new opportunities for activism. While the government might still have considerable control over society, it is obligated to respond to public discontent in ways that it would not have had to previously. MaBaTha's protests against a planned development project near Yangon's iconic Shwedagon Pagoda led to the cancellation of the project.[32] Protests against Time magazine's controversial 2013 cover that labelled U Wirathu the "face of Buddhist terror" brought strong condemnation from the Myanmar government, with then-President Thein Sein stating that he considered the monk a "son of the Buddha."

In addition to pressure on public officials to support or allow Buddhist activism, the 2015 election created incentives for politico-religious partnerships. Many MaBaTha and 969 monks spoke out strongly in support of then-President Thein Sein and the USDP government, and against the NLD, even as the organization's official spokesmen maintained political neutrality. But smaller parties such as the National Democratic Force (NDF) emphasized their religious *bona fides* in an attempt to win public support; the NDF not only endorsed MaBaTha's four laws, but also made the “protection of race and religion” a central plank of its platform. Overall, the reorganization of democratic space in Myanmar since 2011 has created situations in which Buddhist activist groups have been able to effectively use new rights to freedom of speech and expression and also put pressure on public officials as necessary, allowing them to expand their activism and influence significantly.

Anxiety About Buddhism

The word that Theravada Buddhists use to describe their religion in its entirety is *sasana*, which includes not just the sacred texts and commentaries, doctrines and values, monks and sacred sites, but also the lived experience of Buddhism within the population, something that effectively encapsulates Buddhist identity. The Buddha preached that, like everything else that comes into existence, even his teachings and the religious practice that has grown up around them, are temporary and impermanent. There are different interpretations of exactly how long he predicted the religion would last, but the dominant view in Myanmar seems to be that Buddhism is on the downswing and every effort must be made to preserve Buddhist teachings and strengthen moral practice.

Anxiety about Buddhism is not new in Myanmar. After the British colonial administration, which consolidated control over the entire country in 1887, refused to support the institution of the monkhood in the same way that Burmese kings had, and sought to supplant the monastic role in education, many Burmese Buddhists worried that the result would be a decline in monastic discipline and in inculcating Buddhist values in children. One way that Buddhists responded to these fears about the decline and disappearance of Buddhism was to look inward and attempt to strengthen their own practice. The first few decades of the twentieth century saw an unprecedented expansion of lay Buddhist social activism, as well as increased lay involvement in Buddhist practices that had previously been largely reserved for monks.[33]

By contrast, as the nationalist movement gathered strength in the 1920s and 1930s, another perspective was dominant, the idea that Burmese Buddhists constituted a particular community, one defined by religion, but also language, a shared history, and by birth into a particular culture. Nationalist riots in the 1930s were directed first against Indians and later more specifically against Muslims (although more generally, people with darker skin and features associated with South Asian descent were targeted in both cases), coding these populations as foreigners, outside of a national community that had occasionally flexible boundaries but was generally defined in terms of both Burmese (meaning non-Indian and non-Chinese) nationality and the Buddhist religion.

Nationalist Buddhist groups in Myanmar today justify discrimination and, implicitly, even violence against Muslims as a necessary response to what they see as the imminent threat of Islam's expansion in Asia, and its encroachment upon the *sasana*, the Buddhist community. They often make reference to a fabricated historical narrative in which places such as Iraq, Afghanistan, and Indonesia were formerly Buddhist countries but were conquered by Muslims and forcefully converted to become the Islamic-majority states we see today. This narrative is false, but it contains enough references to actual historical events that it can be convincing, especially when preached by those with religious authority in a place like Myanmar that has been closed for decades and which has a rote education system strongly influenced by Buddhism.

This existential fear, that Buddhism itself is in danger of disappearing, is what underlies an implied argument that the ends (preserving Buddhism) justify means that might seem to be counter to some core Buddhist values. And any specific anxieties about Buddhism are reinforced by other anxieties related to the transition more broadly, including concerns about power, access, influence, economic development, and a host of other issues. Because Buddhism is such a core part of many people's identities, but also appears to be controllable in a way that many of these other globalized processes are not, many of the diverse transitional anxieties and uncertainties in Myanmar are channelled through a very particular fear about the disappearance of the *sasana*, the Buddhist religion.

Threats to Monks' Authority and Role in Society

One additional consideration of how Myanmar's recent political changes might have affected the religious sphere has to do with moral and cultural authority and the legitimation of power, especially the role of monks as mediators. The traditional Theravāda Buddhist model of politics has been referred to by scholars as the "two wheels of *dhamma*."[34] In this idealized configuration, the wheel of moral authority was embodied by the *sangha*, the community of monks. Their role was to both restrain and legitimize the actions of the wheel of secular authority, personified by the king. In this way, they could encourage the king to rule according to the Buddha's teachings and act in a mediating role between the laity and the political authority.

This was a system that was guided by a logic of *kamma*, a word that literally means "action" but refers more broadly to the Buddha's teachings on cause and effect. Kings and others with worldly authority were in their positions of power due to having performed great acts of goodness in previous lives. Lay people were simply subjects to be ruled and guided, as the general Buddhist conception of human nature is of the *puthujjana*, human beings as morally flawed, controlled by desire and craving, and likely to act in self-centered ways, hurting themselves and others. Monks had a liminal existence, having stepped outside of the normal realm of human activity by taking their vows and engaging in practices of renunciation and moral development. While the king (or political authority) might be at the apex of the pyramid, it was the monk with whom people would interact on a more daily basis, as teacher, guide, and moral exemplar.

Equally important in this relationship was the existence of monks as "fields of merit," or targets of donations. Because they are prohibited from working, owning property, or having money, monks are completely reliant on the laity for their material existence. Traditionally, kings or political authorities have been the most generous and consistent donors. Not only would donations to monks bring merit (or good *kamma*) to the donor, donations have been a way for political authorities to shore up their legitimacy in the eyes of their subjects. In the traditional model, kings were expected to support the monkhood, and scholarship has pointed to recent examples in Myanmar where, even though previous military governments were reviled by much of the population, their considerable religious donations generated some goodwill, or at the least feelings of ambivalence because they were seen to be acting as a good Buddhist political authority ought to.[35]

It is important to remember that this was an idealized model that comes to us primarily through texts written by kings, ministers, and monks, designed to reinforce royal and monastic authority. But even if the extent of its central legitimating nature is overstated, it is certainly true that even today, monks enjoy a great deal of prestige, moral authority, and influence over the Buddhist lay population. Their teachings about moral conduct in everyday life are relevant not only for daily interactions, but for people's political decision-making and engagement as well. In this context, it is reasonable to consider whether the structural changes that accompany democratization might have effects on this set of relationships.

Indeed, this is what Bénédicte Brac de La Perrière, a scholar of religion in Myanmar, argues is precisely the case in the country, in a passage worth citing at length:

> … the opening of a legal field of action for politics legitimized by popular vote creates a new situation, notably regarding the fact that legitimatization of power no longer directly depends on the monks as 'fields of merit', which breaks the symbiotic nature of the link between the state and the sangha. Moreover, if political action is now authorized for laypeople within the constitutional framework, it is not authorized for members of the sangha who, as in Thailand, are even excluded from voting due to their status of renouncer.[36]

On the surface this seems to be a compelling reason and the important legitimating role that we know monks play in Burmese society suggests that we should seriously consider monastic anxiety over loss of status as a potential reason for the anti-democratic views and actions of some monks over the past few years.

However, on closer examination, there doesn't seem to be much evidence that this is the case, or at least that this is a motivation for anti-Muslim or anti-NLD activities. First, while monastic views regarding democracy are varied and complex,[37] even many anti-Muslim monks have not necessarily expressed skeptical views regarding democracy or its legitimating mechanisms, simply about the place of certain non-Buddhist populations in Myanmar's polity. Second, the formal legitimating mechanisms between state and *sangha* have likely been weakening for decades, at least since the colonial period irreversibly ended monarchical rule in Burma. Many monks both supported and engaged in democratic politics during the Parliamentary period in Burma between 1948–58 and 1960–62, not necessarily seeing a challenge to their mediating role in that transitional period.

It is certainly true that monks are excluded from voting by the Constitution, which prohibits them from either voting or running for office. Yet, this couldn't be experienced as a loss, since monks have never had this privilege in modern Burmese political history. Furthermore, although occasionally in the past few years Burmese monks have suggested that they ought to be allowed to vote, these comments have been relatively rare and usually only in juxtaposition to what they perceive as the injustice of "foreign" Rohingya populations being allowed to vote when "patriotic" monastics are not. While there have been no formal studies of lay or monastic attitudes towards monastic voting in Myanmar, overwhelmingly consistent anecdotal evidence suggests that there is very little support, at least at the moment, for monks receiving the franchise.

In all likelihood, to the degree that monks are experiencing anxiety regarding the erosion of their legitimating roles or traditional authority or influence, it is related to various aspects of modernity and modern communication more generally, rather than the specific changes wrought by Myanmar's gradual democratic transition. Monks are having to compete with online games and other entertainment to gain the attention of a population that is not only newly freed from decades of isolation, but globally connected at an astonishing rate. The democratic nature of the country's current political changes certainly relates to the speed with which opportunities for communication are opening up, but as of yet, it is not clear that the anxieties that monks have been expressing through primarily anti-Muslim and anti-Rohingya demonstrations are related to their perceived loss of legitimating status in the transition.

Conclusion

It seems clear that several aspects of Myanmar's transition created conditions that were ripe for the rapid ascendancy of Buddhist activist groups such as 969 and MaBaTha. Yet the electoral victory of the NLD in November 2015 brought to power a very different government, one that has, at times, appeared more willing to use its political authority and influence to restrict anti-Muslim speech and activity in certain ways, particularly targeting MaBaTha. Specifically, occasional pressure from NLD government officials on Buddhist authorities to take some sort of action has signalled a significant shift from the permissive environment for religious activism and anti-Muslim activity that was characteristic of the previous USDP government. However, it remains important to understand that an NLD victory did *not* represent a complete rejection of either MaBaTha or its general narrative of Buddhism under threat. At best, it suggested that voters did not accept the most extreme MaBaTha argument that the "pro-Muslim" NLD aimed to usher in an era of "Islamization" in Myanmar, or even the weaker version in which a vote for the NLD was a vote against the interests of Buddhists. But the more cautious overall interpretation is that most voters' desire for overall political change ranked higher than their concerns about religious issues, at least for the moment.

Besides changes in the government's stance, we might also consider changes in the overall political landscape and within MaBaTha itself. The group benefitted from being able to organize around a key issue, the four "Laws for the Protection of Race and Religion" that Parliament passed in stages earlier in 2015. As the organization has diversified its methods and the issues it addresses, there have also been signs of divergent priorities among the group's leadership and membership. After the 2015 election,

U Wirathu stated that he would continue to work in the political arena to pass legislation that would ban Muslim dress and other customary practices. Other monks connected to MaBaTha have discussed a campaign to give monks and nuns the vote, something that would be very controversial in Myanmar and unlikely to garner much lay support. The campaign against cattle slaughtering also reportedly produced a dispute within the organization. The popular Sitagu Sayadaw used his speech at the MaBaTha rally on 4 October 2017 to endorse a push make Buddhism the state religion, raising yet another potentially controversial issue. The divergent individual and institutional responses within the organization to the 2017 MaHaNa order to change its name suggest that the field of religious activism in Myanmar remains heterogeneous, only galvanizing around particular issues, but riven due to localized and personalized interests.

Furthermore, official actions (whether from the government or religious authorities) designed to respond to persistent religious conflict and discrimination have been sporadic, unfocused, and defensive in nature. By early 2018, it seemed from interviews and media reports that MaBaTha's leadership was less sanguine about its earlier dominant position in Myanmar's religio-political space. However, the group remains influential, particularly at the grassroots level, due primarily to its involvement and association with so many activities seen as essential to the protection and propagation of Buddhism.

It is also important to remember that an endorsement of the NLD's political project is not inconsistent with anti-Muslim politics more broadly, or discrimination against other religious, ethnic, or national identities (Chinese, for example, continue to be targeted). In addition to strengthening community networks that can respond to violence and instigation, and fostering a discourse of defending Buddhism that is not anti-Muslim or hostile to non-Buddhists, those interested in advancing political reform in Myanmar must ensure that the NLD does not succumb to pressure from groups like MaBaTha or to anti-Muslim individuals in its own ranks or among its allies.

This concern can be seen particularly in the NLD government's indefensible lack of response to continued abuses against vulnerable Rohingya Muslims, including its strong endorsement of punitive military action after alleged attacks by Islamic militants against security outposts in Rakhine State in October 2016, and the efforts of its leaders to undermine Rohingya claims of abuse and discrimination that have only multiplied and become more credible since that time. This suggests that the NLD has no intention of acting to stop the targeting of *certain* Muslim groups, even as it takes (limited) action against MaBaTha and a few of its most prominent voices.

Myanmar's nascent democratic transition has been a remarkable opportunity that unfolded more rapidly than most observers expected, but has also failed to live up to certain minimal expectations. Some aspects of the transition clearly assisted the rise of Buddhist activist groups such as 969 and MaBaTha, both of which have contained problematic anti-Muslim orientations, in addition to more accepted and acceptable stances towards the development of Buddhism and Buddhist practice more generally. MaBaTha in particular was able to step into a religio-political vacuum to take advantage of widespread anxieties regarding threats to Buddhism, but might have overstepped its bounds in being seen to move more explicitly into the realm of politics in the lead-up to the 2015 election. While the initial years of the transition created opportunities for these groups to emerge and rise to prominence, a shifting political landscape and an expansion of the field of religious activism will likely further splinter MaBaTha and its offshoots, even as the sentiments motivating its rise persist in influencing Myanmar's politics for the foreseeable future.

Notes

1. On this subject, see an excellent essay by Bénédicte Brac de la Perrière. "An Overview of the Field of Religion in Burmese Studies," *Asian Ethnology* 68, no. 2 (2009): 185–210.
2. International Crisis Group, *Counting the Costs: Myanmar's Problematic Census* (Yangon/Brussels, 2014).
3. The full data can be found in the Republic of the Union of Myanmar, *The 2014 Myanmar Population and Housing Census; The Union Report: Religion; Census Report Volume 2C* (2016). It should be noted that these figures include a non-enumerated population in Rakhine State of 1.09 million, assumed in the analysis to be mostly, if not entirely, Muslim.
4. For a more detailed examination of this phenomenon, with particular attention to Myanmar, see Matthew J. Walton and Michael Jerryson, "The Authorization of Religio-political Discourse: Monks and Buddhist Activism in Contemporary Myanmar and Beyond," *Politics & Religion* 9, no. 4 (2016): 794–814.
5. As described below, in June 2017, MaBaTha was officially renamed the "Buddha Dhamma Parahita Foundation." In this chapter, I continue to refer to the group as MaBaTha, as this shorthand is still used both by analysts and the group's adherents and supporters.

6. Juliane Schober, "Buddhist Just Rule and Burmese National Culture: State Patronage of the Chinese Tooth Relic in Myanmar," *History of Religions: An International Journal for Comparative Historical Studies* 36, no. 3 (1997): 218–43; Hiroko Kawanami, "Charisma, Power(s), and the Arahant Ideal in Burmese-Myanmar Buddhism," *Asian Ethnology* 68, no. 2 (2009): 211–37; and Guillaume Rozenberg, *Renunciation and Power: The Quest for Sainthood in Contemporary Burma* (New Haven, CT: Yale University Southeast Asia Studies, 2010).
7. Josefine Roos, *Conflict Assessment in Rakhine State* (Danish Refugee Council Report, 2013).
8. Bill Davis et al., *Massacre in Central Burma: Muslim Students Terrorized and Killed in Meiktila* (Physicians for Human Rights Report, 2013).
9. Jared Ferrie and Min Zayar Oo, "Myanmar Buddhist Committee Bans Anti-Muslim Organizations," *Reuters*, 11 September 2013 <http://www.reuters.com/article/us-myanmar-buddhism-idUSBRE98A0EP20130911> [accessed 2 June 2017].
10. Matt Schissler, Matthew J. Walton, and Phyu Phyu Thi, "Threat and virtuous defence: Listening to narratives of religious conflict in six Myanmar cities," *Myanmar Media and Society Project*, Working Paper 1:1 (2015).
11. Swe Win, "With official help, Myanmar's radical Buddhists target Muslim-owned businesses," *Myanmar Now*, 17 November 2015 <http://www.myanmar-now.org/news/i/?id=9ba61afc-285d-49bd-8f73-8b9efaf941c0> [accessed 2 June 2017].
12. Although technically, official MaBaTha spokesmen were careful to separate the views of individual member monks from the position of the group as a whole, to avoid violating election laws mandating the separation of religion and politics.
13. Aung Kyaw Min, "Minister rebukes Ma Ba Tha," *Myanmar Times*, 15 July 2016 <http://www.mmtimes.com/index.php/national-news/21399-minister-rebukes-ma-ba-tha.html> [accessed 2 June 2017].
14. Lucy Purdon, "Challenge of Criminalising Hate Speech," *Myanmar Times*, 16 August 2016 <http://www.mmtimes.com/index.php/opinion/21962-challenge-of-criminalising-hate-speech.html> [accessed 2 June 2017].
15. Matthew J. Walton and Aung Tun, "What the State Sangha Committee Actually Said About Ma Ba Tha," *Tea Circle*, 29 July 2016 <https://teacircleoxford.com/2016/07/29/what-the-state-sangha-committee-actually-said-about-ma-ba-tha/> [accessed 2 June 2017].
16. Radio Free Asia. "Buddhist Authorities Ban Myanmar's Ultranationalist Ma Ba Tha Group," *Radio Free Asia*, 23 May 2017 <http://www.rfa.org/english/news/myanmar/ban-05232017152958.html> [accessed 2 June 2017].
17. Mratt Kyaw Thu, "What Next for Ma Ba Tha?" *Frontier Myanmar*, 23 June 2016 <http://frontiermyanmar.net/en/what-next-for-ma-ba-tha> [accessed 2 June 2017].

18. Mratt Kyaw Thu, "Ma Ba Tha Forms New Affiliate, Threatens Critics with Legal Action," *Frontier Myanmar*, 17 May 2017 <http://frontiermyanmar.net/en/ma-ba-tha-forms-new-affiliate-threatens-critics-with-legal-action> [accessed 2 June 2017].
19. See, for example, Matthew J. Walton, 'Misunderstanding Myanmar's Ma Ba Tha," *Asia Times*, 9 June 2017 <http://www.atimes.com/article/misunderstanding-myanmars-ma-ba-tha/> [accessed 18 February 2018]; International Crisis Group, "Buddhism and State Power in Myanmar," *International Crisis Group*, Asia Report No. 290, 5 September 2017.
20. C4ADS, *Sticks and Stones: Hate Speech Narratives and Facilitators in Myanmar* (C4ADS Report, 2016).
21. Schissler et al., "Threat and Virtuous Defence," pp. 17–19.
22. Kei Nemoto, "The Concepts of *Dobama* (Our Burma) and *Thudo-Bama* (Their Burma) in Burmese Nationalism, 1930–1948," *Journal of Burma Studies* 5 (2000): 1–16.
23. Nathan Lean, *The Islamophobia Industry: How the Right Manufactures Fear of Muslims* (New York: Pluto Press, 2012).
24. En-Chieh Chao, "The-Truth-About-Islam.Com: Ordinary Theories of Racism and Cyber Islamophobia," *Critical Sociology* 41, no. 1 (2014): 57–75.
25. Aye Thein, "Putting Myanmar's 'Buddhist Extremism' in an International Context," *Tea Circle: An Oxford Forum for New Perspectives on Burma/Myanmar*, 1 September 2017 <https://teacircleoxford.com/2017/09/01/putting-myanmars-buddhist-extremism-in-an-international-context/> [accessed 18 February 2018].
26. Matt Schissler, "On Islamophobes and Holocaust Deniers: Making Sense of Violence, in Myanmar and Elsewhere," in *Conflict in Myanmar: War, Politics, Religion*, ed. Nick Cheesman and Nicholas Farrelly (Singapore: ISEAS Publishing, 2016), p. 298.
27. David Scott Mathieson, "Burma: the clash of church, state and society," *Open Democracy*, 9 July 2014 <https://www.opendemocracy.net/david-scott-mathieson/burma-clash-of-church-state-and-society> [accessed 2 June 2017].
28. Radio Free Asia, "Buddhist Group Comes Under Fire From Myanmar Politicians, Activists," *Radio Free Asia*, 25 September 2015 <http://www.rfa.org/english/news/myanmar/buddhist-group-comes-under-fire-from-myanmar-politicians-activists-09252015170114.html> [accessed 2 June 2017].
29. Jonah Fisher, "Myanmar's Ma Ba Tha monks flex their political muscle," *BBC News*, 8 October 2015 <http://www.bbc.co.uk/news/world-asia-34463455> [accessed 2 June 2017].
30. Andrew R.C. Marshall, "Special Report: Myanmar gives official blessing to anti-Muslim monks." *Reuters*, 27 June 2013 <http://uk.reuters.com/article/us-myanmar-969-specialreport-idUSBRE95Q04720130627> [accessed 2 June 2017].

31. Freedom House. "Myanmar's Ban on Public Speech by Monk Undermines Basic Rights," *Freedom House*, 2 April 2015 <https://freedomhouse.org/article/myanmar-s-ban-public-speech-monk-undermines-basic-rights> [accessed 2 June 2017].
32. Kyaw Phyo Tha, "Ma Ba Tha threatens nationwide protests against Shwedagon highrise projects," *The Irrawaddy*, 12 June 2015 <https://www.irrawaddy.com/news/burma/ma-ba-tha-threatens-nationwide-protests-against-shwedagon-highrise-projects.html> [accessed 2 June 2017].
33. Erik Braun, *The Birth of Insight: Meditation, Modern Buddhism, and the Burmese Monk Ledi Sayadaw* (Chicago: The University of Chicago Press, 2013); Alicia Marie Turner, *Saving Buddhism: The Impermanence of Religion in Colonial Burma* (Honolulu: University of Hawai'i Press, 2014).
34. Frank Reynolds, "The Two Wheels of Dhamma; a Study of Early Buddhism," in *The Two Wheels of Dhamma; Essays on the Theravada Tradition in India and Ceylon*, ed. Gananath Obeyesekere, Frank Reynolds, and Bardwell L. Smith (Chambersburg, PA: American Academy of Religion, 1972).
35. Schober, "Buddhist Just Rule," 1997; Ingrid Jordt, *Burma's Mass Lay Meditation Movement: Buddhism and the Cultural Construction of Power* (Athens: Ohio University Press, 2007).
36. Bénédicte Brac de La Perrière, "A Generation of Monks in the Democratic Transition," in *Metamorphosis: Studies in Social and Political Change in Myanmar*, ed. R. Egreteau and F. Robinne (Singapore: NUS Press, 2015).
37. For an examination of monastic views on democracy in Myanmar, see Matthew J. Walton. *Buddhism, Politics, and Political Thought in Myanmar* (Cambridge: Cambridge University Press, 2016), especially pp. 163–91.

References

Aung Kyaw Min. 2016. "Minister rebukes Ma Ba Tha." *Myanmar Times*, 15 July. <http://www.mmtimes.com/index.php/national-news/21399-minister-rebukes-ma-ba-tha.html> [accessed 2 June 2017].

Aye Thein. 2017. "Putting Myanmar's 'Buddhist Extremism' in an International Context." *Tea Circle: An Oxford Forum for New Perspectives on Burma/Myanmar*, <https://teacircleoxford.com/2017/09/01/putting-myanmars-buddhist-extremism-in-an-international-context/> [accessed 18 February 2018].

Brac de la Perrière, Bénédicte. 2009. "An Overview of the Field of Religion in Burmese Studies." *Asian Ethnology* 68, no. 2: 185–210.

______. 2015. "A Generation of Monks in the Democratic Transition." In *Metamorphosis: Studies in Social and Political Change in Myanmar*, ed. R. Egreteau and F. Robinne Singapore: NUS Press.

Braun, Erik. 2013. *The Birth of Insight: Meditation, Modern Buddhism, and the Burmese monk Ledi Sayadaw*. Chicago: The University of Chicago Press.

C4ADS. 2016. *Sticks and Stones: Hate Speech Narratives and Facilitators in Myanmar*. C4ADS Report.

Chao, En-Chieh. 2014. "The-Truth-About-Islam.Com: Ordinary Theories of Racism and Cyber Islamophobia." *Critical Sociology* 41, no. 1: 57–75.

Davis, Bill, Holly Atkinson, and Richard Sollom. 2013. *Massacre in Central Burma: Muslim Students Terrorized and Killed in Meiktila*. Physicians for Human Rights Report, May.

Ferrie, Jared and Min Zayar Oo. 2013. "Myanmar Buddhist Committee Bans Anti-Muslim Organizations." *Reuters*, 11 September. <http://www.reuters.com/article/us-myanmar-buddhism-idUSBRE98A0EP20130911> [accessed 2 June 2017].

Fisher, Jonah. 2015. "Myanmar's Ma Ba Tha monks flex their political muscle." *BBC News*, 8 October. <http://www.bbc.co.uk/news/world-asia-34463455> [accessed 2 June 2017].

Freedom House. 2015. "Myanmar's Ban on Public Speech by Monk Undermines Basic Rights." *Freedom House*, 2 April. <https://freedomhouse.org/article/myanmar-s-ban-public-speech-monk-undermines-basic-rights> [accessed 2 June 2017].

International Crisis Group. 2014. *Counting the Costs: Myanmar's Problematic Census*. Asia Briefing No. 144, Yangon/Brussels.

———. 2017. *Buddhism and State Power in Myanmar*. Asia Report No. 290, Yangon/Brussels, 5 September.

Jordt, Ingrid. 2007. *Burma's Mass Lay Meditation Movement: Buddhism and the Cultural Construction of Power*. Athens: Ohio University Press.

Kawanami, Hiroko. 2009. "Charisma, Power(s), and the Arahant Ideal in Burmese-Myanmar Buddhism." *Asian Ethnology* 68, no. 2: 211–37.

Kyaw Phyo Tha. 2015. "Ma Ba Tha Threatens Nationwide Protests against Shwedagon Highrise Projects." *The Irrawaddy*, 12 June. <https://www.irrawaddy.com/news/burma/ma-ba-tha-threatens-nationwide-protests-against-shwedagon-highrise-projects.html >[accessed 2 June 2017].

Lean, Nathan. 2012. *The Islamophobia Industry: How the Right Manufactures Fear of Muslims*. New York: Pluto Press.

Marshall, Andrew R.C. 2013. "Special Report: Myanmar gives official blessing to anti-Muslim monks." *Reuters*, 27 June. <http://uk.reuters.com/article/us-myanmar-969-specialreport-idUSBRE95Q04720130627> [accessed 2 June 2017].

Mathieson, David Scott. 2014. "Burma: the clash of church, state and society." *Open Democracy*, 9 July. <https://www.opendemocracy.net/david-scott-mathieson/burma-clash-of-church-state-and-society> [accessed 2 June 2017].

Mratt Kyaw Thu. 2016. "What Next for Ma Ba Tha?" *Frontier Myanmar*, 23 June. <http://frontiermyanmar.net/en/what-next-for-ma-ba-tha> [accessed 2 June 2017].

———. 2017. "Ma Ba Tha Forms New Affiliate, Threatens Critics with Legal Action." *Frontier Myanmar*, 17 May. <http://frontiermyanmar.net/en/ma-ba-tha-forms-new-affiliate-threatens-critics-with-legal-action> [accessed 2 June 2017].

Nemoto, Kei. 2000. "The Concepts of *Dobama* (Our Burma) and *Thudo-Bama* (Their Burma) in Burmese Nationalism, 1930–1948." *Journal of Burma Studies* 5: 1–16.

Purdon, Lucy. 2016. "Challenge of Criminalising Hate Speech." *Myanmar Times*, 16 August. <http://www.mmtimes.com/index.php/opinion/21962-challenge-of-criminalising-hate-speech.html> [accessed 2 June 2017].

Radio Free Asia. 2015. "Buddhist Group Comes Under Fire From Myanmar Politicians, Activists." *Radio Free Asia*, 25 September. <http://www.rfa.org/english/news/myanmar/buddhist-group-comes-under-fire-from-myanmar-politicians-activists-09252015170114.html> [accessed 2 June 2017].

———. 2017. "Buddhist Authorities Ban Myanmar's Ultranationalist Ma Ba Tha Group." *Radio Free Asia*, 23 May. <http://www.rfa.org/english/news/myanmar/ban-05232017152958.html> [accessed 2 June 2017].

Republic of the Union of Myanmar. 2016. "The 2014 Myanmar Population and Housing Census, The Union Report: Religion, Census Report 2-C," Department of Population, Ministry of Labour, Immigration and Population, July.

Reynolds, Frank. 1972. "The Two Wheels of Dhamma; a Study of Early Buddhism." In *The Two Wheels of Dhamma; Essays on the Theravada Tradition in India and Ceylon*, ed. Gananath Obeyesekere, Frank Reynolds, and Bardwell L. Smith. Chambersburg, PA: American Academy of Religion.

Roos, Josefine. 2013. *Conflict Assessment in Rakhine State*. Danish Refugee Council Report, February/March.

Rozenberg, Guillaume. 2010. *Renunciation and Power: The Quest for Sainthood in Contemporary Burma*. New Haven, CT: Yale University Southeast Asia Studies.

Schissler, Matt. 2016. "On Islamophobes and Holocaust Deniers: Making Sense of Violence, in Myanmar and Elsewhere." In *Conflict in Myanmar: War, Politics, Religion*, ed. Nick Cheesman and Nicholas Farrelly. Singapore: ISEAS Publishing.

Schissler, Matt, Matthew J. Walton, and Phyu Phyu Thi. 2015. "Threat and virtuous defence: Listening to narratives of religious conflict in six Myanmar cities." *Myanmar Media and Society Project*, Working Paper 1:1.

Schober, Juliane. 1997. "Buddhist Just Rule and Burmese National Culture: State Patronage of the Chinese Tooth Relic in Myanmar." *History of Religions: An International Journal for Comparative Historical Studies* 36, no. 3: 218–43.

Swe Win. 2015. "With official help, Myanmar's radical Buddhists target Muslim-owned businesses." *Myanmar Now*, 17 November. <http://www.myanmar-now.org/news/i/?id=9ba61afc-285d-49bd-8f73-8b9efaf941c0> [accessed 2 June 2017].

Turner, Alicia Marie. 2014. *Saving Buddhism: The Impermanence of Religion in Colonial Burma*. Honolulu: University of Hawai'i Press.

Walton, Matthew J. 2016. *Buddhism, Politics, and Political Thought in Myanmar*. Cambridge: Cambridge University Press.

———. 2017. "Misunderstanding Myanmar's Ma Ba Tha," *Asia Times*, 9 June. <http://www.atimes.com/article/misunderstanding-myanmars-ma-ba-tha/> [accessed 18 February 2018].

Walton, Matthew J. and Aung Tun. 2016. "What the State Sangha Committee Actually Said About Ma Ba Tha." *Tea Circle*. 29 July. <https://teacircleoxford.com/2016/07/29/what-the-state-sangha-committee-actually-said-about-ma-ba-tha/> [accessed 2 June 2017].

Walton, Matthew J. and Jerryson, Michael. 2016. "The Authorization of Religio-political Discourse: Monks and Buddhist Activism in Contemporary Myanmar and Beyond." *Politics & Religion* 9, no. 4: 794–814.

SECTION FOUR

The Rohingya Crisis

CHAPTER 10

Motherhood, Home, and the Political Economy of Rohingya Women's Labor

Shae A. Frydenlund

As military clearance operations in northern Rakhine state killed thousands and displaced over 700,000 people in August 2017, Rohingyas have again become the objects of a variety of gazes, both within and outside Myanmar. Widely circulated views of Rohingya experiences, including their seemingly prior "stateless" condition, overlook one key historical fact: that Rohingyas once had access to formal citizenship status. This status afforded them the opportunity to vote, be elected to political office, and hold government jobs before, but was actively revoked when citizenship became linked to membership in a "national race" in 1982 (Cheesman 2017). Similarly, academic knowledge about Rohingyas often focuses on their ethnic identity, refugee-ness, and exclusion while ignoring the material conditions of *inclusion* within a violent political economy, thereby erasing vital aspects of Rohingya identity. Moreover, when racialized ethnic and religious exclusion is the central question framing academic knowledge about Rohingyas, this knowledge evokes Katherine McKittrick's observations on the fixation on black/non-white death, in which such death becomes necessary to "prove the brutality of racism."[1] In the case of Rohingyas, a fixation on death and exclusion proves the brutality of the military violence and Bamar supremacy.

This chapter attends to the actual lifeworlds of Rohingya women struggling to exist in northern Rakhine state and in the diaspora. Such a focus allows us to perceive their existence in a more detailed way, so revealing the ways that exclusion from formal wage labor instantiates the insidious exploitation and expropriation of gendered and unwaged

Rohingya labor, which is enrolled in wider processes of capitalist accumulation. Yet this inclusion is far from complete. Drawing on bell hooks'[2] writing on Black home-space as a site of refuge and resistance, I explore the Rohingya home and religious clothing as spaces of sanctuary, and Rohingya women's commitment to their identities as mothers, Muslims, and homemakers as acts of dignity amid conditions of surveillance and death. Analyzing the political economy of Rohingya women's labor alongside their everyday lives has the added benefit of re-socializing and contextualizing lives that have been reduced in academic and journalist renderings alike to abject bodies.

To accomplish this task, the chapter traces the contours of knowledge about Rohingyas, pointing to the fissures and interstitial spaces from which critical, humanizing understandings of Rohingya women's material lives and labors can emerge. The first section discusses extant literature on Rohingya identity, political positioning, and the causes and conditions of Rohingya exclusion and suffering—both in Myanmar and in the diasporic locales in which they have found themselves. The second section offers a feminist political economy analysis of Rohingya labor and social reproduction, examining the cases of Rohingya refugee women in different, yet inextricably linked, places. Their experiences reveal the uniquely gendered mode of Rohingya dispossession and the group's often-overlooked inclusions within broader capitalist economies. The final section extends and augments this political economy approach by attending to the complex and multidimensional aspects of Rohingya women's lives, work, and their identities as mothers, women of faith, and home-makers.

Methods

I conducted research in Myanmar, Bangladesh, Malaysia, and the United States from August 2017 to October 2018, and employed ethnographic methods of interview and observation alongside feminist participatory and community-based research methods (CBR)[3] of discussion groups and community meetings. Broadly, feminist methodology challenges the production and politics of knowledge, and prioritizes the home and the scale of the everyday as site of scholarly knowledge production. My use of feminist methods and CBR allowed me to incorporate a diversity of Rohingya women's views and opinions into research design and the implementation of research activities. I lived with three Rohingya women in a refugee shelter in Kuala Lumpur and with a refugee family in Aurora,

Colorado. I conducted 45 semi-structured interviews altogether, and facilitated five women's discussion groups. This chapter therefore aims to reflect attentiveness to critical understandings of Rohingya positioning within labor markets while also attending to deeper meanings and acts of resistance nested within women's multidimensional experiences of exclusion and inclusion, specifically the importance of motherhood, religious clothing, and the home as spaces imbued with multiple cultural and political meanings.

Rohingya Belonging and Exclusion

There is a rapidly growing body of scholarship that discusses the histories of Islam and Muslim groups in Rakhine state,[4] the relationship between Islam and the Myanmar state,[5] and the relationship between race, power, Islam, and Buddhism in Myanmar.[6] The history of the Rohingya ethnonym itself[7] and the presence or absence of a named Rohingya ethnic group in various accounts of Rakhine history remain at the forefront of both scholarly and public debates over Rohingya-ness and the legitimacy of Rohingya claims of belonging within the Myanmar nation. There is also a significant body of work written in Burmese language about Islamic history, politics, and culture. However, the diversity of literature on Islam in Myanmar is not yet reflected in Anglophone literature about Rohingyas. Furthermore, amid scholarly examinations of Rohingya belonging within or exclusion from the Myanmar polity, the articulation of inclusion with exclusion has yet to be examined.

Extant literature on Muslim exclusion in Myanmar has argued that their marginality within and expulsion from the Myanmar body-politics has been made possible in part through the racialization of ethnic identities, where Buddhism and Burman-ness are equated with belonging in the Myanmar nation and ethnic minorities are understood to be deviant, different, and disloyal. Matthew Walton[8] argues that Burman-ness is similar to whiteness in the US in the former's structural and discursive effects, resulting in the institutionalized dominance of Burmans and the institutionalized exclusion of ethnic minorities. Walton's use of critical race theory identifies the racialized hierarchies that underpin Bamar supremacy, but also obscures the complexity of Muslim and non-Muslim ethnic minority positioning in Myanmar. Elliott Prasse-Freeman[9] challenges such clean and static hierarchies, arguing that the Rohingyas are being conjured as constitutive others to aid in the creation of a cohesive

Burmese "us" that transcends ethnic particularism. Nationalists stress common identities, performing what Glen Sean Coulthard[10] has identified as a politics of recognition, where difference and diversity is indexed, but simultaneously depoliticized and subordinated beneath a dominant identity and within colonial/capitalist relations. Furthermore, upland ethnic minorities are positioned differently than Muslims within the discourse of *taingyinthar*, which is undergirded by a blood-based folk theory that all peoples of Burma, much like the lost tribes of Israel, were "originally" of the Buddha's Sakkya clan.[11] Hence, minority Christianity and animism is understood to be an aberration that can be repaired. The key distinction is that while non-Muslim ethnic groups are certainly discriminated against, their experiences vary considerably than those of Muslims, especially Rohingyas, whose alterity is presented as inassimilable and irrefragable.

Writing against the use of ethnic and religious identity as a sole heuristic for understanding Muslim experiences and political positioning in Myanmar, Melissa Crouch[12] confronts misconceptions about Muslims by examining the everyday politics of belonging, inclusion, and the embodiment of state power. She argues against rigid, ethnic-based assumptions about Muslims in Myanmar, instead emphasizing the continuum of relations with the state and the diversity of relations therein. Muslims have long been defined by ethnic categories in Myanmar, and Crouch suggests that Muslim experiences should be understood vis-à-vis their degree of affiliation with the state. For example, she argues that Bamar and Bamar-adjacent Muslims, including Panthay, express their Burmese-ness through culture, language, and dress, and are more likely to hold administrative positions that render them more proximate to the Myanmar state than Rohingyas, whose framing as "problems" external to the Myanmar body-politic renders them further afield.[13] By reconfiguring conceptualizations of Muslims in scholarship, Crouch aims to recover Muslim contributions to Myanmar from discourses that represent Muslims as a threat to the state. Crucially, despite their exclusion from the benefits of citizenship, Myanmar's remaining Rohingyas (and those living in displacement in Bangladesh and Malaysia) live in very close proximity to the state. Rohingyas are emplaced, counted, and surveilled heavily by multiple state and non-state actors. Building on critical understandings of Muslim exclusion in Myanmar, this chapter examines how exclusion from full citizenship and formal labor markets facilitates multiple, often violent, inclusions.

While there is extensive scholarship written on Rohingyas' political positioning and experiences of exclusion vis-à-vis the Myanmar state,

Rohingyas' intimate, everyday lives, and cultural identities have been largely overlooked. In a notable exception, Kazi Fahmida Farzana[14] examines the construction of Rohingya identities on their own terms while considering their positioning within the broader historical-geographic workings of the Myanmar and Bangladesh states. In her textual and discursive analysis of content from drawings, folk songs, and oral histories, she finds the space of the border to be vital in the formation of Rohingya ethnicity, political identity, and Rohingyas' informal strategies of resistance to oppression and conditions of marginality. Her analysis is uniquely powerful because her methodology prioritizes Rohingya identity, culture, and agency at the scale of the everyday.

Farzana's work also highlights importance of research methods and their material implications. As a historian of ancient Arakan and contemporary Rakhine, Jacques Leider has also studied the genesis of Rohingya ethnicity and political movements. However, he relies heavily on colonial records and positivist knowledge production, which ignore indigenous modes of knowledge production and storage (for example, oral histories and folk songs), thereby reinscribing colonial relations into the present.[15] Colonial records encapsulate positivist epistemology, or a way of knowing that dismisses the complexity of knowledge and the power relations that shape how information is represented (or not) and understood. Positivist epistemology is also based upon a masculinist ontology, which prioritizes the public over the private, time over space, and civilization over "uncivilized" while simultaneously depoliticizing the political.[16] As Michael Charney's (2009) work on Rohingya ethnonyms demonstrates, the use of colonial records is in no way necessary for a rigorous historical analysis of Rohingya political identity. Farzana's pathbreaking use of oral data and participatory research methods rejects colonial and masculinist modes of knowledge production to open new, embodied ways of understanding Rohingya identities and experiences.

The concept of *taingyinthar*, often translated as "national race," is central to understanding Rohingya experiences of exclusion from the Myanmar nation, as well as Rohingya struggles for political rights. Ardeth Thawnghmung[17] examines the emergence of indigeneity as a political identity articulated with the concept *taingyinthar*, where both Rohingya *and* Rakhine Buddhist political parties assert their ethnic groups' nativeness to Rakhine in order to assert their belonging in the Myanmar nation and access political privileges. By investigating the centrality of concepts of indigeneity in Rakhine, she shows that communal violence there is not solely the result of cultural differences, competition for resources, or the political opening since 2011 that allowed for the release of pent-up frustrations—rather, Rohingya and Rakine antagonisms are the result of the ongoing debate about the legitimacy of Rohingyas as *taingyinthar*. However, as Nick Cheesman[18] convincingly argues, a genealogy of *tainyinthar* reveals a complex history that elides a unified, stable definition as a category of national belonging. Rather, *taingyinthar* is imbricated with political and juridical agendas, and its contingency as an interpellative device for national belonging points to the irony of simultaneous invitation to and omission from the Myanmar nation.

Thawnghmung's analysis of indigeneity as it circulates within debates over Rohingya belonging and exclusion is a valuable contribution that animates broader discussions about ethnicity, place, and power in Myanmar, but this work also reflects broader themes within the field of Burma studies, specifically scholarly imaginations of neutrality and the liberal democratic ideals that accompany them. Thawnghmung, like those operating within the valences of government, politics, and private investment in Myanmar, emphasizes non-governmental, humanitarian, and developmentalist interventions that privilege the so-called "rule of law" in addressing the conflict and so-called "Rohingya problem." There are two issues with this mode of analysis. First, Thawnghmung and others[19] have neglected the problematic aspects of humanitarian, charity, and non-governmental interventions in Myanmar, specifically the reinscription of colonial power relations and Buddhist Bamar supremacy. As Jennifer Hyndman[20] observes in her study of refugee management in Kenya, the relationship between UNHCR staff and local people is often characterized by domination and discipline. Second, although Thawnghmung's article was written before the October 2016 killing of Burmese military border guards and long before the events of August 2017, "rule of law" discourses have been suspect in Myanmar for a long time, as the Tatmadaw's history of rights abuses is well known.[21] Videos of extrajudicial killings, rape, and the "Four Cuts" strategy of burning villagers' homes documented on smart phones have been streaming from social media for years, and the events since August 2017 have revealed the horrific violence imbricated within Burma's "rule of law," precluding its utility as a solution to the conflict. Meanwhile, state-sponsored media in Myanmar continues to deny accusations of military misconduct and genocide, citing international bias and misinformation, and infamously suggesting that Muslims burned their own homes to incite international sympathy.

Taken together, research about Rohingyas has mostly reflected the use of what critical geographer Ruth Gilmore identifies as "doomed" methods, which foreground dispossession and naturalize the death and suffering of racialized bodies.[22] Within literature about Rohingyas, a focus on ethnicity, exclusion, and refugee-ness elides the other dimensions of Rohingya lives and reinforces singular representations of refugees as bare, stateless life. The majority of scholarly writings about Rohingyas analyze either their ethnic identities or their experiences of exclusion from the space of the good life in Myanmar.[23] However, few analyses have considered Rohingyas' everyday lifeworlds. Through attendance to the everyday, we can see both exclusion *and* hypercontrol, as well as moments of dignified living etched out of violent conditions. Bringing together Marxian political economy and feminist and anti-racist geography literature with feminist methods, this chapter extends and augments critical literature on Rohingya positioning within and outside Myanmar by exploring the gendered contours of Rohingya labor alongside Rohingya motherhood, religiosity, and homemaking. As this chapter will show, attendance to Rohingyas' everyday lives reveals that their positioning as constitutive outsiders is accompanied by *inclusion* as exploitable and expropriable labor in restructured labor markets, where unfree Rohingyas work for low wages, or none at all.

Gender, Labor, and Social Reproduction

Silvia Federici and other Feminist-Marxists enhanced Marx's foundational writings by theorizing the relationship between patriarchy, gender, and capitalism, arguing that unwaged social reproduction work performed by women, and the gendered division of labor more broadly, is the foundational form of labor exploitation upon which capitalism depends.[24] Developing alongside second wave feminist movements in the 1970s, feminist political economy troubles concepts such as economy, work, mobility, and resources by interrogating the gendered spatial division of labor and the articulation of capitalism and gendered power relations.[25] Hence, gendered, racial, and sexual hierarchies are understood as central processes through which capitalism is mediated spatially. Just as Marx shows that the wage hides the unpaid labor that creates profit, measuring work with a wage also hides how family and social relations are subordinated to the relations of production. Taken together, feminist geography literature challenges and expands understandings of capitalism and the relationship between gender, labor, and dispossession. This section applies Marxist-Feminist theorizations of the relationship between dispossession, labor, and Rohingya women's social reproduction work to shed light on the multiple ways that Rohingya exclusion from citizenship and formal wage labor enables their *inclusion* through exploitation, expropriation, and surveillance, specifically by intensifying unwaged labor burdens among Rohingya women. This analysis also reveals the multiple ways that Rohingya women's unwaged labor circulates within and outside their immediate communities to subsidize low wages and facilitate capital accumulation elsewhere.

The experiences of Rohingya women exemplify the gendered violence of labor market restructuring in Sittwe and Cox's Bazaar, which is characterized by footloose labor dependent upon wages from dangerous, low-wage work. Their navigations of waged and unwaged labor also capture what Nancy Fraser[26] identifies as the relationship between labor exploitation and expropriation:

> Distinct from Marxian exploitation, but equally integral to capitalist development, expropriation is accumulation by other means. Dispensing with the contractual relation through which capital purchases "labor power" in exchange for wages, expropriation works by *confiscating* capacities and resources and *conscripting* them into capital's circuits of self-expansion (2016: 166).

Echoing Federici's theorization of the relationship between women's subjugation and capital accumulation, Fraser argues that Marx's theorization of labor exploitation does not account for the *racial* oppression that strips people of assets and protections again and again. Moreover, Fraser argues, the concept of expropriation sheds light on the ongoing (forcible) conscription of unwaged and gendered labor necessary for capital accumulation. Assets forcibly expropriated include means of production and land, as well as human bodies and their reproductive abilities, which are injected into capital in the form of both slavery and unwaged labor in the semi-proletarianized home.

Rohingya labor is marked as expropriable, that is, stripped of protections afforded to formal wage labor as a result of their racialized political positioning, but is also explicitly gendered. For Rohingya women, the dual articulation of exploitation and expropriation appears in their inclusion within informal wage work *and* the simultaneous intensification of women's unwaged social reproduction labor. Though spatially disparate, the experiences of Rohingya women in Myanmar, Bangladesh, Malaysia, and the United States reflect the unified, ugly logic of exclusion-cum-inclusion, reflecting what Fraser and Federici point to as the gendered, racialized scaffolding of capital.

The spaces and scales of labor exploitation and expropriation matter greatly. The lives and labor of semi-proletarian and proletarian Rohingya women in Myanmar, Bangladesh, Malaysia, and the United States, among other diasporic places, are inextricably linked as women's care work and emotional labor in the home subsidize low wages and facilitate multiple forms of economic development. For instance, studies of transnational labor migration have shown that women working as migrant laborers often provide valuable remittances and act as agents of economic development for home countries in the so-called Global South,[27] yet there is also considerable evidence that economic development in wealthy countries like the United States and Canada is undergirded by labor performed by immigrants and their relatives in poorer countries.[28] In her study of an Illinois town transformed by immigrant laborers who were recruited to a Cargill pork processing plant, Faranak Miraftab shows that this transformation is underpinned by what she calls the "respatialization of life cycle stages,"[29] in which immigrants spend their most productive years working in the United States and their home countries become de facto "cribs and infirmaries" for workers at the beginning and end of their life cycles. United States companies like Cargill and JBS, major employers of refugees in Aurora, also avoid paying the full cost of reproducing immigrant labor by inducing what Miraftab identifies as the "global restructuring of social reproduction."[30] Miraftab's conceptualization of immigrant labor illuminates a more nuanced examination of the ways that Rohingya women's unwaged labor is expropriated and enrolled in capital accumulation at various scales. As the following section shows, Rohingya women's intensified unpaid case work and household labor subsidize low wages paid by brick factories and leather tanneries in Sittwe and Cox's Bazaar, as well as the meatpacking factories that employ large numbers of refugees in the United States.

A Transnational Political Economy of Rohingya Women's Labor

Since fleeing Maungdaw, Rakhine State for Cox's Bazaar, Amina's[31] husband occasionally finds work as a day laborer in nearby Bengali-owned brickmaking factories that are well known for their low wages, labor abuses, and even the rumored murder of a Rohingya worker and its subsequent cover-up by local police. Journalist accounts[32] have noted the prevalence of informal labor markets in Cox's Bazaar, specifically the hiring of Rohingya laborers for around half the 600 thaka[33] daily wage, a practice that has angered local Bengali workers and precipitated several protests calling for the repatriation of job-thieving, wage-depressing refugees. Of course, as many Marxian labor scholars have noted, the capitalist factory owner, not the laborers themselves, profits from injections of vulnerable labor. And yet, while the owners of the means of production in Cox's Bazaar profit from Rohingya men's labor, Bengali households profit from the availability of Rohingya refugee girls to work as low-wage domestic labor. Many girls now work as maids in Bengali homes in the nearby resort town of Cox's Bazaar, their low wages affording middle and even lower-class Bengali households with household labor that is orders of magnitude cheaper than Bengali labor.[34] Echoing Geraldine Pratt's study of the political economy of low-wage Filipina domestic labor in Canada and Pheng Cheah's study of Filipinas in Singapore,[35] Rohingya girls' labor "frees" Bengali women for work in the fields or outside the home, thereby subsidizing the Bengali domicile.

Rohingya men and girls' inclusion in local wage labor markets rest upon an intensification of unwaged labor activities among Rohingya women in Kutupalong. Indeed, as Marx[36] describes about the intensification of labor extraction in "The Working Day," Rohingya women in the camps must spend *more* hours every day hauling water, cooking, cleaning, waiting in ration lines, and tending to children if they or their relatives join the labor force. Taken together, Rohingya women in Cox's Bazaar create the conditions immediately necessary for their families' survival while also indirectly subsidizing the cost of the "good life" for local capitalists, farmers, and lower-class women. The experiences of Rohingya women in Cox's Bazaar reveal similarities and important differences in the ways that domestic labor exploitation occurs between residents of the Global South. The exploitation of Southern women in both the Global North and the Global South depend upon women's vulnerability, but when women labor migrants from the South travel to the North, their labor subsidizes middle-class women who work as professionals; in Bangladesh, my research suggests that Rohingyas' domestic labor enables family farming productivity and the semi-proletarianization of Bangladeshi households as extended family members are relieved of care work. However, the causes and conditions of Rohingya domestic labor in Bangladesh warrant deeper scholarly inquiry.

When I hosted discussion groups in two Rohingya villages outside Sittwe in January of 2018, Rohingya women's experiences with labor markets echoed those of Rohingya women in Cox's Bazaar. Many have lost their husbands to military violence, illness, or work accidents in Saudi Arabia or Malaysia, and are compelled to engage in wage work outside the home. The women agreed that prior to 2012, when violence wracked the city and 100,000 Rohingyas were moved to camps outside the city, things were good: "Back then we could support ourselves with farming and feed our families," Rafika, a 38-year-old mother of three said, "we were happy, we could stay at home." Rafika now joins her husband to work in a Rakhine-owned brickmaking factory nearby, though she only does so out of extreme necessity, while also retaining her responsibilities of cooking, cleaning, and attending to the needs of the children. Although these two adjacent communities were not displaced in 2012, residents are unable to travel without a permit, which made farming an untenable source of livelihood.

Like Rafika, Raihana, a 40-year-old mother of four, used to cultivate her family's land, but their inability to bring produce to market reduced their capacity to pay workers on the farm, and their fields now lie fallow. Following their confinement to the village, Raihana had attempted to earn extra income as a seamstress—she has a sewing machine that was given to her by a non-profit company several years ago—but since the NGO left and people in her village are too poor to buy clothing for her to tailor, the machine is idle most of the time. She now works as a leather tanner for a Rakhine businessman, and her husband works at a Rakhine-owned brick factory for about 5,000 kyat[37] per day, but in the rainy season, he gets only 2,500 kyat per day working on a Rakhine fishing boat. Raihana cooks, cleans, looks after the children, and sews when she can for significantly less than what she earned before—only 250 kyat or so per week. Rafika and Raihana's experiences point to the intensification of demands for Rohingya women's labor in Rakhine, while also highlighting the fact that they are effectively if not literally dispossessed of their land: separated from the means of production and "freed" for incorporation into wage work that is mostly controlled by Rakhines.

Local business owners and consumers of domestic services in Rakhine and Bangladesh are not the only beneficiaries of the unwaged labor that reproduces Rohingya lives under conditions of severe duress. Those who have been resettled in third countries, especially the United States, very much depend on the care work, emotional support, and even the financial help of Rohingya women living in diaspora in Malaysia. In 2008, Roshida and her sister, Nur, fled Rakhine State for Kuala Lumpur, where they registered as refugees with the UNHCR and were placed on a waiting list for resettlement in a third country. Their elderly mother joined them several years later. In 2015, Roshida's sister and elder daughter were resettled in Aurora, Colorado and Sheboygan, Wisconsin, respectively, but

Roshida and their mother remained on the waiting list in Kuala Lumpur. Roshida cares for her mother, who, like many refugee elders, suffers from multiple health problems including dementia. It is quite common for elders and the infirm to remain behind in countries of origin or in secondary countries while relatives leave to work abroad. Because the UNHCR requires that an entire family be present to be considered for resettlement, elders who do join their children after several years cannot be placed in the UNHCR file without the entire family starting the process over. Thus, elders are often permanently left behind and cared for by their daughters or daughters-in-law.

While we talk in the family's three-room apartment in Selayang, a town on the northern outskirts of Kuala Lumpur well known for its large Rohingya population, Roshida notices that her mother has entered the bedroom and turned off the light. She gets up to see what her mother is doing, then murmurs: "She is like a child. I must watch her all the time." Each month, Roshida must take her mother to the clinic at least three times, requiring multiple Grab rides (a service like Uber that is popular in Southeast Asia) and costs totaling 300 RM, or US$50. Given their income from her husband's occasional electrician work is 1,000 RM per month, and rent is 600 RM per month, they are facing extreme hardship. Not only is Roshida's solely responsible for elder care, her sister Nur is unable to send any money from the United States to Roshida in Kuala Lumpur to help pay for their mother's expenses.

In fact, several years later Roshida used her savings to send Nur nearly US$600 in gold and mobile phones when Nur could not pay her bills. Refugee assistance varies by state, city, and non-profit partner, which is sub-contracted by the state to manage refugee resettlement. In Aurora, Lutheran Family Services, the International Rescue Committee, and African Community Centers arrange housing and provide limited cash aid for new arrivals, but the privatization and neoliberalization of refugee resettlement programs pushes refugees to find immediate employment to "support themselves." In order to fulfill grant requirements and attract donor funding, refugee organizations seek high employment rates among refugees, regardless of job quality or compensation.

Nur's husband, Hafiz, works at JBS in Greeley, Colorado, a meatpacking plant, but his wages are barely enough to cover the high cost of rent and other living expenses in Aurora. Roshida sends Nur clothing, makeup, and food from Malaysia: "I bought her Thanaka (a traditional makeup from Myanmar) and clothes from the market here. She works so much, so she doesn't have time to shop. And everything is so expensive in America." Roshida's situation is not unique. I conducted 15 interviews and extended observation sessions with Rohingya and Myanmar Muslim refugee women (in Malaysia?), most of whom provided care for an elderly parent or parent-in-law who was not resettled in the United States, and none of whom received remittances significant enough to alleviate financial hardship. Rohingya refugees cited Malaysia's restrictive immigration policies as the primary reason they chose to apply for resettlement in a third country. In Malaysia, they are unable to work legally, access affordable healthcare, or send their children to public schools. From 2011 to 2015, the United States accepted a large number of refugees from Malaysia and Thailand, although some were resettled in Europe or Australia. Most Rohingya refugees knew that life in the United States was not going to be easy, but many had genuine hope for success and better opportunities for themselves and their children in the United States. With respect to economic security, few find life in the United States any easier. In fact, many are significantly poorer than they were in Kuala Lumpur. Nur's husband reflects on their new life in the US: "In Malaysia, I had a decent business distributing goods from the market, I had a truck and a motorcycle," and Nur adds, "Here we have to work to death just to pay the bills." Nur and Hafiz hope to buy a house one day, but for now they are in debt and are barely making ends meet.

Tosima and her husband live in a two-bedroom high-rise apartment in Selayang. She has a 18-month-old daughter and also cares for her elderly mother-in-law. Tosima expressed sympathy for her brother-in-law, who lives in Aurora and works at a palette construction company: "He is also very poor and has a family to take care of. He can't afford to send us money or support grandmother. It's hard living there." Tosima's mother-in-law is very sick with diabetes, and is currently in the hospital. She takes a 30 RM Grab car to the hospital almost every day, and spends an hour or more cooking homemade meals to bring to her mother-in-law. When her mother-in-law is at home, Tosima walks her to the bathroom, feeds her, and keeps her company all day. In addition to caring for her child and mother-in-law, Tosima also spends about 40 minutes on the phone with her sister-in-law each evening. Her sister-in-law needs her encouragement, Tosima says.

Rohingya women's stories underscore the material effects of their exclusion from citizenship, commodity markets, and labor markets in Myanmar, which ironically facilitates their heightened surveillance and expropriation as informal workers and unwaged home-makers. While the material conditions of displacement and the political economy of gendered, (un)waged labor undeniably serve the interests of capital at multiple scales, Rohingya women's own views of their everyday lives complicate our understandings of the relationship between labor, gender, and dispossession. The next section expands this discussion of labor to attend more carefully to the lifeworlds, identities, and dignity of Rohingya women themselves as they navigate emplacement, displacement, and resettlement.

Motherhood, *Niqab*, and the Rohingya Home

Rohingya women living throughout Southeast Asia share similar experiences of scarcity and limited opportunity. As discussed above, their experiences and articulations of agency reveal the incompleteness of their exclusion and the existence of lives carved out within, outside, and parallel to structures of violence and oppression. A feminist political economy analysis reveals that Rohingya expulsion from the Myanmar body politics and their exclusion from formal wage labor enables insidious *inclusions* as Rohingyas are impoverished, confined, and surveilled by the Myanmar and Bangladesh militaries. Yet, the texture of Rohingya women's everyday lives as mothers, observant Muslims, and home-makers also sheds light on their resilience and resistance to Burmanization and the development interventions that follow dispossession.

Drawing on Doreen Massey and the broader fields of feminist geography and cultural geography, Blunt and Dowling[38] illustrate the multi-scalar nature of home as it is socially constructed through interrelations with other scales, ideas, and places. A relational understanding of space opens a radical re-consideration of home as a generative site of consent and dissent in wider cultural, socio-economic, and political struggles. By refuting fixed, hierarchical notions of scale, feminist geographies of home also open possibilities for understanding the home as central to the production of capitalism, nation, empire, as well as the production of identities. Most importantly, constructions of home are crucial in producing social inclusion and exclusion—Rohingya women's struggles over their autonomy in the interconnected spheres of home and motherhood illustrate the incomplete character of state, military, and non-governmental modes of power over Rohingya lives and draw our attention to the interstitial spaces from which dignified understandings of Rohingya life can emerge. This section engages feminist geography and feminist and postcolonial political economy to unpack Rohingya women's articulation of motherhood, home, and positioning as (un)waged workers in relation to thorny questions of agency, resistance, and the pervasive crush of capital.

Nuraini has been interviewed many times by journalists and other visitors to the Butukhali refugee camp in Cox's Bazaar, Bangladesh. She appears in a BBC film and several other publications about Rohingya refugees, tearfully recounting the murder of her husband, 9-year-old son, infant son, and her own near death. When I arrive at her house, she begins to remove her headscarf and roll up her sleeves, asking if I want to photograph her scars. I politely decline. Nuraini is still distraught about the massacre of her family, but instead of talking about her own suffering as a victim of violence, she talks at length about her regrets as a mother and her concerns for her young daughter. A few weeks before the military came to her village, her son had asked her for a *longyi*, but she did not buy it for him. Now he is dead, she says, she regrets not spending a few thousand kyat to make him happy. Like all the refugee women I have spoken with, Nuraini is concerned about her child's well-being: "What about my daughter? She saw everything. I'm worried about her future. I want her to have an education." Nuraini's emphasis on her responsibilities as a mother points to an important aspect of Rohingya identity, and humanity, that has been obfuscated by a focus on Rohingya ethnicity and refugee-ness.

Echoing Fahmida Kazi Farzana's descriptions of Rohingyas novel expressions of resistance, Nuraini has developed several strategies for improving her condition in the camps and avoiding would-be exploiters. When I ask her if she gave her consent for the local NGO worker and fixer to arrange our meeting, she responds that she did—but that she has refused to see a journalist who promised to bring her a shawl, but failed to deliver: "I heard him knocking but I didn't come to the door," she said. Nuraini also fills her kerosene tank using money from various visitors (including, reportedly, a KPop star and Chinese actress), relatives, and neighbors who help support her, since her injuries prevent her from gathering wood for cooking and hauling water. The *mazee* (Rohingya village leader) of her camp block ensures that she receives UNHCR rations, and her brother-in-law carries the rice and lentils to her house. As they sit with grief and sadness, Nuraini and other Rohingya refugee women also spend a lot of time thinking about their identities as mothers and home-makers. In fact, motherhood is the first thing that many women mention with respect to their own understandings of the effects of violence, confinement, and state surveillance, as well as their hopes, fears, and dreams for a better life.

Rohingya motherhood and the Rohingya home also appear at the center of debates over Rohingya-ness and the Myanmar nation. Popular narratives circulating within social media and the teashops of Yangon and Sittwe often link Rohingya practices of motherhood and occupation of home-space with a perceived intensification in conservative Islamic views. Foreign and local non-governmental workers, journalists, students, and even academics have told me that Rohingyas are becoming more conservative Muslims as a result of their isolation and inability to travel between villages in Rakhine state. Ben, an anthropologist who has worked in Rakhine with MSF and other smaller NGOs as a research consultant, explained:

> Rohingyas used to be able to visit their relatives in other villages, and they got more diverse views and information. Now they need permits to travel, and are only getting information from religious leaders. They are becoming much more conservative and Islamic. Now the women wear *burqa*—they didn't used to. The women are having more children and don't want birth control, they come to the centers only for handouts.

More than one non-governmental worker has denied claims that Rohingya women reject birth control, and that they only visit clinics and support centers to get "handouts." In fact, an employee at IRC told me that women in Sittwe camps are "desperate" for birth control, and that NGO centers and offices provide much-needed social interaction and emotional support. Regardless, Ben's assertions seem increasingly common, even among "modern" Rohingyas themselves. I have observed the performance of what Stacy Leigh Pigg[39] describes as the credible and "developed" knowledge that is framed in opposition to "backward" and credulous local knowledge in conversations with both Burmese and Rohingya individuals who speak English and work in close proximity with foreign development agencies. Salam and Amina, both Rohingyas, explained to me that Rohingyas did not used to wear *burqa*, and that "backward" Rohingyas need to be educated to put an end to the oppression of women in their conservative culture. Notably, the incorporation of Rohingya women into waged labor markets is overwhelmingly cited as an important "solution" to liberate them from their backwardness and oppression in the home.

While Rohingya women's practices of *purdah*, *burqa*, and family decisions to keep young girls at home are often explained as a function of backwardness, ignorance, and the inherently sexist nature of Islam, Rohingya mothers themselves tell a different story. Sitting in a circle of 15 Rohingya women living in Kutupalong camp, Sairah explains why she didn't send her daughter to school back home in Maungdaw:

> As a mother I am always worried about sending my children to school —I was afraid they will be robbed. I send my sons to school, but I can't send my daughters to school past 8 or 9 because there is no secure environment—we are afraid they will be harassed or raped. I cannot give my son money or a mobile phone because he will be robbed and it will be stolen.

Sairah's views show that her family's decision to keep her daughter at home is not just a function of conservative views about gender and education, or symptoms of an imagined Islamic radicalization. Were it not for the constant fear of harassment, the women say they would certainly send their girls to be educated past the age of 8 or 9.

Women's decisions to stay in the home and wear *burqa* also reflect strategies for dealing with their own trauma while nurturing their own identities. Raziyah, 35, fled Rakhine for Kuala Lumpur in 2012, and has recently begun wearing *niqab*, a black veil that covers the face and has a small horizontal slit for the eyes. She explains her decision: "the veil gives me peace in my mind. I have so many worries and fears, but when I wear *niqab* I feel calm." Raziyah's perspective on covering and faith is echoed by many Rohingya women, for whom the traumas of war are compounded by constant harassment and surveillance in secondary countries and displacement camps. Like the space of the home, Islamic clothing provides a space of sanctuary and dignity. Like Raziyah, Hamina, 48, takes pride in her decision to cover herself and practise *purdah*, which generally entails the visual and spatial seclusion of women from strangers and men who are not close relatives, though there is significant diversity in the practice across south and southeast Asia.

> As Rohingya women, we stay in *purdah*. It's dignity for us. We have bamboo fences for showers in our yards—the military came and tore down our bamboo fences—we had no privacy as women. It was shameful.

Hamina also emphasized that she does not want to work outside the home because there is no women-only workplace that is accessible to her: "I would have to work alongside men at the brick factory, and I would be ashamed." When I ask her about why she would feel ashamed, she clarifies that by "ashamed"—or *shorom* in Rohingya, she means her own discomfort being outside the home with men who are not relatives. Were it not for conditions of extreme poverty, all the Rohingya women I spoke with in Sittwe would prefer to stay in the home and take care of their families: "at home I feel comfortable and safe," Hamina says. Noor, a single mother of 5, echoes Hamina's views, explaining that Rohingya women have different values than Rakhine women:

> We are not like Rakhine women, who can go out and visit, go and do all the things they want. We don't do this. I only go out to work because I need to survive, because it's such hard times. Given the choice, I would stay inside. I don't want to go out.

Hamina and Noor's views point the important and inextricable relationship between dignity and space in Rohingya women's lives. Most women who now live in Kutupalong came from smaller villages of several hundred or a thousand people. The women I spoke with outside Sittwe didn't wear *burqa* or even *hijab* inside their villages (they preferred a simple cloth headscarf tied around their hair)—but will cover if they "go to town." Far from the quiet hometowns and villages, Kutupalong-Butukhali is a bustling "city" home to nearly a million people. Hence, it is not unreasonable to expect that Rohingya women would feel compelled to cover themselves in a new, strange place filled with new, strange faces where they seldom have the privacy they were accustomed to in their rural homes.

Unsurprisingly, few Rohingya women are eager to work outside the home in the camps. Of course, "Rohingya women" is not a monolith, and there is considerable diversity among women's views of religion, politics, identity, and work. Some women in Kutupalong do wish they had access to paid work outside the home, but for them the doors of wage work remain closed at every turn, as Kalyan Sanyal (2006) wrote of the capital's constitutive others. Shafika, who has a college degree in biochemistry from Sittwe University and lived in Maungdaw's town center, wants to find a job in Kutupalong, but has felt discriminated against as an observant Muslim woman:

> Because we wear veils, we can't get jobs. Not even at NGOs. We could work as teachers, but we face discrimination. It's not formal discrimination, but we don't get opportunities because we choose to wear *burqa*.

Discussions with Rohingya women revealed that, on one hand, deeply held views of Muslim faith and dignity often preclude employment opportunities, while on the other hand Rohingya women are denied access by virtue of the increasing demands of life in confinement and displacement. Hence, Rohingya women are doubly-excluded from opportunities to earn cash income to supplement their livelihoods while unpaid labor burdens expand.

Rohingya experiences of confinement in Kutupalong-Butukhali reveal a significant increase in demands for Rohingya women's unwaged social reproduction labor and the extension of Rohingya women's working days. According to interviews and community meetings, women in Kutupalong-Butukhali spent more than four hours per day hauling water from wells that are in the "valleys" between the camp's steep hills, making work outside the home nearly impossible. An employee at a major international aid organization in Cox's Bazaar expressed frustration with failed attempts to recruit women for jobs to improve the camp infrastructure: "They don't want to work. They need money, but we can't just give it to them. They have to do something." I pointed out that they were in fact doing many other things, and (unsuccessfully) suggested wages for doing housework.

Conclusion

Rohingya women's uneven experiences of work, motherhood, and home in Rakhine, Bangladesh, Malaysia, and Aurora point to a key process overlooked by scholars of dispossession and primitive accumulation: that women are never wholly confined to the realm of waste, surplus populations, and the made-to-die. Of course, many of the world's women continue social reproduction work within the spaces of what Kalyan Sanyal[40] would call wasteland. However, an examination of the specific condition of confinement faced by refugees, who are widely considered "wasted" people given their forceful exclusion from formal wage labor markets and their spatial confinement to camps, reveals their positioning as producers and reproducers. Their social reproduction labor (non-capital) is continuously enrolled in broader relations of capitalism and the capitalist mode of production, even though this production may be several scales removed from the immediate orbit of Rohingya women's daily lives.

Stories of motherhood, home, and Rohingya women's faith therein not only illuminate the complex and multi-dimensional aspects of Rohingya women's identities, they also contradict dominant narratives of Rohingya radicalization that continue to justify Myanmar military operations in Rakhine state, the ongoing surveillance and confinement of Rohingyas in Sittwe and Cox's Bazaar, and development interventions that presuppose Rohingya backwardness and women's uniform experiences of oppression by co-ethnic men. This chapter aimed to interrogate the materiality and multiplicity of Rohingya labor to shed light on the uniquely gendered aspects of Rohingya displacement, dispossession, and emplacement while simultaneously recognizing the incompleteness of this dispossession. My use of feminist, community-based methods aims to prioritize Rohingya women's own views of their identities, experiences, and practices of making and supporting life, which place at the center possibilities for decolonized knowledge and practical acts of resistance.

I have argued that by sitting with Rohingya women's labors and everyday lives, it is possible to enhance our understandings of how Rohingya exclusion—displacement and dispossession—accompanies a reciprocally incomplete inclusion vis-à-vis gendered labor exploitation and expropriation, specifically in the unseen spaces of the domicile. Through the use of feminist and CBR methods, I also aim to support ethical and beneficial research about Rohingyas while emphasizing novel spaces for collective resistance. In Myanmar, collective class struggle has been broadly eclipsed by a focus on individual ethnic group grievances and the restoration of citizenship rights[41]; however, as Cresa Pugh[42] compellingly argues, the restoration of full citizenship and recognition as *taingyintha* is unlikely to ensure Rohingyas' safety or prosperity. Rather, Soe Lin Aung and Stephen Campbell[43] point to the successes of labor movements that are shifting terrains of struggle for workers in Myanmar and elsewhere. Given that Rohingya exploitation and expropriation is taking place largely outside the formal wage contract, an extension of collective struggle into the intimate spaces of the everyday offers valuable opportunities for reconfiguring Rohingya positioning vis-à-vis oppressors. No doubt, Rohingyas face formidable structural barriers to their emancipation, not least of which is heavy-handed state violence. Drawing inspiration from bell hooks, who writes of Black women who make homes where Black families can be subjects and not objects, practices of Rohingya homemaking, religiosity, and motherhood become visible as processes that restore dignity that is denied to Rohingyas. Amid confinement and exclusion, the home, the wardrobe, the camp, and the kitchen, rather than the court or the factory floor, present themselves as spaces within which acts of meaningful resistance and refusal can emerge.

Notes

1. K. McKittrick, "On Plantations, Prisons, and a Black Sense of Place," *Social & Cultural Geography* 12, no. 8 (2011): 953.
2. Bell Hooks, "Homeplace: A site of resistance," *Undoing Place? A Geographical Reader*, ed. Linda McDowell (New York: Arnold, 1997).

3. See, for example, K.J. Strand, N. Cutforth, R. Stoecker, S. Marullo, and P. Donohue, *Community-Based Research and Higher Education: Principles and Practices* (London: John Wiley & Sons, 2003).
4. Michale Charney, "Theories and Historiography of the Religious Basis of Ethnonyms in Rakhaing (Arakan), Myanmar (Burma)," Paper given at "The Forgotten Kingdom of Arakan: A Public Seminar on the People of Present Day Arakan State of Myanmar," Bangkok, 23 November 2005; Thibut d'Hubert and Jacques Leider, "Traders and Poets at the Mrauk-U Court: Commerce and Cultural Links in Seventeenth-century Arakan," in *Pelagic Passageways: The Bay of Northern Bengal Before Colonialism*, ed. Rila Mukherhjee (New Delhi: Primus Books, 2011); Jacques Leider, "These Buddhist Kings with Muslim Names," in *Études Birmanes en Homage à Denise Berno*, ed. Pierre Pichard and Francois Robinne (Paris: École Française d'Extrême-Orient, 1998); J. Leider, "Competing Identities and the Hybridized History of the Rohingyas," in *Metamorphosis: Studies in Social and Political Change in Myanmar*, ed. Renaud Egreteau and François Robinne (Singapore: NUS Press, 2015), pp. 151–78; Moshe Yegar, *The Muslims of Burma*, Schriftenreihe des Südasian-Instituts der Universität Heidelberg (Wiesbaden: Otto Harrassowitz, 1972); Moshe Yegar, *Between Integration and Secession: The Muslim Communities of the Southern Philippines, Southern Thailand, and Western Burma/Myanmar* (Lanham and Oxford: Lexington Books, 2002).
5. Melissa Crouch, ed., *Islam and the State in Myanmar: Muslim-Buddhist Relations and the Politics of Belonging* (Oxford: Oxford University Press, 2016); Andrew Selth, "Burma's Muslims and the War on Terror," *Studies in Conflict & Terrorism* 27, no. 2 (2004): 107–26; Nick Cheesman, "How in Myanmar 'National Races' Came to Surpass Citizenship and Exclude Rohingya," *Journal of Contemporary Asia* 47, no. 3 (2017): 461–83.
6. Matthew J. Walton, "The 'Wages of Burman-ness': Ethnicity and Burman Privilege in Contemporary Myanmar," *Journal of Contemporary Asia* 43, no. 1 (2013): 1–27; Matt Schissler, Matthew Walton, and Phyu Phyu Thi, "Reconciling Contradictions: Buddhist-Muslim Violence, Narrative Making and Memory in Myanmar," *Journal of Contemporary Asia* 47, no. 3 (2017): 376–95.
7. Charney 2005: 23; M.W. Charney,"Where Jambudipa and Islamdom Converged: Religious Change and the Emergence of Buddhist Communalism in Early Modern Arakan (Fifteenth to Nineteenth Centuries)," Doctoral dissertation, University of Michigan, 1999.
8. Walton 2013: 5.
9. Elliott Prasse-Freeman, "Scapegoating in Burma," *Anthropology Today* 29, no. 4 (August 2013).
10. Glen Sean Coulthard, *Red Skin, White Masks: Rejecting the Colonial Politics of Recognition* (Minneapolis: University of Minnesota Press, 2014).

11. Elliott Prasse-Freeman, "Bad Blood and the Muslim Beef: Deterritorialization, Nationalist Reinscription, and Right-Wing Movements in Contemporary Burma," American Anthropology Association Annual Conference, San Jose, California, 14–18 November 2018.
12. Crouch 2016.
13. See also Francis Wade, *Myanmar's Enemy Within: Buddhist Violence and the Making of a Muslim 'Other'* (London: Zed Books, 2017).
14. Kazi Fahmida Farzana, "Music and Artistic Artefacts: Symbols of Rohingya Identity and Everyday Resistance in Borderlands," *Austrian Journal of Southeast Asian Studies* 4, no. 2 (2011): 215; Kazi Fahmida Farzana, "Boundaries in Shaping the Rohingya Identity and the Shifting Context of Borderland Politics," *Studies in Ethnicity and Nationalism* 15, no. 2 (2015): 292–314.
15. For an elaboration on this point, see Shae Frydenlund, "On the Uses of (Neo)liberalism in Myanmar and the Promise of Radical Feminism," *Oxford Tea Circle*, 2017.
16. Doreen Massey, *For Space* (London: Sage, 2005).
17. A.M. Thawnghmung, "The Politics of Indigeneity in Myanmar: Competing Narratives in Rakhine State," *Asian Ethnicity* 17, no. 4 (2016): 527–47.
18. Cheesman 2017: 468.
19. See for example Ian Holliday, "Addressing Myanmar's Citizenship Crisis," *Journal of Contemporary Asia* 44, no. 3 (2014): 404–21; and Gerard McCarthy, "Buddhist Welfare and the Limits of Big 'P' Politics in Provincial Myanmar," in *Conflict in Myanmar: War, Politics, Religion*, ed. Nick Cheesman and Nicholas Farrelly (Singapore: ISEAS Publishing, 2015).
20. Jennifer Hyndman, *Managing Displacement: Refugees and the Politics of Humanitarianism* (Minneapolis: University of Minnesota Press, 2000).
21. Cheesman 2015: 4.
22. Ruth Wilson Gilmore, *Golden Gulag: Prisons, Surplus, Crisis, and Opposition in Globalizing California* (Berkeley: University of California Press, 2007).
23. Michael McIntyre and Nast Heidi, "Bio (Necro)polis: Marx, Surplus Populations, and the Spatial Dialectics of Reproduction and 'Race'," *Antipode* 43, no. 5 (2011): 1465–88.
24. Silvia Federici, *Revolution at Point Zero: Housework, Reproduction, and Feminist Struggle* (Oakland: PM Press, 2012).
25. Doreen Massey, *Spatial Divisions of Labor: Social Structures and the Geography of Production* (New York: Routledge, 1995); L. McDowell, "The Lives of Others: Body Work, the Production of Difference, and Labor Geographies," *Economic Geography* 91, no. 1 (2015): 1–23.
26. Nancy Fraser, "Expropriation and Exploitation in Racialized Capitalism: A Reply to Michael Dawson," *Critical Historical Studies* 3, no. 1 (2016): 163–78.
27. Rhacel Parreñas, *Servants of Globalization: Woman, Migration, and Domestic Work* (Stanford: Stanford University Press, 2001); Rachel Silvey, "Power,

Difference, and Mobility: Feminist Advances in Migration Studies," *Progress in Human Geography* 28, no. 4 (2004): 490–506; Rachel Silvey, "Consuming the Transnational Family: Indonesian Migrant Domestic Workers to Saudi Arabia," *Global Networks* 6, no. 1 (2006): 23–40; Rachel Silvey and R. Elmhirst, "Engendering Social Capital: Women Workers and Rural–Urban Networks in Indonesia's Crisis," *World Development* 31, no. 5 (2003): 865–79.

28. G. Pratt, *Families Apart: Migrant Mothers and the Conflicts of Labor and Love* (Minneapolis: University of Minnesota Press, 2012).
29. Miraftab 2016: 140.
30. Ibid.: 141.
31. Pseudonyms are used to protect the identity of human subjects.
32. For example, see Katie Arnold, "Traffickers Prey on Lost Rohingya Children in Bangladesh Camps," *Reuters*, 7 November 2017; Tommy Allard and Thomas Wilkes, "$6 for 36 Days of Work: Child Exploitation Rife in Rohingya Camps," *Reuters*, 12 November 2017.
33. About US$7. One US$ is about 85 Bangladesh Thaka.
34. Allard and Wilkes 2017: 3.
35. Pheng Cheah, *Inhuman Conditions: On Cosmopolitanism and Human Rights* (Cambridge: Harvard University Press, 2006).
36. Karl Marx and Friedrich Engels, *Capital: Volume I* (New York: Dover Publications, 2011).
37. About US$4. One US$ is about 1,300 Myanmar kyat.
38. Alison Blunt and Robyn Dowling, *Home* (New York and London: Routledge, 2006).
39. Stacy Leigh Pigg, "The Credible and the Credulous: The Question of 'Villagers' Beliefs' in Nepal," *Cultural Anthropology* 11, no. 2 (1996): 160–201.
40. Kalyan Sanyal, *Rethinking Capitalist Development: Primitive Accumulation, Governmentality and Post-colonial Capitalism* (London: Routledge, 2006).
41. Elliott Prasse-Freeman and Phyo Win Latt, "Class and Inequality in Contemporary Myanmar," *The Routledge Handbook of Contemporary Myanmar*, ed. Ian Holliday, Nicholas Farrelly, and Adam Simpson (Oxon and New York: Routledge, 2018), pp. 404–18.
42. Cresa Leonard Pugh, "Is Citizenship the Answer? Constructions of Belonging and Exclusion for the Stateless Rohingya of Burma," International Migration Institute (IMI), Oxford Department of International Development (QEH), University of Oxford, 2013.
43. Soe Lin Aung and Stephen Campbell, "The Lady and the Generals," *Jacobin*, 13 January 2016; Stephen Campbell, "Cross-ethnic Labour Solidarities among Myanmar Workers in Thailand," *Sojourn: Journal of Social Issues in Southeast Asia* 27, no. 2 (2012): 260–84; Stephen Campbell, "Articulating Grievance in Southeast Myanmar," in *Civil Wars in South Asia: State, Sovereignty, Development*, ed. Aparna Sundar and Nandini Sundar (New Delhi: SAGE Publications India, 2014), p. 240.

References

Allard, Tommy and Thomas Wilkes. 2017. "$6 for 36 Days of Work: Child Exploitation Rife in Rohingya Camps." *Reuters*, 12 November.

Arnold, Katie. 2017. "Traffickers Prey on Lost Rohingya Children in Bangladesh Camps." *Reuters*, 7 November.

Blunt, Alison and Robyn Dowling. 2006. *Home*. New York and London: Routledge.

Campbell, Stephen. 2012. "Cross-ethnic Labour Solidarities among Myanmar Workers in Thailand." *Sojourn: Journal of Social Issues in Southeast Asia* 27, no. 2: 260–84.

———. 2014. "Articulating Grievance in Southeast Myanmar." In *Civil Wars in South Asia: State, Sovereignty, Development*, ed. Aparna Sundar and Nandini Sundar. New Delhi: Sage Publications, pp. 240–63.

Charney, Michael. 2005. "Theories and Historiography of the Religious Basis of Ethnonyms in Rakhaing (Arakan), Myanmar (Burma)." The Forgotten Kingdom of Arakan: A Public Seminar on the People of Present Day Arakan State of Myanmar. Bangkok, 23 November.

Cheah, P. 2006. *Inhuman Conditions: On Cosmopolitanism and Human Rights*. Cambridge: Harvard University Press.

Cheesman, Nick. 2015. *Opposing the Rule of Law*. Cambridge: Cambridge University Press.

———. 2017. "How in Myanmar 'National Races' Came to Surpass Citizenship and Exclude Rohingya." *Journal of Contemporary Asia* 47, no. 3: 461–83.

Coulthard, Glen Sean. 2014. *Red Skin, White Masks: Rejecting the Colonial Politics of Recognition*. Minneapolis: University of Minnesota Press.

Crouch, Melissa, ed. 2016. *Islam and the State in Myanmar: Muslim-Buddhist Relations and the Politics of Belonging*. Oxford: Oxford University Press.

D'Hubert, Thibaut and Jacques Leider. 2011. "Traders and Poets at the Mrauk-U Court: Commerce and Cultural Links in Seventeenth-century Arakan." In *Pelagic Passageways: The Northern Bay of Bengal Before Colonialism*, ed. Rila Mukherjee. Delhi: Primus Books.

Farzana, Kazi Fahmida. 2011. "Music and Artistic Artefacts: Symbols of Rohingya Identity and Everyday Resistance in Borderlands." *Austrian Journal of Southeast Asian Studies* 4, no. 2: 215.

———. 2015. "Boundaries in Shaping the Rohingya Identity and the Shifting Context of Borderland Politics." *Studies in Ethnicity and Nationalism* 15, no. 2: 292–314.

Federici, Silvia. 2012. *Revolution at Point Zero: Housework, Reproduction, and Feminist Struggle*. Oakland: PM Press.

Fraser, Nancy. 2016. "Expropriation and Exploitation in Racialized Capitalism: A Reply to Michael Dawson." *Critical Historical Studies* 3, no. 1: 163–78.

Gilmore, Ruth Wilson. 2007. *Golden Gulag: Prisons, Surplus, Crisis, and Opposition in Globalizing California*. Berkeley: University of California Press.

Henue, Siobhan. 2018. "Rohingya Girls Targeted by Child Traffickers at Bangladesh Border Crossings." *ABC News*, 7 February.

Hooks, Bell. 1997. "Homeplace: A Site of Resistance." In *Undoing Place? A Geographical Reader*, ed. Linda McDowell. New York: Arnold.

Holliday, Ian. 2014. "Addressing Myanmar's Citizenship Crisis." *Journal of Contemporary Asia* 44, no. 3: 404–21.

Hyndman, Jennifer. 2000. *Managing Displacement: Refugees and the Politics of Humanitarianism*. Minneapolis: University of Minnesota Press.

Leider, Jacques. 1998. "These Buddhist Kings with Muslim Names." In *Études Birmanes en Homage à Denise Berno*, ed. Pierre Pichard and Francois Robinne. Paris: École Française d'Extrême-Orient.

Marx, Karl and Friedrich Engels. 2011. *Capital: Volume I*. New York: Dover Publications.

Massey, Doreen. 2005. *For Space*. London: Sage.

McCarthy, Gerard. 2015. "Buddhist Welfare and the Limits of Big 'P' Politics in Provincial Myanmar." In *Conflict in Myanmar: War, Politics, Religion*, ed. Nick Cheesman and Nicholas Farrelly. Singapore: ISEAS publishing.

McDowell, L. 2015. "Roepke Lecture in Economic Geography: The Lives of Others: Body Work, the Production of Difference, and Labor Geographies." *Economic Geography* 91, no. 1: 1–23.

McIntyre, Michael and Heidi Nast. 2011. "Bio (necro) Polis: Marx, Surplus Populations, and the Spatial Dialectics of Reproduction and 'Race'." *Antipode* 43, no. 5: 1465–88.

Miraftab, Faranak. 2016. *Global Heartland: Displaced Labor, Transnational Lives, and Local Placemaking*. Bloomington: Indiana University Press.

Parreñas, Rhacel. 2001. *Servants of Globalization: Woman, Migration, and Domestic Work*. Stanford: Stanford University Press.

Pigg, Stacy Leigh. 1996. "The Credible and the Credulous: The Question of 'Villagers' Beliefs' in Nepal." *Cultural Anthropology* 11, no. 2: 160–201.

Prasse-Freeman, Elliott. 2013. "The Futile and Violent Search for 'Authenticity' in Burma." *DVB*, 12 July.

______. Forthcoming. "Bad Blood and the Muslim Beef: Deterritorialization, Nationalist Reinscription, and Right-Wing Movements in Contemporary Burma." American Anthropology Association Annual Conference, San Jose, California, 14–18 November 2018.

Pratt, Geraldine. 2012. *Families Apart: Migrant Mothers and the Conflicts of Labor and Love*. Minneapolis: University of Minnesota Press.

Pugh, Cresa Leonard. 2013. "Is Citizenship the Answer? Constructions of Belonging and Exclusion for the Stateless Rohingya of Burma." International Migration Institute (IMI), Oxford Department of International Development (QEH), University of Oxford.

Sanyal, Kalyan. 2006. *Rethinking Capitalist Development: Primitive Accumulation, Governmentality and Post-colonial Capitalism*. London: Routledge.

Silvey, Rachel. 2004. "Power, Difference, and Mobility: Feminist Advances in Migration Studies." *Progress in Human Geography* 28, no. 4: 490–506.

———. 2006. "Consuming the Transnational Family: Indonesian Migrant Domestic Workers to Saudi Arabia". *Global Networks* 6, no. 1: 23–40.

Silvey, Rachel and R. Elmhirst. 2003. "Engendering Social Capital: Women Workers and Rural–Urban Networks in Indonesia's Crisis." *World Development* 31, no. 5: 865–79.

Selth, Andrew. 2004. "Burma's Muslims and the War on Terror." *Studies in Conflict & Terrorism* 27, no. 2: 107–26.

Schissler, Matt, Matthew Walton, and Phyu Phyu Thi. 2017. "Reconciling Contradictions: Buddhist-Muslim Violence, Narrative Making and Memory in Myanmar." *Journal of Contemporary Asia* 47, no. 3: 376–95.

Soe Lin Aung and Stephen Campbell. 2016. "The Lady and the Generals." *Jacobin*, 13 January.

Strand, K.J., N. Cutforth, R. Stoecker, S. Marullo, and P. Donohue. 2003. *Community-Based Research and Higher Education: Principles and Practices.* London: John Wiley & Sons.

Wade, Francis. 2017. *Myanmar's Enemy Within: Buddhist Violence and the Making of a Muslim 'Other'*. London: Zed Books.

Walton, Matthew J. 2013. "The 'Wages of Burman-ness': Ethnicity and Burman privilege in Contemporary Myanmar." *Journal of Contemporary Asia* 43, no. 1: 1–27.

Yegar, Moshe. 1972. *The Muslims of Burma*. Schriftenreihe des Südasian-Instituts der Universität Heidelberg. Wiesbaden: Otto Harrassowitz.

———. 2002. *Between Integration and Secession: The Muslim Communities of the Southern Philippines, Southern Thailand, and Western Burma/Myanmar.* Lanham and Oxford: Lexington Books.

CHAPTER 11

Two Sides of the Same Arakanese Coin: "Rakhine," "Rohingya," and Ethnogenesis as Schismogenesis

Elliott Prasse-Freeman and Kirt Mausert

> "Bengalis do not have any characteristics or culture in common with the ethnicities of Myanmar."
>
> – Senior General Min Aung Hlaing, 19 March 2018[1]

> "The patterns of behavior associated with elimination of other groups may be assimilated into their culture so that they are impelled to eliminate more and more."
>
> – Gregory Bateson, 1935[2]

Introduction: A Theory of Longue Duree Ethnogenesis

In the wake of ongoing cycles of ethnic cleansing of Myanmar's Rohingya minority, the most recent of which saw over 700,000 driven out of Myanmar's Rakhine State into Bangladesh beginning in August 2017, the world has been searching for answers to what has motivated these brutal pogroms. Journalistic and academic accounts have generally characterized the violence as deriving from some mixture of internecine conflict (between Buddhist Rakhine and Muslim Rohingya) and state-sponsored military cleansing operations. Although the modality of violence is quite different across these explanations, what they have in common is reducing the conflict to Buddhists versus Muslims, and the autochthonous Rakhine (with backing of their co-religionists, the Bamar, amongst other "national races" of Burma) versus the putatively allochthonous Rohingya.

The problem with these accounts is that while religion and indigeneity have certainly proven to be potent discourses for mobilizing the violence, an exclusive focus on them ultimately obscures factors that would illuminate other central motivations of the conflict. Specifically, while both folk and academic histories draw on particular interpretations of official British colonial records and Arakanese royal chronicles to present the Rakhine and Rohingya as unrelated ethnic groups—a division that has allowed elites of both to make political claims to autonomy within Myanmar—reexamination and retheorization of historical sources, linguistic patterns, archaeological records, and anthropological data casts doubt upon that conclusion and the very epistemological stance that insists upon such a project of categorization. Instead, we suggest that after the migration of the Mranma people to Arakan around the 9th century,[3] processes of schismogenesis[4] (creation through differentiation) has been underway which has resulted today in the binary Rakhine/Rohingya, with the former considered "native" and the latter "foreign" to Arakan. We suggest here that both *emblems* in fact are intimately related to one another rather than either preceding the other in a meaningful sense.

Hence, contemporary conflicts over the status of the Rohingya—of the validity and legitimacy of the emblem itself—are animated by a misapprehension of the centuries-long process whereby the Rakhine identity (imagined as an ethnic group in relation to Burma's other national "races," chiefly the Bamar) has gone through fundamental change as its proponents appropriated as their *exclusive cultural patrimony* many of the symbols of the general "Arakanese" culture that preceded it. "Arakan" here is the name given to the political kingdoms derived from the preceding "Indic"[5] kingdoms which variously incorporated Buddhist, Hindu, and, later, Muslim subjects and symbols in what is now Rakhine State[6] and southeastern Bangladesh. While Rakhine/Rohingya *should* index changes in the complex trans-ethnic political-cultural system[7] constituted by Arakan/Chittagong over a millennium, the dyad *instead* stands for the aggrandizement of the first term at the expense of the latter's erasure.

But even as we encourage the consideration of the Arakan/Chittagong system, it is also ensconced in other systems. The Rakhine ethnogenetic project of cultural-symbolic appropriation, the other side of which has been the denial of indigeneity to this proto-Rohingya Muslim population[8] has been labeled "Irrawaddy-ification" by Michael Charney.[9] Charney describes this as a process deriving from the historical contingencies of the 17th- and 18th-century decline of Arakan,[10] followed by the policies of the Bamar conquerors that began with the annexation of Arakan in

1784/85. A review of the recent relative explosion of research on 17th-century Arakan and Bengal[11] brings those initial cycles of schismogenesis into focus—in which conceptions of difference were generated, boundaries drawn, borders established that re-oriented Arakan towards the Irrawaddy on one hand, and Chittagong (just across the Naf river from Arakan[12]) towards Bengal and the wider Muslim world to the west on the other. The early 19th-century British colonial occupation that followed the Bamar conquest further exacerbated these divisions, compelling additional cycles of ethnogenesis often achieved through violent projects of separation. The British gave way to a further intensification of the essentialization of Rakhine identity in the post-colonial era, as Rakhine nationalists have sought to affirm their place within the post-colonial Myanmar state's "national races" pantheon, an imaginary animated by an ideology which privileges Buddhism and concomitant narratives of indigeneity. This has occurred while Rohingya elites have insisted upon the ethnonym "Rohingya" and privileged Muslim identity over non-Muslim traditions as a connection to Arakan. We conclude by arguing that the Rohingya/Rakine conflict can be perceived as microcosmic of a broader anxiety in Myanmar society about indigeneity—itself a metonym for belonging in the polity, in which the ability to claim membership may be the only way of securing access to scarce resources and opportunities. This is particularly potent given the current inefficacy and irrelevance of formal citizenship status.[13] Deconstructing "Rakhine" and contesting Rohingya exclusion together unravel the flimsy fabric with which Myanmar's indigeneity discourse is currently woven.

To describe these various processes, this chapter will proceed in a speculative vein, drawing from a four-fields (Biological, Linguistic, Archaeological, Sociocultural) anthropological methodology. This project, while ambitious in its theorization, is also humble—in that we are re-reading work generated by others, reassembling texts arranged by those who have come before us, and proposing new trajectories for research that either we have just begun (through an ongoing multi-sited ethnographic project in Cox's Bazaar, Kuala Lumpur, and Yangon) or which we ourselves cannot follow. By examining earlier claims, we hope to ask: *are there other reasonable ways of interpreting these data?* Such questioning can critique current interpretive theories and advance alternative ones, based on what we know from fieldwork conducted elsewhere in Burma (and beyond). This is especially necessary when many current arguments about the ethnogenesis of the Rohingya take colonial records as dispositive,[14] or fixate on the existence of the *ethonyms* "Rohingya" and "Rakhine" in various archives without considering the potential for, on one hand, radical cultural differences *within* those respective terms across time and space, and on the other, the existence of groups of people sharing culture, dress, religion, language despite the *absence* of a consistent ethnic name inscribed within discursive traditions.

Part I: Dueling Indigeneities

This section seeks to sketch features of Rakhine and Rohingya nationalist historiography to illustrate how *both* traditions seek to establish their bona fides as authentic ethnic groups within the purview of the modern racialized post-colonial Myanmar state. Although our ethnographic research suggests these are elite discourses that may not penetrate to the grassroots,[15] these narratives circulate and hence affect political conditions, making deconstruction imperative. While scholarly debate has fixated on Rohingya nationalist claims,[16] we argue that by critiquing both ethnonyms, the presumption that "Rohingya" is constructed while "Rakhine" is trans-historically consistent (that is, *ahistorically* eternal) can be contested.

Rakhine and Rohingya Historiographies

Rakhine historiography elides the ethnogenic process by asserting narratives of timeless, essentialist ethno-communities.[17] Here indigeneity is formulated in a linear historical framework in which authenticity correlates to antiquity, securing the group's, and by proxy an individual's, position within Myanmar society.[18] Consequently, Rakhine nationalist historians assert some variety of the claim that "Rakhaing [sic] culture is older and more advanced than that of Burma,"[19] seeking to situate the Rakhine as the more "pure" and direct descendants of the progenitors of the modern Bamar "race." For instance, for Buddhist monk-cum-historian Ashin Nyanuttara, "Ancient Rakhaing entered into Rakhaing strip from the north-eastern parts of India," and while *other* races—"Aryans and Mongoloids"—may have "cohabited" with one another and "entered into Rakhaing strip," at no point did "the races [mix] *after* they entered into the Rakhaing strip."[20] Nyanuttara invokes here a popular folk theory that the name "Rakhine" refers to upholding the "racial purity" of the group.[21] Similarly, many Rakhine nationalist historians assert that their dialect is identical with the earliest Burmese dialect, a fact refuted by linguistic analysis.[22] Further, while Rakhine vernacular histories ground themselves in Rakhine royal chronicles,[23] these have undergone various modern revisions and adjustments.[24]

Such maneuvers stand as attempts to account for the obviously Indic character of the earliest Arakanese civilization while simultaneously inoculating themselves from the taint of *kala* (the term, often used as a slur, for South Asians or Muslims), by arguing that the Rakhine can trace a "pure," impregnable channel to the Buddha through royal "Aryan" blood.[25] For instance, the emblems of the Rakhine State flag and state seal bear iconic likeness with the symbols found on the coinage of the earliest (pre-Mranmaic migration) periods of Arakanese civilization,[26] symbols that bear a striking correspondence to the emblems found on coinage from the neighboring and associated Harikela kingdom, north of Chittagong.[27] Critically, this linkage with symbols of Indic civilizations to the Buddha's homeland is more a mytho-cosmological than a historical one. Rakhine nationalists assert a genealogical relatedness to Indian (*qua* Aryan) royalty, even claiming that the Rakhine originate in India itself, while they fiercely reject links with actual South Asian *people*.

While Rohingya historiography often interprets the same sources in different ways,[28] positing that Rohingya predated the Rakhine, it reflects a commitment to the same indigeneity imperative that privileges ancient origins.[29] A common trope here is that shipwrecked Arabs brought their faith with them to Arakan in the late 8th century AD, establishing themselves as the progenitors of modern Rohingya. The lack of corroborating historical or archaeological records renders this claim highly speculative, however. While the claim appears reasonable—shipwrecks were common along Arakan's shores for many centuries; Arab traders were in communication with the Bay of Bengal even before the advent of Islam—the primary tradition of Islam practised in areas where maritime Muslim Arab traders introduced the faith, Shafi'i, differs from the Hanifi tradition of Islam in Southeastern Bengal and Arakan.

Rohingya nationalists, for their part, in developing a theory of ethnogenesis linked first and foremost to the introduction of Islam to Arakan, dissociate themselves from those pre-existing Hindu-Buddhist Vedic cultural emblems, thereby amplifying the complementary schismogenic process (abdicating those emblems to Rakhine nationalists). Moreover, Rohingya historiography's focus on Islam, seeking to emphasize a distinctive and essential Rohingya identity, laminates "religion" on "race," excluding Arakanese Hindus and Buddhist Mramagyi (the latter a recognized "national race" of Myanmar), groups which both share mutually intelligible dialects and common genealogical ancestry with Rohingya Muslims. This sacrifices a broader, more inclusive, notion of the Rohingya identity by adhering to the dominant model of authentic ethnic groupings under the "national races" ideology of the Myanmar state.

While the Rohingya and Rakhine historiographies hence stand as mutually exclusive, they can be displaced by reconceptualizing ethnogenesis as a historical and cultural, rather than an essentially biological or genealogical, process. We turn next to what such a pursuit might look like.

Part II: Early Peopling of Arakan

The Arakan littoral has for millennia played an important role in connecting diverse populations divided by the imposing geographic barrier of the Himalayas' associated ranges, as groups traversed this narrow band of coastline.[30] Ancestors of peoples now populating Bangladesh's Chittagong Hill Tracts and the Arakan Yoma range reached the region well before lowland agricultural states,[31] suggesting they may have fled to the hills when such states did come. And come they did: by approximately 500 CE, an Indic civilization organized around wet rice cultivation and modeled on city-states found across the Bay of Bengal had been established along the littoral. There has, since this period, been a continuous presence of wet rice cultivators organized by cosmologies, religions, and models of political authority of Indic provenance,[32] indisputably attested to in scripts evident in inscriptions by the engraved deities, and even in the urban plans of the capitals of kings with Sanskritic titles and mythic lineages.

While the archaeological record clearly testifies to Arakan's Indic sources, the history of its *peopling* remains controversial. Human population genetic surveys including Rakhine and neighboring populations have begun to clarify our understanding of peopling events in the history of the region, resolving some questions left open by historical and archaeological records. Critically, contrary to the theory that a small group of migrants from the Irrawaddy moved into the Arakan littoral in the mid-1st millennium CE,[33] these surveys suggest that a relatively large group reached the region,[34] changing Arakanese social demographics through either migration, invasion, or both.[35] These studies further suggest that Rakhine retain a greater degree of the shared genetic heritage traceable to peoples of present-day southwestern China than the markedly more genetically diverse Bamar group, indicating that Mranmaic migrants from the Irrawaddy to Arakan branched off from an ancestral population relatively early in the history of such peoples in the Irrawaddy valley.[36] The divergences between the modern Rakhine and Burmese dialects show evidence of continuous exchange and influence, mostly of Burmese on Rakhine, and a mid-10th century basal dialectal split is consistent with these findings.[37] All surveys so far clearly indicate that both Rakhine and Burmese populations carry non-trivial genetic contributions of South Asian origins, however,[38] pointing to an earlier Indic population pre-dating Rakhine's Tibeto-Burman speaking ancestors in the region that coincides with evidence from the archaeological record, and continuous gene flow since.[39]

Part III: Hindu/Muslim Arakanese History and Iterative Schisms

While such deep history is speculative for lack of primary source material, Thibaut d'Hubert's recent work on Muslims at the 17th-century Arakanese court sheds some light on the historical presence of non-Buddhists in Arakan. D'Hubert has illuminated that these Muslims were not a cloistered "foreign" elite, as has long been assumed. D'Hubert refutes the assumption that they constituted "a community of foreign merchants only;" rather, Muslims "were present at virtually all levels of Arakanese society,"[40] from the court to the fields, where hundreds of thousands of slaves that were gathered from contemporary eastern Bengal were settled.[41] Regarding those elites, they generated a robust set of institutions—educational, religious, and legal—reflected in "a local administrative and political multilingual idiom [that] appears on coins, in inscriptions, and in later literary texts."[42] As such they formed identities as *Arakanese Muslims* in particular,[43] carving out a liminal position—by facilitating foreign trade—that was essential to the kingdom's prosperity. In this, d'Hubert observes that "it is not that Bengali Muslims were completely assimilated into Arakanese nobility; their otherness was crucial to their roles as cultural intermediaries."[44]

But mid-17th century political-economic changes[45] deeply affected Muslim social positioning. First, Muslims' lynchpin role in that foreign trade was displaced, as the Dutch VOC asserted itself in the Bay of Bengal, allowing Arakanese elites to "trade directly with the European and other foreign merchants of the Bay of Bengal networks"[46] rather than through Arakanese Muslim middlemen. This decrease in Muslim importance to the kingdom dovetailed with Arakan's first "Buddhification," instigated by Narapati (1638), who "strove to appear as a pious king."[47] D'Hubert's readings of the Arakanese Muslim poet Alaol's corpus of texts allows us to see how Buddhification and the declining role of Muslims in trade drove changes in Buddhist and Muslim self-identification, resulting in a "crystallization of religious identities."[48] The Mughal invasion (1660–66) of Arakan exacerbated these divisions, leading d'Hubert and Leider to observe that "Bengali Muslims were suspected to be on the Mughal side. A clear distinction was made between the Buddhist Arakanese power and the non-Arakanese Muslims."[49] Charney finds a parallel process occurring for Buddhists, noting that King Sanda-thu-dhammaraza, previously impious and fairly disinterested in Buddhism, "after the turbulent 1660s ... stressed [his] personal devotion to Buddhism" and made the Crown Prince ordain as a monk.[50] The liminal position enjoyed by the Arakanese Muslims (previously simultaneously both integrated and differentiated from Arakanese Buddhist majority culture) seems to have then experienced a reorientation towards marginalization. Hence language, religion, and dress that had marked their difference perhaps took on additional meanings, becoming what we could call proto-ethnic material.

After the Mughal occupation of Chittagong the decline of Arakan was swift, increasing ossification of religious identification. Charney finds that as central power waned, rural gentry became comparatively stronger, waging incessant mobilizations for domination of vulnerable villages and control of the crown itself. The destabilization wrought by these various conflicts led to a decline in food production, which spurred reinforcing cycles of food insecurity (even famine), and population flight,[51] but it also led to "people consciously defin[ing] themselves according to their commitment to one or another religion."[52] For instance, rural gentry encouraged followers to "conver[t] to their own faith"—which meant either Buddhism and Islam.[53] After a Bengali (either Hindu or Muslim) named Gadra took the throne in 1737 and proceeded to destroy Buddhist images and occupy monasteries, "some Buddhist elites (many perhaps in association with monks), encouraged a closer identification between the kingship and Buddhism."[54]

Leider identifies certain texts emerging at this time that attempted to fortify and buttress the Buddhist quality of Arakan.[55] The fact that apocrypha emerged is suggestive itself, indexing potential intention by social actors to intervene in standard narratives. Leider identifies the particular text he analyzes as emerging *before* the 1784/85 Bamar invasion, and hence ascribes the source of the Arakan anxiety about Buddhism to the mid-18th century political context in which both *internal* Arakan instability and the looming presence of non-Buddhists in Chittagong and further west manifested threat. It is noteworthy in this context that the author of the apocryphal sermon in question emplaces many Buddha relics around Arakan state, the effect of which was to not only demarcate the political contours of Arakan dynastic rule, but also to construct "a representation of the ... 'Buddhicized' parts of Arakan," both "sanctify[ing] the land," and "mark[ing] the territorial appropriation of the land by the Buddha ... thus defin[ing] the topography of a fully 'Buddhicized' territory."[56]

Even as the Arakanese side was emphasizing Buddhist idioms and its (new) separation from Chittagong and the greater Bengal world, a parallel process on the western side of the Naf commenced. Rishad Chaoudhury describes a "cultural reification of the frontier,"[57] relaying how discourse written only decades after the Mughal invasion recasts Arakan as fundamentally other, a land of infidels and demonic treachery. D'Hubert describes a parallel project in which 19th-century Islamic "reformist movements ... reject[ed] the Arakanese past of Bengali Muslims,"[58] noting that Bengal rejected Arakan Muslim culture due to its ostensible Hindu roots.[59] When combined with Bengal's early 18th century state centralization project—involving the building of military installations and the expansion of taxation that "pressed Chittagong more tightly into the purview of Bengal proper"[60]—we see a concomitant process of cleansing the memory of the other. Today, as Swapna Bhattacharya tells us, Bengalis maintain a popular imaginary of Rakhine (or "Magh") that "recalls the dreadful memory of Luso-Arakanese piracy and slave raiding during the sixteenth to eighteenth centuries," adding that the "concept of a Magh community is inextricably linked with the still current Bengali expression Mager Muluk, i.e. world of disorder."[61] Such cultural texts served to establish a new frontier between civilizations where fluidity and interchange had prior defined societal relations. Leider and Kyaw Minn Htin's identification that certain foundational myths of Bengali Muslim domination of Arakanese kings are both false and yet also persistent is consistent with this ideological project.[62] Finally, the case of the Marma community dwelling in the Chittagonian Hill Tracts, "who share [with the Rakhine] the same culture and practice the same religion" and yet "have developed a distinctive identity and are individualized by a different name 'Marma',"[63] can also be interpreted as an outcome of this split, a process Kyaw Minn Htin calls "de-Arakanization."

Part IV: The Colonial Projects – Bamar and British

The purification project continued and was accelerated with the Bamar colonization of Arakan that began with the 1784/85 occupation. Badawpaya's regime did not rule at a distance through intermediaries, but displaced existing institutions and replaced them with its own.[64] Charney identifies two sources of purification at the elite level: first, that Burmese occupiers *literally re-wrote* Arakanese history themselves, privileging narratives of Irrawaddy dominance.[65] Second, the Arakanese also rewrote their own history and redesigned their own cultural narratives to make these conform to the occupiers' standards. Leider highlights Arakanese resistance to Burmese rule after occupation, finding that it did not simply take the form of armed insurgency, but had cultural, symbolic, and discursive components that stressed ethnic/political autonomy of (Buddhist) Arakan. Leider demonstrates how Arakanese historiography sought to conform to the genre conventions of Burmese chronicles.[66]

As Irrawaddy's influence on Rakhine intensified, the British further exacerbated ethno-religious distinctions between Rakhine and Muslims "by identifying religious sites as either Muslim or Buddhist and granting their caretaker-ship on the basis of one or the other religious affiliation."[67] Further, the British identified Rakhine as "indolent" and Bengalis as "thrifty,"[68] favoring the latter in agricultural schemes, and in the 1880s facilitated massive resettlement from Chittagong to exploit new lands.

Summing up the state of Arakan after the successive colonizations, Leider identifies an explicit project forged by Arakan Buddhist elites intended to rehabilitate the status of Buddhism by improvising new legitimating stories and inscribing them in authoritative texts.[69]

Moreover, after the British claimed Arakan in 1824, Charney outlines a diffusion of this purification sentiment to local levels by identifying a two-stage process in which dislocations wrought by colonialism separated local clients from their patrons after which Buddhist institutions reinscribed those abandoned subjects. Specifically, people were mobilized to solve collective action failures through intra-religious bonds rather than inter-religious (community) ones, as had been the case previously under local leadership (see Buchanan's 1798 account for an example[70] of a patron organizing religiously diverse clients; Charney argues that such bonds soon thereafter "evaporated"[71]). Further, "Buddhist monastic education affected the rural population spatially and socially: monastic schools in large villages strengthened the Buddhist presence in rural areas and also provided a uniform influence upon elites and non-elites in such villages and towns."[72] As a result of these changes, locals sought prestige by patronizing religious institutions rather than village ones;[73] the fact that they extended this patronage beyond the village, sponsoring temple repairs far away, for instance, indicates that "Buddhist Arakanese had come to view themselves as part of a larger Buddhist community."[74]

Ultimately, by the end of the 19th century, Muslim and Buddhist had become communal identities which policed inter-marriage and conversion. Charney finds that "the overwhelming majority of Arakanese villages in 1891 appear to have been religiously endogamous," and that communities threatened "social exclusion to those who sought to change their religious identity."[75]

Part V: Theorizing Ethnogenesis

Contemporary accounts of the nature of the ongoing ethnic cleansing in Rakhine state typically skip the genealogy outlined above that shows increasing schismogenesis, to implant themselves exclusively in the British era (1824–1947). Such accounts emphasize how the British colonial project altered the ethnic relationships that existed in Arakan state—and indeed the entire country—due to the British endeavor to classify the peoples it subjugated according to a theory of ethnicity with roots in European/British anthropology. This theory attempted to establish the existence of distinct races of humans of which White Europeans were the most superior.

Much has been made of colonization's putative impact on ethnicity in Myanmar. Anthropologist Michael Gravers is representative of many scholars when he argues that "culture and ethnicity became reified and bounded, based on absolute differences in race, religion and mentality."[76] But Gravers, citing Furnivall, also notes another, often overlooked, aspect of the colonial system that compels us to reassess his own "reification thesis": namely that "ethnic groups were bound together by the market economy and by the colonial administration."[77] Donald Horowitz, scholar of ethnic conflict, elaborates this point in his seminal comparative volume: "What the colonialists did that was truly profound, and far more important for ethnicity, was to change the scale of the polity by several fold."[78] This new scale meant that ethnicities were *produced*, as localized identities were aggregated and amalgamated into supra-local categories more capable of participating efficaciously in the colonial (and ultimately post-colonial) state political economy.[79] The question of what happens to those *local* identities after they are aggregated into larger ones is a function of the forms and degrees of intensity of states' respective governmentalities[80]: strong states either obliterate local identities altogether or displace them to marginal domains ("cultural" or "folklore"); but when state projects are weak, inconsistent, or desultory (as with the British colonizers, whose ethnic categorization project was woefully confused[81]), to then become occasionally despotic but infrastructurally unsophisticated (as with the post-colonial regime[82]), we have a situation such as Burma's, where "transvestite" ethnic identities[83] can coexist. In other words, the reification thesis implies *exhaustive* ascriptive categorization, ignoring the evidence of people retaining the ability to maneuver within the field of ethnic categorization, holding multiple identities at different scales simultaneously, and fractionally.

Tellingly, various forms of identification are still being generated and renegotiated in Myanmar today.[84] We have found in our ethnographic fieldwork that not only do Burmese persons often inhabit multiple ethnicities at once, but new identifications may presently be in the process of being formed: people often describe how their *lu-myo* (their race or "type of person") is "Buddhist,"[85] for instance, an identity that does not neatly fit the schema described above by those such as Gravers.

Fortunately, ethnographic and theoretical research on Burma has long provided us with powerful tools for thinking about this kind of ethnic mutability and mutation. Edmund Leach's pathbreaking study of the Kachin/Shan oscillatory system demonstrates how the "unstable equilibria" that define ethnic relations allow singular individuals to embody *multiple* ethnic identities, being "simultaneously Kachin and Shans."[86] F.K. Lehman's observation that ethnicity in Burma must be conceptualized as "reticulate"—such that a given ethnicity's "connection with Burma proper was systematically mediated by some third [ethnicity]"[87]—helps us understand that ethnicities take diverse meanings in different contexts depending on how they nest within broader networks and emerge under various circumstances.

Given these foundations, common dismissals of Rohingya claims to an authentic ethnicity appear less valid, even disingenuous. For instance, Leider argues that, "Contemporary Rohingya writers claim that a local Rakhine Muslim identity to be called 'Rohingya' has existed for centuries, because they argue for the recognition of distinct ethnic credentials. But at the same time, they point to the great diversity of ethnic origins and social backgrounds of Muslims during the pre-modern period which makes the hypothesis of a single identity rather unlikely."[88] But if identities are *not* mutually exclusive, as Leach stresses, there is no reason why there cannot be a diversity of ethnicities *and* a super-ordinate ethnicity (eventually called "Rohingya") that brings them together under certain conditions.

This is particularly relevant when we consider Mandy Sadan's research on the problematic exonym "Kachin." Sadan begins by identifying the now classic, but still regularly (willfully) ignored, fact that domineering textual cultures often define oral ones without their consent or participation[89]—relevant for those who spuriously find in the absence of evidence of the ethnonym Rohingya in colonial records the evidence of the non-existence of the people who came to see themselves as Rohingya. Sadan then explains a double-bind for those Kachin who recognize that "Kachin" "has so singularly failed to attain status as an indigenous form" for people labeled Kachin,[90] even as the term is politically expedient, even *necessary*, for Kachin autonomy projects in the context of a de facto imperial state that has demonstrated preference for ruling through division.[91] Relevant for our Rohingya discussion is that Sadan shows that those labeled "Kachin" have searched for an indigenous term, finding some success in "Wunpawng," "a relatively recent innovation ... derived from a nationalist interpretation of archaic oral tradition."[92] The conceptual parallels between "Wunpawng" and "Rohingya" are apparent: both groups have been labeled ("Kachin" in the former case, "Bengalis" in the latter case) in ways they reject. The critical difference, of course, is that "Kachin," imperfect as it might be, confers belonging in the polity as *taing-yin-tha* (indigenous). "Bengali," of course, does not.

The task becomes to consider the empirical data vis-à-vis Rohingya given these theoretical tools. It is commonly asserted that the British instalment of a system of migrant agricultural labor in Arakan, a region which remains relatively underpopulated compared to the neighboring Irrawaddy valley and the Bengal delta, imported the "Bengalis" who would eventually become those who claim "Rohingya" identity today. Indeed, even those historians who acknowledge the existence of Muslims before this period assert, albeit without evidence, that the mass migration facilitated by the colonial agricultural machine effectively overran previous Muslim society and culture, replacing it with Chittagonian Bengali.[93]

Yet the community of Muslims east of the Naf spoke and continue to speak a different dialect than Chittagonian,[94] and have aggressively denied that they are precisely the same as those on the Chittagonian side. Colonial records, for instance in the 1923 census, tell us as much: "the race of Arakan-Mahommedans, numbering 24 thousands ... object to being classed with their co-religionists the Chittagonians, and consider themselves much more closely related to the Arakanese Buddhists amongst whom they live."[95] Later the census writers elaborate further: "Although so closely connected with Chitagonians racially the Arakan-Mahomedans do not associate with them at all; they consequently marry almost solely among themselves and have become recognized locally as a distinct race."[96] It seems that in the 1920s, after most of the British-facilitated immigration, the local Arakanese Muslims (the proto-Rohingya) thought of themselves as distinct. Given that the Rohingya of today speak a different dialect and continue to differentiate themselves from Chittagonian Bengalis, it seems a slow process of ethnogenesis was occurring even amidst mass immigration, and that this migration may even have fed into the complementary schismogenic process of differentiation between Rakhine and Rohingya, as contrastive icons have been accumulatively subordinated under each emblem.

The post-colonial period has only seen more schismogenesis, with Rakhine and Rohingya differentiation proceeding along both spatial and social-institutional forms. In regards to the former, Leider shows how inter-communal violence under the Japanese occupation in 1942 effectively led to a project of mutual ethnic cleansing, sending Rakhine Buddhists south, and Rohingya north to areas bordering Bangladesh.[97] Regarding sociocultural appropriation, everything from coins, to flags, to wrestling has been rendered exclusively Rakhine. For example, de Mersan's study of Rakhine spirit cults shows how Rakhine are in the process of "writing out" the Chittagonian from their myths, re-construing a historically linked world as separate.[98] "Rakhine traditional wrestling" is increasingly restricted to Rakhine people, even though Rohingya had long participated in it;[99] our interviews reveal that some Rohingya insist that Rakhine "stole" it from them, and similar forms of wrestling culture exist in Chittagong.[100] Finally, for all the insistence on ethnic impregnability, intermarriage continues: Wade presents Rohingya "becoming" Rakhine,[101] while our interviews have found that both Rakhine men and women have crossed the ethnic threshold the other direction.

Part VI: Post-colonial Struggles for Recognition

Ultimately, rather than imagining ethnicities as billiard balls—impregnable and rigid, such that when they smash together ("Chittagonian Muslim" meets "Arakanese Muslim"), one breaks the other—we consider the possibility of the production of hybridity, particularly considering their intermingled pasts. In general this orientation is necessary in the context of a multi-ethnic country in which many ethnic groups share co-ethnics across borders (and who should not "lose" status as "belonging" because of complex histories of intercourse across those cartographic lines). This is not to dismiss the possibility of complete absorption by "Chittagonians" and the eradication of Arakanese Muslim (Rohingya) traces, but this is theoretically unlikely. More importantly, given that people today call themselves Rohingya, it seems strange to advance the claim that they were absorbed by "Chittagonians" simply because the term "Rohingya" did not gain wide purchase as an ethnonym during the colonial moment.

And yet, there is a disheartening tendency in much academic literature to assume that Rohingya claims of indigeneity are invalidated because Chittagonians assimilated and adopted Rohingya patterns of life and speech. Or to go further and suggest, without evidence, that Chittagonians subsumed "Rohingya," and/or that inter-ethnic mixing is so recent that "Rohingya" is a mere cynical ideology. We turn here to writings on the Rohingya by Jacques Leider, a scholar who has, on one hand, laudably contested an international discourse that reduces all Rakhine to incorrigible racists,[102] but has, on the other, made claims about the Rohingya that warrant retheorization so as to open up ways of both understanding ethnogenesis and of interrogating extant historical materials.

While Leider notes that, "The building of a communal identity referred to as 'Rohingya' is … a social process that has hitherto not been studied by anthropologists,"[103] he effectively proceeds in his writings to make a number of anthropological claims that he does not support with evidence. For example, Leider argues that Rohingya ethnicity was a political movement that remained cloistered in elite circles, "mostly associated with Muslim guerrilla organizations fighting against the Burmese government."[104] He claims that while Rakhine and Muslim tension across the post-independence period—which the government apparently prevented from developing into full-blown internecine conflicts[105]—made "individuals beg[i]n to produce exclusive narratives to describe their history and identity,"[106] it was only "leaders of the Muslim diaspora of Arakan" who "became the mainstay of the acclaimed Rohingya identity."[107] "Muslims in Arakan," conversely, "kept on identifying primarily as Muslims."[108] Leider also claims that the "visceral rejection of the Rohingya identity by the Buddhists in Arakan and by many ethnic groups of Myanmar has a lot to do with the distortions and contradictions built into the political DNA of the Rohingya movement."[109]

The obvious problem with these claims is that none are supported by evidence. When Leider claims that after independence "Muslims in Arakan" continued identifying as *Muslim* (rather than Rohingya), he not only does not substantiate the claim, but elsewhere he acknowledges that there is little known about how average Muslims conceived of their identity, conceding his own claims are *impossible to confirm*.[110] Yet, despite all that we do *not* know about Rohingya, Leider asserts that the Muslims in Rakhine state, indoctrinated by "Rohingya ideology" essentially constituted a *Chittagonian Bengali* society.[111]

The deeper problem with such claims[112] is that they refuse to imagine different explanations. This compels us to ask, in turn: why is there such an insistence, on the part of both nationalists and certain researchers, to see the Rohingya as irredeemably infested with the taint of "Bengaliness" —and hence allochthony? We suspect it stems from the subtleness, even slipperiness, of our argument—that admittedly could be construed as trying to "have it both ways," in the sense that we are identifying that Rohingya are claiming ethnic *difference* from Chittagonian Bengalis (and hence indigeneity), while also showing that there is enough *similarity* between the groups that when they interacted over generations in Rakhine state, the latter amalgamated into the Rohingya.

But this is not such a fanciful claim when we consider it within the social systems or "transethnic" model urged by Robinne and Sadan.[113] When broadening our consideration of what the Arakanese/Chittagonian world looked like *before* the tyranny of the map compelled many to see Rakhine "belonging" in Arakan and Muslims "belonging" in Bengal (later, Bangladesh), the apparent mutability/differentiation paradox dissolves. The view of the colonist—the map and the census and the ethnic categorization chart—sees a horde of Muslims "invading" Arakan. But if we expand our view back in time, to the Indic civilizations of Vesali and Lemro of ancient Arakan, we might say that these Bengalis were not invading, but *coming home*. This "homecoming" is not meant to be construed in terms of "ancestral homelands" nor for those *specific* persons, but as a reconstitution of the stubborn Chittagong that was always already within Arakan, a reminder of that past that has been effectively reterritorialized elsewhere, where not obliterated entirely.

Part VII: Conclusion: Unraveling Indigeneity Discourses

Yet, a persistent broader question remains:[114] why does the rest of the country so intently reject the Rohingya? We propose that the generalized hatred of the Rohingya illuminates the entire system of belonging in the Myanmar polity, even as the conflict generates changes in that system. Not only does the eager participation of Rakhine nationalist elites in Rohingya exclusion elevate the former's standing in the system, but nationalists of all ethnic orientations have capitalized on processes of formal democratization and a liberalization of the public sphere to generate a robust, if revanchist, national conversation over belonging in the polity which enhances each group's position within it.[115] As other ethnic groups in Burma have uniformly rejected the Rohingya, discourses that a shared primordial "blood" subtends superficial differences in ethnic groupings and religious affiliations amongst officially ratified "national races" are increasingly prevalent.[116] By establishing the Rohingya as the extimate other, these groups inscribe themselves inside.

But that only addresses the in-group forming inertia that motivates Rohingya exclusion. Burma's trans-social antipathy—spanning right-wing nationalists to former political prisoners—goes far beyond that project. Rather, the hatred suggests an anxiety that the constitutive foundation of belonging in Myanmar is corrupted and collapsing, incoherent and increasingly consumed by its own internal contradictions. Following Rene Girard's theory of the scapegoat,[117] the Rohingya are not hated because they are *different*, but because there is fear that they are actually the *same*, revealing that purportedly natural categories are, indeed, arbitrary emblems. Consequently, "Rohingya" contests the entire colonialist cartographic ontology in which "races" belong to certain territorial domains. In so doing, the Rohingya threaten to expose a gaping hole in this logic. The question is whether, even as this unraveling produces violent attempts to restitch the torn fabric, space is created in the caesura for other idioms and foundations—a broader sense of indigeneity, a broader sense of cultural citizenship—to take their place.

Notes

1. Quoted in Democratic Voice of Burma, "Min Aung Hlaing warns against anti-military sentiment," *Democratic Voice of Burma*, 21 March 2018.
2. Gregory Bateson, "Culture Contact and Schismogenesis," *Man* (1935): 178–83.
3. Pamela Gutman, "Ancient Arakan, with special reference to its cultural history between the 5th and 11th centuries," Diss., Australian National University, 1976.
4. "A process of differentiation in the norms of individual behavior resulting from cumulative interaction between Individuals," in Gregory Bateson, *Naven*, 2nd ed. (Stanford, California: Stanford University Press, 1958).
5. The role of people and traditions emanating from ancient Bengal played a central role in these earlier polities.
6. Parts of Myanmar's southern Chin State and areas now incorporated into India which were once part of the ancient kingdom of Harikela were associated with early Arakan, just as the kingdom extended its influence to present-day Bago, or Pegu, at the height of its power.
7. Francois Robinne and Mandy Sadan, "Postscript: Reconsidering the dynamics of ethnicity through Foucault's concept of 'spaces of dispersion'," in *Social dynamics in the highlands of Southeast Asia: Reconsidering political systems of highland Burma by ER Leach*, ed. Francois Robinne and Mandy Sadan, Vol. 18 (Leiden: Brill, 2007a).
8. The Kaman, another Muslim minority of Arakan, are however recognized as a "national race."

9. Charney uses the term in "Beyond State-Centered Histories in Western Burma, Missionizing Monks and Intra Regional Migrants in the Arakan Littoral, c. 1784–1860," in *The Maritime Frontier of Burma Exploring Political, Cultural and Commercial Interaction in the Indian Ocean World, 1200–1800*, ed. Jos Gommans and Jacques Leider (Amsterdam: KITLV Press, 2002). While he describes the process as "Burmanization" in "Where Jambudipa and Islamdom Converged: Religious Change and the Emergence of Buddhist Communalism in Early Modern Arakan (Fifteenth to Nineteenth Centuries)," Doctoral dissertation, University of Michigan, 1999, many of the arguments and materials therein are relevant.
10. Charney 1999.
11. Thibaut d'Hubert, *In the Shade of the Golden Palace: Alaol and Middle Bengali Poetics in Arakan* (Oxford: Oxford University Press, 2018); Rishad Choudhury, "An eventful politics of difference and its afterlife: Chittagong frontier, Bengal, c. 1657–1757," *The Indian Economic & Social History Review* 52, no. 3 (2015): 271–96.
12. This border was established by Mughal invaders in 1666, who fixed, for the first time in Arakan's history, this East/West divide.
13. Nick Cheesman, "How in Myanmar 'National Races' Came to Surpass Citizenship and Exclude Rohingya," *Journal of Contemporary Asia* 7, no. 3 (2017): 461–83.
14. The colonial encounter and its forms of knowledge creation are often privileged by national and foreign researchers alike, despite the incompetence of such categorization (that the colonists themselves acknowledged), and the potential for subjects to evade state enumerating exercises. See Derek Tonkin, "Exploring the Issue of Citizenship in Rakhine State," in *Citizenship in Myanmar: Ways of Being in and from Burma*, ed. Ashley South and Marie Lall (Singapore: ISEAS-Yusof Ishak Institute, 2018). For a brief critique, see Elliott Prasse-Freeman, "The Rohingya Crisis," *Anthropology Today* 33, no. 6 (December 2017).
15. Our fieldwork indicates that non-elite Rohingya do *not* relay common tropes described by Rohingya elites. Many convey, simply, that they are Rohingya of Myanmar, and trace no origin story beyond their family's experiences in Rakhine.
16. Jacques Leider has critiqued Rohingya narratives on a number of occasions without attending to the constructed nature of "Rakhine" [see, *inter alia*, "Background and Prospects in the Buddhist-Muslim Dissensions in Rakhine State of Myanmar," in *Ethnic Conflict in Buddhist Societies in South and Southeast Asia*, ed. K.M. de Silva (Kandy: International Centre for Ethnic Studies, 2015b), pp. 25–55. Nick Cheesman, who admittedly has different objectives, juxtaposes a key Rohingya text with a sermon by a Burman monk ["The Right to Have Rights," in *Communal Violence in Myanmar* (Yangon: Myanmar Knowledge Society and Australia National University,

2015)]. Ardeth Thawnghmung ["The politics of indigeneity in Myanmar: competing narratives in Rakhine state," *Asian Ethnicity* 17, no. 4 (2016): 527–47] gets the closest to deconstructing Rakhine by critiquing how a particular Rakhine text *elides* a discussion of its own historical origins by focusing on refuting Rohingya claims to authenticity.

17. Myat Moe, "Striving to achieve lasting peace," *Global New Light of Myanmar*, 7 February 2018.
18. As Cheesman (2015) notes, citizenship rights are literally tied to an individual's status as indigenous.
19. Nyanuttara, *A Study of Buddhism in Arakan*, 2014.
20. Ibid., emphasis added.
21. Michael Charney, "Theories and Historiography of the Religious Basis of Ethnonyms in Rakhaing (Arakan), Myanmar (Burma)," The Forgotten Kingdom of Arakan: A Public Seminar on the People of Present Day Arakan State of Myanmar, Bangkok, 23 November 2005.
22. Maung Tha Hla, *The Rakhaing*, Buddhist Rakhaing Cultural Association, 2004. Both modern Rakhine and Burmese are Mranmaic dialects derived from Old Burmese (Nathan Hill, "The merger of Proto-Burmish *ts and *č in Burmese," SOAS Working Papers in Linguistics, Vol. 16, 2013), John Okell states that, "the probability is that the earlier inscriptions were written by a people who had no ethnic or linguistic connection with the Arakanese." This conclusion not only "remove[s] the aura of age from [Rakhine] culture," but also suggests connections with the Bengali social system—as recent scholarship on epigraphic evidence appears to confirm (Griffiths 2015: 286).
23. Nyanuttara 2014; similarly, San Tha Aung follows dynastic lists taken at face value from Rakhine royal chronicles to conclude, in the absence of any corroborating archaeological evidence, that the royal lineage of ancient Rakhine kings extends to "about 3000 B.C." (San Tha Aung, *The Buddhist Art of Ancient Arakan*, 1979), a date which quite conveniently situates Arakan within the ancient Indic *oecumene* of the historical personage of the Buddha.
24. "Rakhine dynastic lists linked to a succession of 'capitals' are desperately messy and inconclusive" (Leider 2015b).
25. Maung Tha Hla, for instance, allows that "the inhabitants of Rakhaing assimilated immigrants Aryans such as Kan Razagree and his followers."
26. See generally Pamela Gutman, "The ancient coinage of Southeast Asia," *Journal of the Siam Society* 66, no. 1 (1978): 8–21.
27. Robert S. Wicks, *Money, Markets, and Trade in Early Southeast Asia: The Development of Indigenous Monetary Systems to AD 1400*. SEAP Publications, No. 11, 1992, pp. 91–2.
28. Leider 2015b.
29. See Ba Tha, *A Short History of Rohingya and Kamas of Burma*, trans. A.F.K. Jilani, ed. Mohd. Ashraf Alam (Rakhine: Kaladan News, 2007 [1963]). Many Rohingya elite texts do not, as Nick Cheesman puts it, "question the

premises on which the taxonomy is based, and argue for a new formula for political membership." The "problem is not the taxonomy itself, but the exclusion of Rohingya from it" (2015: 142).

30. Li, Y.C., et al. "Ancient inland human dispersals from Myanmar into interior East Asia since the Late Pleistocene," Scientific Reports, Vol. 5, Article number: 9473 (2015).
31. N. Gazi, et al. "Genetic Structure of Tibeto-Burman Populations of Bangladesh: Evaluating the Gene Flow along the Sides of Bay-of-Bengal," *PLoS ONE* 8, no. 10 (2013); Gutman 1976.
32. Gutman 1976.
33. Michael Charney (1999) made this tentative proposal.
34. Gazi 2013.
35. "Invasion" here is used in the sense of being undertaken and organized by a military.
36. Monika Summerer, et al. "Large-scale mitochondrial DNA analysis in Southeast Asia reveals evolutionary effects of cultural isolation in the multi-ethnic population of Myanmar," *BMC Evolutionary Biology* 14, no. 17 (2014); Li Yu-Chun 2015.
37. Heidi Davis, "Consonant Correspondences of Burmese, Rakhine and Marma with Initial Implications for Historical Relationships," MA Thesis, University of North Dakota, 2014.
38. Ibid.
39. Arlo Griffiths, "Three More Sanskrit Inscriptions of Arakan: New Perspectives on Its Name, Dynastic History, and Buddhist Culture in the First Millennium," *Journal of Burma Studies* 19, no. 2 (2015): 281–340.
40. d'Hubert 2018: 30.
41. Charney 1999: 152–72.
42. d'Hubert 2018: 45–6; see also Thibaut d'Hubert, "The Lord of the Elephant: Interpreting the Islamicate epigraphic, numismatic, and literary material from the Mrauk U period of Arakan (ca. 1430. Thibaut 1784)," *Journal of Burma Studies* 19, 2 (2015): 341–70.
43. D'Hubert 2018: 64–5.
44. Ibid.: 68.
45. Charney 1998, 1999; Stephan van Galen, "Arakan at the Turn of the First Millennium of the Arakanese Era," in *The Maritime Frontier of Burma Exploring Political, Cultural and Commercial Interaction in the Indian Ocean World, 1200–1800*, ed. Jos Gommans and Jacques Leider (Amsterdam: KITLV Press, 2002).
46. D'Hubert 2018: 123.
47. Ibid.: 102.
48. Ibid.: 100.
49. D'Hubert and Leider 2011: 93.
50. Charney 1999: 207.

51. Ibid.: 228–33.
52. Ibid.: 219. This was a marked change from previous eras when affiliations that may have appeared religious often were merely associated with patron-client relationships (Charney 1999: 216).
53. Charney 1999: 224.
54. Ibid.: 244.
55. Jacques Leider, "Relics, Statues, and Predictions: Interpreting an Apocryphal Sermon of Lord Buddha in Arakan," *Asian Ethnology* 68, no. 2 (1999): 333–64.
56. Leider 2009: 341.
57. Rishad Choudhury, "An eventful politics of difference and its afterlife: Chittagong frontier, Bengal, c. 1657–1757," *The Indian Economic & Social History Review* 52, no. 3 (2015): 271.
58. D'Hubert 2018: 10.
59. Ibid.: 158–9.
60. Choudhury 2015: 287.
61. Swapna Bhattacharya, "Myth and History of Bengali Identity in Arakan," in *The Maritime Frontier of Burma Exploring Political, Cultural and Commercial Interaction in the Indian Ocean World, 1200–1800*, ed. Jos Gommans and Jacques Leider (Amsterdam: KITLV Press, 2002), p. 201.
62. Jacques Leider and Kyaw Minn Htin, "King Man Co Mvan's Exile in Bengal: Legend, History and Context," *Journal of Burma Studies* 19, no. 2 (2015): 371–405.
63. Kyaw Minn Htin, "The Marma from Bangladesh: A 'de-Arakanized' Community in Chittagong Hill Tracts," *Suvannabhumi* 7, no. 2 (December 2015): 133.
64. Jacques Leider, "Politics of Integration and Cultures of Resistance. A Study of Burma's Conquest and Administration of Arakan," in *Asian Expansions: The Historical Experiences of Polity Expansion in Asia*, ed. Geoffrey Wade (London: Routledge, 2015a), pp. 184–213.
65. Charney 2002: 216.
66. Leider 2015a: 201.
67. Charney 1999: 270.
68. Ibid.: 284.
69. Leider 2008: 440.
70. Willem van Schendel, ed., *Francis Buchanan in Southeast Bengal (1798): His Journey to Chittagong, the Chittagong Hill Tracts, Noakhali and Comilla* (Dhaka: University Press Limited, 1992), p. 89.
71. Charney 1999: 320.
72. Ibid.: 292.
73. Ibid.: 297
74. Ibid.: 299.
75. Ibid.: 300, 301.

76. Michael Gravers, "Introduction: Ethnicity against State – State against Ethnic Diversity?" in *Exploring Ethnic Diversity in Burma*, ed. Mikael Gravers. NIAS Studies in Asian Topics Series, 39 (Copenhagen: NIAS Press, 2007), p. 14.
77. Gravers 2007: 14.
78. Donald Horowitz, *Ethnic Groups in Conflict* (Berkeley: University of California Press, 2001), p. 76.
79. Horowitz 2001: 82.
80. Prasse-Freeman 2017.
81. The 1921 census enumerators commented on their own significant mistakes: that the differences in "the numbers tabulated at previous census as Mahomedad-Arakanese" across the years "indicate 0 Messages enumeration of the Arakan-Mahomedans at previous censuses under other descriptions; in the census tables of 1901 it is impossible to identify them. Probably they have been entered as Sheikh or possibly under Other Mahomedan tribes in all the three earlier censuses mentioned in the table" [S.G. Grantham, *Census of India, 1921*, Vol. X (Rangoon: Office of the Superintendent, Government of Burma, 1923), p. 214]. For a thorough discussion of the errors in categorization, see Erin Lynn McAuliffe, "Caste and the quest for racial hierarchy in British Burma: An analysis of census classifications from 1872–1931," Masters thesis, University of Washington, 2017.
82. See Elliott Prasse-Freeman, "Power, Civil Society, and an Inchoate Politics of the Daily in Burma/Myanmar," *Journal of Asian Studies* 71, no. 2 (2012): 371–97.
83. Benedict Anderson, *Imagined Communities* (New York: Verso, 2006), p. 166.
84. Francis Wade, *Myanmar's Enemy Within: Buddhist Violence and the Making of a Muslim 'Other'* (London: Zed Books, 2017).
85. For other evidence of "Buddhist lu-myo," see Charles Carstens, "Religion," in *Handbook of Contemporary Myanmar* (Routledge, 2018).
86. E.R. Leach, *Political Systems of Highland Burma* (Oxford and New York: Berg, London School of Economics Monographs on Social Anthropology #44, 1959), p. 2; for important critiques, see those assembled in Sadan and Robinne 2007b.
87. Lehman 1967: 119.
88. Leider 2013: 230.
89. Mandy Sadan, "Constructing and Contesting the Category 'Kachin' in the Colonial and post-Colonial Burmese State," in *Exploring Ethnic Diversity in Burma*, ed. Michael Gravers. NIAS Studies in Asian Topics Series, 39 (Copenhagen: NIAS Press, 2007), pp. 34–76, 39; see also James Scott, *The Art of Not Being Governed* (New Haven: Yale University Press, 2009).
90. Sadan 2007: 42.
91. Ibid.: 35.
92. Ibid.: 54.

93. Leider 2013: 229–30. Leider contradicts this claim elsewhere, instead asserting—also without evidence—that this putative absorption took place a number of decades later: "Bengali Muslim immigrants from Chittagong who settled in the north of Arakan ... assimilated, *after independence*, the precolonial Muslim community in northern Arakan" (Leider 2015a: 204, emphasis added).
94. While the fact of dialectal variation alone does not *prove* that a sociologically-meaningful ethnic distinction exists (Robinne and Sadan 2007a: 304), it is held up by Rohingya themselves as a way of marking difference, as a way of generating, constituting, and defending ethnic identity.
95. Grantham 1923: 22.
96. Ibid.: 213.
97. Leider 2018.
98. Alexandra de Mersan, "Ritual and the Other in Rakhine Spirit Cults," in *Myanmar's Mountain and Maritime Borderscapes*, ed. Su-Ann Oh (Singapore: ISEAS-Yusof Ishak Institute, 2016).
99. Arani Chowdhury, et al. "Power structures, class divisions and entertainment in Rohingya society," *BBC Media Action*, August 2018, p. 24.
100. Mahbubul Haque, "Bali Khela," in Sirajul Islam and Ahmed Jamal, *Banglapedia: National Encyclopedia of Bangladesh* (Asiatic Society of Bangladesh, 2012).
101. Wade 2017: ch. 10.
102. We enthusiastically support Leider in these endeavors and have also written against such simplistic and obfuscating discourses. On considering the Rakhine plight and perspective, see Elliott Prasse-Freeman, "A Senseless Census in Burma," *Foreign Policy*, 21 December 2013b; on not reducing Rakhine to racists, see Elliott Prasse-Freeman, "Fostering an Objectionable Burma Discourse," *Journal of Burma Studies* 18, no. 1 (June 2014): 118, fn 49.
103. Leider 2013: 232.
104. Jacques Leider, "Transmutations of the Rohingya Movement in the Post-2012 Rakhine State Crisis," in *Ethnic and Religious Identities and Integration in Southeast Asia*, ed. Ooi Keat Gin and Volker Grabowsky (Chiang Mai: Silkworm Books, 2017), pp. 199–200.
105. Leider 2017: 205.
106. Ibid.: 200.
107. Ibid.: 201.
108. Jacques Leider, "Conflict and Mass Violence in Arakan (Rakhine State): The 1942 Events and Political Identity Formation," in *Citizenship in Myanmar: Ways of Being in and from Burma*, ed. Ashley South and Marie Lall (Singapore: ISEAS-Yusof Ishak Institute, 2018), p. 206. Years earlier scholar Aye Chan made (also without providing evidence) a similar claim: "the majority

of the ethnic group, being illiterate agriculturalists in the rural areas, still prefers their identity as Bengali Muslims" [Aye Chan, "The Development of a Muslim Enclave in Arakan (Rakhine) State of Burma (Myanmar)," *SOAS Bulletin of Burma Research* 3, no. 2 (2005): 396–420, 415].

109. Jacques Leider, "Competing Identities and the Hybridized History of the Rohingyas," in *Metamorphosis: Studies in Social and Political Change in Myanmar*, ed. Renaud Egreteau and Francois Robinne (Singapore: NUS Press, 2016), pp. 160–1.
110. At one point Leider argues there is "a lack of detailed sources to explore the inner life of the Rohingya organizations to give us a deeper understanding of political and ethnic dynamics" (Leider 2015: 37–8).
111. As quoted earlier, Leider 2013: 229–30.
112. The point of highlighting Leider's various assertions about Rohingya is to use them, following Shae Frydenlund, for theorizing the Rohingya issue ["On the uses of (neo)liberalism in Myanmar and the promise of radical feminism," *Oxford Tea Circle*, 25 October 2017].
113. Robinne and Sadan 2007a.
114. Elliott Prasse-Freeman, "Scapegoating in Burma," *Anthropology Today* 29, no. 4 (August 2013).
115. Ibid.
116. Gustaaf Houtman, *Mental Culture in Burmese Crisis Politics*, ILCAA Study of Languages and Cultures of Asia and Africa Monograph Series No. 33, 1999: chapter 5.
117. René Girard, *The Scapegoat* (Baltimore: Johns Hopkins University Press, 1986).

References

Anderson, Benedict. 2006. *Imagined Communities: Reflections on the Origin and Spread of Nationalism*. New York: Verso.

Aye Chan. 2005. "The Development of a Muslim Enclave in Arakan (Rakhine) State of Burma (Myanmar)." *SOAS Bulletin of Burma Research* 3, no. 2: 396–420.

Ba Tha. 2007 [1963]. *A Short History of Rohingya and Kamas of Burma*, trans. A.F.K. Jilani, ed. Mohd. Ashraf Alam. Rakhine: Kaladan News.

Bateson, Gregory. 1935. "Culture Contact and Schismogenesis." *Man* 35: 178–83.

Bhattacharya, Swapna. 2002. "Myth and History of Bengali Identity in Arakan." In *The Maritime Frontier of Burma Exploring Political, Cultural and Commercial Interaction in the Indian Ocean World, 1200–1800*, ed. Jos Gommans and Jacques Leider. Amsterdam: KITLV Press.

Carstens, Charles. 2018. "Religion." In *Handbook of Contemporary Myanmar*. Routledge.

Charney, Michael. 1998. “Crisis and Reformation in a Maritime Kingdom of Southeast Asia: Forces of Instability and Political Disintegration in Western Burma (Arakan), 1603–1701.” *Journal of the Economic and Social History of the Orient* 41, no. 2: 185–219.

———. 1999. “Where Jambudipa and Islamdom Converged: Religious Change and the Emergence of Buddhist Communalism in Early Modern Arakan (Fifteenth to Nineteenth Centuries).” Doctoral dissertation, University of Michigan.

———. 2002. “Beyond State-Centered Histories in Western Burma, Missionizing Monks and Intra Regional Migrants in the Arakan Littoral, c. 1784–1860.” In *The Maritime Frontier of Burma Exploring Political, Cultural and Commercial Interaction in the Indian Ocean World, 1200–1800*, ed. Jos Gommans and Jacques Leider. Amsterdam: KITLV Press.

———. 2005. “Theories and Historiography of the Religious Basis of Ethnonyms in Rakhaing (Arakan), Myanmar (Burma).” The Forgotten Kingdom of Arakan: A Public Seminar on the People of Present Day Arakan State of Myanmar, Bangkok, 23 November.

———. 2015. “The Right to Have Rights.” In *Communal Violence in Myanmar*. Yangon: Myanmar Knowledge Society and Australia National University.

———. 2016. “State and Society in Arakan since the Fourteenth Century: From Inclusion to Polarisation and Exclusion.” Paper delivered at “Myanmar's Democratic Transition and the Rohingya Persecution,” Oxford University, 11 May.

———. 2017. “How in Myanmar ‘National Races’ Came to Surpass Citizenship and Exclude Rohingya.” *Journal of Contemporary Asia* 7, no. 3: 461–83.

Choudhury, Rishad. 2015. “An eventful politics of difference and its afterlife: Chittagong frontier, Bengal, c. 1657–1757.” *The Indian Economic & Social History Review* 52, no. 3: 271–96.

D'Hubert, Thibaut. 2015. “The Lord of the Elephant: Interpreting the Islamicate epigraphic, numismatic, and literary material from the Mrauk U period of Arakan (ca. 1430–1784).” *Journal of Burma Studies* 19, no. 2: 341–70.

———. 2018. *In the Shade of the Golden Palace: Alaol and Middle Bengali Poetics in Arakan*. Oxford: Oxford University Press.

D'Hubert, Thibaut and Jacques Leider. 2011. “Traders and Poets at the Mrauk U Court: Commerce and Cultural links in Seventeenth-Century Arakan.” In *Pelagic Passageways: The Northern Bay of Bengal Before Colonialism*, ed. Rila Mukherjee. Delhi: Primus Books, 2011.

Davis, Heidi. 2014. “Consonant Correspondences of Burmese, Rakhine and Marma with Initial Implications for Historical Relationships.” MA Thesis, University of North Dakota.

De Mersan, Alexandra. 2016. “Ritual and the Other in Rakhine Spirit Cults.” In *Myanmar's Mountain and Maritime Borderscapes*, ed. Su-Ann Oh. Singapore: ISEAS-Yusof Ishak Institute.

Democratic Voice of Burma. 2018. "Min Aung Hlaing warns against anti-military sentiment." *Democratic Voice of Burma*, 21 March.

Frydenlund, Shae. 2017. "On the uses of (neo)liberalism in Myanmar and the promise of radical feminism." *Tea Circle*, 25 October.

Gazi, N.N., et al. 2013. "Genetic Structure of Tibeto-Burman Populations of Bangladesh: Evaluating the Gene Flow along the Sides of Bay-of-Bengal." *PLoS ONE* 8, no. 10.

Girard, René. 1986. *The Scapegoat*. Baltimore: Johns Hopkins University Press.

Grantham, S.G. 1923. *Census of India, 1921*, Vol. X. Rangoon: Office of the Superintendent, Government of Burma.

Gravers, Michael. 2007. "Introduction: Ethnicity against State – State against Ethnic Diversity?" In *Exploring Ethnic Diversity in Burma*, ed. Mikael Gravers. NIAS Studies in Asian Topics Series, 39. Copenhagen: NIAS Press.

Griffiths, Arlo. 2015. "Three More Sanskrit Inscriptions of Arakan: New Perspectives on Its Name, Dynastic History, and Buddhist Culture in the First Millennium." *Journal of Burma Studies* 19, no. 2: 281–340.

Gutman, Pamela. 1976. "Ancient Arakan, with special reference to its cultural history between the 5th and 11th centuries." Diss., Australian National University.

Haque, Mahbubul. 2012. "Bali Khela." In *Banglapedia: National Encyclopedia of Bangladesh*, ed. Sirajul Islam and Ahmed Jamal, 2nd ed. Asiatic Society of Bangladesh.

Hill, Nathan. 2013. "The merger of Proto-Burmish *ts and *č in Burmese." SOAS Working Papers in Linguistics, Vol. 16.

Horowitz, Donald. *Ethnic Groups in Conflict*. Berkeley: University of California Press, 2001.

Houtman, Gustaaf. 1999. *Mental Culture in Burmese Crisis Politics: Aung San Suu Kyi and the National League for Democracy*. ILCAA Study of Languages and Cultures of Asia and Africa Monograph Series, No. 33.

Irvine, Judith and Susan Gal. 2000. "Language Ideology and Linguistic Differentiation." In *Regimes of Language: Ideologies, Polities, and Identities*, ed. Paul V. Kroskrity. Oxford: James Currey Publisher, pp. 35–83.

Kyaw Minn Htin. 2015. "The Marma from Bangladesh: A 'de-Arakanized' Community in Chittagong Hill Tracts." *Suvannabhumi* 7, no. 2 (December): 133–53.

Leach, E.R. 1959. *Political Systems of Highland Burma*. Oxford and New York: Berg, London School of Economics Monographs on Social Anthropology #44.

Lehman, F.K. 1967. "Ethnic Categories in Burma and the Theory of Social Systems." In *Southeast Asian Tribes, Minorities, and Nations*, ed. Peter Kunstadter. Princeton, NJ: Princeton University Press, 1967, pp. 93–124.

Leider, Jacques. 2008. "Forging Buddhist Credentials as a Tool of Legitimacy and Ethnic Identity: A Study of Arakan's Subjection in Nineteenth-Century

Burma." *Journal of the Economic and Social History of the Orient* 51, no. 3: 409–59.

______. 2009. "Relics, Statues, and Predictions: Interpreting an Apocryphal Sermon of Lord Buddha in Arakan." *Asian Ethnology* 68, no. 2: 333–64.

______. 2013. "Rohingya: the name, the movement, the quest for identity." In *Nation Building in Myanmar*. Yangon: Myanmar EGRESS/Myanmar Peace Center, pp. 204–55.

______. 2015a. "Politics of Integration and Cultures of Resistance. A Study of Burma's Conquest and Administration of Arakan." In *Asian Expansions: The Historical Experiences of Polity Expansion in Asia*, ed. Geoffrey Wade. London: Routledge, pp. 184–213.

______. 2015b. "Background and Prospects in the Buddhist-Muslim Dissensions in Rakhine State of Myanmar." In *Ethnic Conflict in Buddhist Societies in South and Southeast Asia*, ed. K.M. de Silva. Kandy: International Centre for Ethnic Studies, pp. 25–55.

______. 2016. "Competing Identities and the Hybridized History of the Rohingyas." In *Metamorphosis: Studies in Social and Political Change in Myanmar*, ed. Renaud Egreteau and Francois Robinne. Singapore: NUS Press.

______. 2017. "Transmutations of the Rohingya Movement in the Post-2012 Rakhine State Crisis." In *Ethnic and Religious Identities and Integration in Southeast Asia*, ed. Ooi Keat Gin and Volker Grabowsky. Chiang Mai: Silkworm Books, pp. 191–239.

______. 2018. "Conflict and Mass Violence in Arakan (Rakhine State): The 1942 Events and Political Identity Formation." In *Citizenship in Myanmar: Ways of Being in and from Burma*, ed. Ashley South and Marie Lall. Singapore: ISEAS-Yusof Ishak Institute.

Leider, Jacques and Kyaw Minn Htin. 2015. "King Man Co Mvan's Exile in Bengal: Legend, History and Context." *Journal of Burma Studies* 19, no. 2: 371–405.

Lewis, M. Paul, ed. 2009. *Ethnologue: Languages of the World*, 16th ed. Dallas, Texas: SIL International.

Li, Yu-Chun, et al. 2015. "Ancient inland human dispersals from Myanmar into interior East Asia since the Late Pleistocene." *Scientific reports* 5.

Maung Tha Hla. 2004. *The Rakhaing*. Buddhist Rakhaing Cultural Association.

McAuliffe, Erin Lynn. 2017. "Caste and the quest for racial hierarchy in British Burma: An analysis of census classifications from 1872–1931." Masters Thesis, University of Washington.

Myat Moe. 2018. "Striving to achieve lasting peace." *Global New Light of Myanmar*, 7 February. <http://www.globalnewlightofmyanmar.com/striving-achieve-lasting-peace/>.

Nyanuttara, Ashon. 2014. *A Study of Buddhism in Arakan*. Wheaton, IL: Oo Thein Maung.

Okell, John. 1995. "Three Burmese Dialects." *Pacific Linguistics. Series A. Occasional Papers* 83: 1–138.

Prasse-Freeman, Elliott. 2012. "Power, Civil Society, and an Inchoate Politics of the Daily in Burma/Myanmar." *Journal of Asian Studies* 71, no. 2: 371–97.

———. 2013a. "Scapegoating in Burma." *Anthropology Today* 29, no. 4 (August).

———. 2013b. "A Senseless Census in Burma." *Foreign Policy*, 21 December.

———. 2014. "Fostering an Objectionable Burma Discourse." *Journal of Burma Studies* 18, no. 1 (June).

———. 2017. "The Rohingya Crisis." *Anthropology Today* 33, no. 6 (December).

Robinne, Francois and Mandy Sadan. 2007a. "Postscript: Reconsidering the dynamics of ethnicity through Foucault's concept of 'spaces of dispersion'." In *Social Dynamics in the Highlands of Southeast Asia: Reconsidering Political Systems of Highland Burma by ER Leach*, ed. Francois Robinne and Mandy Sadan, Vol. 18. Leiden: Brill.

———, eds. 2007b. *Social Dynamics in the Highlands of Southeast Asia: Reconsidering Political Systems of Highland Burma by ER Leach*, Vol. 18. Leiden: Brill.

Sadan, Mandy. 2007. "Constructing and Contesting the Category 'Kachin' in the Colonial and post-Colonial Burmese State." In *Exploring Ethnic Diversity in Burma*, ed. Michael Gravers. NIAS Studies in Asian Topics Series, 39. Copenhagen: NIAS Press, pp. 34–76.

Saga Wa. 2013. "The Rakhine people are protecting the union's culture, customs, and traditions in addition to its autonomy and the ownership of the land" (author's translation), *Myawady*, 30 September. <http://www.myawady.com.mm/allnews/headline/item/26678-2013-09-30-08-44-12>.

San Tha Aung. 1979. *The Buddhist Art of Ancient Arakan*. Rangoon: Ministry of Education.

Scott, James. 2009. *The Art of Not Being Governed*. New Haven: Yale University Press.

Singer, Noel. 2008. *Vaishali and the Indianization of Arakan*. Delhi: APH Publishing.

Summerer, Monika, et al. 2014. "Large-scale mitochondrial DNA analysis in Southeast Asia reveals evolutionary effects of cultural isolation in the multi-ethnic population of Myanmar." *BMC Evolutionary Biology* 14.17.

Thawnghmung, Ardeth Maung. 2016. "The politics of indigeneity in Myanmar: competing narratives in Rakhine state." *Asian Ethnicity* 17, no. 4: 527–47.

Tonkin, Derek. 2018. "Exploring the Issue of Citizenship in Rakhine State." In *Citizenship in Myanmar: Ways of Being in and from Burma*, ed. Ashley South and Marie Lall. Singapore: ISEAS-Yusof Ishak Institute.

Van Galen, Stephan. 2002. "Arakan at the Turn of the First Millennium of the Arakanese Era." In *The Maritime Frontier of Burma Exploring Political, Cultural and Commercial Interaction in the Indian Ocean World, 1200–1800*, ed. Jos Gommans and Jacques Leider. Amsterdam: KITLV Press.

Van Schendel, Willem, ed. 1992. *Francis Buchanan in Southeast Bengal (1798): His Journey to Chittagong, the Chittagong Hill Tracts, Noakhali and Comilla*. Dhaka: University Press Limited.

Wade, Francis. 2017. *Myanmar's Enemy Within: Buddhist Violence and the Making of a Muslim 'Other'*. London: Zed Books.

Wicks, Robert S. 1992. *Money, Markets, and Trade in Early Southeast Asia: The Development of Indigenous Monetary Systems to AD 1400*. No. 11. SEAP Publications.

CONTRIBUTORS

Adam Simpson is Program Director: Master of Communication in UniSA Creative and Senior Lecturer: International Studies in UniSA Justice and Society at the University of South Australia. He has held a 6-month Visiting Research Fellowship at the Centre for Southeast Asian Studies, Kyoto University, and Visiting Scholar positions at SOAS, University of London, Queen Mary, University of London and Keele University. His research adopts a critical perspective and is focused on the politics of the environment and development in Southeast Asia. He has published in international journals such as *Society & Natural Resources*, *Third World Quarterly*, *Environmental Politics* and *Pacific Review*. He is the author of *Energy, Governance and Security in Thailand and Myanmar (Burma): A Critical Approach to Environmental Politics in the South* (Routledge, 2014; updated paperback edition, NIAS Press, 2017) and is lead editor of the *Routledge Handbook of Contemporary Myanmar* (2018) and *Myanmar: Politics, Economy and Society* (Routledge, 2020).

Aung Tun, a native Burmese, is an independent researcher/scholar in Myanmar, working on economic governance, conflict, and ethnic politics. He holds a degree in international studies from the University of Massachusetts, Boston. He also contributes his pieces to different media outlets including *Asian Times Online* and *The Diplomat*.

Bo Bo Nge is a native of Yangon, and a PhD candidate in the field of Financial and Management Studies at the School of Oriental and African Studies (SOAS). From 2014 through 2016, Bo Bo was head of Research and Risk Management Departments in the banking industry in Myanmar. Prior to that, he had worked as a portfolio manager and financial analyst for eight years in the United States. He studied international economics and international relations at Johns Hopkins University in 2004–06 for his graduate degree. He was Levy Economics Institute Scholar at

Bard College, New York, where he studied economics for his Bachelor's degree. Bo Bo is a fellow at Kennedy School of Government at Harvard University since 2014. He is also a member of the National Economic Co-ordination Committee (NECC) of the Union of Myanmar since its formation in 2016. His primary interest is in the economic and development issues of his native land and people.

Elliott Prasse-Freeman is assistant professor in Sociology/Anthropology at the National University of Singapore. He completed his PhD in Anthropology at Yale University, where his dissertation used ethnographic fieldwork on social movements in Myanmar to consider novel conceptions of politics in semi-authoritarian contexts. His articles on Myanmar politics have appeared in the *Journal of Asian Studies*, *Journal of Burma Studies*, and various edited volumes.

Fumiharu Mieno is professor of Economics at the Center for Southeast Asian Studies, Kyoto University. He obtained his doctorate degree from Hitotsubashi University. Previously, he worked as research associate at Hitotsubashi University, associate professor at Hosei University, and professor at Kobe University. He was also visiting professor at Thammasat University and Columbia University. His research areas are financial system in economic development and financial sector in Southeast Asia, in particular Thailand and Myanmar. His major publications are *Economic Transition in Myanmar After 1988: Market Economy Versus State Control* (Singapore: NUS Press, 2009), *Financial Reform and Southeast Asia: Analyzing Regional Long-term Trends and Corporate Finance* (in Japanese, Keiso Shobo, 2015), "Fund Mobilization and Investment Behavior in Thai Manufacturing Firms in the Early 1990s," *Asian Economic Journal* 20, no. 1 (2006), and "Toward Myanmar's New Stage of Development: Transition from Military Rule to the Market," *Asian Economic Policy Review* 8, no. 1 (2013).

Kirt Mausert is an independent researcher based in Cox's Bazaar, Bangladesh. He holds a BA in Linguistics from Binghamton University (SUNY), and an MA in Anthropology from the University of Pennsylvania, for which he conducted ethnographic research related to royal authority and national politics in Bangkok, Thailand. Previously based in Yangon, Myanmar from 2010–17, his research interests have focused on the contemporary Rohingya nationalist movement and the social semiotics of race and national identity in Myanmar.

Marjanneke Vijge is assistant professor at the Copernicus Institute of Sustainable Development, Utrecht University. Marjanneke's current research focuses on policy coherence around the Sustainable Development Goals in developing countries. She analyzes the consequences for the poorest and most vulnerable in the fields of climate and food security. Marjanneke received her PhD degree from Wageningen University on the topic of forest and climate governance, with her main field work conducted in India. After her PhD, she was selected for a 1-year Niels Stensen Fellowship with which she conducted post-doctoral research in Myanmar on the governance of the extractive industries sector. This resulted in articles in *Global Environmental Politics and Resources Policy* on the effects of the Extractive Industries Transparency Initiative (EITI) in Myanmar, one of which was selected as runner-up to the Oran R. Young Prize 2018. Following her post-doctoral research, Marjanneke worked as climate policy expert with the Food and Agriculture Organization of the United Nations (FAO). Marjanneke has been visiting scholar at three institutes in India, Indonesia and Myanmar, and worked with different UN agencies in Italy, Myanmar, and Kenya.

Matthew J. Walton is assistant professor in Comparative Political Theory at the Department of Political Science, University of Toronto. Prior to this, he was the Aung San Suu Kyi Senior Research Fellow in Modern Burmese Studies at St Antony's College. He received his PhD in Political Science from the University of Washington and previously taught at the George Washington University. His research focuses on religion and politics in Southeast Asia, with a special emphasis on Buddhism in Myanmar. His first book, *Buddhism, Politics, and Political Thought in Myanmar*, was published in 2016 by Cambridge University Press. His articles on Buddhism, ethnicity, and politics in Myanmar have appeared in *Politics & Religion*, *Journal of Burma Studies*, *Journal of Contemporary Asia*, *Journal of Contemporary Buddhism*, and *Asian Survey*.

Moe Thuzar is lead researcher (socio-cultural) at the ASEAN Studies Centre of ISEAS-Yusof Ishak Institute and an ISEAS Fellow. She is concurrently co-coordinator of the Myanmar Studies Program at ISEAS. Prior to joining ISEAS, she headed the Human Development Unit at the ASEAN Secretariat. At ISEAS, she has co-authored *Myanmar: Life After Nargis* with Pavin Chachavalpongpun (2009), and co-edited *Urbanisation in Southeast Asia: Issues and Impacts* with Yap Kioe Sheng (2012). Moe has contributed extensively to compendia and edited volumes on ASEAN and Myanmar. Under her ASEAN research, Moe monitors regional integration moves under the ASEAN Socio-Cultural Community. Moe monitors Myanmar's ongoing transition issues, and was involved in advising Myanmar's ASEAN chairmanship in 2014. A former diplomat, she is researching Burma/Myanmar's post-World War II diplomatic history for her PhD.

Patrick McCormick is currently an independent researcher. He was formerly affiliated with the Department of Comparative Linguistics at the University of Zurich where he worked on a research project funded by the Swiss National Science Foundation. He was the representative of the École Française d'Extrême-Orient in Yangon from 2014–16. He has been living in Yangon since 2006 and has also worked as a consultant in the areas of education, mother-tongue education, peace building, and governance.

Patrick Strefford is associate professor of International Relations at Kyoto Sangyo University. He earned his BA at Hull University, his MA at Leeds University, and his PhD at Kobe University. At Kyoto Sangyo University, Strefford teaches course on International Relations, International Development and the Theory of Knowledge. His research focuses on Myanmar's foreign relations, particularly aid donors' policies and practices towards Myanmar. He has recently published articles on Japanese diplomacy towards Myanmar, Myanmar's transition and the international ODA regime, and on capacity development in Myanmar, among others. From 2013 to 2016, Strefford was the principal researcher on a Japan Society for the Promotion of Sciences grant to conduct research in international aid to support the transition in Myanmar, focusing on donor assistance to capacity building in the public sector.

Pavin Chachavalpongpun is associate professor at the Center for Southeast Asian Studies, Kyoto University. Earning his PhD from the School of Oriental and African Studies (SOAS), Pavin is the author of *A Plastic Nation: The Curse of Thainess in Thai-Burmese Relations* and *Reinventing Thailand: Thaksin and His Foreign Policy*. He is also the chief editor of the online journal, *Kyoto Review of Southeast Asia*, the only journal which presents all articles in English, Japanese, Thai, Bahasa Indonesia, Filipino, and Vietnamese. He is the editor of the forthcoming *Routledge Handbook of Contemporary Thailand*.

Shae A. Frydenlund is a PhD candidate in Geography at the University of Colorado, Boulder. Her work examines race, gender, and labor in Myanmar and the Himalayas. As a National Science Foundation doctoral fellow, her current research explores the relational linkages between Rohingya refugee women's unwaged labor and urban change. She is the author of "Labor and Race in Nepal's Indigenous Nationalities Discourse: Beyond 'Tribal' vs 'Peasant' Categories" in the journal *Himalaya*.

Yoshihiro Nakanishi is associate professor at the Center for Southeast Asian Studies, Kyoto University. His research focuses on politics and civil-military relations in Myanmar and Pakistan. Nakanishi previously worked with the Institute of Developing Economies (IDE-JETRO) and was a visiting scholar at the Paul H. Nitze School of Advanced International Studies, a division of Johns Hopkins University. He was also a visiting professor at the University of Yangon, Myanmar. He is the author of *Strong Soldiers, Failed Revolution: The State and Military in Burma, 1962–1988* (Singapore and Japan: NUS Press and Kyoto University Press, 2013).

INDEX

KYOTO-CSEAS SERIES ON ASIAN STUDIES
Center for Southeast Asian Studies, Kyoto University

List of Published Titles

The Economic Transition in Myanmar after 1988: Market Economy versus State Control, edited by Koichi Fujita, Fumiharu Mieno, and Ikuko Okamoto, 2009

Populism in Asia, edited by Kosuke Mizuno and Pasuk Phongpaichit, 2009

Traveling Nation-Makers: Transnational Flows and Movements in the Making of Modern Southeast Asia, edited by Caroline S. Hau and Kasian Tejapira, 2011

China and the Shaping of Indonesia, 1949–1965, by Hong Liu, 2011

Questioning Modernity in Indonesia and Malaysia, edited by Wendy Mee and Joel S. Kahn, 2012

Industrialization with a Weak State: Thailand's Development in Historical Perspective, by Somboon Siriprachai, edited by Kaoru Sugihara, Pasuk Phongpaichit, and Chris Baker, 2012

Popular Culture Co-productions and Collaborations in East and Southeast Asia, edited by Nissim Otmazgin and Eyal Ben-Ari, 2012

Strong Soldiers, Failed Revolution: The State and Military in Burma, 1962–88, by Yoshihiro Nakanishi, 2013

Organising Under the Revolution: Unions and the State in Java, 1945–48, by Jafar Suryomenggolo, 2013

Living with Risk: Precarity & Bangkok's Urban Poor, by Tamaki Endo, 2014

Migration Revolution: Philippine Nationhood and Class Relations in a Globalized Age, by Filomeno V. Aguilar Jr., 2014

The Chinese Question: Ethnicity, Nation, and Region in and Beyond the Philippines, by Caroline S. Hau, 2014

Identity and Pleasure: The Politics of Indonesian Screen Culture, by Ariel Heryanto, 2014

Indonesian Women and Local Politics: Islam, Gender and Networks in Post-Suharto Indonesia, by Kurniawati Hastuti Dewi, 2015

Catastrophe and Regeneration in Indonesia's Peatlands: Ecology, Economy and Society, edited by Kosuke Mizuno, Motoko S. Fujita & Shuichi Kawai, 2016

Marriage Migration in Asia: Emerging Minorities at the Frontiers of Nation-States, edited by Sari K. Ishii, 2016

Central Banking as State Building: Policymakers and Their Nationalism in the Philippines, 1933–1964, by Yusuke Takagi, 2016

Moral Politics in the Philippines: Inequality, Democracy and the Urban Poor, by Wataru Kusaka, 2017

Liberalism and the Postcolony: Thinking the State in 20th-century Philippines, by Lisandro E. Claudio, 2017

Networked: Business and Politics in Decentralizing Indonesia, 1998–2004, by Wahyu Prasetyawan, 2018

Writing History in America's Shadow: Japan, the Philippines, and the Question of Pan-Asianism, by Takamichi Serizawa, 2020